Louis Véron and the Finances of the

Perspektiven der Opernforschung

Herausgegeben von Jürgen Maehder und Thomas Betzwieser

Band 9

PETER LANG

Frankfurt am Main · Berlin · Bern · Bruxelles · New York · Oxford · Wien

John D. Drysdale

Louis Véron and the Finances of the Académie Royale de Musique

PETER LANG

Europäischer Verlag der Wissenschaften

Bibliographic Information published by Die Deutsche Bibliothek
Die Deutsche Bibliothek lists this publication in the Deutsche Nationalbibliografie; detailed bibliographic data is available in the internet at <http://dnb.ddb.de>.

Abbildung auf dem Umschlag:
»Cliché Bibliothèque nationale de France, Paris«.

ISSN 0930-2174
ISBN 3-631-39866-2
US-ISBN 0-8204-6027-3

© Peter Lang GmbH
Europäischer Verlag der Wissenschaften
Frankfurt am Main 2003
All rights reserved.

Printed in Germany 1 2 3 4 6 7

www.peterlang.de

Dedicated to Professor Roderick Swanston who
inspired my initial interest in musicology

TABLE OF CONTENTS

PREFACE

The purpose of this book, which is the revised version of a thesis completed in 2000, is to show how the entrepreneur Louis Véron wrought substantial changes to the Opera in Paris at the *Salle le Peletier*. For a brief period, from 1 June 1831 to 31 August 1835, he changed the culture of maladministration and malpractices which had flourished at the Opera during the Restoration period. He reduced the bloated costs of the fixed personnel by a programme of brutal redundancies, retirements and salary reductions; he reduced the costs of scenery for new productions by renegotiation of the tariff for scene-painting and by the use of old materials to build the sets; and he reduced the costs of materials to make the costumes by changing most of the suppliers and enforcing substantial price reductions in the materials supplied. Concurrently, Véron staged successful new productions which especially appealed to his new self-confident bourgeois audiences; changed many of the seat prices to attract them; and reduced the number of free seats which had become a flagrant abuse under the former regime. The result was that he did indeed make a fortune, but as he was so narrowly focused on this single aim, he breached the terms of his appointment and aroused resentment, jealousy and envy. He was politically maladroit in that he failed to carry the authorities with him. Having attempted to resign in 1833, he finally resigned on 31 August 1835 with twenty-one months of his six year contract still to run.

Research into the primary sources has thrown light on how the Opera was managed under Véron's concession and brings into question some previous comments on this subject. For example, William Crosten claimed that the Opera was run as a business for the benefit of predominantly bourgeois audiences.[1] Jane Fulcher, on the other hand, placed the emphasis on the role of the State and the need for the Opera to convey the correct political message.[2] It is noticeable, however, that Crosten failed even to mention the *Commission de Surveillance* which supervised Véron on behalf of the State. Equally Fulcher made no attempt to explain or highlight the vigorous entrepreneurial action taken by Véron to reduce costs and raise receipts. The evidence used by these two authors to justify their assertions could thus be said to be rather partial, and a more balanced assessment emerges in this book as a result of a more detailed study of the relevant primary sources.

The method adopted to prove the contention that a dramatic change took place at the Opera under Véron's leadership is to compare and contrast the two regimes and to detail the practical effects of this transformation. Chapter 1 focuses entirely on the Restoration period, with its weak management, poor finances and stifling bureaucracy. This was balanced, however, by the progress which the Opera made towards the end of the 1820s in two specific areas. First, the new productions moved on from the traditional *tragédie lyrique* in that they were based on historical subjects and were staged with scenery and costumes which reflected a new regard for historical accuracy.

---

1   William L. Crosten, *French Grand Opera: An Art and a Business* (New York, 1948, reprint 1972).

2   Jane F. Fulcher, *The Nation's Image: French Grand Opera as Politics and Politicized Art* (Cambridge, 1987).

Second, the finances, as revealed by an analysis of the annual accounts, undoubtedly improved towards the end of the regime. Loans were written off, outstanding debts were paid by the *Maison du Roi*, and successful new productions raised receipts. Chapter 2 describes how Véron became director of the Opera and how he used the freedom granted to him, as a concessionaire under the new regime, to enforce changes across the board in order to reduce his cost-base, raise his receipts and make a fortune. His decline and fall is also described. Finally, an analysis of the Annual Accounts 1831–32 to 1834–35 proves that he did indeed make a fortune, although the last year showed clear signs of a reversal of this favourable trend. Chapter 3 takes the general points already made in the first two chapters down to a more detailed level. It compares and contrasts the cost-structure of the scenery and costumes during the two regimes, and shows that the changes wrought by Véron were indeed dramatic. A new tariff for scene-painting was negotiated, which reduced the costs substantially. Furthermore, Véron refused to pay the scene-painters' bills in full which further reduced the cost. He also made substantial use of old sets to build his new sets and saved a lot of money thereby. As for the costumes, it was clear that Véron changed most of the suppliers of materials and negotiated lower prices for the materials supplied. Lastly, chapter 4 takes the general points made in the first three chapters and applies them to a detailed analysis of new productions under the two regimes. The impact of Véron's cost reductions becomes clear here and can be both compared and contrasted.

Véron directed the Opera in Paris from 1 March 1831 to 31 August 1835, and his total gross income is estimated at around FF 936.000.[3] Was this a fortune and how did it compare with the deceased estates of the Parisian wealthy?

An attorney-at-law, who lived in the Marais and died in 1832, left an estate worth FF 450.000.[4] As a member of the *haute bourgeoisie*, Véron would have hoped to attract him to the Opera. He had inherited two houses in Paris and had a country house at Charenton. The family lived in an apartment on two floors which was rented for FF 2.500 per annum. It had seven main rooms, servants' quarters and offices from which he conducted his legal practice. He had at least two domestic servants, kept a luxurious table, owned a good cellar and had a library of some 2.000 books. His wife dressed very well. While not among the very rich, the family lived extremely comfortably. He had a *cens* of over FF 1.000.

The *cens* defined the electorate in France and was evidence of a man's standing, influence and wealth.[5] It was a tax on landed property, the *impôt foncier*, and on business premises, the *patente*. Under the July 1830 Revolution, a man was entitled to vote provided he was over twenty-five years of age and had a *cens* of FF 200 or more. Noticeably, neither salary nor position were criteria for the franchise. In 1842, there were 18.138 such electors in Paris, and a *cens* of between FF 1.000 and FF 3.000 was indicative of a fortune of between FF 200.000 and FF 1.000.000. Of the 18.138 electors, 2.428 had a *cens* of over FF 1.000 and were regarded as *grands notables*. Of these, fifty

3   See text, p.110.

4   Adeline Daumard, *La Bourgeoisie Parisienne 1815–48* (Paris, 1963), p. 173.

5   Daumard, op. cit., pp. 31–58.

per cent were property-owners, twenty-nine per cent merchants and industrialists and twelve per cent came from the professions.[6] A hierarchy of wealth was thus established by the *cens* and the deceased estates. The *petite bourgeoisie*, mostly shopkeepers and the like, were defined as having wealth of between FF 2.000 and FF 20.000, the *classes moyennes*, the middle classes, of between FF 20.000 and FF 500.000, and the rich or very rich of FF 500.000 and above.[7]

Estimates of the cost of living should be treated with caution as times and wants have changed so much since the early nineteenth century. Nevertheless, some prices are indicative. A litre of wine cost around sixty-eight centimes in 1830 and white bread was eighty centimes for two kilos. First quality beef cost around fifty-eight centimes a pound. A coach and coachman could be hired for between FF 450 and FF 600 a month and a local letter of up to seven and a half grammes cost ten centimes.[8] A male servant could cost around FF 430 per annum and a female servant FF 300 per annum, while a spacious apartment could cost up to FF 3.000 per annum to rent.[9]

It was noticeable that salaries were placed very low in the social hierarchy and a salaried position was, as the *cens* showed, not highly esteemed. The banker, lawyer, merchant or doctor, none of whom were salaried and all of whom could make a fortune, counted as the *grands notables* among the *haute bourgeoisie*. Véron's salary of FF 12.000 per annum was useful to him, but his aim was to make a fortune from his concession.

By all accounts, Véron lived very well and kept a celebrated cook called Sophie.[10] Unless he squandered his income from the Opera, which seems unlikely given his character, he did indeed make a fortune and joined the ranks of the *grands notables* in Paris.

The research for this book was drawn for the most part from primary sources in Paris at the *Archives Nationales* and the *Bibliothèque de l'Opéra*. As for the secondary sources, I should like to pay a special debt of gratitude to Yves Ozanam, who gave permission for me to read his thesis on the Opera in the Restoration period, part of which covered the financial position but none of which compared or contrasted this position with that under Véron's regime. I am also indebted to the Bodleian Library in Oxford, which is close to my home and which made many secondary sources available to me. The quotations in French throughout the thesis have, with advice, been corrected wherever possible to reflect modern usage.

As I started my thesis at the age of sixty, having had a career in merchant banking for thirty years, I needed, and obtained, a great deal of encouragement and support to embark on such a project. I should like to pay tribute to Professor Roderick Swanston,

---

6   Daumard, op. cit., pp. 149 and 164.

7   Adeline Daumard, *Les Fortunes Françaises aux XIXᵉ Siècle* (Paris, 1973), p. 211.

8   Guillaume de Bertier de Sauvigny, *Nouvelle Histoire de Paris. La Restauration, 1815–1830* (Paris, 1977), pp. 101–125.

9   Daumard, *La Bourgeoisie Parisienne*, pp. 138 and 139. Cited in relation to a retired pork-butcher who died in 1840 and left a net estate of FF 854.000.

10 Crosten, op.cit., p. 23.

whose courses on History of Music and Harmony and Counterpoint inspired an initial interest in musicology, and who persuaded me that a doctoral thesis was attainable; to Professor Brian Trowell who first gave me the idea that research into the finances of the Opera during the early nineteenth century could yield interesting results; and to Professor Cyril Ehrlich who pointed me towards a supervisor who might be sufficiently interested in my subject to take me on. It is therefore with great pleasure that I should like to pay especial tribute to my excellent supervisor, Professor Mark Everist. With his own interest in nineteenth-century French music, he provided just the right combination of carrot and stick, and was never-failing in his support and interest. Further assistance was also provided by Brenda Thornton in Oxford who gave good editing advice, and Amanda Jones and Muriel Ranivoalison, both of whom helped with the French translation. Lastly, I should like to thank my wife, Gay, who, as it turned out, rather fancied being married to a Doctor of Philosophy and author. She was very supportive throughout, not least on my many visits to Paris.

CHAPTER 1

The *Académie Royale de Musique,* henceforth called the Opera, occupied a special place in Paris during the Restoration period. It was the leading Royal theatre at a time when opera was the most prestigious of lyric theatre genres, and its management structure and budget procedures were clearly defined. Nevertheless, the institution was mismanaged and a culture of waste and inefficiency prevailed throughout the Restoration period, especially when Emile-Timothée Lubbert was director from 1827 to 1831. Despite a large subsidy and other financial assistance, most of the 1820s saw a continual shortfall in receipts, exacerbated by the prevalence of free seats. The consequence was that the Opera, despite the fact that it was not called on to pay any of the costs of the new *Salle le Peletier* theatre when it was built after the 1820 assassination of the Duc de Berry, was a persistent drain on the resources of the *Maison du Roi*. It had a chronic inability to pay its debts, some of which should have been paid by the *Théâtre Italien* prior to its separation from the Opera in September 1827. The Opera also faced challenges on the amount of tax which it should pay to the poor in Paris, the *droit des indigents*, and on the levy which it raised from the secondary theatres in Paris, the *redevance des théâtres secondaires*. Nevertheless, and despite all these problems, the Opera's finances improved greatly in the late 1820s due to vigorous action taken by Baron de La Bouillerie, the head of the *Maison du Roi*, and to higher receipts from successful new productions. The July 1830 Revolution then paved the way for the arrival of Louis Véron as the new director in early 1831, an entrepreneur who made sweeping changes and a fortune for himself as well.

Unlike the many private boulevard theatres in Paris which flourished and drew large audiences during the Restoration period[1] the five Royal theatres enjoyed special privileges, not least that of being subsidised by the *Budget des théâtres Royaux.* These Royal theatres, with the exception of the *Théâtre Français*, were authorised to stage different genres of opera. The *Théâtre Italien*, as the name implied, specialised in Italian opera sung in the original language; the *Odéon* sometimes staged foreign operas, notably from the German repertoire and these were sung in French; the *Opéra Comique* had a monopoly over opera which was sung in French and mixed with spoken dialogue; and the Opera staged operas in French which were sung throughout, usually of the genre *tragédie lyrique,* and ballets.[2]

---

1   Jane F. Fulcher, op. cit., pp. 16–17.

2   Yves Ozanam, *Recherches sur l'Académie royale de Musique (Opéra Français) sous la seconde Restauration* (Thèse, École des Chartes (Paris, 1981), 3 vols, I, p. 2. The background to the Opera's position in Paris, as well as extensive research into the management and finances of the Opera are covered, pp. 1–106, and I am indebted to M. Ozanam for his assistance with my research.

As the voice was deemed superior to pure orchestral or chamber music,[3] opera was a paramount feature of musical life in Paris during the Restoration period. Thus the famous salons in Paris, which in general favoured literature rather than music, tended, when music was performed, to attract the famous opera singers of the day, who then sang arias and ensembles from operas currently in favour at the Opera and the *Théâtre Italien*.[4] Chamber music, which naturally lent itself to these salons, was also performed, but the era of the popular virtuoso was one which only came into vogue after 1830.[5] Public concerts of pure music were also very infrequent, partly due to this lack of interest, but also due to the *droit des indigents*, which taxed public concerts at one-quarter of the gross ticket price for the benefit of the poor in Paris, and to the *redevance des théâtres secondaires*, which was levied by the Opera on public concerts at one-fifth of the gross ticket price after deduction of the *droit des indigents*. As a result, given, say, a gross price of FF 6 for a ticket to a public concert, the promoter had to pay away FF 2.40 for this tax and levy. The result was that few such concerts were performed:

> ... il ne pouvait se donner de bal ni de concert sans que l'Opéra ne perçût un cinquième de la recette brute .... L'impôt sur les concerts, sans distinction, fut – alors comme aujourd'hui – une mesure des plus funestes au développement de la musique symphonique et de la musique de chambre en France; il en rendait les auditions publiques quasi impossibles.[6]

Although Pierre Baillot had, for example, succeeded in promoting chamber concerts for trios, quartets and quintets since 1814, even these were limited to four a year by

3 «Ce culte de la voix, fétichiste chez certains, dogmatique chez beaucoup d'autres, est à la base de l'esthétique musicale de ce quart de siècle.» ("This cult of the voice, fetishist with some and dogmatic with many others, is at the root of the musical aesthetic of this quarter of a century.") Claude Laforêt, *La Vie musicale au Temps romantique (Salons, Théâtres et Concerts)* (Paris, 1929), p. 204.

4 «Les salons les plus fameux de l'époque romantique étaient des salons littéraires.» ("The most famous salons of the Romantic period were the literary salons.") Laforêt, op. cit., p. 171. «D'une façon générale, l'attrait de ces soirées musicales repose sur deux éléments: l'audition d'un ou de plusieurs virtuoses à la mode, artistes de l'Opéra ou des Italiens, ... et l'exécution de mélodies ou d'ensembles empruntés aux répertoires des deux scènes lyriques favorites du public: Opéra et Théâtre-Italien.» ("As a general rule, the attraction of the musical evenings rested on two factors: the performance of either one or several virtuosi singers from the Opera or the *Théâtre Italien*, ... and the rendition of tunes or arias taken from the two lyrical repertories which were most favoured by the public at that time, namely, the Opera and the *Théâtre Italien*.") Laforêt, op. cit., p. 171.

5 Laforêt, op. cit. Chopin, for example, arrived for the first time in Paris in 1831 and gave his first concert in early 1832, p. 151. Paganini gave the first of his eleven 1831 concerts at the Opera on 9 March 1831, and then his six concerts at the Opera in the spring of 1832, p. 165. On the other hand, Liszt gave his first Paris concerts in 1823 at the age of 12, at the salons of the Duchesse de Berry and the Duc d'Orléans.

6 ("... it was impossible to give a ball or a concert without the Opera taking a fifth of the gross ticket price .... The tax on the concerts, with no differentiation between them, was, both then as now, one of the most disastrous steps in the development of symphonic music and chamber music in France. It made public concerts almost impossible.") Jacques-Gabriel Prod'homme, *L'Opéra (1669–1925)* (Paris, 1925), p. 36. If one were to add the effect of the *droit des indigents*, then Prod'homme's comment becomes even more apposite.

1829.[7] Even after the *Société des Concerts du Conservatoire* had been formed, following an *arrêté* from Vicomte Sosthène de La Rochefoucauld on 15 February 1828, and had, under Habeneck, given its first concert on 9 March 1828 – which included Beethoven's *Eroica* symphony – matters were not greatly improved in the short run as the Society was limited to six concerts a year.[8] The prevailing view remained that opera was the truest and most complete expression of music,[9] but that this music was itself of only equal importance to an opera's libretto, scenery, costumes and ballet. It has been said that this was merely a reflection of a somewhat superficial musical taste which required instant pleasure without any great effort.[10] Given that opera embraced many arts in one form, it can also be argued that this musical taste was, in fact, a sophisticated one which was sustained in the 1820s despite Royal indifference. Neither Louis XVIII nor Charles X showed much interest in music and rarely attended an opera, let alone instrumental music.[11]

The Opera occupied a special position among the five Royal theatres, not least because it cost the most and attracted the biggest annual subsidy. Its importance was emphasised in a report to the King by La Rochefoucauld in October 1824, in which he defined a double role for the Opera. First, to the outside world it should sustain the glory and superiority of French painting, poetry, music, theatre and dance. Second, within France itself it should exalt the virtues of the power of the monarchy which was so generous in supporting it.[12] In keeping with this double role, the French language should always be used and *tragédie lyrique* remained a genre whereby the monarchy could proclaim and extol its legitimacy and virtues.

---

7   Jean Mongrédien, *La Musique en France des Lumières au Romantisme* (Paris, 1986). Translated by Sylvain Frémaux, *French Music from the Enlightenment to Romanticism 1789–1830* (Portland, 1996), pp. 248–251.

8   Arthur Dandelot, *La Société des Concerts du Conservatoire de 1828 à 1897. Les grands concerts symphoniques de Paris* (Paris, 1898), pp. 2–10.

9   «L'Opéra peut être considéré comme l'expression la plus vraie, la plus complète de la musique.» ("Opera can be considered the truest and most complete expression of music.") Joseph d'Ortigue, *Le Balcon de l'Opéra* (Paris, 1833), p. II.

10 Jean Chantavoine and Jean Gaudefroy-Demombynes, *Le Romantisme dans la musique européenne* (Paris, 1955), pp. 491–501.

11 "Louis XVIII's and Charles X's major problem was surely that they neither set the tone for a musical policy nor went to any effort to encourage one by attendance." Patrick Barbier, *La vie quotidienne à l'Opéra au temps de Rossini et de Balzac: Paris, 1800–1850* (Paris, 1987). Translated by Robert Luoma, *Opera in Paris 1800–1850. A Lively History* (Portland, 1995), pp. 15–18.

12 «... soutenir ... cette gloire et cette supériorité que nous nous sommes acquises dans les arts de la peinture, de la poésie, de la musique, et dans l'art théâtral et la danse ... il doit exalter les vertus du pouvoir monarchique, si généreux à son égard.» ("... enhance ... the glory and superiority which we have achieved in the art of painting, poetry, music, theatre and dance ... it should glorify the virtues of the power of the monarchy which is so generous in its support.") *Rapport à sa Majesté*, La Rochefoucauld, October 1824, (O^3 1666 IV).

Management and Budgets

Management Structure and Personalities

It was only to be expected that the Opera was under the control of the King through the *Maison du Roi*, and that the management structure created by the restored Bourbon dynasty should hark back to the *ancien régime*. An *arrêté* in March 1780 was embodied in an *ordonnance* of the King on 18 March 1817.[13] This *ordonnance* confirmed the principle of three levels of management. At the first level was the minister who directed the *Maison du Roi;* at the second level was his representative who had direct responsibility for the Opera as well as for the other Royal theatres; and at the third level was the director of the Opera, or, as was the case from 1817 to 1821, the joint-directors.

Although the director of the *Maison du Roi* was not directly in charge of the Opera at the first level of management, he remained its supreme authority. The Marquis de Lauriston, director from 1820 to 1824,[14] took over from the Comte de Pradel, director from 1815 to 1820. He thus signed the 5 May 1821 *Règlement* which decreed, among many other matters, that decisions on personnel, finance and repertoire could not be put into effect without his approval.[15] Lauriston's role was to ratify decisions rather than to take them, but for this purpose he, or any other director, had the power to appoint specialist Commissions to advise him. An example was the *Commission des Théâtres Royaux*, created in August 1827[16] to study the financial problems of all the Royal theatres. La Bouillerie, *Intendant général de la Maison du Roi* from 1827 to 1830,[17]

---

13 «Article 1. Conformément aux dispositions de l'arrêt du Conseil d'État du Roi, en date du 17 mars 1780, Notre Académie Royale de Musique est maintenue, ainsi qu'elle a été dès l'origine, sous les ordres immédiats du Ministre Secrétaire d'État de Notre Maison, et sous la surveillance de telle Personne qu'il aura choisie pour le représenter. Article 2. L'Administration de cette Académie se compose d'un Administrateur ayant titre d'Administrateur du Matériel et des deniers, et un Régisseur ayant titre de Régisseur de la scène et du Personnel des artistes, assisté d'un Secrétaire Général et d'un Comité d'Administration.» ("Article 1. As agreed in the decree of the *Conseil d'État du Roi*, 17 March 1780, our Opera is maintained, as it has been right from the beginning, by the personal authority of the Minister of our *Maison du Roi* and is under the supervision of any person whom the above-mentioned Minister may have chosen as his representative. Article 2. The Administration of the Opera comprises a Director of Material and Finance and a Manager who is both stage-manager and staff-manager, aided by a General Secretary and an Administrative Committee.") *Ordonnance Royale,* 18 March 1817, (AJ^{13} 109 I).

14 Appointment of the Marquis de Lauriston, 1 November 1820. *Bulletin des lois, 2ème semestre 1820,* no. 428, p. 965.

15 *5 mai 1821 Règlement pour l'Académie royale de Musique et le service de l'Opéra.* Articles 4, 8, 23 to 27, (AJ^{13} 1186).

16 *Commission des Théâtres Royaux*, 14 August 1827, (O^3 1601).

17 Appointment of the Baron de La Bouillerie, 23 May 1827. *Bulletin des lois, 1er semestre 1827,* no. 163, p. 557. He was appointed as *Intendant général.*

having taken over from the Duc de Doudeauville, director from 1824 to 1827,[18] was advised by this Commission. As a result, a supplement of FF 400.000 was provided by the Civil List to clear the backlog of debts overdue to suppliers by all the Royal theatres.[19] At the second level of management, the representative of the director was, from 1815 to 1824, Baron de La Ferté who held this position as the *Intendant de l'Argenterie, Menus-Plaisirs et Affaires de la Chambre du Roi*.[20] In August 1824, the *Département des Beaux-Arts* was created and Doudeauville appointed his son, La Rochefoucauld, as its first director.[21] Among his many duties, La Rochefoucauld thus had direct responsibility for the five Royal theatres. The name of his department was changed in 1829 to *Direction générale des Beaux-Arts*.[22] At the third level of management came the director of the Opera although, as noted, this position was held jointly by two people from 1817 to 1821.[23] After two more directors – Viotti and Habeneck – Duplantys was appointed from 1824 to 1827[24] and Lubbert from 1827 to 1831.[25]

Although a formal structure was created for the management of the Opera in the Restoration period it was the interplay of personalities, combined with their weaknesses and strengths, which was more significant. La Rochefoucauld, for example, was given considerable latitude by his father, but came under increasing pressure once La Bouillerie had taken over in 1827. Evidence for this lay, for example, in the way in which the Opera's annual budget was approved. Until 1824, the director of the *Maison du Roi* had signed these instead of La Ferté but thereafter La Rochefoucauld signed the 1825, 1826 and 1827 budgets instead of Doudeauville.[26] Once La Bouillerie had taken over, however, the pendulum swung against La Rochefoucauld. He had to submit the 1830 budget to La Bouillerie for approval[27] but well before then the latter had taken a more direct interest in the Opera. The personality of La Rochefoucauld had much to do with this. On the one hand, he deserved much credit for his championing of Rossini and for the way he moved the Opera forward artistically. On the other hand, he was a weak director and both he and his department were not skilled in supervising the Royal theatres in general nor the Opera in particular, being naïve in commercial and financial

---

18 Appointment of the Duc de Doudeauville, 4 August 1824. *Bulletin des lois, de juillet à septembre 1824*, no. 687, pp. 110–111.

19 La Bouillerie to La Rochefoucauld, 5 April 1828, (O^3 1599).

20 Decision, 6 March 1815, (O^3 1644 VII).

21 Decision, 28 August 1824, Doudeauville to Habeneck, 6 September 1824, (AJ^{13} 114 II).

22 *Ordonnance*, 31 January 1829, La Rochefoucauld to Lubbert, 14 February 1829, (AJ^{13} 122 I).

23 Ozanam, op. cit., p. 31.

24 *Nominations et cessations de fonctions consécutives à la réforme décidée le 26 novembre, 1824*, (AJ^{13} 109 I).

25 *Arrêté*, La Rochefoucauld, 12 July 1827, (AJ^{13} 109 I). Lubbert was already *Directeur du Personnel*, and Article 2 of this *arrêté* stated that the Director of Personnel would have the title of Director of the Royal Academy of Music.

26 Budgets of the Opera, 1825 – 1827, (O^3 1696).

27 Budget of the Opera, 1830, (O^3 1708).

affairs.[28] With his father at the *Maison du Roi*, La Rochefoucauld was protected, but the arrival of La Bouillerie showed up his weaknesses, caught as he was between a strong director above him and an incompetent one below him. Thus although La Rochefoucauld had created a system of *inspecteurs* and *sous-inspecteurs* who had the right to examine all aspects of the Opera,[29] and Duplantys had kept him fully informed through daily letters,[30] all of this was to no avail once Lubbert took over. Not only did Lubbert take a much more independent line as director, but as the extent of his unauthorised activities in matters of finance and personnel became ever more exposed to bureaucratic disapproval, so La Rochefoucauld found himself in an uncomfortable position. On the one hand, he had to solicit La Bouillerie for supplements to the budget and to defend Lubbert's maladministration. On the other, he had to castigate Lubbert for putting him in this unenviable position. The more Lubbert failed to keep La Rochefoucauld informed, the more plaintive the letters became. At the same time, the tone of La Bouillerie's letters to La Rochefoucauld became one of exasperation mixed with threats.

The overall impression gained of these relationships was of a strong director in La Bouillerie who sought to impose discipline and economies on the Opera, but of two unsatisfactory directors in La Rochefoucauld and Lubbert at the second and third levels; the first because he was weak and ineffective and the second because he was a poor manager, especially in financial affairs.

---

28 There were many references to La Rochefoucauld's deficiencies as director of the *Beaux-Arts*. a) "He brought to his government of the *Académie royale de Musique* all the incapacity of a nobleman.... One could dupe him easily, but he would deceive no one." François Henri Joseph Castil-Blaze, *L'Académie Impériale de Musique* (Paris, 1855), 2 vols, II, p. 189, quoted by Crosten, op. cit., p. 15; b) "... the unfortunate and virginal Viscount who lengthened the skirts of the dancers at the Opera and with his own patrician hands applied a modest plaster to the middle of all the statues." Théophile Gautier, *Mademoiselle de Maupin* (Paris, 1834), preface, quoted by Crosten, op. cit., p. 15; c) Frederic W. J. Hemmings, *Theatre and State in France, 1760–1905* (Cambridge, 1994), pp. 177–181. He described the building of a theatre for the *Opéra Comique*, called the *Salle Ventadour*, started in 1826 and completed in 1829. "The circumstances surrounding the erection of the new building into which the *Opéra Comique* moved in 1829 provided an object lesson in the dangers inherent in negotiations between the Crown and a thrusting commercial concern, particularly when the Crown is represented by an incompetent aristocrat like the Duc de La Rochefoucauld, Minister of the Royal Household. The civil servants in the Royal Household were outwitted at every turn by the businessmen with whom they were negotiating;" d) «... mais sa dévote passion s'en prenait aux jupes des danseuses qu'il faisait rallonger pour ne point donner aux spectateurs de coupables pensées.» ("... but his pious mentality recoiled against the dancers' dresses which he had lengthened so as not to arouse shameful thoughts in the audience.") Alphonse Royer, *Histoire de l'Opéra* (Paris 1875), pp. 138–139.

29 La Rochefoucauld created, 4 April 1825, a system of inspectors and sub-inspectors who had the right to examine all areas of activity, and the Opera was visited regularly by Edouard Leconte, (AJ[13] 109 I).

30 Duplantys to La Rochefoucauld, daily letters which kept the latter informed, (O[3] 1678).

Budgets

There were three levels of budget. First, the *Budget des théâtres Royaux*; second, the budget of the Opera itself; and third the budgets of individual productions. The second level, in particular, was a highly bureaucratic ritual. Provided it conformed to the elaborate regulations laid down over the years, and especially to the 5 May 1821 *Règlement*, the annual budget was usually accepted by the authorities, even although they were fully aware of the abuses and inefficiencies, and appointed various Commissions to look into these problems.

Throughout the Restoration period there were five Royal theatres, each of which received a subsidy. They were the Opera, *Théâtre Italien*, *Théâtre Français*, *Opéra Comique* and *Odéon*. The subsidies were paid to them out of the *Budget des théâtres Royaux* which formed part of the annual budget of the *Maison du Roi* and the Ministry of the Interior.[31] This budget was debated and approved by the Chamber of Deputies as part of the overall annual budget of the State. Having been approved, the *Budget des théâtres Royaux* was then administered by the *Maison du Roi* which distributed the subsidies to the five Royal theatres. It also distributed the subsidies to two schools of music, paid some pensions and maintained an emergency fund called the *fonds de réserve*.

The State was in the advantageous position of finding the money to fund its share of the *Budget des théâtres Royaux* from a tax on gambling in Paris, the collection of which was called *la ferme des jeux*. This was carried out by the City of Paris which then handed over the tax to the Treasury:

> Au début de la Restauration, les recettes de la ferme des jeux avaient été divisées en deux parts; l'une d'elles fut destinée à la liste civile, chargée d'acquitter les subventions aux théâtres. L'ordonnance du 4 août 1818 ayant concédé le privilège de l'exploitation des jeux à la Ville de Paris, celle-ci assuma la charge de payer les subventions aux théâtres royaux (FF 1.300.000) que distribuait le Ministre de la Maison du Roi. La loi de finance du 19 juillet 1820 attribua définitivement aux théâtres les revenus de la ferme des jeux et, pour la première fois, en 1821, mais sans détail les subventions figurèrent au budget .... Les jeux supprimés après 1830, l'État soutint seul de ces ressources les cinq grands théâtres de Paris.[32]

The proportion of this tax which was used to subsidise the Royal theatres varied from year to year. In 1824, for example, it was noted that FF 5.500.000 was paid to the

---

31 *Budget des théâtres Royaux*   1820–1827, (O^3 1650). 1828, (F^{21} 1075). 1829, (O^3 1681 II). 1830, (O^3 1601). For 1820–1824, there was reference to the *second Théâtre Français*; thereafter, the reference was to the *Odéon*.

32 ("In the early years of the Restoration, the receipts from the tax on gambling were divided into two parts and one part went to the Civil List which was responsible for subsidising the theatres. Since the City of Paris had acquired the right, 4 August 1818, to levy the tax on gambling, the City now took on the responsibility of paying the subsidy to the Royal theatres – a sum of FF 1.300.000 – which was distributed by the Minister of the *Maison du Roi*. The finance law of 19 July 1820, definitely awarded the income from the gambling tax to the theatres and in 1821, for the first time, the subsidies were mentioned in the budget but with no details .... When gambling was abolished after 1830, the State alone provided the funds for the five grand theatres of Paris.") Pierre Bossuet, *Histoire des théâtres nationaux* (Paris, 1909), p. 123.

Treasury and that FF 1.460.000 of this was used to fund the *Budget des théâtres Royaux*.[33] This level of funding was not automatic, however, being subject to scrutiny and possible amendment in the Chamber of Deputies. Lauriston appeared before the Chamber's *Commission du Budget* on 14 May 1824, both to try and get reinstated a FF 200.000 cut in the funding and to head off a proposed further cut of FF 100.000. He pointed out that the five Royal theatres could not carry on without subsidy and presented a note which showed the extent to which the Civil List had provided extra funds to these theatres. This included FF 174.000 which was mentioned in the 1824 *Budget des théâtres Royaux*. The Minister of the Interior, on the other hand, opposed the reinstatement of the FF 200.000 and this proposal was carried by the Chamber of Deputies. The proposed further cut of FF 100.000 was, however, opposed by the Minister and this was also carried.[34]

The State funded the total of the *Budget des théâtres Royaux* until 1824 when it became clear that the Civil List also contributed a proportion to the total, being the FF 174.000 already mentioned.[35] It was also clear that the FF 1.460.000 contributed by the State in 1824 was FF 200.000 less than in previous years as the total annual budget from 1818 to 1822 was FF 1.660.000.[36] Equally, although the 1823 budget totalled FF 1.800.000, included within it was FF 141.176, being a reimbursement of advances made to the Opera by the Civil List. The implication here was that the State contributed its FF 1.660.000 and also reimbursed the Civil List for a loan which the latter had previously made to the Opera.[37] Unfortunately for the *Maison du Roi,* however, once the principle had been established that the Civil List should contribute to this budget, it found itself in an unenviable position. Until 1828 the State continued to contribute FF 1.460.000 and as the 1826 and 1827 totals remained constant at FF 1.659.000, the Civil List contributed the balance of FF 199.000.[38] In 1828, however, the budget rose to FF 1.750.000 and the Civil List had to contribute FF 290.000 as the State's contribution remained at FF 1.460.000.[39] In 1829, by virtue of a law passed in August 1828,[40] the

---

33 *Archives de la Chambre des Députés des Départements. Procès-verbaux des séances de la Commission du Budget, session de 1824, 24 avril–9 juillet,* (C733). The session on 7 May 1824 noted that *la ferme des jeux* brought in an annual sum of FF 5.500.000 for the City of Paris, and that of this total, FF 1.460.000 went to subsidise the Royal theatres. One deputy contrasted this with the FF 50.000 which went to subsidise primary education.

34 *Archives de la Chambre des Députés des Départements,* op. cit., sessions on 14 May 1824 and 11 June 1824, (C733).

35 *Budget des théâtres Royaux,* 1824, (O³ 1650). The total budget for 1824 was FF 1.634.000 and it was noted, for the first time, that the State contributed FF 1.460.000 and the *Budget de Notre Maison* – that is to say the Civil List – contributed FF 174.000. The budget was signed on 13 March 1824 by the King and Lauriston.

36 Benselin to Lauriston, 12 May 1824, (O³ 1599).

37 *Budget des théâtres Royaux,* 1823, (O³ 1650).

38 *Budget des théâtres Royaux,* 1826 and 1827, (O³ 1650).

39 *Budget des théâtres Royaux,* 1828, (F²¹ 1075).

40 *Extrait du Budget des théâtres,* 1830, (O³ 1601). A letter, 18 October 1830, to the Minister of the Interior, was attached to this extract of the 1830 budget. The subsidy of FF 1.300.000 was justified by reference to the *loi du 7 août 1828* which reduced the subsidy from FF 1.460.000 to FF 1.300.000.

State's contribution fell to FF 1.300.000 and the Civil List had to contribute FF 452.000 out of the revised final total of FF 1.752.000.[41] In 1830, the total budget rose to FF 1.884.306, the State's contribution remained at FF 1.300.000 and the Civil List was forced to contribute the balance of FF 584.306.[42] This was especially painful as a provisional budget had shown a total budget of only FF 1.724.844.[43]

The *Budget des théâtres Royaux* subsidised all the five Royal theatres and the Opera consistently absorbed well over half of the total subsidy, with the figure oscillating around sixty per cent:[44]

	%		%
1820	65	1826	59
1821	57	1827	60
1822	58	1828	62
1823	49	1829	62
1824	58	1830	54
1825	58		

Furthermore, as the section on Deficits, Supplements, Loans and Debts will show, the *Maison du Roi* was forced to come to the direct rescue of the Opera through funding over and above its contributions to the *Budget des théâtres Royaux*. It was bad enough that the contributions of the *Maison du Roi* to the subsidies of all the Royal theatres had risen due to an increase in the budget itself and to a reduction in the State's contribution, but the Opera's chronic inability to pay its debts was a further drain on the resources of the *Maison du Roi*.

At the second level came the budgets of the Opera itself which have, for the Restoration period, already been researched in depth by Yves Ozanam.[45] Each year the Opera, having gone through an extensive exercise of budget preparation which entailed detailed reports and recommendations from the heads of the various departments, submitted a *projet de budget* to the authorities.[46] This estimated the budgeted receipts

---

41 *Budget des théâtres Royaux,* 1829, (O^3 1681 II). This was attached in a letter from La Bouillerie to La Rochefoucauld, 8 May 1829, and put the total at FF 1.752.000. A previous budget, included in a letter from La Bouillerie to La Rochefoucauld, 13 February 1829, had put the provisional budget at FF 1.744.000, of which the *Maison du Roi* was due to contribute FF 444.000.

42 *Extrait du Budget des théâtres,* 1830, (O^3 1601).

43 *Projet de budget,* 1830, (F^{21} 1075). The total was FF 1.724.844 and the budget was signed by La Bouillerie, 16 December 1829.

44 These percentages have been calculated from:

1820–1827	O^3 1650
1828	F^{21}1075
1829	O^3 1681 II
1830	O^3 1601

45 Ozanam, op. cit., pp. 39–55.

46 *Projet de budget.* Some examples: 1824, (O^3 1716 IV). 1826, (AJ^{13} 118 II). 1828, (AJ^{13} 146 III). 1829, (O^3 1681). 1830, (AJ^{13} 124 VI).

and expenses for each category contained within the budget and gave the reasons which lay behind the figures. The estimated budget was then finally approved by the authorities[47] and credits were opened for each category of expense. The basis for this approval was that the receipts and expenses should balance although an approved budget could be revised during the year. If certain expense categories were likely to be higher than estimated, then credit supplements were created, approval having first been gained from the authorities. This was especially true of the 1829 budget, as shown by an analysis of the budget and Annual Accounts for that year.[48] Modifications within the budget could also take place, even although the total expenses figure remained the same.[49] If the receipts were likely to be higher than the budget, these could also be included in a revision.[50]

The *projet de budget* was an elaborate budgetary process, the details of which are further explored in the analyses of the annual accounts 1827–1830. The fact was, however, that this process was a bureaucratic ritual and not one which paid keen attention to the ways in which expenses could be reduced and receipts increased. Provided it conformed to the regulations, the annual budget was unlikely to be changed materially by the authorities prior to approval. It was, however, a different matter after La Bouillerie had taken over. Changes made during the year were subject to severe scrutiny by him and were another cause for disaffection between the three levels of management.

The Consequences of Mismanagement

The previous section placed the emphasis on the management structure, the personalities and the budgets. To what extent the management problems at the Opera were a consequence of these or whether they had more to do with a deep-seated culture of waste and abuse of the system, it is hard to judge. What can be said, however, is that there was no lack of awareness of the situation, nor of advice on what to do, nor of analysis of the inefficiencies and malpractices which were rife during the Restoration period. La Rochefoucauld was very clear about this when he wrote a report to the King in October 1824, soon after he was appointed. His first paragraph was as follows:

> Des rapports et des renseignements précis, m'ayant fait connaître la mauvaise situation administrative et financière de l'Académie Royale de Musique, j'ai pensé qu'un des premiers actes de mon administration devait avoir pour objet de réformer les abus nombreux qui ont amené

---

47 Budgets of the Opera. Some examples: 1821–1826, (O³ 1696). 1829, (O³ 1696). 1830, (O³ 1708).

48 Budget and Annual Accounts 1829. Budget, (O³ 1696); Annual Accounts, (AJ¹³ 146 IV).

49 *Rapport*, 28 July 1828, (O³ 1680 I). This approved various changed categories of expense, although the total remained the same.

50 *Rapport au Roi*, 9 March and 10 April 1830 (O³ 1708). The 1829 receipts were higher than budgeted, so the budget was changed.

cet état de choses, et dont l'existence est devenue publique. Cette mesure m'a, d'ailleurs, paru indispensable dans l'intérêt du trésor du Roi.[51]

La Rochefoucauld was advising the King that he had been briefed on the poor administrative and financial situation at the Opera and that one of the first acts of his administration would be to correct the many abuses which had led to this state of affairs, not least in the interests of the King's Treasury. Maybe La Rochefoucauld had already read the report by Dubois about the overall situation at the Opera and the detailed analyses provided in 1821 and 1822 by Du Rais, the head of material at the Opera. In 1826, Leconte, an inspector, also provided insights into how the Opera was run.

The prevailing culture of abuse and inefficiency was vividly described by Dubois, the head of material at the Opera after Du Rais and subsequent manager of productions. This report, May 1824, was sent to the Comte de Lastoret.[52] In that it was a polemic, it would be a mistake to accept Dubois' views in their entirety. Nevertheless, they were a fascinating insight into the way in which the Opera was managed, or rather mismanaged, and deserve a prominent place in any discussion of the Opera's finances in this period.

Dubois started with a general observation. As it was a complex matter to manage a theatre, there was a need for stability and certainty in order to make lasting improvements. He then pointed out that the Opera was not achieving this due to the rapid turnover of directors, and questioned whether this way of doing things was beneficial. As he then explained, the answer was quite the opposite as everything worked to destroy any benefit. As soon as a new director arrived, the staff welcomed him and celebrated the change. Initially there was hard work, obedience, even respect. But no-one should be deceived. This initial outburst of zeal had little to do with any confidence inspired by the new director and everything to do with hatred of the previous one. The staff were so triumphant about the latter's fall from power that they were in a mood to be accommodating with the new director, whoever he was and however he acted. The cycle then began anew. In the first year the staff, hoping for goodwill, or rather feebleness, from the new director, were obedient, seemed satisfied, and gave the impression of regarding the new director as their liberator. Meanwhile the director, in order to gain the support of the staff, made no complaints, directed without too much severity and tolerated the staff's many malpractices. He directed, in effect, in a paternalistic way. In the second year, as a result of his observations of what was going on, he then started to make some changes, and the staff began to realise that the director had not shut his eyes as they had thought. They thus began to murmur, demonstrate their fears, try some slander. Their obedience was carried out with bad grace and was strained. Sick-time grew again, complaints of tiredness made themselves heard, and the director was regarded as demanding and unjust. These two years having passed, the

---

51   ("Detailed reports and information have made me aware of the parlous administrative and financial situation of the Opera and I considered that one of my administration's first actions should be to reform the numerous abuses which have led to this state of affairs and which are now common knowledge. This step has furthermore appeared essential to me in the interest of the *Trésor du Roi*.") *Rapport au Roi*, La Rochefoucauld, October 1824, (O³ 1666 IV).

52   *Rapport*, Dubois to the Comte de Lastoret, 3 May 1824, (AJ¹³ 114 I). See Appendix I.

third year arrived and the revolution then became general. The director, having noted in every detail the vices and abuses which existed, felt it was his duty to carry out a decisive coup and to tolerate no longer those illicit favours with which reason and economy should do away. Ring-leaders were sidelined, some staff dismissed and new duties were outlined to those who remained or had come in as replacements. This new system was then criticised, ridiculed and slandered, and the new duties led to anarchy. The director was loudly declared to be unaccommodating and incapable, and only thought of as someone to be replaced. Thereafter, the slander, the anonymous letters and the articles in the press reached the ears of higher authority. Assailed with denunciations, poisoned words and false testimony, confidence and goodwill seeped away and a new director was appointed.

Dubois remarked that his account was not an exaggeration. It was a realistic and true description of the situation. Worse was to follow as the old director, who had just embarked on considerable changes, could not even console himself that such changes would be preserved. Confusion arising from such changes became disorder as the old director had not had the time to explain his intentions and to put his plans and projects into place. His changes were thus blamed for the disorder and the old ways were re-established in full force. Thus what could have been fruitful seemed bad, and everyone was amazed that the previous director could have been so misguided as to have had such detrimental ideas and such disorderly projects.

It was thus inevitable that a rapid turnover of directors would produce such tiresome results. How could one expect the staff to sustain a steadfast loyalty and enthusiasm when they knew that the authorities would change the director every two or three years? The staff, working towards the undoubted downfall of each director, did their duties without enthusiasm. The directors, in the middle of such storms, pursued their daily tasks with secret unease, aware of the fate predicted for them and which had brought down their predecessors. Dubois thought that the only way to remedy this instability was to contract out the direction of each of the Royal theatres for a fixed number of years. As for the Opera, history had shown that this was not an innovation, and Dubois suggested that an assured ten-year *privilège* would cause the constant malpractices to cease in the face of a sustained management effort which was free of impediment. Meanwhile, the *Maison du Roi,* having guaranteed the jobs of those granted the *privilège,* except in the case of embezzlement, could insist on an accurate account of their tenure which was long enough to profit both art and economy.

This idea of a *privilège* granted to someone who would manage the Opera *en régie intéressée,* being a leasehold concession negotiated between that individual and the *Maison du Roi*, was prophetic in that Véron took over the Opera on that basis in 1831, although it was the State rather than the *Maison du Roi* which granted the concession. It was also an idea which recurred throughout the 1820s. Lubbert suggested in 1827 that he should manage the Opera for three years at his own risk and peril with an annual subsidy of FF 840.000. La Rochefoucauld accepted the idea in principle, but nothing was done.[53] Some, like Fétis, argued against such a change. He felt that the Opera was

---

53   Lubbert to La Rochefoucauld, 2 August 1827, and La Rochefoucauld's acceptance, (O³ 1672 IV).

an institution which, by its very vocation, was likely to be in deficit and could not be managed according to the rules of a profitable enterprise.[54] Others argued in favour[55] but in the end no changes were made under the Restoration[56] and the malpractices remained in place.

Another aspect of the prevailing culture at the Opera was also revealed by Dubois in a letter to La Rochefoucauld on 17 November 1824. Although the Opera's subsidy for 1823 had been cut from FF 750.000 to FF 546.000, it had been made clear by Lauriston that the *Maison du Roi* would always come to the rescue in a case of urgent need.[57] This was indeed so. The 1823 subsidy was restored and the *Maison du Roi* continued to bail out the Opera throughout the 1820s. The consequence was that the Opera rightly believed that despite its profligacy and malpractices, sufficient money would always be found. The authorities might talk toughly about the need to make economies but this was never followed through with robust action. The Opera thus had no real incentive to improve itself and the abuses continued until the arrival of Véron in 1831.

Du Rais, as head of material prior to Dubois, also provided ample evidence of management inadequacies and abuses of the system when he wrote three detailed reports in 1821 and 1822.[58] These were a veritable catalogue of detailed problems which complement the broader picture painted by Dubois. His analysis of the new 1822 tariff for scene-painting led him to conclude that the previous system was thirty-nine per cent cheaper on average: he had compared the actual cost for scene-painting of six old productions with the cost which would have been incurred were the new tariff to have been applied. Were a new system to be in place, whereby artists were given a personal allowance to maintain and clean their costumes and accessories such as

---

54 *Revue musicale, publiée par M. Fétis* .... (Paris, 1828), III, pp. 289–299.

55 *Lettre sur l'Opéra et sur le danger auquel il n'a pas encore échappé, adressée à l'auteur d'un écrit sur l'Opéra et sur le danger auquel il vient d'échapper* (Paris, 1829), 12 pp. ("A letter about the Opera and about the danger it has not yet escaped, addressed to the author of an article on the Opera and on the danger from which it has just escaped.")

56 *Sur l'Opéra et sur le danger auquel il vient d'échapper* (Paris, 1829), 8 pp. ("The Opera and the danger from which it has just escaped.")

57 Dubois to La Rochefoucauld, 17 November 1824, (O³ 1707 I). He noted that the 1823 subsidy from the *Budget des théâtres Royaux* had been cut from FF 750.000 to FF 546.000 and that this was at a time when, due to the success of the *Théâtre Italien,* the Opera «... a perdu la plus grande partie de la faveur publique et presque toute sa location à l'année.» ("... has lost a substantial amount of public support and nearly all its seats and boxes rented on an annual basis.") Dubois also pointed out that in March 1823, Lauriston had assured the Opera «... qu'en cas de besoin urgent, il pourvoirait à l'insuffisance de la subvention par un secour extraordinaire.» ("... that if needs be, he would provide for the inadequacy of the subsidy by means of an extra payment.") Lauriston to Habeneck, 19 March 1823, (O³ 1663 I).

58 a) *Rapport,* Du Rais to Lauriston, December 1821, (AJ¹³ 144 IV); b) *Rapport, Du Rais à M.M. les membres chargés de l'examen et de l'apurement des comptes de cette administration.* n.d. ("Report, Du Rais to the members responsible for the analysis and audit of the accounts of this administration.") This report was subject to some *Observations extraites,* n.d.,which have been archived, (O³ 1707 I); c) *Rapport à la Commission chargée de rechercher les moyens d'améliorer le Régime de l'Opéra.* n.d. ("Report to the Commission responsible for finding ways of improving the management of the Opera.") Du Rais sent some comments on this report to Vicomte de Sennones, *Secrétaire Général du Ministère de la Maison du Roi,* September 1822, (O³ 1707 I).

tights, stockings, shoes and feathers, then the cost to the Opera could fall by fifty per cent, not least because there would be a substantial reduction in the cost of replacing costumes which had been allowed to deteriorate. There were serious abuses of the system whereby material delivered to make new costumes was taken in and out of the storerooms. There were abuses of the 5 May 1821 *Règlement* which laid down detailed procedures for the withdrawal of costumes from the storerooms and for their return. Many singers and dancers just took the costumes home, or stored them in their changing rooms so that it was easier to use them again. In any event, these artists had no incentive to look after these costumes and they quickly deteriorated. The cost of wood for heating was exorbitant and could, with better control, be reduced by thirty-three per cent. The payment of *comparses* (extras) was not well controlled. Some were paid twice-over and some were paid who had not actually performed. There was a real abuse in the remuneration of the scene-changers. Their annual salaries, according to Du Rais, totalled around FF 43.800 but payments for extra work added a further FF 39.700 and it needed much firmer management from Gromaire, the head *machiniste*. Finally, although the 5 May 1821 *Règlement* was very precise over the numbers to be employed at the Opera, these limits had already been exceeded in certain areas.

Further evidence of maladministration came from Leconte, an inspector from the *Beaux-Arts*, through a series of reports in 1826 to La Rochefoucauld.[59] Looking at the preliminary 1825 accounts, he discovered that a double-counting of expenses totalling FF 28.986 had been missed; that forty-one items of expense totalling FF 24.253 had not been entered in the books at all and that bills totalling FF 17.809 had come to light since the accounts were drawn up. As a result, he concluded that the day-book was full of mistakes and that he had little faith in the book-keeper, Bonnemer. Leconte also looked at the 1825 costs of scene-painting and costumes. He pointed out that although the budget allocation had been FF 200.000, the actual result was FF 313.845 and he made a very revealing analysis of why this was so. Scene-painting for new productions had cost FF 86.370 but maintenance at FF 26.603, and extra payments at FF 31.052, had taken this total to FF 144.025. As for costumes, new productions had cost only FF 24.315, maintenance a staggering FF 135.967 and overtime FF 9.538 to give a total of FF 169.820. Compared with 1824, the maintenance of scenery and costumes had cost FF 78.184 more and overtime FF 12.507 more. The lack of control implied by these figures was obvious and Leconte called for a redress of these weaknesses.

Leconte also wrote a highly critical report in September 1826 on the extra costs incurred by Gromaire, the head *machiniste*, whose department ordered the materials, built the sets, and operated the stage machinery.[60] His main complaint was that Gromaire was in a position of such power that no-one could control his activities and challenge his department's expenses. When, for example, he ordered materials for building the sets, no-one could say whether or not he was spending too much. Although he had two assistants, Bursay and Châtizel, neither of them knew what was going on as

59 Leconte to La Rochefoucauld, 12 May 1826, 19 May 1826, 21 May 1826, 24 July 1826, (O³ 1672 IV).

60 Leconte to La Rochefoucauld, 14 September 1826, (O³ 1676 II).

Gromaire kept all the information to himself. Were he to die or to have an accident, then the whole operation could grind to a halt. Leconte also pointed out that the 5 May 1821 *Règlement* had limited the number of staff to sixty-one but that Gromaire had got round this limitation. He paid his staff overtime, amounting to some FF 7.000 per annum, and employed external workers who, although supposedly temporary, were paid as though they worked throughout the year. Leconte identified nineteen such workers who, in the first seven months of 1826, had cost FF 13.910 for an annualised total of FF 23.844. In 1825 this total had been FF 20.230 and the hourly rates paid to these workers were such that it would have been cheaper to employ them as full-time staff on annual salaries. Leconte then made his recommendations to La Rochefoucauld. Bursay, the so-called deputy, should be retired and a stronger man brought in alongside Gromaire. He should learn all about the operations and succeed Gromaire when he retired or were he to have an accident. La Rochefoucauld, however, did not agree with this solution.[61] He suggested instead that Bursay should be officially appointed *adjoint* (deputy-head) and be the person to succeed Gromaire. Leconte was horrified.[62] Bursay, he wrote, was completely useless and quite the wrong person to promote. He had allowed Gromaire to trample all over him because he had too feeble a character to resist. What was needed was a man who could stand up to Gromaire, although Leconte acknowledged that La Rochefoucauld would have the final say in the matter and that Bursay would be chosen. As for the overtime and the external workers, Leconte had spoken to Gromaire in the presence of Duplantys. He had made the point that it was inconceivable that staff should be paid overtime at a time when external workers were employed all the year round. Gromaire had then put his side of the story. Whereas previously one opera and one ballet had been staged on the same evening, now there was often one opera and two ballets and there were more scene-changes. He also said that the flies and below-stage facilities had been extended which meant more work. Be that as it may, Leconte still felt that all the external workers could be sacked without any compromise to the quality of work although he realised that this was too extreme a solution. In the end he suggested to La Rochefoucauld that six should go. La Rochefoucauld wrote to Duplantys with this suggestion[63] and although the latter rehearsed Gromaire's arguments again, including the one that all the external workers should be taken on as permanent staff,[64] La Rochefoucauld stood by his decision.[65] Nevertheless, Gromaire won in the end. His staff totalled sixty-one in 1826, the year of Leconte's report. By 1827 the total had risen to seventy-two and by 1829 to seventy-six.[66]

The conclusion to be drawn from this section is clear. Although the authorities were fully aware of the culture of abuse and inefficiency which prevailed under the

---

61   La Rochefoucauld to Leconte, 20 September 1826, (O^3 1676 II).

62   Leconte to La Rochefoucauld, 9 October 1826, (O^3 1676 II).

63   La Rochefoucauld to Duplantys, 13 October 1826, (O^3 1676 II).

64   Duplantys to La Rochefoucauld, 28 October 1826, (O^3 1676 II).

65   La Rochefoucauld to Duplantys, 2 November 1826, (O^3 1676 II).

66   Personnel classified by category of employment, 1826, 1827, 1829, (PE2 (698)).

Restoration, they seemed powerless to do anything about it. If anything, matters got worse under Lubbert despite La Bouillerie's efforts, and it took the arrival of Véron to change the culture and correct many of these malpractices.

The Infractions of Lubbert

Lubbert's background had encouraged La Rochefoucauld to think that he would make a good director. Born in Bordeaux on 8 February 1794, of a family which, having been rich, was ruined by Napoleon, he obtained a position as *Inspecteur de la loterie au Ministère des finances.*[67] He did a course in harmony and counterpoint and put on a one-act comic opera at the *Théâtre Feydeau*, 14 April 1823, called *Amour et Colère*. It was not successful. He wrote another opera on a Scribe libretto but this was not performed. Having first been director of personnel at the Opera, he took over from Duplantys in July 1827[68] and showed an initial interest and enthusiasm. According to Fétis he was, however, basically idle[69] and the Opera soon fell into sloppy ways, especially in financial matters. In 1827, he had made the proposal to manage the Opera for three years at his own risk and peril and although this new way of managing the Opera was finally accepted in 1831, he then lost out to Véron.[70] He became director of the *Opéra Comique* on a similar basis, but this ruined him. He went to Cairo and died there in 1859.

In the early months of Lubbert's tenure as director, La Rochefoucauld set up a *Comité consultatif* composed of Lubbert as chairman and of various other members of the Opera's staff.[71] La Rochefoucauld must have lived to regret the inclusion of Article 3 in his *arrêté*. Under this clause, Lubbert had the right not to conform to the majority view, although he had to give his reasons for doing so. In February 1828, Lubbert's traits of indolence, maladministration and independence were maybe not so apparent but as the *arrêté* had placed a lot of power in his hands, his natural inclination to independence would have been reinforced. Both La Bouillerie and La Rochefoucauld finally became disenchanted with Lubbert's independent actions and their letters reflected a mounting sense of exasperation and frustration.

In May 1829, La Rochefoucauld complained to La Bouillerie that Lubbert was not keeping him in touch as the regulations demanded. He was also put out by the fact that Lubbert had written directly to La Bouillerie.[72] A long letter to Lubbert in October 1829 was full of complaints about Lubbert's management failures:

> C'est toujours avec un nouveau regret, Monsieur, que je me trouve dans l'obligation de vous rappeler à l'observation des règles de l'ordre administratif que je vous ai tant de fois recommandé

---

67   Jean Gourret, *Ces Hommes qui ont fait l'Opéra 1669–1984* (Paris, 1984), pp. 114–115.

68   As already described in n. 25.

69   François-Joseph Fétis, *Biographie universelle des musiciens et bibliographie générale de la musique* (Paris, 1863), 8 vols, *Tome V*, p. 359.

70   Louis Véron, *Mémoires d'un bourgeois de Paris,* (Paris, 1856), 6 vols, III, pp. 168–173.

71   *Arrêté*, La Rochefoucauld, 18 February 1828, (O³ 1680 I).

72   La Rochefoucauld to La Bouillerie, 9 May 1829, (O³ 1694 I).

de suivre dans votre gestion, comme étant le seul qui puisse en assurer les résultats et leur imprimer un caractère légal.[73]

Whether it was a failure to keep La Rochefoucauld informed about the costumes, scenery and budget for the new ballet *Manon Lescaut*; or the unauthorised use of the English ambassador's box by *les Gentilshommes de la Chambre*; or the abuses of free seats which kept out the paying public; or a failure to submit a daily report, this letter was a veritable catalogue of complaints. In November 1829, La Rochefoucauld wrote again at length to La Bouillerie with another lengthy catalogue of complaints against Lubbert and his failure to keep to the regulations.[74] It went into considerable detail, not least in the matter of three orchestral players, Le Carpentier, Manuel and Renat who were supposed to have been made redundant on 1 July 1829, but were kept on without authorisation, thus being paid illegally. Their salaries formed part of a total of FF 135.136 of unauthorised expenses which Lubbert incurred, having illegally used an equivalent total of receipts which had not first been handed over to the *Maison du Roi* as the regulations required. Later that month Lubbert wrote to La Rochefoucauld.[75] It was one of his less obfuscatory letters in that he admitted irregularities in exceeding the budget and employing personnel without authorisation. On the other hand, he pointed to his success with new productions which had led to a much higher level of receipts. He also referred to previous years when there were many deficits and compared those years with his own successful tenure as director. On the same day, two more letters were sent by Lubbert to La Rochefoucauld which admitted further infractions. The first referred to a singer called Pouilley.[76] Lubbert had regretted Pouilley's retirement on 1 July 1829 and encouraged by Hérold, the head of singing, he had re-employed him without authorisation. The second referred to the singer Bonel who was also due to retire on 1 July 1829. His last role was in *Guillaume Tell* for performance in April 1829 but as the production was delayed, rehearsals had not begun until June.[77] At this point Rossini had insisted that Bonel should stay on as he had composed the music for the role of Melchtal with Bonel's voice and capabilities in mind.[78] Lubbert gave way and Bonel performed the part. Lubbert felt he had been a bit reckless in such disobedience and hoped that La Rochefoucauld would excuse this fault of an excess of zeal. The further interest here was that the salaries of both singers were not authorised from July onwards and formed part of the FF 135.136 paid directly, and therefore illegally, out of receipts. Another letter, this time from La Bouillerie to La Rochefoucauld, made the latter look out-of-touch and foolish especially as the tone of the letter was rather sarcastic.[79] It pointed out that although La Rochefoucauld had sought authorisation

---

73 ("Sir, it is again with renewed regret that I have to remind you of the administrative regulations which I have, on countless occasions, recommended that you should follow in your management of the Opera, as you are the only one who can achieve results and give them an air of legality.") La Rochefoucauld to Lubbert, 31 October 1829, (AJ^{13} 123 I).

74 La Rochefoucauld to La Bouillerie, 13 November 1829, (O^3 1685 I).

75 Lubbert to La Rochefoucauld, 19 November 1829, (O^3 1685 I).

76 Lubbert to La Rochefoucauld, 19 November 1829, (O^3 1685 I).

77 Lubbert to La Rochefoucauld, 19 November 1829, (O^3 1685 I).

78 Rossini to Lubbert, 1 July 1829, (O^3 1685 I).

79 La Bouillerie to La Rochefoucauld, 20 November 1829, (O^3 1681 I).

from him for some pension payments, La Bouillerie had heard, indirectly, that Lubbert had already paid them and so his authorisation had become completely useless. He went on to criticise Lubbert for being irresponsible in that he had completely lost sight of his duties and responsibilities. Again, in November, came another long letter from La Rochefoucauld to Lubbert, full of complaints about Lubbert's failure to keep him informed and of his continued flouting of procedures.[80] Nine days later on 30 November, he had to write a letter to La Bouillerie which highlighted his weak position as the man sandwiched between Lubbert's maladministration and La Bouillerie's exasperation.[81] On the one hand he complained about Lubbert's independent actions over personnel yet, on the other, he had to seek approval for five ballet dancers, illegally employed as not previously authorised, namely Scio, Bégrand, Fuchs, Gilmain and Monet. These dancers had already been paid directly, and therefore illegally, out of the Opera's receipts, and also formed part of the total of FF 135.136. By this time Lubbert had lost the confidence of both La Bouillerie and La Rochefoucauld and the responsibility for finance and material was transferred to the secretary-general, d'Aubignosc, who thus became responsible for the budget and the flow of financial information to the *Direction générale des Beaux-Arts*.[82] The complaints against Lubbert continued, however, as shown by a letter written in January 1830.[83] La Rochefoucauld complained that, having already written twice in December 1829, he was still not getting any satisfaction from his request for a weekly summary of performances and receipts and went on to suggest that Lubbert might have a hidden interest in not making this information available. In a further letter of the same date, he ordered the secretary-general to keep a special register, itemising daily the subject-matter submitted to Lubbert for approval.[84] A summary of this register should be sent to La Rochefoucauld every fortnight.

The above letters, only a selection of the many written at that time, gave credence to the view that Lubbert was a poor administrator, being especially dilatory in financial matters, and that La Rochefoucauld was an ineffective director at the second level of management. The fact is, however, that the malaise went deeper than that. Previous directors of the Opera were also not well qualified to run a complex organisation such as the Opera and did not stay long enough to effect lasting improvements. There

---

80   a) «... vous multipliez les obstacles au lieu d'applanir les difficultés, vous compromettez gratuitement votre responsabilité financière;» b) «En dernière analyse, vous regardez comme superflu l'envoi que je vous ai demandé d'un tableau hebdomadaire de vos opérations;» c) «Le temps consumé à des discussions sur ce qui n'a pas été fait, sera bien plus avantageusement employé à faire régulièrement ce qui doit être fait ....»

a) ("... you increase the difficulties instead of smoothing out the problems, you recklessly compromise your responsibility for the finances;") b) ("Finally, you consider my request superfluous when I asked you for a weekly account of your activities;") c) ("The time wasted in these discussions about what has not been done would be spent to greater advantage in regularly ensuring that what ought to be done, is done ....") La Rochefoucauld to Lubbert, 21 November 1829, (AJ[13] 123 I).

81   La Rochefoucauld to La Bouillerie, 30 November 1829, (O[3] 1685 I).

82   La Rochefoucauld to Lubbert, 24 December 1829, (O[3] 1685 I).

83   La Rochefoucauld to Lubbert, 12 January 1830, (AJ[13] 122 I).

84   La Rochefoucauld to Lubbert, 12 January 1830, (O[3] 1685 I).

was thus neither competence nor continuity. Of the five directors or co-directors from 1815 to 1824, four – Choron, Persuis, Viotti and Habeneck – were musicians with few administrative or personnel skills. Duplantys, on the other hand, director from 1824 to 1827, was at the other extreme in that he had had no musical or theatrical experience, having previously been the manager of a workhouse.[85] A sense of *noblesse oblige* also led to the undesirable result that an ex-director could be kept on in another capacity. Duplantys, for example, successfully made representations to La Rochefoucauld after Lubbert was appointed director in his stead,[86] and became treasurer of the Opera.[87] According to one comment, it seemed as though he was more suited to this latter job:

> M. Duplantys juge la musique comme une addition, la peinture comme un compte courant, et la poésie comme une facture.[88]

Two Financial Problems

The finances of the Opera fell into deficit in the early 1820s and debts mounted to such an extent that the *Maison du Roi* was forced to supplement the annual subsidy and to make further grants and loans. It also had to pay some creditor suppliers directly as the Opera had run out of cash. This situation was made worse by the fact that the Opera supported the *Théâtre Italien*, with which it had formed an alliance in 1818. By the end of the 1820s, however, La Bouillerie had managed to improve the Opera's finances although Lubbert, who continued to be irresponsible in financial matters, broke the regulations yet again in late 1829. He precipitated a further financial embarrassment which required yet another loan.

In the best traditions of operatic drama, the sudden assassination of the Duc de Berry, a nephew of Louis XVIII, on 13 February 1820, provoked a chain of events which caused the Opera to plunge into substantial deficit. He had been attending the Opera for a programme which contained the one-act opera, *Le Rossignol* and two ballets, *Le Carnaval de Venise* and *Les Noces de Gamache*. Since 1794 the Opera had been housed at the *Salle Richelieu* which was opposite the *Bibliothèque Nationale* and it was there that the Duc de Berry was stabbed in the chest by Louis-Pierre Louvel, a saddlemaker who was a devotee of Napoleon and had sworn to exterminate the Bourbons. The Duc de Berry had escorted his wife to her carriage as she had felt tired and wished to leave early, and he was stabbed on the steps of the *Salle Richelieu*. He died in the director's office, having received the last rites. Among those who attended him was a M. Roullet, the proprietor of the Opera's shop, who later recorded his

---

85   Ozanam, op. cit., p. 34.

86   Duplantys to La Rochefoucauld, 9 July 1827, (O³ 1678).

87   La Rochefoucauld to Lubbert, 24 July 1827, (AJ¹³ 119 I).

88   ("Monsieur Duplantys considers music to be like a bill, painting like a current account and poetry like an invoice.") Jean-Toussaint Merle, *Lettre à un compositeur français sur l'état actuel de l'Opéra* (Paris, 1827), pp. 42–43.

impressions for official purposes.[89] Louis XVIII ordered that all performances should cease at the *Salle Richelieu*[90] and that the building should be pulled down. As a result, it was decided that the Opera should move on 9 April 1820 to the *Salle Favart*,[91] but for security and other reasons[92] performances did not begin until 19 April.[93] The Opera moved again, briefly, to the *Théâtre Louvois*, 11–15 May 1821, for four performances,[94] and then finally to its new home at the *Salle le Peletier* which opened on 16 August 1821.

Cost of the *Salle le Peletier*

Many sites and plans had been considered for the new theatre and the site of the *hôtel de Choiseul* was finally chosen. The intention was that the new theatre would be a temporary conversion, the cost of which would be low when compared with that of building an entirely new theatre. In fact the *Salle le Peletier* remained the successful home of the Opera until burnt down in 1873.

The tangled saga of the cost of this conversion, and the dispute over who should pay the bills are sufficiently interesting to merit detailed study. There is much to be learnt from this about the Opera's financial problems in the early 1820s, not least because it suffered substantial deficits as a result of the closing of the *Salle Richelieu*.

The architect François Debret was chosen to carry out the conversion and he submitted an approximate budget which was accepted by Baron Hély d'Oissel, the director of public works.[95] The total was FF 872.804, which included a provision of FF 200.000 to build new storage space for the scenery as well as new administrative offices. It also included a FF 50.000 contingency and a deduction of FF 150.000, being the estimated value of fittings to be taken from the *Salle Richelieu* prior to its demolition. Based on this budget, an *ordonnance du Roi* was issued on 9 August 1820 which, among other things, authorised the opening of a credit of FF 900.000 with the Ministry of the Interior.[96] It was clear that this Ministry was in overall charge of the project and would thus pay the bills based on Debret's budget. On this basis work

---

89   This chain of events was described in various publications. a) Rebecca S. Wilberg, *The 'Mise en scène' at the Paris Opéra – Salle Le Peletier (1821–73) and the Staging of the First French Grand opéra: Meyerbeer's "Robert le Diable"*. Ph.D. diss., Brigham Young University, 1990, pp. 27–30; b) Ozanam, op. cit., pp. 72–73; c) Pierre N. Roullet, *Récit historique des événements qui se sont passés dans l'administration de l'Opéra, la nuit du 13 février 1820* (Paris, 1820); d) Barbier, op. cit., pp. 34–35.

90   Director, *Maison du Roi*, to Minister of the Interior, 25 February 1820, (O^3 1605).

91   Director, *Maison du Roi*, to Minister of the Interior, 3 March 1820, (O^3 1605).

92   Courtin to La Ferté, 14 April 1820, (O^3 1651 II).

93   *Journal usuel de l'Opéra 1791–1850* (Paris, *Bibliothèque de l'Opéra*).

94   La Ferté to Lauriston, 4 April 1821, (O^3 1655 IV).

95   *Devis approximatif*, signed by Debret, totalling FF 872.804, n.d., (F^{13} 1273).

96   *Ordonnance du Roi*, 9 August 1820, (AJ^{13} 185). Article 3 authorised the credit of FF 900.000. Curiously, the *ordonnance* referred to a budget of FF 800.072. Whether this was a simple error – Debret's budget was for FF 872.804 – or not, is unclear.

started on 13 August 1820,[97] but it soon became apparent that the budget was totally inadequate. Hély d'Oissel had to go back to the Chamber of Deputies in April 1821, not only to explain what had happened but also to seek an increase in the 1820 credit of FF 900.000.[98] He explained that an entirely new theatre would have cost FF seven to eight million and that the *hôtel de Choiseul* had been chosen as the conversion cost would be so much cheaper. This had, however, been a hurried decision and the budget summary from Debret had been accepted without sufficient scrutiny. As a result, he was seeking to double the 1820 credit to FF 1.800.000. The detailed reasons he gave were many and various. The foundation work had proved to be much more expensive especially due to the water level; the conversion of the *hôtel de Choiseul* had exceeded estimates; changes in the design during the course of construction had entailed extra costs; there had been no provision in the budget for the cost of stage machinery; and the price of labour and materials had risen due to shortages, especially as two new boulevard theatres were under construction at the same time. The Minister then presented a *projet de loi* which sought to double the 1820 credit to FF 1.800.000 and assured the deputies that this would be sufficient. Despite the Minister's efforts at persuasion, however, and the recommendation of Vicomte Héricart de Thury, president of the Chamber's Commission which reported that this *projet de loi* should be adopted, there were not enough votes to approve it and it therefore lapsed. There was likely to be a long delay before it could be re-presented and an *ordonnance du Roi* on 20 June 1821 recognised this unpalatable fact, while noting that bills of FF 600.000 were outstanding.[99] A provisional extra credit of FF 300.000 was opened at the Ministry of the Interior, although this necessitated a temporary loan of FF 150.000 from the *Maison du Roi,* which was, however, soon repaid.

After the *Salle le Peletier* had opened on 16 August 1821, the *projet de loi* was re-submitted to the Chamber of Deputies on 9 November 1821.[100] The same arguments were put forward but no progress was made. It was not until 1 March 1822 that the credit of FF 1.800.000 was approved although not without an objection from a deputy called Labbey de Pompières.[101] The law itself was promulgated on 31 March 1822,

---

97 Wilberg, op. cit., p. 36.

98 *Chambre des Députés. Exposé des Motifs du Projet de loi présenté par son Excellence le Ministre Secrétaire d'État au Département de l'Intérieur. Séance du 26 avril 1821,* (F^{21} 1073).

99 *Ordonnance du Roi,* 20 June 1821, (F^{13} 1273).

100 a) Re-submission of the *projet de loi,* together with an explanation of the background, November 1821, (F^{21} 1073). b) This episode was covered in detail by Lauriston in the report to the Minister of the Interior, 27 September 1822, (F^{21} 1073). The report set out the various attempts to present the *projet de loi* to the Chamber of Deputies, and its final adoption by the Chamber.

101 *Archives Parlementaires, 2. Série (1800–1860), Tome 35,* 26 February–29 March 1822. *Séance,* 1 March 1822. The President proposed the adoption of «... un crédit supplémentaire de FF 1.800.000 ...,» to be added to the 1820 budget. In the ensuing debate, one deputy, Labbey de Pompières, objected. «Sur 30 millions de français, il y en a peut-être 29 millions qui ignorent qu'il existe un Opéra, et vous voulez leur en faire payer la construction!» ("Out of thirty million Frenchmen there are probably twenty-nine million who do not know of the existence of the Opera and you want them to pay for its construction!") Nevertheless, Article 1er of the budget was adopted, with some eight to ten members of the left opposing.

having also been adopted by the Chamber of Peers. Meanwhile, and despite the previous assurances given to the Chamber of Deputies that F1.800.000 would be sufficient, costs had risen well above this ceiling. As early as November 1821, Hély d'Oissel had estimated a new total of FF 2.432.705 based on approximate figures supplied by Debret, and had allocated FF 1.972.820 of this to the Ministry of the Interior and FF 459.885 to the *Maison du Roi*.[102] At this stage, Hély d'Oissel seemed to have no doubt that Lauriston would approve the latter figure.[103] One government department, which had also received these figures, noted some extra costs which took the total to FF 2.462.442. It pointed out, however, that as these figures were still approximate, it was premature to allocate the costs as suggested by Hély d'Oissel.[104] By 1 June 1822, the estimate had risen to FF 2.533.195 and a total of only FF 1.304.075 had been paid to contractors and suppliers whose total bills, before scrutiny, revision and cut-back, had amounted to FF 3.201.718.[105] Hély d'Oissel then wrote to the Minister of the Interior in August 1822.[106] He had problems over finalising the final total as many suppliers had still to submit the details of their bills for checking, analysis and revision. He confirmed the provisional total of FF 2.533.195 which included entirely new flooring for the stage. It had been hoped that the flooring from the *Salle Richelieu* could have been used but this proved to be impossible. As for the FF 487.495 which was allocated to the *Maison du Roi*, it might have been possible to offset the value of fittings used from the *Salle Richelieu* estimated at FF 300.000 to FF 400.000, but a recent new law had allocated this value to the *Trésor Royal*. The *Maison du Roi* would thus have to pay the

---

102 a) Hély d'Oissel, *Directeur des Travaux publics,* charged with building the *Salle le Peletier,* to Baron Mounier, 9 November 1821, (F^{13} 1273); b) «État approximatif des travaux faits pour la construction de l'Académie royale de Musique par la Direction des Travaux publics de Paris ....» ("Approximate account of the work undertaken for the construction of the Opera under the supervision of the Director of Public Works of Paris ....") (F^{13} 1273). The total was FF 1.882.820 and the document was signed by Debret, 27 October 1821; c) «État approximatif des travaux exécutés au compte de l'administration de l'Académie royale de Musique ....» ("Approximate account of the work carried out for the Management of the Opera ....") (F^{13} 1273). The total was FF 459.885. Within this total was the cost of fire-hydrants and other safety measures required by the *Préfet de police*; extra work on offices and other facilities requested by the Opera's administration; the stage machinery, which cost FF 182.122; and other extras. The document was signed by Debret, 27 October 1821; d) A further FF 90.000 was due, according to Hély d'Oissel, for fees to architects and inspectors, to give an overall total of FF 2.432.705. This FF 90.000 was for the account of the Ministry of the Interior, thus raising its total to FF 1.972.820, (F^{13} 1273).

103 In the same report, Hély d'Oissel stated: «Tant de moyens d'accroître les recettes, de diminuer les dépenses, et de nouvelles facilités pour l'exploitation du Théâtre, détermineront sans doute M. le Marquis de Lauriston à faire, sans regrets, le sacrifice que les circonstances semblent imposer au crédit dont il dispose.» ("So many means of increasing receipts, of reducing expenses and of finding new ways to use the theatre better will no doubt oblige the Marquis of Lauriston to make the sacrifice, with no regrets, which circumstances seem to impose on the credit he has available.") (F^{13} 1273). In other words, the *Maison du Roi* would pay its share.

104 *Direction Générale de l'Administration départementale et de la police*, to Hély d'Oissel, 8 December 1821, (F^{13} 1273).

105 *État de situation des dépenses pour la construction de la nouvelle Salle, au 1 juin 1823, Règlement provisoire*, (F^{13} 1273) . These figures were confirmed in the document, 22 August 1822, (F^{21} 1073).

106 Hély d'Oissel to the Ministry of the Interior, 22 August 1822, (F^{21} 1073).

FF 487.495 in full. It was clear, again, that Hély d'Oissel had no doubt that the *Maison du Roi* would pay its share of a request for FF 447.490 to pay creditors.   FF 214.540 was allocated to the *Maison du Roi* and FF 232.950 to the Ministry of the Interior. By September 1822 this idea was accepted by the Ministry of the Interior which set about authorising the FF 232.950.[107]

A bombshell was then dropped by Lauriston. Any idea that the *Maison du Roi* would pay the FF 487.495 was dismissed in a powerful, well-argued report to the Minister of the Interior on 27 September 1822.[108] He went over the history of the whole affair and made, in principle, three points. First, the *ordonnance* of August 1820 clearly gave the exclusive task of constructing the new *Salle le Peletier* to the Ministry of the Interior and the credit for FF 900.000 was opened for this purpose. Second, Hély d'Oissel, who was in charge of the construction, had failed to communicate his ideas about the allocation of costs to the *Maison du Roi*. Lauriston expressed himself:

> … justement surpris de l'annonce inattendue d'une pareille charge, sur laquelle il ne m'avait été fait jusqu'à ce jour aucune ouverture et que rien ne pouvoit me faire prévoir.[109]

Third, when the *projet de loi* was presented to the Chamber of Deputies to double the 1820 credit to FF 1.800.000, it was represented that this new credit would cover all the costs and no mention was made of any allocation to the *Maison du Roi*. Indeed, included among the reasons for the new credit was the cost of the stage machinery, yet this cost, finally totalling FF 182.122, was included in the FF 487.495. The report by de Thury to the Chamber of Deputies had made specific reference to this and to the fact that the *Maison du Roi* could not pay due to its own considerable deficit. This was a convincing report by Lauriston and admitted as such by an internal report within the Ministry of the Interior which found Lauriston's points well-substantiated.[110] There was nothing for it but to go back to the Chamber of Deputies with a *projet de loi* which requested a supplementary credit of FF 733.000, being the difference between FF 1.800.000 and the provisional total of FF 2.533.195. A draft unsigned *ordonnance du Roi* was drawn up in early 1823 to authorise the supplementary credit,[111] and the *Commission des Comptes de la Chambre des Députés* sought further details on this request.[112]

---

107   Ministry of the Interior, report, 13 September 1822, (F^{21} 1073).

108   Lauriston to the Minister of the Interior, 27 September 1822, (F^{21} 1073).

109   ("… most surprised by the unexpected announcement of such an expense about which there had been no mention until that day and which I could in no way have foreseen.")

110   *Rapport,* Ministry of the Interior, 2 December 1822, (F^{21} 1073).

111   *Ordonnance du Roi,* unsigned, 1823, (F^{21} 1073).

112   M. de Bouville, *Président de la Commission des Comptes de la Chambre des Députés*, to the Ministry of the Interior, 24 February 1823 and 3 March 1823, (F^{21} 1073).

After various exchanges of letters, the final amount was reduced, first to FF 2.378.393 and then, in a very detailed schedule, to a definitive total of FF 2.375.894.[113] After a new *projet de loi* had been presented and discussed by the Chamber of Deputies, the supplementary credit of FF 575.894 was adopted on 29 June 1824 by a *Résolution de la Chambre*,[114] after a discussion and vote.[115] It was then added to the 1823–24 budget. This long saga was thus finally resolved. The *Maison du Roi* contributed nothing to the capital cost, the whole of which fell on the Ministry of the Interior.

This detailed analysis of the cost of the *Salle le Peletier* reveals discrepancies in the research already published on this subject.[116] Even more important, however, was the evidence of mismanagement in financial affairs, in this case by the Ministry of the Interior. Lauriston fought his corner with skill and success, but elsewhere the *Maison du Roi* was itself revealed as incompetent in financial affairs. It was also culpable of mismanagement and waste through its inability to control the Opera's finances.

Free Seats

The proliferation of free seats and boxes became an increasing financial problem for the Opera during the Restoration period and culminated during Lubbert's tenure as director from 1827 to 1831:

À Paris, la porte des abus est incessamment ouverte aux exigences des courtisans. Dans les dernières années de la Restauration, l'insuffisance des recettes allait sans cesse s'accroissant, parce qu'il n'y avait pas d'homme titré qui n'employât tous les moyens possibles pour obtenir des

---

113 *État des Dépenses pour la construction de la nouvelle Salle de l'Opéra*, n.d., (F^{13} 1273).

114 *Chambre des Députés, Résolution de la Chambre*, 29 June 1824, (C 733).

115 *Archives Parlementaires, 2. Série (1800–1860), Tome 41*, 28 May–6 July 1824. There was a short debate on 29 June 1824 on the supplementary credit of FF 575.894. The President then stated: «Aucun amendement n'ayant été proposé sur le projet de loi, je vais faire lecture de l'article 1er qui est ainsi conçu:» ("As no amendment has been proposed for the *projet de loi*, I am going to read Article 1 which is drafted thus:") i. «Article 1er. Il est accordé au Ministre de l'Intérieur sur les fonds du budget de 1823 au delà des crédits qui lui ont été ouverts pour les dépenses ordinaires de cet exercice par la loi du 17 août 1822, un supplément de FF 575.894, pour solder les travaux de construction et de dispositions intérieures de la nouvelle salle de l'Académie royale de Musique.» ("Article 1. In addition to the funds from the 1823 Budget and over and above the credit made available for the expenses of this undertaking by the decree of 17 August 1822, a supplementary credit of FF 575.894 is granted to the Minister of the Interior so as to pay for the construction works and interior refurbishment of the new Opera house.") ii. «Cet article est mis aux voix et adopté sans discussion.» ("This proposition was put to the vote and adopted without discussion.")

116 a) Félix Martin, *Historique des Salles de l'Opéra* (Paris, *Bibliothèque de l'Opéra*, Rés 1049 [4]), pp. 104–105. According to Martin, the total cost of the *Salle le Peletier* was FF 2.287.495. He considered that the 1821 proposed credit of FF 1.800.000 was only approved in June 1824 by the Chamber of Deputies, and that the Civil List was charged with the balance of FF 487.495; b) Wilberg, op. cit., pp. 31–38. She considered that Debret's original budget was FF 800.072, as detailed in the *Ordonnance du Roi*, 9 August 1820, and that this should be combined with the credit of FF 900.000 to make a total of FF 1.700.072, which was FF 99.928 short of the FF 1.800.000 requested in 1821. She also put the final cost at FF 2.287.495, and, following Martin, wrote that the credit of FF 1.800.000 was finally approved in 1824, and that the *Maison du Roi* paid the excess of FF 487.495.

loges à l'Opéra sans les payer. Ce résultat déplorable de l'avarice du grand monde fut cause qu'en 1828 et 1829 la caisse de la liste civile ajouta près de FF 400.000 pour les déficits de l'Opéra.[117]

These had always been available, even in Napoleon's time, and he made strenuous efforts to try and eradicate them.[118] Matters, however, got much worse after 1815. The aristocracy treated the Opera like a salon which was an extension of the Court and into which entry should be free.[119] Furthermore, it was not only these free seats and boxes *per se* which caused a problem. There were also four separate but related issues which caused concern. The first, discussed fully in the next section, was the attempt to levy the *droit des indigents*, the poor tax, on free tickets. The second was the undoubted malpractice of selling these free tickets on the black-market for cash often at a discount to the face value. The third was the practice whereby those who had rented seats or boxes made such seats available to friends who, in the opinion of the Opera, could well afford to pay, thus depriving it of potential receipts. The fourth was the practice of selling rented boxes on the black-market. It took the arrival of Véron and a sweeping reduction in the number of free seats and boxes to improve the situation and restore lost receipts to the Opera.

Free seats were divided into two categories. Those which were *inscrites*, that is officially approved and registered on lists, and those which were *non-inscrites* or *entrées de tolérance*, that is not officially registered but sanctioned by custom and tacit approval. The first category was itself divided into two, being *entrées de droit*, entry by right, and *entrées de faveur*, entry by favour. The former were, in principle, given to people by virtue of the office or position which they held. The right did not attach to a particular person and the beneficiary changed as and when the holder of that office or

---

117 ("In Paris, the door of abuse is constantly opened by the demands of members of the Court. During the last years of the Restoration, the lack of receipts increased ever more because there was not a single titled aristocrat who did not use every means possible to obtain a box at the Opera without paying for it. The sorry outcome of the avarice of the aristocracy was the main reason why the Civil List was increased in 1828 and 1829 by nearly FF 400.000 to help pay the Opera's debts.") André L. Malliot, *La Musique au Théâtre* (Paris, 1863), p. 81. If this referred to the FF 400.000 found from the Civil List to pay the pre-1828 debts of all the five Royal theatres, then this comment is not quite accurate.

118 a) E. M. de Lyden, *Le Théâtre d'autrefois et d'aujourd'hui. Cantatrices et Comédiens, 1532–1882* (Paris, 1882), p. 190, quoted by Frederic W.J. Hemmings, *The Theatre Industry in Nineteenth-Century France* (Cambridge, 1993), part 1, p. 21. "Napoleon Bonaparte wrote in December 1802, at the foot of the list of free seats for the Opera which contained seventeen boxes and ninety-four names, that as from 21 December all these boxes should be paid for by those who occupied them. He set an example by paying FF 15.000 for his own box;" b) Hemmings, op. cit., part 1, p. 21. "... the decree on the theatres, 1 November 1807, abolishing 'all reserved boxes, free entries, complimentary tickets and like facilities at all four of the major theatres;'" c) Barbier, op. cit., p. 38. "As early as 1802 the prefect of police was startled, when analysing one Friday evening's performance, to count takings of only FF 4.600, even though the auditorium had been filled. After a closer look, he realised that only 20 out of 150 orchestra seats had been paid for, 300 out of 600 pit seats, 26 out of 150 balcony seats, and not a single one out of 200 seats along the sides. The Emperor intervened many times to try to remedy the situation and even paid for his own box himself, but the problem remained unsolved."

119 "Under Louis XVIII and Charles X, the situation became even worse, as the aristocracy treated the Opera as their salon. They made themselves comfortable and strutted about as though they were at Court. Every evening, people of rank occupied the boxes and balconies without paying, completely oblivious that their right to enter might be contested." Barbier, op. cit., p. 39.

position changed. On the other hand, *entrées de faveur* were granted to individuals in their own right and it was possible, with the Opera's agreement, to cede this right to someone else. It was noticeable from an analysis of the official lists, however, that the distinction between the two lists was not fully maintained.[120] An undated list of *entrées de faveur*, which contained references to changes made in 1830, was instructive.[121] There were 325 names on the list, but these included some members of the *Conseil du contentieux, Jury littéraire,* and *Comité de mise en scène.* Against the names of these members the word *droit* had been put and although the second and third committees were dissolved after Véron took over, it was clear that members of the *Comité du contentieux* were, in accordance with the definition described above, included in the new list of *entrées de droit.*[122] This total of 325 names for *entrées de faveur* can be compared with the list for 1826, which totalled only 184,[123] and was indicative of the expansion of names under Lubbert.

As for the second category, it was itself divided into three, being *entrées d'échange, billets de faveur* and *billets de service* and all three came under the general heading of *entrées de tolérance.* *Entrées d'échange*, entry by exchange, were free tickets exchanged with the other Royal theatres, namely the *Théâtre Français,* the *Opéra Comique,* the *Odéon* and the *Théâtre Italien,* as well as with certain secondary theatres. Although it might be thought that these should have been officially registered, and certainly lists were exchanged between the theatres, these free tickets were described as *non-inscrites* and were subject only to a verbal contract.[124] Evidence for these exchanges showed, for example, that the *Théâtre Français* had a list for 1830 and 1831 of seventy-five people who could enjoy a free seat at the Opera,[125] while the *Opéra Comique* had a list of seventy-three names for 1827 and 1828.[126] An 1831 report from

120 Ozanam, op. cit., pp. 217–218.

121 *Liste des entrées de faveur,* n.d., (F^{21} 1067).

122 *Entrées de droit, 1831,* (AJ^{13} 180 IX).

123 *Entrées de faveur, 1826,* (AJ^{13} 118 V). Two lists signed by La Rochefoucauld, 10 August 1826 and
     23 September 1826.

124 Edmond Cavé to the Minister, 20 May 1831, (AJ^{13} 180 IX).

125 *Liste des entrées de la Comédie Française à l'Académie Royale de Musique, pour l'année théâtrale
     1830 et 1831,* (AJ^{13} 218). The list comprised:

Sociétaires	25
Acteurs pensionnaires	13
Sociétaires retirés	20
Conseil judiciaire	10
Administration	7
	75

126 *Liste des entrées par échange du Théâtre Royal de l'Opéra Comique à l'Académie Royale de
     Musique, pour l'année 1827, 1828,* (AJ^{13} 218). The list comprised:

Administration	5
Sociétaires retirés	18
Sociétaires en activité	17
Pensionnaires	20
Chefs d'Orchestre, chant, ballets, Régisseur	5
Conseil judiciaire	8
	73

Edmond Cavé, secretary to the Commission, indicated that a total of 146 names from other theatres enjoyed free seats at the Opera and that a total of 126 free seats were available to nominated members of the Opera for use at the other theatres.[127] There were no lists for *billets de faveur*, tickets by favour, as these were given out according to circumstance. For instance, a very high number were given out for the first night of a new production with the clear aim of "papering the house", and this was repeated on subsequent nights if felt necessary. This could be regarded as a legitimate tactic by the management of the Opera. On the other hand, this ability of the director to use his discretion on *billets de faveur* could be greatly abused and Lubbert did exactly that. *Billets de service*, tickets for service, were supposed to be given to members of the Opera's administration and to those responsible for various departments at the Opera such as singing, the ballet, the orchestra and stagehands. Each person was normally entitled to two tickets per performance but this was abused. The artists also received *billets de service* for each performance in which they appeared,[128] but malpractices abounded here. Authors and composers received free seats for performances of their works, and could well have an *entrée de droit* as well. Again, as will be shown, authors and composers took advantage of these free seats, to the indirect detriment of the Opera's finances.

The subject of free seats at the Opera in the Restoration period has already been substantially researched by Ozanam, both in principle and in detail.[129] Use was not made, however, of the findings of Cavé. This Commission came into being at the same time as Véron was appointed as the new director on 1 March 1831, and one of its first decisions was to direct Cavé to look into the whole question of free seats through research into Lubbert's tenure as director. The background to this request was that the Commission and Véron were very concerned about the malpractices which had proliferated and were determined to curb them. Cavé's findings made fascinating reading in that they laid bare these malpractices and put the whole problem of free seats into context.

First of all, he presented to the Minister the officially registered lists of *entrées de droit* and *entrées de faveur* which had been in use under Lubbert. These totalled 502, a much higher total than, for instance, the 1826 total of 239 divided into 55 *entrées de droit* and 184 *entrées de faveur*. Cavé explained that the total of *entrées de faveur* was especially high as many names had been added by Lubbert which should have remained as unregistered *entrées de tolérance*. He then presented his findings on these *entrées de tolérance non-inscrites* and commented that no lists could be found, either because they had never existed or because they had been destroyed. He made a comprehensive analysis of the way in which these free seats had been allocated and of, by implication, the abuses which had flourished under Lubbert. At every performance Lubbert had given a minimum of fourteen free boxes to friends, protectors and journalists. For the first three performances of a new production, the auditorium had been just about full of

---

127 Cavé to the Minister, 20 May 1831, (AJ[13] 180 IX).

128 Ozanam, op. cit., p. 229. *Billets de service alloués au personnel de l'Opéra à partir du 1er avril, 1821.*

129 Ozanam, op. cit., pp. 217–234.

people with free seats. For other performances, Lubbert had given a minimum of 350 free seats per performance, being *billets de faveur* for journalists, friends and certain employees of the Opera, and *billets de service* for artists. This figure can be confirmed from various lists.[130] Apart from an official free box, the Civil List enjoyed *loges de faveur* and 200 free seats per month, while *les Gentilshommes de la Chambre du Roi*, who had the free use of a box paid for by the King, also enjoyed a further forty-five free seats per month. Quite apart from the official *entrées de droit* accorded to the *Commissaire de Police des Tuileries, l'état-major de la place* and *l'état-major de la garde nationale*, a further eighteen to twenty *cartes d'entrées* per performance were allocated to their staffs. Members of the claque had traditionally been given free seats through *billets de service* from artists but more recently they had received *billets de faveur* from Lubbert himself. Many suppliers of goods and services to the Opera enjoyed *billets de faveur* without any authorisation and with nothing written down. A considerable number of former artists, directors and staff, including orchestral players, could enter the Opera without paying. The same privilege was granted to their parents, widows and children which was a clear abuse of the system. The parents, spouses and friends of current artists and staff could also enter freely, not only into the auditorium, but also backstage. Apart from the *entrées de droit* officially given to authors and composers, the custom had been established for each author and composer to enjoy a free box at every performance of their works and members of the *Jury littéraire, Conseil du contentieux* and *Comité de mise en scène* also enjoyed free entry.

The new administration had every reason to paint as dark a picture as possible of the abuses under Lubbert, and Cavé's report certainly did that. Nevertheless, the extent of these abuses was undoubted and the Commission took immediate action to try and eliminate them.

Aside from those listed in Cavé's report there were many other malpractices, most of which caused financial loss to the Opera. A particular one was the sale of *billets de service* and *billets de faveur* to third parties, thus depriving the Opera of cash to which it had a right.[131] This abuse had long been recognised by the authorities but little had been done to correct it. The management of the *Odéon*, for example, had observed that this was a major abuse which the police did nothing to eradicate.[132] A report to La Rochefoucauld in July 1826 recommended that the free tickets issued to authors, composers and artists should be reduced,[133] and Duplantys suggested that a fine should

---

130 *Relevé sommaire des billets de service ou de faveur délivrés qui sont entrés, ou qui n'ont pas été présentés pendant le mois,* (O³ 1681 II). These monthly summaries had been requested by La Rochefoucauld. For October 1828, the summary showed a total of 5.082 free tickets issued, of which 4.273 were utilised. As there were fourteen performances, this represented an average of 363 issued per performance. For November 1828, the figures were 3.815 free tickets, of which 3.274 were utilised. As there were ten performances, the average per performance was 382.

131 Ozanam, op. cit., p. 231. He cited the case of Brocard who had sold *billets de service* on the black-market and was deprived of free seats for fifteen days, (AJ¹³ 116 IV).

132 *Théâtre Royal de l'Odéon* to La Rochefoucauld, 16 December 1826, (O³ 1672 V).

133 Leconte to La Rochefoucauld, 12 July 1826, (O³ 1620).

be levied equivalent to the price of the ticket.[134] Nothing was done, however, and the whole question was revisited in 1828. A meeting of the *Comité consultatif* on 17 June 1828 recommended that a circular should be sent to all personnel at the Opera,[135] although Lubbert subsequently advised La Rochefoucauld that fines and a withdrawal of free tickets would be a delicate matter given the status of certain soloists.[136] In the interim, certain administrative measures were put in place to combat this abuse,[137] but La Rochefoucauld remained dissatisfied. He felt his instructions had either been ignored or misunderstood.[138] Lubbert, in reply, used the example of Adolph Nourrit, the famous tenor: were he to be fined or have his free tickets withdrawn, he could find himself 'indisposed' and performances would have to be cancelled. In any event, wrote Lubbert, a theatrical company should not be run like a military operation.[139] Finally, a circular was sent to all personnel. Those found guilty of selling free tickets would, for the first offence, receive no free tickets for fifteen days; for the second offence, for two months; and for the third offence, a withdrawal of the privilege.[140] It was, however, questionable whether this circular had the desired effect. In April 1829 La Bouillerie could still refer to the scandalous traffic in free tickets and felt, like the management of the *Odéon* in 1826, that the surest way of stopping the abuse was through active measures from the *Préfet de Police*.[141]

Another abuse was the over-supply of free seats whereby a recipient obtained more free seats than was his or her due.[142] The sale of *contremarques,* cardboard passes

---

134 Duplantys to La Rochefoucauld, 5 September 1826, (O^3 1676 I).

135 «Monsieur le Directeur présente de nouveau au Comité la nécessité de prendre un moyen pour empêcher la vente des billets de service donnés aux artistes.» ("The Director again presents to the Committee the need to adopt a measure which prevents the sale of the free tickets given to performers.") *Comité consultatif*, meeting 17 June 1828, with Lubbert as President, (O^3 1681 II). After a discussion, it was decided to issue a circular to the Opera's staff which set out a range of penalties for this abuse.

136 Lubbert implied that certain artists would be difficult if the measures were imposed. «… je ne puis me dissimuler que l'application de ces moyens seroit dans certains cas, sinon impossible, au moins très délicate et difficile vis-à-vis de certains sujets.» ("… I cannot hide the fact that the application of these measures would be, in certain cases, if not impossible, then at least very delicate and difficult as regards some artists.") Lubbert to La Rochefoucauld, 25 September 1828, (O^3 1681 II).

137 Lubbert to La Rochefoucauld, 1 October 1828, (O^3 1681 II). Various measures had been taken to control the free tickets. Each ticket had the recipient's name on it, and entry would be refused if this were not so. Each day, a list of free tickets, being *billets de faveur* and *billets de service* would be compiled and a monthly list would be sent to La Rochefoucauld. Officials at the door were instructed to scrutinise all tickets scrupulously.

138 La Rochefoucauld to Lubbert, 2 October 1828, (O^3 1681 II). He felt the abuse of the sale of free tickets was greater than ever and felt that Lubbert had been negligent.

139 «Une troupe dramatique ne sauroit être conduite avec la régularité d'une troupe militaire.» ("A theatrical company should not be managed with the precision of the military.") Lubbert to La Rochefoucauld, 4 October 1828, (O^3 1681 II).

140 Circular, Lubbert to the Opera's personnel, 7 November 1828, (O^3 1681 II).

141 La Bouillerie to La Rochefoucauld, 10 April 1829, (O^3 1707 I).

142 Report on irregularities committed by Solomé, November 1829, (O^3 1599).

issued during the intervals so that members of the audience could go outside the theatre, was commonplace especially if the production was a popular one or there was more than one production during the same evening.[143] Those who had rented boxes or seats could take advantage of their position. It was the practice for lessees who were not regular attendees to make these boxes available to their friends and relatives. This was not an abuse as boxes rented in this way were the personal property of the lessees who had the right to dispose of them to friends.[144] Furthermore, the Opera had already received the rental and suffered no direct loss of receipts. La Rochefoucauld pointed out, however, that those who were given these free seats by lessees were those most able to pay.[145] Lessees did abuse the system, however, when they sold their boxes for an evening's performance on the black-market. This was a flourishing practice as Véron later ruefully explained:

> Pendant le grand succès de *Robert le Diable*, une dame du beau monde venait dans sa voiture aux abords de l'Opéra, entre cinq et six heures du soir, mettre presqu'aux enchères sa loge de six place aux premières en face. Je tiens pour certain que, plus d'une fois, des marchands de billets lui achetèrent cette loge deux cent francs, et même jusqu'à trois cent francs; c'était plus que le triple de ce qu'elle coûtait au bureau.[146]

A Tax and a Levy

Droit des Indigents

There was one category of expense at the Opera which was subject to considerable dispute from 1826 onwards and which also threw some light on the extent to which free seats were sold on the black-market. This was the *droit des indigents*, a tax on tickets which was collected by the *Hospices et Secours à domicile de Paris* and then distributed to the poor. It was introduced under the *ancien régime* and levied on theatrical performances, balls, concerts and other public spectacles in Paris. It was suspended in

---

143 Hemmings, op. cit., part 1, pp. 59–60.

144 "A box rented in this way became the lessee's personal property for that night: no one else was allowed to occupy it even if it remained empty …. In his absence, he had the right to dispose of this box to friends." Hemmings, op. cit., part 1, p. 16.

145 La Rochefoucauld to La Bouillerie, 9 March 1830, (O^3 1691). La Bouillerie to La Rochefoucauld, 2 April 1830, (O^3 1691). La Rochefoucauld deplored the fact that the *premiers Gentilshommes de la Chambre du Roi* had allowed their box to be used by other members of Court who gained free seats yet were those most able to pay. La Bouillerie replied by remarking that this was a regular practice and that, in any case, the box had been paid for by the King.

146 ("During the great success of *Robert le Diable*, a society lady used to come close to the Opera, between five and six o'clock in the evening, in order to auction off her box for six people in the centre of the first level. I know for certain that more than once the ticket touts bought this box for two hundred francs, and even up to three hundred francs; that was more than triple the cost of the box at the box-office.") Véron, op. cit., III, p. 326.

1789[147] but a law of 27 November 1796 reintroduced the tax for a temporary six-month period.[148] Given the subsequent dispute between the *Hospices* and the *Maison du Roi*, it would be relevant to quote the French text in full.[149] At this stage, the law was clear. One-tenth was added to the net ticket price – or, what was the same thing, one-eleventh was deducted from the gross price – for all performances, theatrical or otherwise. It was also clear that it was levied only when a seat had been paid for, either for one performance or for a specific period of time. A further law, 26 July 1797, overrode that of 27 November 1796.[150] Again the text is important, given the subsequent dispute, as there were three significant changes.[151] First, a distinction was made between theatrical performances and other spectacles such as balls and concerts. Second, the tax for the former remained the same, being the one-tenth addition to the net ticket price, whereas that for the latter was changed to one-quarter of the gross total receipts. Third, and crucially, the words *en payant* were only included for the non-theatrical performances. An *arrêté* of 9 December 1809 confirmed the two rates of tax and the methods of calculation and decreed that the tax was permanent, rather than one which was renewable annually.[152] Finally, *la loi de finance*, 13 June 1825, also confirmed these details and again the words *en payant* were only applied to non-theatrical

---

147 Ozanam, op. cit., p. 45, who also quoted Malliot, op. cit., p. 231.

148 *Conseil Général d'Administration des Hospices et Secours à domicile de Paris. Séance du 17 mai 1826*, (O³ 1672 V). This meeting quoted the texts of the various laws.

149 The law of 27 November 1796, quoted in minutes of the meeting, 17 May 1826. «Article 1er. Il sera perçu un droit d'un décime par franc en sus du prix de chaque billet d'entrée, pendant six mois dans tous les spectacles où se donnent des pièces de théâtre, des bals, des feux d'artifice, des concerts, des courses et exercises de chevaux, pour lesquels les spectateurs paient .... La même perception aura lieu sur le prix des places louées pour un temps déterminé.» ("Article 1. A tax of one-tenth of a franc is to be levied on the price of each entrance ticket, for six months, at all performances where there are plays, balls, firework displays, equestrian events, for which spectators pay .... The same tax will be levied on the price of seats reserved for a specific period of time.")

150 *Conseil Général d'Administration des Hospices et Secours à domicile de Paris. Séance du 17 mai 1826*, (O³ 1672 V).

151 The law of 26 July 1797, quoted in minutes of meeting, 17 May 1826. «Article 1er. Le droit d'un décime par franc, établi par la loi du 27 novembre 1796, continuera à être perçu jusqu'au 26 novembre 1797, en sus du prix de chaque billet d'entrée et d'abonnement, dans tous les spectacles où se donnent des pièces de théâtre. Article 2ème. Le même droit d'un décime par franc établi et prorogé par les mêmes lois à l'entrée des bals, des feux d'artifice, des concerts, des courses et exercises de chevaux, et autres fêtes où l'on est admis en payant, est porté au quart de la recette jusqu'au dit jour, 27 novembre 1798.» ("Article 1. The tax of one-tenth of a franc, established by the law of 27 November 1796, will continue to be levied on the price of each entrance ticket and season ticket until 26 November 1797, for all shows where theatrical performances are given. Article 2. The same tax of one-tenth of a franc levied and extended by the above laws on balls, firework displays, concerts, equestrian events and other spectacles where one pays to enter, is raised to a quarter of the receipts up to and including 27 November 1798.")

152 This *arrêté*, 9 December 1809, was also quoted in the meeting of the *Conseil Général*, 17 May 1826, already referred to, (O³ 1672 V).

performances.[153] The quantum of the tax collected from the Paris theatres, and the calculations of the one-tenth share, were included in various schedules.[154]

As from 1 January 1826, a new collector of the tax called Locré de St. Julien was appointed for five years. He agreed to raise a minimum of FF 672.000 per annum, even to the extent of meeting any shortfall out of his own pocket. In return, he was to be paid one per cent of the gross tax collected.[155] Locré de St. Julien immediately sought ways of increasing the tax revenue and two of them concerned the Opera. First, it had been the custom for the Opera to pay only one-tenth of the gross receipts from its balls and other spectacles, rather than the one-quarter prescribed by law. After various exchanges between the *Hospices* and La Rochefoucauld, this point was conceded.[156] Second, and of much greater significance, there was an attack on the whole question of free seats, especially those distributed by the Royal theatres. It was claimed, for the first time ever, that the *droit des indigents* should be collected on these *billets de service et de faveur*. The basis for this claim was set out in a *Note* which put forward a new construction of the law, namely that the tax should be charged on a theatre's free tickets just as much as on those which had been sold.[157] The grounds for this construction were subtle. The *Note* pointed out that one-quarter of the gross receipts was payable for non-theatrical performances whereas the exact wording for the theatres was one-tenth of a franc added

---

153 *La loi de finance,* 13 June 1825, also quoted in the meeting of the *Conseil Général,* 17 May 1826, (O^3 1672 V).

154 a) Monthly schedules showing total receipts for all sixteen theatres in Paris, (O^3 1672 V). For example:

March 1826	
Total gross receipts	FF 516.776
Droit des indigents	
Tax on cash at box office	50.700
Tax on *abonnements*	2.659
Monthly total	53.359
October 1826	
Total gross receipts	583.610
Droit des indigents	
Tax on cash at box office	53.454
Tax on *abonnements*	1.446
Monthly total	54.900

b) Books of daily receipts at the Opera, (O^3 1662).

10 December 1823	
Gross total receipts	FF 2.584
One-eleventh of gross	235
Net receipts, to which one-tenth added	2.349

155 *Conseil Général, Séance du 17 mai 1826,* (O^3 1672 V).

156 *Conseil Général, Séances,* 15 March 1826, (O^3 1672 V). 26 July, 6 September 1826, (O^3 1676 V). Chabrol, *Préfet de la Seine,* to La Rochefoucauld, 1 August 1826, 15 September 1826, (O^3 1676 V).

157 *Administration Générale des Hôpitaux, Hospices et Secours à domicile de Paris.* «Note sur les moyens de réprimer les infractions à la loi qui a établi la taxe des pauvres sur les spectacles et autres lieux publics de divertissement.» n.d. ("A note on the measures to stop the breaking of the law which has imposed a poor tax on theatrical performances and other public places of entertainment.") (O^3 1672 V).

to the net price of each ticket. This implied that it was the price on the ticket that mattered, whether or not it had been paid for, and that the tax should be levied on the person who had the seat by virtue of this ticket and not levied on the theatre. After all, the tax was included in the price on the ticket and it was immaterial whether the price was paid for or not. In any event, the spirit of the law, which was designed to help the poor and destitute, demanded that everyone who had a ticket for the theatre should pay the tax. It followed from this construction that anyone who did not pay the tax on his free ticket was breaking the law. No-one, affirmed the *Note,* should enter a theatre without paying the tax as that person was, in effect, a creditor of the *Hospices.* The *Note* also pointed to an abuse whereby many free tickets were sold on the black-market for cash, thus depriving both the theatre and the *Hospices* of any revenue. This fraudulent abuse was practised pretty well openly by the secondary theatres so as to evade the law and no-one had the courage to suppress such impudence. The *Note* astutely made the point that it was not against free tickets as such. It was merely that the tax should be collected on them and that they should not be resold. It then calculated that some FF 1.000.000 of free tickets were given away in Paris by the theatres each year, thus depriving the *Hospices* of around FF 100.000. Following on from this *Note,* the *Conseil Général* of the *Hospices* proposed that the collection of the tax should be made according to the law and without any exemption or reduction. It also proposed an elaborate set of rules and procedures whereby any holder of a free ticket would be forced to pay the tax when the ticket was presented at the theatre.[158]

The *Maison du Roi,* whose Royal theatres were most prone to give away free tickets, took issue with this construction of the law in a *Note* of its own.[159] Needless to say, its own construction affirmed that the tax should only be levied on those tickets which had been paid for. To substantiate this, it relied heavily on the original 17 November 1796 temporary law which clearly stated that the charge of one-tenth on the net price only covered those tickets which had been sold, whether for theatres, balls, concerts or any other spectacle. The construction of this law, according to the *Maison du Roi,* was clear. No tax should be levied on free tickets however much subsequent laws had modified the text. What was more, it was the theatres which should pay the tax, not the ticket-

---

158 *Conseil Général, Séance, 17 mai 1826.* «Projet de Règlements pour assurer la perception du droit des pauvres sur les spectacles et fêtes.» ("A plan to regulate and ensure the collection of the poor tax on theatrical performances and other entertainments.") (O³ 1672 V).

159 «En effet, la taxe imposée aux établissements publics dont il est question, en vertu des diverses lois qui ont régi la matière, n'a jamais dû frapper que les billets payants, et ce principe qui fait toute la question, est explicitement indiqué dans ces lois. Il résulte de tous ces termes bien précis, que la loi n'a réellement frappé d'une taxe que les billets payants, les entrées et les loges louées désignées sous le titre général de places louées pour un temps déterminé, et qu'en conséquence les billets gratis, dont il n'est pas fait mention dans la loi, ne peuvent être assujettis à cette taxe.» ("In reality, the tax imposed on public places of entertainment which is under discussion because of the various rules which govern the issue, has only ever been imposed on tickets which are paid for, and this principle, which is the issue in question, is clearly set out in these laws. It is clear from these well-defined rules that the law has indeed imposed a tax only on tickets which have been paid for and on seats and boxes rented under the general heading of seats rented for a specific period of time. In consequence, free tickets, which are not mentioned in the law, cannot be subject to this tax.") *Note raisonnée sur les prétentions de l'administration des Hospices, relativement au droit des indigents sur le produit des Théâtres.* n.d., (O³ 1691 I).

holder. The word *prix*, as used in the various laws, implied the receipt of cash and not, as the *Hospices* argued, the price as printed on a ticket. The law was clear. The receipt of cash was the basis for the tax. As for the sale of free tickets, which had the effect of tax-avoidance, it was for the police and other authorities to stamp out this abuse. The solution did not lie in charging the tax when the ticket-holder presented it at the theatre. As a final thrust to its argument, the *Maison du Roi* pointed out that the law had stood for thirty years with no tax paid on free tickets. If there had been any ambiguity in the law, the way it should have been construed would already have been resolved.

However much the *Maison du Roi* protested, it was clear that the *Hospices* had influential support. The Ministry of the Interior was in favour and Chabrol, the *Préfet du Département de la Seine*, could write to Doudeauville at the *Maison du Roi* to make this point.[160] He solicited Doudeauville's support for the view taken by the Ministry of the Interior. In any event, the idea that the police could stamp out the abuse of free tickets sold on the black-market rang rather hollow. The *Odéon* had complained about a lack of protection from the police on this very subject:

> Une des causes qui nuisent le plus à la prospérité du théâtre Royal de l'Odéon est, sans contredis, le refus de protection qu'il éprouve journellement de la part de la Police pour réprimer la vente des billets de faveur.[161]

It had asked for the full support of the police and immediate arrest of any individual who sold *billets de faveur*. This should have been easy as the words "Not for sale" had been printed on the ticket, yet the police did nothing. The *Odéon* had requested La Rochefoucauld to contact the *Préfet de Police* to ensure strict enforcement of the law.

This debate dragged on and it was not until 27 August 1829 that the *Conseil de Préfecture de la Seine* decided that the *droit des indigents* should be extended to cover free tickets.[162] The *Maison du Roi* continued to resist and the Opera was instructed not to submit to this new measure.[163] Needless to say, Locré de St. Julien did not accept this and made a claim for FF 8.637, which Lubbert refused to pay.[164] At this point the matter was put in the hands of the *Comité du contentieux de la Liste Civile*, and an advocate called Guichard was instructed to put the case on behalf of the *Maison du Roi*.[165] It would appear that Guichard was not successful and that his successor, an advocate called Ripault, also failed when presenting the same case before the *Conseil de Préfecture de la Seine* in March 1831.[166] Locré de St. Julien then took the matter up with the Commission and met with them on 2 June 1831. He claimed FF 42.514, being

---

160   Chabrol, *Préfet du Département de la Seine*, to Doudeauville, 6 July 1826, (O³ 1672 V).

161   ("One of the causes which most damages the prosperity of the *Théâtre Royal de l'Odéon* is unquestionably the daily refusal of the police to support it in stamping out the sale of free tickets.") *Théâtre Royal de l'Odéon* to La Rochefoucauld, 16 December 1826, (O³ 1672 V).

162   La Rochefoucauld to La Bouillerie, 8 July 1830, (O³ 1690). He referred to the *arrêté* of 27 August 1829.

163   La Rochefoucauld to Lubbert, 23 January 1830, (O³ 1685).

164   Lubbert to La Rochefoucauld, 7 June 1830, (O³ 1690).

165   La Bouillerie to La Rochefoucauld, 16 July 1830, (O³ 1690).

166   Ripault, *Avocat aux conseils du Roi et à la cour de cassation*, to Véron, 7 March 1831, (F²¹ 1075).

the estimated *droit des indigents* owed on *billets de faveur* in the Restoration period as a result of the rulings in his favour. He wanted to know who would pay this amount. The Commission explained that it was not charged with paying the debts of the former regime and advised Locré de St. Julien to go to the *Commissaires Généraux* to seek redress.[167]

The dispute then went before the *Conseil d'État* on 22 July 1831.[168] This time it was the *Théâtre Français* which contested the previous rulings and again it was Ripault who pleaded the case, although it was recognised that all the theatres in Paris would be affected by the court's decision. After the various arguments had been heard, M. Marchant as *Ministère public* gave a view favourable to the theatres in that he considered the price of the ticket was the most important point and that as *prix* meant a price which had been paid, the *droit des indigents* could not be charged on free tickets:

> En effet, l'impôt est établi en sus du prix; le prix est donc le point de départ, la condition première de l'impôt; il sert en même temps à en déterminer la quotité. Si le prix s'élève, l'impôt s'élève; si le prix baisse, l'impôt baisse aussi; enfin si le prix est zéro, l'impôt est zéro.[169]

The *Conseil d'État* then deferred its judgement on the case until it met again on 5 August 1831.[170] It agreed with the argument of the *Maison du Roi* that the law of 27 November 1796 was paramount and concluded that the *droit des indigents* could only be collected on tickets which had been paid for. On the other hand, it agreed with the *Hospices* that the tax was payable by the ticket-holder and not by the theatre. It then made a distinction between tickets which were genuinely free and those which, although issued freely, had then been sold on the black-market for cash or were used to pay expenses. The former should not be subject to the tax whereas the latter, which had been sold for money or money's worth, should attract the tax. It followed from this judgement that the *arrêté* of the *Préfet de la Seine* on 27 August 1829 should be set aside only in respect of free tickets which were handed over without fraud and which conformed to former usage.

This decision was borne out by the *droit des indigents* paid by the Opera under Véron.[171] Initially, he paid by *abonnements*, which reached FF 3.000 per month from January to May 1832. Thereafter, the tax was raised on the actual receipts and ranged between FF 2.700 and FF 3.700 per fifteen days, or FF 5.400 and FF 7.400 per month.

---

167 Commission, minutes of meeting, 2 June 1831, (F²¹ 4633).

168 *Gazette des Tribunaux*, 14 July 1831, (AJ¹³ 1027 I).

169 ("In reality, the tax is levied on the price; this price is therefore the starting point, the main reason for the tax; it also serves to determine the amount of the tax. If the price increases, so does the tax; if the price falls, so does the tax; if the price is zero, so is the tax.") *Gazette des Tribunaux*, 14 July 1831, (AJ¹³ 1027 I).

170 *Recueil des Arrêts du Conseil, par M. Deloche. Tome Premier, 2ème Série, Année 1831. 5 août 1831, Théâtre Français c. les hospices de Paris* (Paris, Conseil d'État, Bibliothèque et Archives), pp. 299–301.

171 Various receipts, signed by Locré de St. Julien for the *droit des indigents* collected from the Opera, (AJ¹³ 291 II).

Redevance des Théâtres Secondaires

By an Imperial decree on 13 August 1811, the Opera became entitled to received a *redevance,* levy, on performances at other places of public entertainment in Paris.[172] The levy was imposed on the so-called secondary and little theatres in Paris at a $\frac{1}{20}^{th}$ or five per cent rate on receipts, the *droit des indigents* having first been deducted. The other Royal theatres were exempted from this levy. It was also imposed on all concerts, balls and other public entertainments at a $\frac{1}{5}^{th}$ or twenty per cent rate on receipts, the *droit des indigents* also having first been deducted. The levy could be paid by an *abonnement* at a rate of $\frac{1}{12}^{th}$ per month and it was for the *Département de la Seine* to make sure that the decree was enforced. The collection of the levy was entrusted to the man who also collected the *droit des indigents.* By 1818 the collector was de Bief and he was entitled to a commission of two and a half per cent on the amount collected.[173]

The special interest about this *redevance* was that, like the *droit des indigents,* it gave rise to a legal challenge. This took place in 1826 and was a very real threat to the Opera given the sums involved. There were other attempts to change the basis of the levy[174] and the way it was collected[175] but these were minor matters compared to the mood of resentment from the theatres which gave rise to the challenge. The legal basis for this was succinctly put in a letter to La Rochefoucauld from Delavau, the *Préfet de Police.* No tax could be collected unless the authority to do so had been included in the annual budget passed into law by the Chamber of Deputies. As the *redevance* had never been included, unlike the *droit des indigents,* its legality was thus in question. Furthermore, the decree of 1811 was not a law and could not be relied upon.[176] Chabrol, the *Préfet du Département de la Seine,* also made these points to Doudeauville and felt that he had to suspend any action against non-payers until the levy had been voted on in the Chamber of Deputies.[177] The challenge was then referred to the Opera's *Conseil contentieux* which, in a ruling favourable to the Opera, made a number of points which rebutted the challenge. First, an *impôt,* tax, was defined as a *contribution publique,* a contribution from the public, which was collected in the name of the State. In this sense the *droit des indigents* was a tax, especially as it was collected throughout France. The *redevance,* on the other hand, was not a contribution from the public as it was levied on certain theatres in Paris and paid to the Opera rather than the State. In this sense it was an indemnity and not a tax. Second, although it was true that the authority to collect a tax was a matter of law and of annual renewal through

172 *Décret Impérial,* 13 August 1811, (AJ[13] 148). See also *Bulletin des lois, 2ème Semestre 1811,* no. 385, pp. 137–138.

173 *Arrêté,* Pradel, 20 January 1818, (AJ[13] 148). *Arrêté,* Lauriston, 4 September 1822, (O[3] 1680 I).

174 A failed attempt to levy the *petits théâtres* at $\frac{1}{5}^{th}$ and not $\frac{1}{20}^{th}$, draft *ordonnance du Roi* with letter, 5 September 1817, (AJ[13] 148).

175 A failed attempt by Locré de St. Julien to take over de Bief's *privilège* as collector. La Rochefoucauld to Locré de St. Julien, 12 January 1826, (O[3] 1676 V). La Rochefoucauld to Duplantys, 12 January 1826, (O[3] 1676 V).

176 Delavau to La Rochefoucauld, 24 May 1826, (O[3] 1676 V).

177 Chabrol to La Rochefoucauld, 2 June 1826, (O[3] 1676 V).

a budget passed by the Chamber of Deputies, the *redevance*, being an indemnity, needed no such legal process. The decree of 13 August 1811, even although it did not constitute a law, was sufficient. Third, a decree had the force of law unless and until legal authority ordained otherwise. In summary, therefore, there was no need for the *redevance* to feature in the annual *loi de finance* as it was a purely local matter unlike the *droit des indigents*. The decree of 13 August 1811 was sufficient and the *Préfet de la Seine* was empowered to take action against non-payers.[178] This line of reasoning was confirmed by a *Tribunal de la Seine* on 2 May 1828, whose judgement was upheld by the *Cour Royale* on 18 August 1828, after an appeal.[179] The Opera thus retained its right to collect the *redevance*, although it was finally abolished by Louis-Philippe in 1831.[180]

There were, however, two problems over the collection of this levy. First, de Bief, the collector, proved unable or unwilling to pay over to the Opera certain sums which he had collected. It had become clear to the authorities that he could cause problems especially as he had lost the privilege of collecting the *droit des indigents*. It was felt by Lubbert in December 1827 that de Bief should put up caution money of around FF 25.000 given that one month's *redevance* was around FF 16.000.[181] La Rochefoucauld agreed[182] but it was too late. Despite de Bief's promise to deliver, given at a meeting with Leconte,[183] he failed to pay over FF 26.796 which was owing and lost this privilege also.[184] He was forced to sell shares which realised FF 18.203 towards a revised total shortfall of FF 26.910 and the balance of FF 8.707 was charged in the 1827 accounts of the *Maison du Roi*.[185] Second, and of more significance, was the refusal of the theatres to pay the *redevance* after the July 1830 Revolution. Handry de Janvry, who had become the new collector of the *redevance*, wrote to *Les Commissaires de la Liste Civile* on 5 April 1831 to explain the position. The *Préfet de la Seine* had again refused to move against non-payers and out of an 1830 total of FF 183.376, there remained FF 85.418 to be collected. A further FF 32.340 was collectable for January and February 1831, to give a total of FF 117.758.[186] According to the summary of accounts as at 1 March 1831, it was unlikely that this would be collected[187] as there was again confusion over the legality of doing so. *Les Commissaires de la Liste Civile* wrote to both the Minister of Finance and the Minister of Commerce and Public Works

---

178   *Conseil contentieux de l'Académie Royale de Musique*, 14 June 1826, (O³ 1676 V).

179   Paul Pélissier, *Histoire administrative de l'Académie Nationale de Musique et de Danse* (Paris, 1906), pp. 124–125.

180   *Ordonnance Royale*, 24 August 1831, (F²¹ 1053).

181   Lubbert to La Rochefoucauld, 18 December 1827, (O³ 1676 III).

182   *Rapport, Maison du Roi, Département des Beaux-Arts*, 27 December 1827, (O³ 1676 III).

183   Leconte to La Rochefoucauld, 21 February 1828, (O³ 1680 I).

184   *Procès-verbal* of meeting, Duplantys, de Bief and Leconte, 30 March 1828, (O³ 1680 I).

185   La Rochefoucauld to La Bouillerie, 30 November 1828, (O³ 1685 I).

186   Handry de Janvry to *Les Commissaires de la Liste Civile*, 5 April 1831, (F²¹ 1053).

187   *Situation et Inventaire au 1ᵉʳ mars, 1831*, (AJ¹³ 228 I).

to seek clarification of its position[188] and the matter was finally resolved by the *ordonnance* from Louis-Philippe on 24 August 1831. This ruled that the *redevance* had been suspended since July 1830.[189]

There is one further comment to make on this subject. Every writer to date has followed Véron and put the annual total of the *redevance* at around FF 300.000,[190] but this was manifestly inaccurate. Not only were there many references to a figure much lower than this in various documents,[191] but the annual accounts clearly showed that the total amount collected oscillated around FF 180.000:[192]

	FF		FF
1820	141.562	1826	164.153
1821	185.280	1827	180.995
1822-			
9 months	125.733	1828	194.673
1823	173.353	1829	188.895
1824	172.739	1830	182.958
1825	173.946		

This was a curious lapse by Véron, given the evidence available.

---

188 *Les Commissaires de la Liste Civile* to the Minister of Commerce and Public Works, 18 April 1831, 7 May 1831, 23 July 1831, (AJ^{13} 180 XI). *Les Commissaires de la Liste Civile* to the Minister of Finance, 7 May 1821, (AJ^{13} 180 XI). This letter put the outstanding *redevance* at FF 117.000.

189 *Ordonnance du Roi*, 24 August 1831, (AJ^{13} 180 XI).

190 a) Pélissier, op. cit., p. 127. He mentioned the sum of FF 300.000; b) «Par ailleurs, Louis-Philippe est décidé à ne plus réclamer des autres théâtres de Paris la redevance annuelle qui, bon an mal an, rapporte de FF 250.000 à FF 300.000.» ("Moreover, Louis-Philippe decided not to claim the annual *redevance* any more from the other Parisian theatres which on average brings in FF 250.000– 300.000.") Maurice E. Binet, *Un médecin pas ordinaire, le Docteur Véron* (Paris, éditions Albin Michel, 1945), p. 105; c) «... malgré la subvention de l'État et les FF 300.000 perçus à titre de redevances sur les théâtres secondaires et sur les spectacles de curiosité.» ("... despite the state subsidy and the FF 300.000 collected as *redevances* on the secondary theatres and on other improvised entertainments.") Royer, op. cit., p. 139; d) «Les produits de la redevance à l'Opéra s'élévaient donc annuellement à plus de FF 300.000.» ("The total tax collected for the Opera therefore rose annually to more than FF 300.000.") Véron, op. cit., p. 164; e) Albert de Lasalle, *Les Treize Salles de l'Opéra* (Paris, 1875), p. 202. He put the *redevance* at over FF 300.000; f) "... to which was added about FF 300.000 taken in tribute from the secondary theatres." Crosten, op. cit., p. 16.

191 a) Lubbert to La Rochefoucauld, 18 December 1827. Lubbert felt that the monthly total was around FF 16.000, (O^3 1676 III); b) *Conseil contentieux de l'Académie Royale de Musique*, (O^3 1676 V). Mentioned an annual total of around FF 160.000; c) Duplantys to La Rochefoucauld, 9 May 1826, (O^3 1676 I). He constructed a table of the *redevance:*

	FF		FF
1818	159.436	1822	178.006
1819	147.516	1823	173.353
1820	141.562	1824	172.739
1821	183.746	1825	173.946

192 The Annual Accounts, total of *redevance.*

Deficits, Supplements, Loans and Debts

The cost of the new *Salle le Peletier* was borne by the Ministry of the Interior, and the *Maison du Roi* was not, in the end, required to pay anything. The Opera was, however, severely affected due to disruptions and relocations, and by 1823 its financial situation was critical. There had been periods when no performances were possible, notably after the assassination of the Duc de Berry on 13 February 1820, and before the re-opening at the *Salle Favart* on 19 April 1820, and also after the Opera left the *Théâtre Louvois* on 15 May 1821, and only re-opened at the *Salle le Peletier* on 16 August 1821. It also became clear that the *Salle Favart* was not a suitable venue. It was too small and the stage was too narrow.[193] The consequence was that by 31 March 1823 the Opera had an accumulated deficit of crisis proportions, due especially to the deficits incurred in 1820 and 1821 of FF 140.670 and FF 158.082 respectively. The total deficit had, according to one document, reached FF 431.707.[194] This comprised debts to suppliers of FF 290.531 and a loan outstanding from the *Maison du Roi* of FF 141.176.[195] Another document mentioned FF 426.649.[196]

All of this was put into stark relief by Du Rais in a report on 20 April 1823 which emphasised the gravity of the situation and used the deficit of FF 431.707 to highlight this.[197] First, the deficit had accrued to the point where confidence and credit were eroding. The situation was so grave that without a prompt and effective remedy it would soon be impossible to carry on. Second, Du Rais referred to the many lost performances after the assassination of the Duc de Berry and to the enormous burden of staging *Aladin ou la Lampe merveilleuse*. Third, he was astonished that the 1823 subsidy had been cut by about a third to FF 545.387 from the FF 791.987 in 1822. It was usually necessary to have total revenues of around FF 1.600.000 to cover all the expenses but the latter had risen to FF 1.702.877 in 1822. On his calculations, the new lower subsidy for 1823 implied expenses of FF 1.494.534 for receipts and expenses to

---

193 a) *Rapport au Roi*, Lauriston, 30 June 1823, (AJ[13] 109 I); b) «Le théâtre Favart était beaucoup trop étroit, il fallait amoindrir la troupe chantante, dansante et sonnante, pour la faire manœuvrer sur une aussi petite scène. Il fallait choisir dans le répertoire les ouvrages qui n'exigeaient pas le déploiement de toutes les forces de notre Académie.» ("The Favart theatre was far too narrow and it was necessary to reduce the number of singers, dancers and musicians to enable them to manœuvre on such a small stage. A choice had to be made from the repertory of those works which did not require the whole company of the Opera.") Castil-Blaze, op. cit., pp. 165–166.

194 *Relevé général des recettes et dépenses*, 1 January 1819–31 March 1823, (O³ 1600).

	Deficits FF		Time period	Months
1819	10.734	-	1 Jan 1819–31 Dec 1820	12
1820	140.670	-	1 Jan 1820–31 March 1821*	15
1821	158.082	-	1 April 1821–31 March 1822	12
1822	62.329	-	1 April 1822–31 Dec 1822	9
1823 – 1ˢᵗ Q.	59.892	-	1 Jan 1823–31 March 1823	3
	431.707			51

Rapport au Roi, 10 January 1821. Changed to 15 months, (O³ 1653).

195 *Rapport, Ministère de la Maison du Roi*, May 1823, (O³ 1708 I).

196 Note to *Ministère de la Maison du Roi*, (O³ 1724).

197 *Rapport fait par M. Du Rais*, 20 April 1823, (AJ[13] 109 I).

balance, and as this was some FF 200.000 less than the 1822 total it was a wholly unrealistic expectation. He estimated that the likely deficit for 1823 could be as high as FF 246.000 especially as that for the first quarter to 31 March had reached FF 59.892. Not to put too fine a point on it, wrote Du Rais, the cash was exhausted, creditors were demanding payment and there was a threat of court proceedings. Were such proceedings to go against the Opera, its financial situation would be revealed, thus exposing it to calumny, ridicule and malice. Du Rais then proposed a novel and imaginative solution. A loan of FF 300.000, authorised by the King, should be placed in tranches of FF 6.000 each with fifty private subscribers. Repayment by the *Caisse des fonds particuliers du Roi* would be over a three-year period at FF 2.000 per subscriber per annum. Each lender would receive, in lieu of interest, a free seat called a *grande entrée*, worth FF 540 per annum, thus yielding an effective nine per cent return. So that the Opera would not suffer the loss of FF 27.000 per annum due to these extra free seats, the official lists of *entrées de droit* and *entrées de faveur* and the unofficial *entrées de tolérance* should be pruned. Du Rais also proposed some further measures: a supplement of FF 100.000 over and above the 1823 annual subsidy which itself should be raised; the write-off of the 1821 loan to the Opera by the *Maison du Roi* of FF 150.000, of which only FF 8.824 had been repaid, leaving FF 141.176; and economies in all areas of the Opera's activities in order to reduce expenses.

Needless to say, the authorities found this package too difficult to accept although the seriousness of the situation was recognised, especially as creditors were indeed pursuing the Opera.[198] Something had to be done but the action taken was not at all as Du Rais had suggested. A decision was taken to raid the pension fund. A June 1823 report to the King, which highlighted the reasons for the Opera's deficit, estimated its debts at FF 600.000.[199] These had exhausted the Opera's cash resources and exceeded any supplementary help which could be given by *les fonds spécials des Théâtres*. Lauriston advised that, having taken legal advice, it would be possible to appropriate the capitalised sum of annual pensions worth FF 16.334 out of the annual total of FF 33.931. He estimated this capitalised sum to be worth FF 285.000 which although only sufficient to clear half of the Opera's debts, would, with extra funds from *les fonds spécials des Théâtres,* prevent total disorder in the finances of the Opera. This idea was approved by the King[200] and a document was drawn up which, in the event, calculated the capitalised sum at FF 302.866.[201]

---

198 Habeneck to Lauriston, 26 February 1823, (O^3 1663 I).

199 *Rapport au Roi,* Lauriston, 30 June 1823, (AJ^{13} 109 I).

200 *Ordonnance du Roi,* 30 June 1823, (F^{21} 1075).

201 *Compte supplémentaire, Recette extraordinaire, 1823,* (AJ^{13} 144 IV). This document referred to the King's approval, 30 June 1823, of Lauriston's request. The capitalised sum was calculated on the basis of two tranches at 5% with an unexplained reduction:

18 July 1823				
Pensions of	FF 11.500	at 5% x 91.275	=	FF 209.932
21 Jan 1824				
Pensions of	4.834	at 5% x 96.125	=	92.934
Total	16.334			302.866

Throughout the 1820s, however, the Opera had to rely on further funds apart from the 1821 loan of FF 150.000 and the raid on the pension fund. These took a number of forms. In 1821, it had received an extra FF 100.000 directly from the *Maison du Roi* in order to help pay its debts.[202] Supplements over and above the annual subsidy were also paid. For example, Du Rais' criticism of the proposed 1823 subsidy, which was echoed by Habeneck,[203] was recognised and supplements were also granted in 1825 and 1826. The total for these three years was FF 476.126:[204]

	Subsidy foreseen FF	Subsidy paid FF	Difference FF
1823	544.787	741.660	196.873
1825	750.000	911.253	161.253
1826	750.000	868.000	118.000
	Total supplements		476.126

The *Budget des théâtres Royaux* also paid extra funds directly to the Opera in 1821, 1823 and 1824 for the running costs of the new heating and lighting at the *Salle le Peletier*. These were FF 104.000, FF 151.317 and FF 50.000 respectively, for a total of FF 305.317.[205]

By 1829 La Bouillerie decided that something must be done to improve the Opera's finances and he called for information on all the various loans and grants. The first report in February 1829 came from Benselin, *le payeur des fonds particuliers du Roi*. According to his researches, extra funds totalling FF 200.000 had been granted to the Opera in 1824 and 1825 through the budget of the Civil List, for the purpose of settling debts incurred prior to 1825.[206] This was indeed true, as archived correspondence has shown.[207] Benselin cautioned, however, that this was not the full story as other departments had also paid extra amounts to the Opera. He asked La Bouillerie to correct this situation and to have any further amounts for the Royal theatres all paid

---

202 Benselin to Lauriston, 25 May 1821, (O³ 1599).

203 Habeneck to Lauriston, 26 February 1823, (O³ 1663 I). He felt the subsidy was too low and asked for an extra FF 151.231 so that the Opera should not fall into another inevitable deficit.

204 Budgets 1823, 1825, 1826, (O³ 1696). Annual Accounts, (AJ¹³ 144 II).

205 *Budget des théâtres Royaux*, 1821, 1823, 1824, (O³ 1650).

206 *Rapport,* Benselin to La Bouillerie, 28 February 1829, (O³ 1694 II). His report reflected payments allocated through the Civil List. These were over and above the subsidy paid through the *Budgets des théâtres Royaux*.

Amount FF	Approved by King	Paid
50.000	17 December 1824	4 February 1825
50.000	10 March 1825	18 March 1825
100.000	6 August 1825	18 August 1825
200.000		

207 *Rapport au Roi*, 12 December 1824, (O³ 1707 I). The King signed his approval for the extra funds totalling FF 200.000 which should be used to pay creditor suppliers. In the event this FF 200.000 was paid in tranches, as Benselin's report showed.

through a single account.[208] A report also came from La Rochefoucauld which, among a number of topics, contained his estimate of the extra loans and grants to the Opera up to 31 December 1827. It was FF 530.583 and La Rochefoucauld requested that the loans included within this total should be written off.[209] A further report in March 1829 corrected this total to FF 578.176 and laid out, very clearly, the nature of the funding:[210]

à titre d'avance remboursable:		FF	FF
Loan made 1 August 1821 repayable in 17 months		150.000	
Less repaid		8.824	141.176
à titre de don ou de secour:			
Fonds de réserve des Beaux-Arts May 1826		47.594	
– Ditto –	September 1826	52.406	
– Ditto –	January 1827	60.000	
Sur les fonds particuliers du Roi September 1826		27.000	187.000
à titre d'avance à régulariser:			
Caisse du Trésor	24 June 1827	90.000	
	24 August 1827	60.000	
	26 October 1827	50.000	
	31 December 1827	50.000	250.000
	Total		578.176

Of this total, grants which totalled FF 160.000 were corroborated in other documents.[211] La Rochefoucauld stated, wrongly, that this was the correct total as he had excluded the FF 200.000 in Benselin's report and the FF 100.000 given in 1821. He again requested that these loans should be written off, as well as amounts due to the Opera by the *Théâtre Italien* of FF 252.409 which were still outstanding after the latter had separated from the Opera on 30 September 1827. La Bouillerie accepted La

---

208 «La différence, qui se trouve, Monsieur le Baron, entre ces renseignements, et ceux qui vous ont été fournis par le département des Beaux-Arts de la Maison du Roi, provient de ce que les dépenses des théâtres Royaux n'ont pas été toutes payées par une seule et même Caisse; que souvent elles ont été non seulement ordonnancées sur le Trésor de la Couronne mais encore payées directement par lui, et que d'autres fois, elles l'ont été payées par la Caisse des fonds particuliers.» ("Sir, the difference between this information and that provided by the *départment des Beaux-Arts de la Maison du Roi*, arises because the expenses of the Royal theatres have not been paid out by one and the same cashier's office; often the expenses have not only been authorised by the *Trésor de la Couronne* but even paid directly by it; on yet other occasions the expenses were paid out of the *Caisse des fonds particuliers*.") *Rapport*, Benselin to La Bouillerie, 28 February 1829, (O^3 1694 II).

209 *Rapport*, La Rochefoucauld to La Bouillerie, 12 February 1829, (O^3 1694 II).

210 *Rapport*, La Rochefoucauld to La Bouillerie, 17 March 1829, (O^3 1694 II).

211 a) *Rapport, Département des Beaux-Arts*, 2 May 1826, (O^3 1672 IV). It was recognised that 1825 had incurred another deficit, partly due to the cost of the opera *Pharamond*, staged for the coronation of Charles X. A request for FF 100.000 to pay creditor suppliers had been made and this was met in two tranches from the *fonds de réserve des Beaux-Arts* of FF 47.594 and FF 52.406; b) Duplantys to La Rochefoucauld, 13 December 1826, (O^3 1707 I). He asked for a further FF 60.000 to pay creditor suppliers. Doudeauville to La Rochefoucauld, 11 January 1827, (O^3 1707 I). He advised that the FF 60.000 had been agreed for payment.

Rochefoucauld's advice, and the latter was able to write to Lubbert and explain, with satisfaction, that La Bouillerie had agreed with him.[212] La Bouillerie then wrote two reports to the King. The first requested that the loan of FF 141.176, already mentioned by Du Rais in 1823, should be written off by the *Trésor de la Couronne*.[213] The second requested that loans totalling FF 250.000 should be similarly treated.[214] These requests were both approved by the King and so, from the Opera's point of view, loans totalling FF 391.176 were cancelled. As for the FF 252.409 and the reference to the *Théâtre Italien*, this was the culmination of a situation which had been in existence since 1818. In that year, it was decided that the *Théâtre Italien* should be annexed by the Opera as the former had fallen into total incapacity.[215] This change of policy was set out in a *Rapport au Roi*[216] as a result of which the two theatres were managed as an alliance until they separated again on 30 September 1827. This meant, for example, that the Opera's chorus was shared with the *Théâtre Italien* although the members remained on full pay with the Opera, and that administrative services were also shared on the same basis. It also meant that the *Théâtre Italien* could make use of the Opera's warehouses for scenery and costumes. This sharing of resources could be seen as a sharing of two national, musical and theatrical cultures which, in the wider context of the cultural and artistic life in Paris, brought great benefits to the city, as Janet Lynn Johnson has explained.[217] The accounting for this sharing was, however, vague and imprecise and led to a situation whereby the Opera paid, on its own account, expenses which should have been allocated to the *Théâtre Italien*. Whether this mattered or not was unclear at the time since:

> … les deux théâtres ne se maintenant que par la munificence Royale et puisant, conséquemment, à la même source, il importe peu que telle ou telle charge pèse sur un établissement plutôt que sur l'autre théâtre.[218]

It was unclear, therefore, whether the amounts owed to the Opera were fictitious in that no distinction should be drawn between the two theatres, or real in that they should have been settled. Practically, however, the result was that the Opera's expenses were overstated and those of the *Théâtre Italien* were understated. This was one of the reasons why the Opera was in permanent financial difficulty, and the reason why the Opera was owed FF 252.409. Or was it? La Rochefoucauld shared the ambivalence described above. He made the point that the two theatres had been under the same

---

212 La Rochefoucauld to Lubbert, 20 May 1829, (AJ[13] 122 VII).

213 *Rapport au Roi,* La Bouillerie, 12 June 1829, (O[3] 1694 II).

214 *Rapport au Roi,* La Bouillerie, 12 June 1829, (O[3] 1694 II).

215 *Rapport au Roi,* Pradel, 26 February 1818, (O[3] 1736).

216 *Rapport au Roi,* 28 February 1818, (F[21] 1112).

217 Janet Lynn Johnson, *The Theatre Italien and Opera and Theatrical Life in Restoration Paris, 1818–1827.* Ph.D. diss., University of Chicago, 1988.

218 Johnson, op. cit., p. 322. She referred to *observations sur les comptes du Théâtre Royal Italien des exercises 1818, 1819, 1820, 1821 et 3 premiers mois 1822,* (AJ[13] 147 III). ("… as the two theatres maintain themselves only by the King's generosity and draw therefore from the same source of funds, it matters little whether any given expense weighs more heavily on one establishment rather than the other.")

administration until 1 October 1827 and described the debt as a fictitious one which should be cancelled.[219] This advice to La Bouillerie was followed up in further letters[220] and the latter finally approved an internal note which recommended this course of action.[221]

A raid on the pension fund, supplements to the annual subsidy, extra grants and written-off loans were all examples of the help given to the Opera in the 1820s over and above the annual subsidy but this was still not the end of the story. The *Maison du Roi* found itself forced to pay some of the Opera's debts to creditor suppliers as, yet again, the Opera's cash had run out.

The background to this was a report by La Bouillerie to the King in August 1827, in which he referred to the latter's desire to create a Commission which should, among other things, examine how the debts of the Royal theatres should be paid. La Bouillerie proposed, and the King agreed, that a *Commission des Théâtres Royaux* should be set up with the power to seek information from the Royal theatre directors and to examine documents. It should then submit its findings to La Bouillerie.[222] This Commission assumed special importance in 1827, when the *Théâtre Italien* separated from the Opera on 30 September. There were great problems in calculating the financial settlement, not only between the Opera and the *Théâtre Italien*, but also because of the outstanding debts to creditor suppliers. Thus although La Rochefoucauld could report in January 1828 that he was able to send to La Bouillerie separate accounts for the Opera and the *Théâtre Italien* for the nine months to 30 September 1827 and that the Commission had finished its work on the Opera for the years 1821 to 1825, work on the two calendar years 1826 and 1827 was not yet completed.[223] To speed matters along, La Bouillerie wrote to Hutteau d'Origny, a Commission member. He stressed how important it was that the finances of the Opera and the *Théâtre Italien* should be sorted out and counted on the Commission's zeal in this regard.[224] As for Lubbert, he was well aware of the need to settle these debts. He had just received in December 1827 the last instalment of FF 50.000 out of the loan of FF 250.000, and with this amount he had been able to calm a discontent which had been simmering for several years and which was about to

---

219 La Rochefoucauld to La Bouillerie, 12 February 1829, (O^3 1694 II).
220 La Rochefoucauld to La Bouillerie, 17 March 1829, (O^3 1694 II). La Rochefoucauld to La Bouillerie, 21 May 1829, (O^3 1694 II).
221 *Intendance Générale de la Maison du Roi, Division de la Maison Civile,* to La Bouillerie, 5 June 1829, (O^3 1694 II).
222 *Rapport au Roi,* La Bouillerie, 14 August 1827, (O^3 1680 I). The members were

M.M.	Amy	*Conseiller d'État, Président.*
	Hutteau d'Origny	*Maître de requêtes.*
	Alphonse La Bouillerie	- ditto -
	Prévost	- ditto -
	De La Salle	*Chef de la cour des comptes.*
	De La Ferté	*Directeur des fêtes et spectacles de la Cour.*
	Benselin	*Trésorier des fonds particuliers du Roi.*

223 La Rochefoucauld to La Bouillerie, 22 January 1828, (O^3 1680 I).
224 La Bouillerie to Hutteau d'Origny, 2 February 1828, (O^3 1680 I).

explode. He also pointed out that this discontent was well-founded. Some suppliers had not been paid for two years and many had not been paid for one.[225] This was in breach of the contract which suppliers had signed with the Opera whereby bills should be paid in the fourth month following the delivery of goods, and the Opera was, according to Lubbert, being dangerously high-handed:

> ... ne point y répondre et ne point les solder, sont des moyens sûr de les exaspérer et de donner lieu à un scandale nuisible et honteux pour un établissement qui doit son existence à la munificence du Roi.[226]

In Lubbert's view, as outstanding debts of the Opera totalled around FF 250.000 and those of the *Théâtre Italien* FF 60.000, extra help would be needed to pay them. On the same day as Lubbert's letter, La Bouillerie also wrote to La Rochefoucauld. He first pointed out that if the Opera and the *Théâtre Italien* had not persistently exceeded their budgets, then suppliers would have been paid on time. Nevertheless, he was able to report that supplementary funds from the Civil List had been found to pay the debts outstanding as at 31 December 1827,[227] and action followed swiftly thereafter. Exchanges of letters showed that outstanding 1826 debts of the Opera totalling

---

225 *État des sommes dues par l'Académie royale de Musique pour les fournitures faites et travaux exécutés pendant les années 1825, 1826, et 9 premiers mois de 1827*, (AJ[13] 144 IV). This very detailed schedule showed the amounts outstanding to each supplier and the totals were:

	FF
	FF
1825	10.497
1826	123.901
1827 to 30 September	217.772
	352.170

Lubbert's letter, 14 February 1828, which stated that the total was FF 250.000 would have reflected the two tranches of FF 50.000 received 26 October 1827 and 31 December 1827, out of the total loan of FF 250.000. The document also corroborated some of the figures in La Rochefoucauld's report to La Bouillerie, 17 March 1829. It showed *sommes prêtées par la Liste Civile*.

		FF	FF
1821	Loan		141.176
1827	Loan June	90.000	
	August	60.000	150.000
			291.176

As the schedule was as at 30 September 1827, it did not include the two further FF 50.000 tranches of the 1827 loan, taking the total to FF 250.000.

226 ("... ignoring their requests and not settling the accounts are a sure way of infuriating them and of creating a damaging scandal which would be embarrassing for an establishment which owes its existence to the generosity of the King.") Lubbert to La Rochefoucauld, 14 February 1828, (O[3] 1680 I).

227 «... je ferai donc payer les sommes dues aux fournisseurs, sur la production, que vous voudrez bien faire, des bordereaux de dépenses appuyés de mémoires justicatifs, vérifiés et certifiés ....» ("... I shall have the amounts owing to the suppliers paid on production of the schedules which you will kindly let me have. The schedules should be supported by bills which have been checked and approved ....") La Bouillerie to La Rochefoucauld, 14 February 1828, (O[3] 1680 I). The supplementary funds of FF 400.000, to settle the pre-1828 debts of all the Royal theatres were referred to in a report to La Bouillerie from the *Division de la Maison Civile*, 15 May 1829, (O[3] 1694 II).

FF 73.183 were paid directly from this supplement.[228] A further exchange of letters cleared 1827 debts of FF 145.740.[229] In 1829, further 1827 debts of FF 110.440 were identified[230] and as La Bouillerie's stated aim was to settle all the Opera's debts to suppliers which were outstanding as at 31 December 1827, approval was sought to pay these.[231] After various reports,[232] Salogne finally wrote to Lubbert. These creditors would be paid directly by the *Maison du Roi* and they should come to the *Caisse du payeur des fonds particuliers du Roi, rue du Carousel,* to collect the FF 110.440 due to them.[233] La Bouillerie had thus done well on behalf of the Opera. Not only had loans totalling FF 391.176 been converted into gifts and written-off by the *Maison du Roi*, but the latter had also paid, on behalf of the Opera, debts totalling FF 329.363.

The Loan of FF 135.136

Towards the end of 1829, both La Bouillerie and La Rochefoucauld would have had reason to be satisfied with the financial position at the Opera, despite Lubbert's shortcomings as director. Outstanding loans had, with the King's approval, been written-off and the back-log of debts to creditor suppliers had been cleared, either through a supplement from the Civil List, or by direct payment again through the Civil List. The financial tangle with the *Théâtre Italien* had also been unravelled. The Opera was also doing better artistically, with three new successful productions, *La Muette de Portici, Le Comte Ory* and *Guillaume Tell*. Although Lubbert had sought, and obtained, a supplementary budget, rising box-office receipts and rentals from boxes made it unlikely that the Opera would actually need a supplement to the annual subsidy. It would thus have been a shock when, in December 1829, it was discovered that Lubbert had yet again flouted the regulations. He had paid expenses directly from receipts and a further loan of FF 135.136 was needed.

The Opera, strictly speaking, had no cash except in the very short term. All receipts were *ordonnancées,* authorised, and handed over to the *Maison du Roi*. All expenses were also *ordonnancées* by the *Maison du Roi* so that cash could be released to the Opera which could then pay these expenses. Lubbert had, however, been paying expenses without going through this process. He had used the cash from receipts to pay

---

228 Lubbert to La Rochefoucauld, 28 February 1828. La Rochefoucauld to La Bouillerie, 1 March 1828. La Bouillerie to La Rochefoucauld, 17 March 1828. Lubbert to La Rochefoucauld, 19 March 1828, (O³ 1680 I).

229 Lubbert to La Rochefoucauld, 8 March 1828. La Rochefoucauld to Lubbert, 2 April 1828. La Bouillerie to La Rochefoucauld, 29 March 1828, (O³ 1680 I).

230 La Rochefoucauld to La Bouillerie, 12 February 1829, (O³ 1694 II).

231 *Rapport, Division de la Maison Civile* to La Bouillerie, 15 May 1829, (O³ 1694 II). It was pointed out that a small credit balance of FF 3.784 was left over from the 1828 FF 400.000 allocation to pay the debts of the Royal Theatres; that the Opera was due FF 13.117 from the secondary theatres; and that there was a small adjustment of FF 2 to be made. The Civil List was thus due to pay FF 93.537 to the Opera.

232 *Rapport au Roi,* La Bouillerie, 20 May 1829. La Rochefoucauld to La Bouillerie, 21 May 1829. *Rapport, Division de la Liste Civile,* to La Bouillerie, 5 June 1829. *Rapport, Intendance Générale* to La Bouillerie, 16 July 1829, (O³ 1694 II).

233 Salogne to Lubbert, 28 July 1829, (AJ¹³ 122 VII).

certain expenses directly. As a result, although all the receipts had been *ordonnancées,* there simply was not the cash to pay over and this shortfall amounted to FF 135.136. On the expenses side, he had paid out an equivalent FF 135.136 but this was illegal as the expenses had not been authorised in the first place. All of this was set out in a report by Salogne to La Bouillerie which showed that receipts authorised up until 30 November were FF 741.727, but that cash paid over was only FF 606.591, the difference having been used to pay these various expenses which were detailed in his report.[234] Salogne then came up with an ingenious solution to resolve this anomaly. He proposed that the *Maison du Roi* should loan FF 135.136 to the Opera before the year-end on 31 December 1829. The Opera would then immediately pay an equivalent amount back to the *Maison du Roi* which would thus eliminate the shortfall of receipts. From an accounting point of view this would solve the problem on the receipts side as the total authorised would be the same as the amount paid over. As for the expenses, these were illegal and should be regarded as recoverable. Salogne then set out the procedures whereby, over a three year period, the Opera should seek to recover the FF 135.136 by instalments while reducing the loan by equivalent amounts. He concluded with a recommendation to La Bouillerie that the Opera should not advance any money to anyone without La Bouillerie's approval and that all receipts should be paid over immediately to the *Maison du Roi.* A further report was sent to La Bouillerie which made a formal request for the loan of FF 135.136.[235] La Bouillerie then wrote a report, countersigned by Salogne, to Benselin, the *payeur des fonds particuliers du Roi.* He instructed Benselin to pay over, by way of loan, FF 135.136 to the Opera. This loan should be repaid through monthly instalments according to an agreed maturity schedule arranged with each beneficiary of the illegal expenses.[236]

Meanwhile La Rochefoucauld also gave his views on this matter to La Bouillerie.[237] He suggested an immediate loan of FF 50.000. His powers had, however, already been curtailed by La Bouillerie's active involvement in the affairs of the Opera and the latter wrote back to him along the lines of Salogne's report.[238] He first referred La Rochefoucauld to the revised way of reporting the Opera's financial affairs, and then advised him that a loan of FF 135.136 had been authorised. This was a provisional loan which must be repaid and he forbad any future loan to anyone and for whatever reason without his special authorisation. In this, as in other matters, La Rochefoucauld was shown to be behind events and was overruled by La Bouillerie.

The fact that Lubbert had paid these expenses illegally, and the way in which the matter was finally handled, were proof of Lubbert's maladministration and of the authorities' propensity to talk toughly but act weakly. The simple fact was that,

---

234 *Rapport,* Salogne to La Bouillerie, 24 December 1829, (O^3 1685 I).

235 *Rapport Division de la Maison Civile* to La Bouillerie, 28 December 1829, (O^3 1685 I).

236 La Bouillerie to Benselin, 29 December 1829, (AJ^{13} 228 I).

237 «... la nécessité de régulariser plusieurs avances faites à des artistes et en même temps, le versement d'une partie de recettes que ces avances ont paralysé.» ("... the need to regularise several advances made to artists and at the same time to pay over a portion of the receipts which these advances have tied up.") La Rochefoucauld to La Bouillerie, 21 December 1829, (O^3 1685 I).

238 La Bouillerie to La Rochefoucauld, 28 December 1829, (O^3 1685 I).

according to the first analysis, FF 29.690 of these expenses were irrecoverable,[239] whatever La Bouillerie may have demanded by way of recovery through monthly instalments. It was not long before the Opera's 1829 budget had been increased to absorb some of these expenses into the Opera's 1829 Annual Accounts. According to a summary of the position as at 14 May 1830, FF 27.390 was thus... *régularisé par ordonnancements et suppléments de crédits.* Meanwhile, FF 2.300 was set against the 1828 surplus as the expenses dated back to that year.[240] Far from being recovered by instalments, a total of FF 29.690 was, according to this summary, treated as a normal expense although this figure was subsequently reduced to FF 29.328. The overall line of thought here was at least consistent. As this total was not originally authorised, it was illegal and thus recoverable. As soon as it had been authorised by inclusion in the 1829 budget, it could be treated as an expense in the normal way.

On 1 March 1831, Véron took over as director. Three days later Lubbert was requested to clarify the whole question of the FF 135.136, and was left in no doubt about the possibility of future claims were he not to do so:

> Vous jugerez sans doute comme nous, Monsieur, qu'il est dans votre intérêt de rendre des comptes qui vous libèrent de toute réclamation ultérieure ....[241]

---

239 *Détail des Avances faites par la Caisse de l'Académie, 22 decembre 1829*, (AJ[13] 228 I).

	FF	FF
Amounts pertaining to 1828:		
Marion de Grandmaison, lawyer, judicial expenses	300	
Scribe, man of letters, supplementary for *Le Comte Ory*	2.000	2.300
Amounts pertaining to 1829:		
Provisional salaries to various artistes	17.390	
Indemnity to buy out Mme. Damoreau's holiday	10.000	27.390
		29.690
Salary advances to be paid back progressively:		
Solomé, *régisseur*	925	
Lafont, *artiste du chant*	4.000	
Damoreau, *artiste du chant*	20.110	
Talon, *concierge de la Direction*	100	25.135
Advances: supplementary budget requested:		
Feux	10.000	
Artistes externes	1.071	
Travaux extraordinaires	5.034	
Droit des Indigents	2.638	
	18.743	
Payments to account for sub-contractors	2.122	
-ditto- for various pensioners	714	
	2.836	21.579
Advances to *la Caisse des Retraites*		58.732
Total		135.136

240 *Décompte de l'avance faite à la Caisse de l'Académie par décision de l'Intendance générale de la Maison du Roi, en date du 29 decembre 1829.* This was dated 14 May 1830, (AJ[13] 228 I).

241 ("Sir, you will no doubt consider it to be in your interest, as we do, to give a full explanation of the accounts which will render you free of any further claims ....") *Les Commissaires de la Liste Civile* to Lubbert, 4 March 1831, (AJ[13] 228 I).

Lubbert replied to this by sending the details so far as he understood them. The overall result was that out of the loan of FF 135.136, the *Maison du Roi* was repaid only FF 36.307. Expenses of FF 29.328 were authorised; Véron assumed the responsibility for the recovery of outstanding loans to staff; and FF 46.004 was assumed as a liability by the authorities.[242]

This episode highlighted a number of points. It showed that Lubbert was incompetent and evasive in financial matters, it showed that the *Maison du Roi*, despite the efforts of La Bouillerie, did an ineffective job in supervising the Opera, and it showed La Rochefoucauld personally in a poor light. Given the cumbersome bureaucracy and weak controls it was, perhaps, an accident waiting to happen.

---

242 Lubbert to *Les Commissaires de la Liste Civile*, April 1831, (AJ[13] 228 I).
The details were as follows:

FF

a) Expenses authorised.   29.328
As already noted in the 14 May 1830 report, FF 29.690 was first authorised. Subsequent to this it was discovered that FF 242 had been wrongly paid to an orchestral player called Barbareau, and FF 120 was wrongly paid to Bonel. This total of FF 362 was paid to the *Caisse des fonds particuliers du Roi*, and deducted from the FF 29.690.

b) Advances to be repaid by instalment.   23.497
According to the 14 May 1830 report, FF 25.135 had been advanced to various artists. By April 1831, FF 1.638 had been recovered and paid over to the *Caisse des fonds particuliers du Roi*. The balance of FF 23.497 was then further reduced by instalments to FF 18.038 repaid out of a loan made to Lubbert to pay petty expenses. This amount was included in the final overall settlement, 1 March 1831, as a result of Véron's arrival and it was for him to recover it.

c) Paid to the *Caisse des fonds particuliers du Roi*.   36.307
The 14 May 1830 report showed that the Opera hoped to gain approval for yet another supplementary budget of FF 20.865 so that these illegal expenses could be authorised. This total was included under reference six, being FF 18.743 plus FF 2.122. In the event, the Opera was not successful. It also repaid FF 12.728 out of the advance to the *Caisse des Retraites*. The FF 36.307 thus comprised:-

	FF
Repaid, as wrongly charged	362
Deductions from salaries	1.638
Repaid as not *ordonnancées*	20.865
Pension fund repayment	12.728
Advance to pensioners	714
	36.307

d) *La Caisse des Retraites.*   46.004
FF 12.728 had been repaid out of the total of FF 58.732, and the authorities then assumed the balance directly.

Total   135.136

The Accounts 1 January 1827 to 1 March 1831

Prior to September 1827, the Opera's accounts were compromised by the alliance with the *Théâtre Italien*. Thereafter, the accounts, even if their absolute accuracy has to be questioned, were more informative in that they related only to the Opera and laid bare the state of its finances. They also revealed the way in which La Bouillerie struggled to impose a new procedure for reporting and supervision, and some of the ways in which Lubbert either flouted, or sought to circumvent, such procedures. 1827, for example, was a year in which the parlous state of the Opera's finances could be analysed. 1828 showed the start of a revival on the receipts side, due to successful new productions, and the overall situation was helped by a higher subsidy. The year showed a small surplus. 1829 produced a mixed result in that much higher receipts were partially offset by Lubbert's inability to control expenses which caused great irritation to La Bouillerie. Nevertheless, there was another small surplus. 1830 reflected the July Revolution, especially as it affected the renting of boxes, and the Opera again fell into deficit. Finally, a summary of these years, together with the two months to 1 March 1831, covered the financial settlement prior to Véron's arrival.

It has been claimed that the Opera was in a very serious financial state in 1830 and up to 1 March 1831 but these annual accounts, combined with the initiatives taken by La Bouillerie, showed otherwise. Véron inherited a much improved financial situation and went on to make his fortune.

1827

This was the year when the *Théâtre Italien* separated from the Opera. There was great difficulty in establishing separate accounts for the two theatres, both for the nine months to 30 September, and for the full calendar year. There was also pressure to conclude these so that debts overdue to creditor suppliers could be identified and use made of the 1828 FF 400.000 extra subsidy from the Civil List, made available to all the Royal theatres to settle such debts.

On the face of it, the 1827 Annual Accounts looked none too bad. The budget for both receipts and expenses had been set at FF 1.725.888 while the accounts showed receipts of FF 1.715.249, expenses of FF 1.742.337 and a small deficit of FF 27.088.[243] Within these figures, however, some fundamental weaknesses were revealed. Receipts from the box-office and the renting of boxes and seats were only FF 547.697 and as this sum covered only thirty-one per cent of total expenses, the *Maison du Roi* had to provide an extra subsidy over and above the FF 750.000 initially granted. A further FF 160.000 was received under *recettes extraordinaires*, even although the detailed accounts correctly recorded this as *à titre de prêt*, being a loan. The long-term underlying weakness of the Opera's finances was also highlighted by the levy on the

---

243 *Bordereau de Situation complémentaire des Recettes et Dépenses de l'Exercise 1827*, (AJ[13] 145 V). See Appendix II.

secondary theatres which totalled FF 180.995, and without which the Opera would have been in deep deficit.

Out of the total receipts of FF 1.715.249, the box-office total was FF 499.707 and as there were 161 performances during 1827,[244] the average per performance was FF 3.103. This average does not, however, reveal the extent to which successful new productions were crucial to the Opera's financial viability. Rossini's *Moïse*, for example, was first staged in 1827 and was a great success. It grossed FF 148.609 at the box-office from thirty-two performances, for an average of FF 4.644. The ballet *La Somnambule*, in which Marie Taglioni made her début, was also a success. Even although it was paired with operas which had been seen many times, it grossed FF 88.901 from twenty-two performances for an average of FF 4.041. These two new productions represented some one in three of all performances yet took nearly fifty percent of box-office receipts. Meanwhile, Rossini's *Le Siège de Corinthe*, first staged to great acclaim in 1826, when it took FF 55.168 from thirteen performances for an average of FF 4.243, was already slipping. It was performed a further thirty-five times in 1827, but average receipts per performance were only FF 2.595.[245] Put another way, the 107 performances in 1827, which excluded *Moïse* and *La Somnambule*, took only FF 262.197 at the box-office, for an average of FF 2.450.

The 1827 Annual Accounts, signed on 21 January 1829, also reflected the poor cash position. The Opera simply did not have the cash to settle the back-log of debts overdue to creditor suppliers although La Bouillerie managed to solve this problem. The extra FF 400.000 from the Civil List in 1828 paid debts of FF 218.923 and direct payments by the Civil List settled further debts of FF 110.440. The burden of these overdue debts fell wholly on the suppliers as all fixed and variable personnel were always paid on time and in full. Major creditors paid in this way were detailed under various categories in the accounts and included lighting FF 25.801, heating FF 19.374, building maintenance FF 17.442 and costumes and scene-painting FF 148.610. This failure to pay creditors on time was contributory to Véron's success in negotiating fixed annual amounts with most suppliers in the first three categories, who preferred certainty of payment even although the contract terms were onerous.

Overall, therefore, the 1827 Annual Accounts showed that the *Maison du Roi* provided an extra FF 489.363 to keep the Opera solvent, and the small deficit in the Annual Accounts of FF 27.088 told only part of the story. There also remained FF 252.409 owed by the *Théâtre Italien* as a result of the separation as at 30 September 1827 and a further FF 90.000 out of the FF 250.000 lent to the Opera in 1827. These were both finally written off by the *Maison du Roi*.

---

244 *Journal usuel de l'Opéra 1791–1850, (Bibliothèque de l'Opéra).*
245 Details of box-office receipts, (CO288 (942) and CO289 (943)).

1828

This was a better year for the Opera. The budget for both receipts and expenses had been set at FF 1.697.925 but the final outcome was receipts of FF 1.705.748, expenses of FF 1.650.178 and a surplus of FF 55.570.[246] The budgeted annual subsidy had been raised from FF 750.000 to FF 850.000 and there was no record of any supplements received during the year. Although box-office receipts were down slightly against budget, FF 522.105 compared with FF 540.000, these receipts were an improvement over the 1827 total of FF 499.709. The rentals from boxes also improved, FF 82.880 compared with FF 50.000, and a comment on the detailed accounts noted that such rentals were the best thermometer of the attitude of high society towards the Opera.[247] Overall, there were 156 performances in 1828[248] and the box-office average per performance was FF 3.347 compared with FF 3.103 in 1827. The main reason for this improvement is not hard to find. The opera, *La Muette de Portici,* first staged in February 1828, was an outstanding success. It grossed FF 252.088 from fifty performances in 1828, some one in three of all performances, and the box-office average was very high at FF 5.042. Meanwhile, Rossini's *Le Comte Ory* was another success. With seventeen performances in 1828, it grossed FF 72.724 for an average of FF 4.278. Such successes were timely as *Moïse,* a triumph in 1827, could only average FF 2.978 from ten performances, and *Le Siège de Corinthe* FF 2.278 from twenty.[249] Meanwhile, a new ballet, *Lydie,* failed and was taken off after five performances.[250]

On the expenses side, there was no record of 1828 creditors having been paid by the *Maison du Roi* and the cost of costumes and scene-painting was down substantially on budget, FF 149.995 compared with FF 180.000. This was a reflection of La Rochefoucauld's insistence that old costumes and scenery should be used wherever possible for new productions. Total expenses were thus below budget and FF 55.050 out of the total surplus of FF 55.570 was paid over to *La Caisse de fonds particuliers du Roi,* FF 42.429 on 21 October 1829 and FF 12.621 on 17 December 1830. There remained FF 520, recoverable directly by the *Maison du Roi* from Laurent, the new director of the *Théâtre Italien.*

---

246 *Bordereau de Situation des Recettes et Dépenses de l'Exercise 1828,* (AJ[13] 146 III). See Appendix II.

247 «L'avantage obtenu par cet article, qui est le meilleur thermomètre de la faveur de la haute société compense seul le désavantage des autres articles, et fait que les recettes, en général, dépasseront les prévisions du budget.» ("The advantage gained by this category of receipts, which are the best barometer of the positive attitude of high society, makes up for the disadvantage of the other categories and means that, on the whole, receipts will exceed the budget's estimates.") Annual Accounts 1828, (AJ[13] 146 III).

248 *Journal usuel de l'Opéra 1791–1850,* op. cit..

249 Details of box-office receipts, (CO288 (942)).

250 Details of box-office receipts, (CO289 (943)).

1829

Although La Bouillerie was successful in putting the Opera's finances onto a sounder footing, Lubbert again flouted the regulations and incurred expenses which were unauthorised and therefore illegal. As a result of La Bouillerie's initiatives, loans by the *Maison du Roi* to the Opera of FF 391.176 were written off and funds were found to pay outstanding debts to creditor suppliers of FF 329.363. He had thus relieved the Opera from a burden of loans and debts which totalled FF 720.539. 1828 had been a better year for the Opera with a surplus of FF 55.570 without the need for any extra help. Nevertheless, La Bouillerie had seen enough to be convinced that administrative changes were necessary. A more strict regime of accounting and supervision was needed, even to the extent of taking this under his direct control. A report to the King in December 1828 set out his thoughts and was approved.[251] The gist of the report was sent to La Rochefoucauld[252] and it was not long before La Bouillerie's fears were realised.

The 1829 budget again reflected the principle that expenses should be matched by receipts, thus creating an equilibrium. Budgeted receipts of FF 1.669.850 were matched by expenses of the same amount,[253] although an anomaly had already crept in. In order to get the budget to balance, *gratifications annuelles,* annual bonuses, were put at FF 55.000 although the detailed calculations showed FF 71.575. Be that as it may, Lubbert was advised that the budget had been approved, first by La Bouillerie and then by the King.[254] He was also put in no doubt by La Rochefoucauld that he must scrupulously conform to the new accounting and reporting regulations. Barely had this budget been approved, however, than Lubbert sought a supplementary budget of FF 82.630,[255] the details of which were contained in a separate letter.[256] La Rochefoucauld submitted this to La Bouillerie and received a withering reply. La Bouillerie expressed astonishment at such a request and the reasons for it. It seemed to

---

251 a) «Cette partie de l'administration échappe ainsi à l'action de surveillance que je m'efforce d'exercer sur tous les autres services de la Maison.» ("This part of the administration escapes the tight control which I am struggling to exert over all the other departments of the *Maison du Roi*;") b) «Sans l'accomplissement de cette condition, il me serait impossible de garantir au Roi que le déficit de l'Académie royale de Musique, qui naguère vient d'être comblé par le Trésor de Sa Majesté, ne se présentera pas de nouveau puisque je n'ai aucun moyen d'en paralyser le retour.» ("Without the fulfillment of this condition I cannot guarantee the King that the deficit of the Opera, which formerly was written off by His Majesty's Treasury, will not again appear since I have no means to prevent its return;") c) «... que cette administration sera considérée à l'avenir dans ses rapports de Comptabilité avec l'Intendance Générale comme un autre service placé dans mes attributions directes ....» ("... that this management will in future be considered, so far as the return of its accounts to the *Intendance Générale* is concerned, as another department under my direct control ....") *Rapport au Roi*, La Bouillerie, 13 December 1828, (O³ 1679).

252 La Bouillerie to La Rochefoucauld, 17 December 1828, (O³ 1679).

253 *Budget des Recettes et Dépenses pour l'année 1829*, (O³ 1696).

254 La Rochefoucauld to Lubbert, 9 March 1829, (AJ¹³ 122 I). La Rochefoucauld to Lubbert, 15 June 1829, (AJ¹³ 122 VII).

255 Lubbert to La Rochefoucauld, 30 July 1829, (AJ¹³ 122 I).

256 Lubbert to La Rochefoucauld, 30 July 1829, (AJ¹³ 122 VII).

him that most of the extra expenses had been incurred prior to the approval of the 1829 budget and some even dated back to 1828. He could not understand why they had not all been included in the 1829 budget and felt it was impossible to approach the King again to gain approval for a supplementary budget.[257] Unusually, he also wrote directly to Lubbert on the same day and on the same subject. He pointed out that these expenses had been incurred without his approval and were therefore illegal. He could not possibly ask the King for more funds to pay for them. He felt most of the blame should fall on Lubbert himself with whom he was most displeased.[258] Meanwhile, La Rochefoucauld replied to La Bouillerie's unwelcome strictures. He could not excuse Lubbert's irregularities but did point out that the Opera had had an uninterrupted success for some time. He hoped that La Bouillerie would not refuse to solicit the King for the necessary financial support.[259] Needless to say, La Bouillerie did finally solicit the King to approve a supplementary budget, giving details of the slightly higher

257 a) «Je ne vous dissimulerai, Monsieur le Vicomte, l'étonnement que me cause une proposition de cette nature, et plus encore la révélation des motifs sur lesquels elle se trouve appuyée.» ("Sir, I cannot conceal from you the amazement which such a suggestion creates in me. Even more so when the explanation of the reasons on which this suggestion is founded is revealed to me;") b) «Je crois donc devoir vous adresser à ce sujet les observations suivantes, qui convaincront, je l'espère, que la marche suivie dans cette instance par l'administration de l'Opéra, serait subversive de tout ordre et de toute régularité, si elle était tolérée.» ("I therefore feel obliged to make the following points to you on this subject which, I hope, will convince you that the course of action adopted in this instance by the management of the Opera would undermine all order and regularity were it to be allowed;") c) «Eh bien, Monsieur le Vicomte, je vois que les mesures, qui ont amené ces dépenses, remontent pour la plupart à une époque antérieure à l'approbation définitive du Budget et que quelques unes même datent de l'année 1828.» ("Well, Sir, I see that the measures which have incurred these expenses go back for the most part to a period before the final approval of the Budget and that some even date back to 1828;") d) «... je crois devoir vous demander, Monsieur le Vicomte, par quel motif cette somme n'a pas été comprise dans le Budget de 1829? » ("... I feel bound to ask you, Sir, why this sum was not included in the 1829 Budget?") La Bouillerie to La Rochefoucauld, 3 September 1829, (O³ 1685 I).

258 a) «... que considérant ces dépenses comme illégales, je ne puis soumettre au Roi la demande des fonds sollicités pour y faire face.» ("... that as these expenses are illegal, I cannot submit a request to the King for further funds to settle the bills;") b) «... je ne me suis pas dissimulé, Monsieur, qu'une partie du blâme que méritent les mesures dont il s'agit, devait retomber sur vous, et je ne crois pas devoir vous en cacher mon mécontentement.» ("... Sir, I cannot conceal my opinion that part of the blame for these expenses under discussion should fall on you and I do not feel duty-bound to hide from you my great displeasure.") La Bouillerie to Lubbert, 3 September 1829, (O³ 1685 I).

259 a) «Je ne m'étois point dissimulé, Monsier le Baron, ce qu'une semblable demande devoit vous causer d'étonnement et je ne chercherai point à excuser des irrégularités qui proviennent d'un oubli, dont Monsier Lubbert reconnoit toute la gravité ....» ("Sir, it comes as no surprise to me that such a request should have amazed you and I will not try to excuse the irregularities which have arisen due to a forgetful moment and of which M. Lubbert recognises the full gravity ...;") b) «... vous ne refuserez pas de solliciter du Roi les secours nécessaires pour assurer le service d'un théâtre dont le succès, non interrompu depuis quelque temps, constate l'heureuse direction qui lui a été imprimée.» ("... you will not refuse to solicit the necessary help from the King to ensure the running of a theatre whose success, uninterrupted for quite some time, shows the favourable direction that has now been instilled into it.") La Rochefoucauld to La Bouillerie, 15 September 1829, (O³ 1685 I).

FF 82.710 required.[260] The King signed his approval, and both La Rochefoucauld and Lubbert were advised of this together with the categories of expense affected.[261]

This episode is interesting because it throws light on the characters involved, and on the deep-seated culture of waste and inefficiency at the Opera. La Bouillerie was a strong administrator who was making a big effort to improve the Opera's financial

---

260 *Rapport au Roi*, La Bouillerie, 31 October 1829, (O³ 1685 I).
This report gave an interesting insight into the way in which this matter was dealt with in the accounts:
a) Details of the various items were as follows:

			FF	FF
Chant	-	Salary for Lafont	7.652	
	-	ditto – Valère	6.750	14.402
Service de la Salle	-			390
Gratifications Annuelles aux premiers sujets				
	-	Glossop	2.667	
	-	Dubadie	1.000	
	-	Jawureck	1.000	
	-	Taglioni	2.000	6.667
Feux	-	Lafont	2.819	
	-	Valère	2.250	5.069
Mobilier et Bâtiment	-			2.500
Dépenses diverses	-	Year's building insurance from 14 May		4.515
Fonds de réserve	-	Baignol of the *Théâtre de Bordeaux* to buy out Lafont's contract		25.000
	-	Maraffa – Fischer due to termination of contract		9.167
	-	*Théâtre de Lyon* to postpone Damoreau's holiday so she can sing in the delayed *Guillaume Tell*		5.000
	-	Grassari due to termination of contract		10.000
				82.710

Each of these items told a story and the failures to include some of them in the original budget arose from a number of causes. The FF 25.000 to the *Théâtre de Bordeaux* related back to 1828 when Lafont was engaged to double Nourrit in *La Muette de Portici*, starting in October. It looked like an oversight that this amount was not included in the 1829 budget, especially as Lubbert had already been making unauthorised payments to Lafont under *mandats provisoires*, which totalled FF 17.500 by the end of July. The termination of Maraffa-Fischer's contract was the subject of a lot of official correspondence and Lubbert made another unauthorised payment of FF 9.167 under a *mandat provisoire*. Lafont's salary and *feux* looked like a further failure to seek authorisation as Lubbert had already been paying Lafont.

b) The FF 82.710 was allocated in the accounts as follows:

	FF
Chant	14.403
Service de la Salle et du Théâtre	390
Gratifications annuelles aux premiers sujets	6.666
Feux ou droit de présence	5.069
Frais de mobilier et bâtiment	2.500
Dépenses diverses	4.515
Fonds de réserve	49.167
	82.710

c) The heading *Complément de subvention des théâtres Royaux*, which was included in the budget for the Royal Theatres, would be increased from FF 507.000 to FF 589.710.

261 La Bouillerie to La Rochefoucauld, 20 November 1829, (O³ 1685 I). La Rochefoucauld to Lubbert, 25 November 1829, (AJ¹³ 122 VII).

position. La Rochefoucauld was shown to be a weak and ineffective supervisor, caught between a strong superior in La Bouillerie and an irresponsible director in Lubbert.[262] As for Lubbert, his cavalier attitude towards financial matters was revealed. The paradox was, however, that despite all, 1829 was a good year for the Opera's finances. On the receipts side, the outcome was much better than budget, FF 1.805.460 compared with FF 1.669.850.[263] Receipts from the box-office totalled FF 574.155 from 155 performances,[264] for an average of FF 3.704 compared with FF 3.347 in 1828 and FF 3.103 in 1827. Rentals from boxes also improved very substantially, FF 129.650 compared with FF 82.880 in 1828. Again, the reasons are not hard to find. The Opera had four successes in 1829. *La Muette de Portici* and *Le Comte Ory* continued to do well, the former still averaging FF 4.013 from forty-one performances. Meanwhile, *Guillaume Tell* was first staged in 1829 and took FF 142.933 from twenty-eight performances for an average of FF 5.104, and the new ballet *La Belle au Bois Dormant* was also a success. It grossed FF 93.740 from twenty-three performances for an average of FF 4.075. It was very noticeable that sixteen of these were paired with old operas, yet these took FF 65.761 for an average of FF 4.100, thus making the ballet a success in its own right as it was paired with *Le Comte Ory* for the other seven performances.[265] These four productions thus accounted for 122 performances out of the total of 155,[266] took FF 497.171 at the box-office out of a total of FF 574.155 and averaged FF 4.075 per performance. The overall effect on receipts was thus very beneficial:[267]

	Budget	Accounts
	FF	FF
Recettes à l'entrée	540.000	574.155
Locations de loges à l'année	75.000	129.650
Recettes extraordinaires	13.000	57.850
	628.000	761.655

Even the King paid for his boxes for the first time: FF 48.000 was included under *recettes extraordinaires* and a suggestion that this amount should be deducted from the annual subsidy was not implemented.[268] As for the expenses, the final budget of

---

262 «Vous n'ignorez pas combien de difficultés faisoient naître l'indécision de ma position primitive, mais ces difficultés s'applanissent chaque jour, et, jaloux de seconder vos plans d'ordre et d'économie, vous devez remarquer le soin extrême que j'apporte à ne point m'écarter de la ligne que je dois suivre.» ("You are not unaware of how many difficulties arose out of the non-resolution of my original position but these difficulties get easier by the day, and, anxious to support your plans for order and economy, you should note the extreme care I take not to stray from the path I must follow.") La Rochefoucauld to La Bouillerie, 15 September 1829, (O³ 1685 I).

263 *Exercise 1829. Compte définitif des Recettes et Dépenses*, (AJ¹³ 146 IV). See Appendix II.

264 *Journal usuel de l'Opéra, 1791-1850*, op. cit..

265 Details of box-office receipts, (CO288 (942) and CO289 (943)).

266 *Journal usuel de l'Opéra, 1791-1850*, op. cit..

267 *Exercise 1829. Compte définitif des Recettes et Dépenses*, (AJ¹³ 146 IV).

268 «Admettant que le prix de la location des Loges du Roi qui, n'ayant pas été prévu au Budget, figure en recettes extraordinaires, doive être déduit de la subvention royale.» ("Allowing for the fact that the rent of the Royal Boxes, which was not budgeted for, appears under extraordinary receipts, it should be deducted from the royal subsidy.") *Compte définitif, Recettes*, (AJ¹³ 146 IV).

FF 1.843.358 was not fully utilised as the final expenses total was only FF 1.770.103 for an apparent saving of FF 73.255.[269] This so-called saving was, however, more apparent than real, as creative accounting ensured that such a saving was bound to emerge. Although every actual expense included in the 1829 Annual Accounts had, ultimately, to be *ordonnancée* and a revised higher budget had to be set which enabled these *ordonnances* to be issued, the reverse was not the same. If a category of actual expense came in below budget, the latter was not lowered. It stayed the same and thus enabled the authorities to show a saving over budget. Costumes and scenery, for example, were budgeted at FF 170.000 and remained at this figure although the actual expense was only FF 137.239, for an apparent saving of FF 32.761. This explained why the final budget for 1829 showed expenses of FF 1.843.358 yet the actual figure in the accounts was only FF 1.770.103.

Quite apart from these budgeting anomalies, the 1829 Annual Accounts showed an actual surplus of FF 35.357 as higher receipts had more than offset the higher expenses. As in 1828, there was no record of any supplement from the *Maison du Roi* over and above the annual subsidy from the *Budget des théâtres Royaux*.

1830

This was the year of the July 1830 Revolution and although the way in which the Opera was managed remained the same until 1 March 1831, both La Bouillerie and La Rochefoucauld resigned. Lubbert remained director but prevailing opinion moved towards the idea of a *régie intéressée*, being a concession awarded on a leasehold basis.

The 1830 Annual Accounts reflected the events of 1830.[270] The budget for receipts and expenses had been set at FF 1.724.844 and actual receipts at the box-office were, surprisingly, only slightly less than budget, FF 553.956 compared with FF 560.000. A note on the 1830 detailed accounts made particular reference to this. The three operas already in the repertory, *La Muette de Portici*, *Le Comte Ory* and *Guillaume Tell* continued to do well at the box-office, while a new *opéra-ballet*, *Le Dieu et la Bayadère*, was another success, especially due to Marie Taglioni. All told, these four productions grossed FF 416.421 from 107 performances for an average of FF 3.891.[271] Given the difficult circumstances in 1830 from July onwards, the Opera had good reason to be satisfied with this result. The new ballet, *Manon Lescaut*, grossed FF 119.370 from twenty-seven performances for an average of FF 4.421. On the face of

---

269 *Intendance Générale de la Maison du Roi. Exercise 1829. Théâtre Royaux*, (AJ[13] 146 IV).

270 a) «Malgré les événements de juillet, les différences des recettes effectuées et des recettes présumées ne sont que de FF 6.045 ....» ("Despite the events of July, the difference between actual receipts and budgeted receipts is only FF 6,045 ...;"). b) «... mais comme les locations se font habituellement pendant les mois d'octobre, novembre et décembre, l'agitation qui s'est manifestée à Paris pendant ce trimestre a départi un coup funeste à des recettes qui n'ont pour but que la tranquillité publique et la sécurité dans la jouissance des loges que l'on a ainsi payées d'avance.» ("... but as rentals are usually renewed in October, November and December, the unrest seen in Paris during this quarter has delivered a serious blow to these receipts. There has to be a feeling of public order and safety for these boxes to be paid for in advance.") *Exercise 1830. Compte général des recettes et dépenses*, (AJ[13] 228 I). See Appendix II.

271 Details of box-office receipts, (CO288 (942)).

it, this was a good result but the figures could be misleading as thirteen performances were paired with *Le Comte Ory*.[272]

On the other hand, the renting of boxes was badly affected, with receipts of FF 57.431 compared with a budget of FF 100.000 and a further note on the 1830 detailed accounts referred to this shortfall. Although the actual amount for 1829 had been better than budget at FF 129.650, the 1830 budget had been set at only FF 100.000 but even this figure proved to be too optimistic. It was noted that rentals were, by custom, renewed in October, November and December, but that the disturbances during that period, which started on 18 October, had caused renewals to fall due to a lack of public order. This first disturbance began when a large crowd gathered at the *Palais Royal* shouting republican slogans and insults at the King. The crowd then marched to the fortress of *Vincennes*, where four Restoration ministers, Chantelauze, Guernon-Ranville, Peyronnet and Polignac, were being held, the Chamber of Deputies having voted to have them tried. In the event, the trial did not open until 15 December amid demands from the mob for the death penalty. During the period which led up to this trial the Chamber of Deputies, which had become a court of justice, collected evidence against the ministers. A tense situation had thus prevailed between October and December[273] and this caused renewals of box rentals to fall. Of further interest on the receipts side was a separate category which showed that Charles X and Louis-Philippe continued to pay an annual total of FF 48.000 for their boxes, and a note that the secondary theatres had, since 1 July 1830, refused to pay their *redevances* to the Opera. FF 85.000 out of a total of FF 182.958 remained to be collected. As for the annual subsidy, the first budget wrongly showed a much reduced figure of FF 630.219[274] compared with FF 817.925 in 1829. A subsidy of FF 148.700 for the funding of pensions was subsequently added for a total of FF 778.919, and an equivalent amount of FF 148.700 was added to the expenses under pension payments.[275] Total receipts as a result of the above were finally FF 1.656.143, being FF 68.701 less than the budget. On the expenses side, the total was FF 1.731.810 for an overall deficit of FF 75.667 which was not funded by a supplement from the *Maison du Roi*. During the course of the year, extra amounts of FF 19.408 had been added to the budget – the buying-out of the singer Cinti-Damoreau's holiday for FF 18.000 was the main reason – but the allocations between the various categories of expense within this revised budget were re-allocated at the year-end. For twenty-eight categories, the budget was revised to reflect the actual expense incurred. For four categories the budget remained the same even although the actual expense differed. An arbitrary figure of FF 1.590 was then added to costumes and scenery so that the increased budget total could remain unchanged at FF 1.744.252 even although the actual expense was FF 1.731.810.

The four years of annual accounts 1827–30 showed an improving situation in the receipts of the Opera although no determined effort was made to reduce the expenses.

272 Details of box-office receipts, (CO289 (943)).

273 Hugh A.C. Collingham, *The July Monarchy, a Political History of France 1830–1848* (New York, 1988), pp. 34–39.

274 *Exercise 1830. Compte général des recettes à l'exercise*, (AJ[13] 228 I).

275 *Budget de l'Académie Royale de Musique pour l'Année 1830*, (PE3 (699)).

Successful new productions were clearly the reason for this improvement, especially in 1828 and 1829, and it is a tribute to La Rochefoucauld and Lubbert that Rossini's four operas were staged to critical and public acclaim. Meanwhile, *La Muette de Portici*, as analysed in chapter 4, built on the new trends initiated by *Le Siège de Corinthe* and remained a great success at the box-office. At the same time, La Bouillerie took the initiative in improving the Opera's overall financial position. The increase in the 1828 annual subsidy to FF 850.000, the write-off of various loans to the Opera and the payment of outstanding debts to suppliers, all helped. The result was that Véron took over the Opera at a time when its finances had already greatly improved.

The Situation as at 1 March 1831

On 1 March 1831, Véron was installed as the new director of the Opera. He had the mandate to manage it for his own profit as from 1 June 1831, as a concession from the State. As part of this change in management, a settlement of the Opera's financial affairs was drawn up as at the same date.[276] This comprised four sections: a retrospective look at the annual accounts for the three years 1828–1830; an estimate of the financial outcome for the two months to 28 February 1831; a summary of the FF 135.136 loan; and a summary of a FF 50.000 loan to Lubbert.

The first section started with the 1828 Annual Accounts and stated that the surplus in that year was FF 55.570, a figure which corresponded to that already identified. This retrospect also confirmed that the surplus had been paid over to *La Caisse des fonds particuliers du Roi*, less the FF 520 to be reclaimed from Laurent, the new director of the *Théâtre Italien*. As for 1829, the surplus of FF 35.357 also corresponded to that already identified. The retrospect stated that the new system of accounting and supervision had brought the Opera's finances under the direct control of the *Maison du Roi* and noted that *redevances* of FF 7.709 remained to be collected from the *Théâtre de la Porte St. Martin* and the *Cirque Olympique*. As for 1830, the deficit was put at FF 62.636 but this was FF 13.031 less than the FF 75.667 already identified. The retrospect showed higher receipts at FF 1.669.174 and the cause of this difference remains a mystery which archived documents have not revealed. The retrospect also noted that FF 95.000, not FF 85.000, remained to be collected from the secondary theatres and that the likelihood of recovery was very uncertain. The implication of this was that the *Maison du Roi* had assumed the responsibility for collecting this amount and that Véron had been absolved from this.

The second section focused on January and February 1831. Actual receipts were FF 79.128, but FF 138.491 remained due, being two months of the annual subsidy at FF 129.820, two months' rentals from the King's boxes at FF 8.000, and FF 671 from the renting of shops. Total receipts, received or receivable were thus FF 217.619. As for expenses, these were FF 237.256, being considerably less than budget due to an underspend on material costs of FF 39.192. The overall deficit for these two months was thus FF 19.637 and was assumed by the *Maison du Roi*.

---

276 *Situation et Inventaire au 1ᵉʳ mars, 1831*, (AJ¹³ 228 I).

The third section dealt with the loan of FF 135.136 and the outcome of this has already been covered. The fourth and final section dealt with a FF 50.000 loan to Lubbert. It was noted that FF 11.169 had already been repaid to the *Caisse des fonds particuliers du Roi*, a figure confirmed in Lubbert's own account of his stewardship.[277] Various outstanding expenses, including loans to Talon and Solomé, were set against this loan which left, rather conveniently, a balance of FF 6.

The above analyses, combined with the successful initiatives of La Bouillerie on behalf of the Opera, make it curious that informed opinion has maintained that the Opera had substantial debts at the time of the July 1830 Revolution. There was no evidence in the analysis of the annual accounts, nor in other primary sources, to support this claim and the estimate of a deficit of FF 1.000.000 or more looks ill-informed and inaccurate.[278] The finances of the Opera had already improved considerably by July 1830 and the final settlement gave no indication of substantial outstanding deficits, loans or debts which either became the responsibility of the old or new administrations or were assumed by Véron himself. This is an important point. Véron did not inherit any back-log of debts and went on to make a fortune for himself after 1 June 1831. He had managed the Opera on behalf of the Ministry of the Interior from 1 March to 31 May 1831 but as from 1 June 1831 he was able to initiate many changes which reduced costs, and to stage new productions which raised receipts.

---

277 *Compte des fonds d'avance de FF 50.000*, (AJ[13] 228 I).

278 See the following: a) "Everyone talked of economies to be made, and the proposals to pare or discontinue those state expenses classified as luxuries of course put the subsidised theatres in an extremely embarrassing position – a position which was not eased any by the discovery of a final deficit of over a million francs in the Opéra accounts." Crosten, op. cit., p. 16; b) «Au moment de la révolution de juillet, l'administration dirigée par Sosthène de La Rochefoucauld était en déficit de plus d'un million.» ("At the time of the July Revolution, the management run by Sosthène de La Rochefoucauld was in deficit by over a million francs.") Auguste Ehrhard, *L'Opéra sous la direction Véron (1831–35)* Extract from the *Revue Musicale de Lyon,* 1907, p. 2; c) "The following year, when the July Monarchy came to power, the new regime was the 'beneficiary' of a FF 1.200.000 deficit." Barbier, op. cit., p. 38.

CHAPTER 2

The financial record of Véron's tenure as concessionaire at the Opera is described here in detail. The terms of his appointment, the subsidies he received and the fines which were imposed provide a backdrop to Véron's policies towards the fixed personnel at the Opera and the various suppliers of goods and services. These policies enabled him to achieve considerable reductions in expenses. Receipts were enhanced by a new policy on free boxes and seats, new seat prices and successful new productions. The reasons for his premature departure and the settlement with the State are then summarised. Finally, an analysis of the annual accounts during his concession, and of the settlement with Duponchel, reveals the size of Véron's fortune.

The July 1830 Revolution which brought Louis-Philippe to the throne was an event which reflected an ambiguity prevalent in France at the time: the majority of middle-class Frenchmen, from small shopkeeper to banker, adhered to the principles of the 1789 Revolution yet feared its consequences. The Restoration from 1815 to 1830 had allayed their fears but had not adhered to those principles, and it took the arrival of Louis-Philippe, who was a prince, patriot and liberal, to give the appearance that this ambiguity had been resolved. On the one hand the *parti du mouvement,* the party of the left, could claim that another Revolution had taken place in that the Bourbons had again been deposed and their claim to legitimacy removed. On the other hand, the conservative *parti de résistance,* the party of the right, could portray the July 1830 Revolution as a mere constitutional change in that no political revolution had taken place. It was just that the new King was a more acceptable alternative to a republic. In either case extremism, in the form of both legitimists and republicans, had been thwarted and France had found a middle way to government. Needless to say, this ambiguity persisted throughout Louis-Philippe's reign, and although the *parti de résistance* held sway initially, this prepared the way for the 1848 Revolution and the final triumph of the republicans.[1]

This ambiguity was also reflected in a new policy towards the Opera. Chapter 1 described the ineffective supervision by La Rochefoucauld and the poor management by Lubbert, both of which led to inflated costs, many malpractices and an inability to get to grips with the problems. By the end of the Restoration period, the idea of placing the management of the Opera in the hands of a director who would manage it as a concession and for his own profit had already been canvassed, not least by Lubbert himself, but nothing was done. The new government, however, was determined to take decisive action to improve matters yet was itself equivocal in the chosen method of doing so. On the one hand, it sought to uphold bourgeois values of economy and good house-keeping through the appointment of a director who would be allowed to manage the Opera for his own profit. In this sense a revolution had taken place which, it was hoped, would help do away with the abuses and failures of the Restoration period. On

---

1   Collingham, op. cit., ch. 1 and 2. I am indebted to Hugh Collingham for his views on the politics of the July 1830 Revolution.

the other hand, the Opera, which was still called the *Académie Royale de Musique*, was perceived as an organ of the State which subsidised it, and of the King who was concerned that his pomp and dignity should be upheld. With this in mind a *Commission de Surveillance,* the Commission, was formed to ensure that these interests were protected. A conflict of interest was thus created between the private enterprise drive for profit through the concession to Véron, and the imperative for both the State and the King that their respective interests should be sustained. This conflict of interest was not resolved during the period from 1831 to 1835 as the two sides could not find a middle way through compromise and mutual respect. This was despite the fact that both had initially subscribed to the idea of a *régie intéressée*, which could be described as a leasehold agreement to a concessionaire:

> L'Opéra entrera en régie intéressée et le Directeur ne sera plus soumis qu'à la surveillance de la Commission chargée de faire exécuter le Cahier des charges dans l'intérêt de l'art et du gouvernement.[2]

The Appointment of Véron

In the early hours of 1 March 1831, the authorities took the decisive step to change the way in which the Opera was managed.[3] Véron was initially appointed manager on behalf of the State and then director, 1 June 1831, for six years at his own risk, peril and fortune. The 28 February 1831 *Cahier des charges* was signed by all parties and this spelt out the ground rules for these new arrangements.[4] The Commission was established with the Duc de Choiseul as president, Hippolyte Royer-Collard, Baron d'Henneville, Armand Bertin and Edmond Blanc as members, and Edmond Cavé as secretary.[5] Royer-Collard resigned on 28 April 1831 due to a conflict of interest: he was also *Chef de la division des Beaux-Arts*, and Kératry, a member of the Chamber of Deputies, was appointed in his place.[6]

Why was Véron appointed and not someone else, including the incumbent Lubbert? The former's character and background have already been well-described both by himself and others,[7] but as he emerged as the pivotal figure in the Opera's early 1830s' transition, a brief summary would also be of interest. He was born on 5 April 1798, the son of a Parisian stationer who practised all the bourgeois virtues of prudence, thrift and money-making. Véron decided to become a doctor and qualified in 1823 but his

---

2 ("The Opera will be managed as a leasehold agreement to a concessionaire and the director will only be subject to the monitoring of the Commission responsible for the execution of the *Cahier des charges* in the interest of art and the government.") Report of the Commission, 1 March 1831, (F[21] 4633).

3 Véron, op.. cit., III, pp. 171–172.

4 *Cahier des charges*, 28 February 1831, (AJ[13] 187 I). See Appendix III for the full text and translation.

5 *Cahier des charges*, 28 February 1831, Article 3, (AJ[13] 187 I). For background on the Commission members, see Fulcher, op. cit., pp. 58–59.

6 Commission, minutes of meeting, 28 April 1831, (F[21] 4633).

7 a) Véron, op. cit.; b) Ehrhard, op. cit., pp. 5–12; c) Crosten, op. cit., pp. 20–23; d) Charles P. Séchan, *Souvenirs d'un homme de théâtre, 1831–1855* (Paris, 1883), p. 190.

entrepreneurial talents soon emerged. He became the friend of a pharmacist called Regnault who had developed a chest paste. When he died, Regnault left the formula to Véron in his will. Entrepreneur that he was, Véron advertised this paste in medical journals and made a modest fortune thereby. He then turned his hand to journalism and after working for various journals, he founded the *Revue de Paris* in 1829 which established him socially and in the world of arts and letters. It has to be said that neither his physique nor his appearance were very attractive and every description of him was somewhat derogatory. "His bearing combined impertinence and unction, an affectation of levity and a touch of arrogance." A fellow journalist called his face "a mould of Regnault paste in a setting of currant jelly," while Heinrich Heine pictured him as "a bulky caricature-like figure, with a head entirely buried in an immense white cravat ... rolling about insolently at his ease." As William Crosten wrote, "few men of Véron's generation were more often described, criticised and ridiculed, but this caused him no displeasure."[8] Indeed he was, according to Charles Séchan, someone who preferred to be spoken of badly rather than not at all.[9]

With this background, and despite his appearance, it was possible to see why, through the Commission's eyes, he would have been a suitable candidate. He had had no connections with the Restoration government and in this he was in a similar position to the members of the Commission. Through his profitable career in private business, he was in harmony with the new bourgeois élite, with its interest in money and successful enterprise. He had a flair for display, prodigious energy and proven administrative skills.[10] He could demonstrate strong financial backing and could put up

---

8   Crosten, op. cit., p. 22. All the quotations are on this page.

9   Séchan, op. cit., p. 190.

10   a) «Véron avait le flair. Il sentait, si l'on peut dire, l'appât que le public désire qu'on lui serve. Il se jettait dessus, le préparait et le lui lançait.» ("Véron had intuition. He felt, so to speak, the bait that the audience desired to be served. He would throw himself on it, prepare it and hurl it at them.") Binet, op. cit., p. 131; b) «Il a réussi, surtout, à contenter les bons bourgeois; à satisfaire les principaux tenants de la nouvelle classe.» ("He succeeded, above all, in keeping the good middle class happy and in satisfying the main upholders of the new class.") Binet, op. cit., p. 139; c) «Son assiduité au travail était légendaire.» ("His diligence at work was legendary.") Gourret, op. cit., p. 122; d) «Il avait l'oeil de maître, intervenait sans cesse et partout, multipliait les conférences avec les peintres, les décorateurs, les machinistes, examinait et visitait lui-même devis et projets, courait à droite et à gauche, stimulait tout le monde et connaissait chacun.» ("He had an expert's eye and would constantly intervene and be everywhere. He would multiply the meetings with the painters, decorators and stagehands, would himself examine and review estimates and projects, would busy himself all over the place, would stimulate everyone and know each one of them.") Gourret, op. cit., p. 122; e) «Bon psychologue, il préférait diriger par la persuasion souriante plutôt que par l'autorité brutale.» ("As a good psychologist, he preferred to direct by smiling persuasion rather than by brutal authority.") Gourret, op. cit., p. 122; f) «Ce qui est incontestable, c'est que le docteur Véron sut admirablement comprendre et satisfaire les goûts de son siècle, bons ou mauvais; qu'il devina l'un des premiers toute la puissance de la presse périodique.» ("What is indisputable is that Dr. Véron understood admirably how to satisfy the tastes of his century, good or bad; and that he was among the first to understand the power of the periodical press.") Séchan, op. cit., p. 194; g) Séchan also wrote about Véron's style of direction. Referring to previous directors: «Ses prédécesseurs avaient presque tous dirigé l'Opéra sans sortir de leur cabinet directorial.» ("His predecessors had almost all directed the Opera without getting out of their director's office.") They had delegated most of the administration to others. Véron, on the other hand, got involved in everything, «... descendant jusqu'aux plus minces détails.» ("... going down to the minutest details.") Séchan, op. cit., p. 198.

the caution money required.   Finally, he had good connections especially with the press.   With these credentials he was, by his own admission, able to convince the Commission that his success at the Opera would redound to the political credit of the new regime.[11] He was also prepared to accept an annual subsidy which would fall over time.   Despite his lack of knowledge and experience of music in general, and of opera and ballet in particular, he was appointed in an atmosphere of mutual trust and confident expectation.

Perhaps inevitably, however, Véron and the Commission soon lost confidence in each other.   Véron thought that he had gained a free hand to direct the Opera for his own profit and underestimated the power of the Minister and the Commission to intervene and change the ground rules.   The Commission thought that the interests of the State and the King were paramount and underestimated the consequences of appointing a man who was single-minded in his desire for profit.[12] Véron was a narrowly-focused man who took too dismissive a view of his State-appointed masters and thus overestimated his powers.   The State was initially attracted by a man of action who could sort out problems but became disenchanted by the ensuing social and political difficulties.   Envy and jealousy also played their parts as Véron did indeed make a fortune.

The Caution Money

When Véron met with the Comte de Montalivet,   Minister of the Interior, and the Commission on 28 February 1831, the question of caution money was raised.   Véron gave the impression in his memoirs that Montalivet had raised this from FF 200.000 to FF 250.000,[13] and this has been accepted by all commentators to date.   A close inspection of the relevant clause in the 28 February 1831 *Cahier des charges*, however, and of subsequent correspondence, reveals another story.   Article 18 set a minimum of FF 150.000 and a maximum of FF 250.000 with the actual amount to be agreed by 1 June 1831.[14] The implication of this Article and of the subsequent sequence of events was that Montalivet was not fixing the actual amount but merely raising the maximum which Véron should put up.   On 10 May 1831 the Commission met to examine the changes to Véron's *Cahier des charges* as proposed by the new Minister,

---

11   Véron, op. cit., III, p. 172.

12   There were many references to Véron's cupidity. a) Séchan quoted a critic of Véron called Philarète Chasles. «Personne, dans notre époque, et après M. de Talleyrand ou Beaumarchais, vers 1750, n'a eu comme Véron le nez au vent pour découvrir le profit, et la rapide course du lévrier pour l'atteindre.» ("No-one in our time, and after M. de Talleyrand or Beaumarchais, around 1750, had such a nose as Véron for sniffing out a profit, nor the speed of a greyhound to reach it.") Séchan, op. cit., p. 192; b) «Ses parents l'initièrent par leur exemple à une religion: celle de l'argent.» ("His parents initiated him by their own example into one religion: that of money.") Ehrhard, op. cit., p. 5; c) «Comme on l'a vu, le sentiment qui domine dans la vie de M. Véron, c'est l'amour de l'argent; il aime l'argent, il en aime le son, la vue, le toucher.» ("As one has seen, the feeling that dominates M. Véron's life is the love of money; he likes money, he likes its sound, its sight and its feel.") Charles de Boigne, *Petits mémoires de l'Opéra* (Paris, 1857), p. 9.

13   Veron, op. cit., III, p. 172.

14   *Cahier des charges*, 28 February 1831, Article 18, (AJ[13] 187 I).

d'Argout,[15] and at its meeting on 16 May, Véron objected to the proposed new Article 18 which fixed the caution money at FF 250.000. In his view it should be fixed at FF 200.000 and not the maximum as stated in the 28 February 1831 *Cahier des charges*.[16] The Commission was inclined to accept Véron's view and Cavé wrote to the Minister accordingly.[17] He first set out the underlying reason for the caution money. It was to give twice the cover needed to pay certain expenses, namely the monthly salaries of fixed personnel, the monthly proportion of the annual insurance premiums and the monthly amount payable for the *droit des indigents*. For that reason the Commission was required to certify to the Minister, on a monthly basis, that the value of the caution money was at least double these expenses. According to Cavé, Véron was asking the Minister to fix the caution money exactly between the maximum and minimum, that is to say at FF 200.000. The Commission had agreed with Véron on this and Cavé commended the FF 200.000 to the Minister. D'Argout, however, clearly insisted that his FF 250.000 should stand, and this was the amount which was included under Article 18 in the first supplement to the 28 February 1831 *Cahier des charges,* 30 May 1831.[18] Of this amount, FF 50.000 was put up by Véron and FF 200.000 by his wealthy financier friend Alexandre Aguado.[19] The Commission had been overruled and Véron received an unwelcome taste of Ministerial power. The Commission with which he had to deal had proved to be a weak link. In this, it harked back to La Rochefoucauld and his weak link with La Bouillerie.

The *Cahier des charges*

This document was a radical departure from the spirit and practices of the Restoration period. It also represented the new regime's perception of the Opera and of its place in the political, civil and artistic life of the nation.[20] Such perceptions have already been well researched[21] and there is no need to repeat them. More important here was Véron's own view that this *Cahier des charges* gave him the freedom to carry out sweeping changes to the management and finances of the Opera. The over-zealous use of this perceived freedom resulted in his premature downfall in 1835 but this had more to do with his personality and political insensitivity than with any failure to improve the Opera's situation. The Commission admitted as much at the time of his resignation:

> Le succès de l'opéra actuel, l'éclat dont il brille, nous feraient considérer comme imprudente la recherche d'un autre mode d'administration.[22]

---

15 Commission, minutes of meeting, 10 May 1831, (F^{21} 4633).

16 Commission, minutes of meeting, 16 May 1831, (F^{21} 4633).

17 Cavé to the Minister, d'Argout, 20 May 1831, (AJ^{13} 187 II).

18 *Cahier des charges,* first supplement, 30 May 1831, Article 18, (AJ^{13} 187 I).

19 Fulcher, op. cit., p. 57.

20 *Cahier des charges*, 28 February 1831, (AJ^{13} 187 I).

21 See, for example: a) Fulcher, op. cit., ch. 2. b) Crosten, op. cit., ch. 2. c) Collingham, op. cit., pp. 282–285.

22 ("The current success of the Opera and the brightness with which it shines would lead us to think that any attempt to find another mode of administration would be imprudent.") Commission to the Minister, 15 August 1835, (AJ^{13} 180 III).

Véron thought he had gained greatly from various omissions in the 28 February 1831 *Cahier des charges*. For example, the numbers to be retained as fixed personnel only covered the chorus, corps de ballet and orchestra. There was no mention of the soloists and, crucially, of the numbers to be employed in the various service departments. This was a marked departure from the Restoration period and seemed to give Véron the freedom to reduce staff numbers:[23]

Règlement, 5 May 1821		*Cahier des charges*, 28 February 1831, Article 6
Chant	21	N/A
Choeurs	66	68
Danse	29	N/A
Ballets	71	72
Orchestre	79	80
Salle et Théâtre	66	N/A
Costumes	52	N/A
Décorations	61	N/A
	445	220

In any event, as his policy was to strengthen the artistic side, the minimum requirements for chorus, corps de ballet and orchestra were in tune with his policy and ambitions. Also omitted was any definition of what fixed personnel actually meant. In the Restoration period there had, of course, been retirements and a few redundancies, but the underlying assumption and practice was that *fixe* meant fixed. In modern parlance it was a job for life. Indeed, this was recognised in Article 5 which enjoined Véron to respect existing employment contracts during his time as manager on behalf of the State from 1 March to 31 May 1831.[24] Thereafter, however, Article 25 seemed to give some freedom to Véron. Although he had to pay some attention to the regulations in respect of the personnel whom he had inherited, no restrictions were placed on those personnel whom he subsequently employed.[25] As it rapidly became apparent, *fixe* was by no means fixed. Véron, who was ruthlessly dedicated to make his fortune, was able to enforce retirements and redundancies on an unprecedented scale. What is more, where minimum numbers were enforced for the chorus, corps de ballet and orchestra, he employed new artists at much lower salaries, thus reducing the overall cost. There was a further omission. Apart from the period from 1 March to 31 May 1831, nothing was written about salary levels. These were, by convention, reviewed annually and Article 25 gave Véron the scope to make significant salary reductions as from 1 June 1831.[26] This was a major freedom when compared with the Restoration period when part of the cumbersome annual budget process entailed a review of all personnel together with salary recommendations for the coming year. Even if a review was very unfavourable, it was unknown for a salary to be reduced.

---

23 Numbers to be retained for fixed personnel, (AJ[13] 1186 and AJ[13] 187 I).

24 *Cahier des charges*, 28 February 1831, Article 5, (AJ[13] 187 I).

25 *Cahier des charges*, 28 February 1831, Article 25, (AJ[13] 187 I).

26 *Cahier des charges*, 28 February 1831, Article 25, (AJ[13] 187 I).

Whereas the 5 May 1821 *Règlement* set out the procedures whereby suppliers were appointed,[27] the 28 February 1831 *Cahier des charges* had nothing to say on this point. This left Véron free of the cumbersome procedures mandatory under the Restoration. He was also free of the requirement to have a principal painter on the payroll and this enabled him to conclude a new contract with Ciceri as well as a new tariff for scene-painting. The result was a significant reduction in the costs of costumes and scenery. The 5 May 1821 *Règlement* and various subsequent *arrêtés* had also laid down detailed procedures for the annual budget round; the presentation of budgets for new productions; the reporting of annual accounts; the accounting for receipts and expenses; and the system whereby the expenses were paid. One result of this was that the Opera, apart from Lubbert's success in obtaining an advance to pay petty expenses, had, strictly speaking, no cash unless, as with Lubbert, it paid expenses directly out of receipts. This was all changed under the new regime. The only reporting requirement in the 28 February 1831 *Cahier des charges* concerned the caution money and the need to report the salaries paid in the previous month, together with the deductions made for pension fund purposes.[28] The first supplement to the *Cahier des charges*, 30 May 1831, added the payments to authors, the instalments of the annual insurance premiums and the *droit des indigents* to this list.[29] Of budgets, accounting procedures and the reporting of annual accounts there was nothing laid down. Véron could thus install his own systems of financial control and was free to open a bank account.[30] As the State still paid an annual subsidy to the Opera, the Commission's ceding of financial control to Véron was a curious lapse.

On the other hand, the 28 February 1831 *Cahier des charges* with its twenty-nine Articles had a great deal to say on many subjects. Three Articles, seemingly unrelated, had a disproportionate effect on the finances and contributed to the souring of relationships between Véron and the Commission. Articles on the annual subsidy, the requirement that new productions should be staged with new sets and costumes, and the fines which could be imposed, also provoked discord and contributed to Véron's early departure.

Articles 2, 9 and 10

Article 2 required that the theatre should be refurbished and repainted,[31] while Articles 9 and 10 covered the number and genre of operas and ballets which should be staged each year.[32] The problem with Article 2 was that although the work had to be completed prior to Véron's 1 June 1831 assumption as concessionaire, the bills would be paid by him during his concession. The question then was who should bear the cost and what

---

27 *5 mai 1821 Règlement,* Article 22, (AJ[13] 1186).

28 *Cahier des charges,* 28 February 1831, Articles 17 & 24, (AJ[13] 187 I).

29 *Cahier des charges,* first supplement, 30 May 1831, Article 17, (AJ[13] 187 I). Commission to the Minister, 20 July 1831, re June payments, (AJ[13] 187 V).

30 Annual Accounts 1831–32, (AJ[13] 228 II). Reference to the *Banque de France* under *Comptes supplémentaires.*

31 *Cahier des charges,* 28 February 1831, Article 2, (AJ[13] 187 I).

32 *Cahier des charges,* 28 February 1831, Articles 9 & 10, (AJ[13] 187 I).

should be the method of payment? The Commission decided that the cost was the government's responsibility[33] and that as Véron would pay the bills, he should be subsidised with the money to do so. The problem with Article 9 was that although the new regime, and therefore Véron, had inherited a contract signed between Meyerbeer and the previous administration to stage *Robert le Diable* it would not be performed until after Véron had taken over as director. The minutes of the Commission's meeting on 6 March 1831 reflected its concerns as to who should pay the expenses of *Robert le Diable*: the Ministry of the Interior or the director?[34]

> Est-il juste que le Ministre de l'Intérieur fasse les frais d'un ouvrage dont M. Véron recueillera les bénéfices?[35]

Véron would not take over until 1 June 1831 and until that date the government directed the theatre through the authority of the Commission. It had been agreed with Meyerbeer that work on *Robert le Diable* should start right away, with some expenses incurred prior to 1 June 1831. The Commission concluded that expenses incurred before 1 June 1831 were an obligation of the government. As for the expenses incurred after 1 June 1831, although *Robert le Diable* could bring profit to Véron, it could also fail and thus penalise him. The Commission felt that it would hardly be just that Véron might pay dearly for a mistake to which he had not been a party. In due course, however, the Commission was to change its view. *Robert le Diable* was a great success and Véron effectively received no subsidy towards it.

As might be expected, Véron played an astute game in all this. Although on the one hand he realised that the new opera could be a great success, on the other hand he publicly gave the impression that he disliked the opera and was most unwilling to stage it.[36] To what extent this influenced the Commission was not clear but, at the same meeting on 6 March 1831, it was finally decided that all the expenses for *Robert le Diable* should be a charge to the government, and that this decision should go to the

---

33   Commission, minutes of meeting, 24 March 1831, (F[21] 4633). As the work would be done during the period 1 March–31 May, the Commission felt that the Government should pay and wrote to the Minister accordingly. Also minutes of meeting, 31 March 1831, which indicated that the Minister, at a meeting with Royer-Collard, had agreed to the Commission's recommendation.

34   Commission, minutes of meeting, 6 March 1831, (F[21] 4633).

35   ("Is it right that the Ministry of the Interior should pay for the expenses of a work from which M. Véron would reap the rewards?") Commission, minutes of meeting, 6 March 1831, (F[21] 4633).

36   a) «Il avait déclaré publiquement en pleine répétition, que la partition lui semblait détestable et qu'il ne la jouerait que contraint et forcé, ou moyennant une indemnité suffisante.» ("He had declared publicly, in the middle of a rehearsal, that the score seemed to him appalling and that he would only have it played if under duress and forced to, or for a high enough indemnity.") Séchan, op. cit., p. 198; b) Séchan then referred to an indemnity of FF 60.000–FF 80.000 and implied that Véron's protestations were a negotiating tool. He wrote that the Minister, d'Argout, had come to understand that Véron did not want to stage *Robert le Diable*; c) However, Véron denied this in his memoirs. Véron, op. cit., III, pp. 179–180; d) The above should be put in the context of the Commission's meeting, 6 March 1831, at which it was agreed, subject to the Minister's approval, that the government should bear the expense of *Robert le Diable*. This approval was noted at the Commission's meeting, 31 March 1831, (F[21] 4633).

Minister for approval. At a later meeting on 15 March 1831, when the Commission reviewed the likely expenses and receipts to 31 May, it noted that it was necessary to add the estimated FF 70.000 required to stage *Robert le Diable*. At a meeting on 31 March 1831, Royer-Collard gave details of his separate meeting with the Minister who had approved the necessary funds, and on that basis the Commission ordered a start to *Robert le Diable:* scenery, costumes, music parts, etc. At the same meeting it also learnt that funds were approved for the refurbishment of the theatre.[37]

A block sum was then made available to subsidise Véron for the expenses of refurbishment and of *Robert le Diable*. It totalled FF 100.000, payable by instalments, and a contract was concluded between Véron and the Commission.[38] The text of the contract contained a number of interesting points. The timetable for the refurbishment was very tight indeed. The theatre had to close on 15 May 1831 and re-open on 1 June. Barely a fortnight was allowed for the considerable amount of work to be done and Véron could not claim any indemnity if the theatre was not able to open on time. The refurbishment was estimated to cost at least FF 40.000 according to an attached budget. When added to the estimated cost of FF 70.000 for *Robert le Diable*, this already made for a total of FF 110.000. Véron was also required to take full financial responsibility for *Robert le Diable*. As the government had refused to acknowledge the former regime's contract with Meyerbeer, this clause enabled it to put any liability onto Véron personally. Altogether the contract was onerous for Véron. He was taking a big financial risk in taking over the Opera and the success of *Robert le Diable* was by no means assured. The extra subsidy of FF 100.000 was to be paid in three instalments, and the first instalment of FF 30.000 was paid on 1 June 1831, which was within the timescale agreed.[39] In the event, however, only one more instalment of FF 30.000 was paid, and the authorities finally deemed that none of the FF 60.000 should be earmarked for the cost of *Robert le Diable*. Not only was this opera not fully subsidised, it was not subsidised at all: a fact which previous research has failed to clarify.[40]

How much did the refurbishment cost? After various names had been submitted to the Minister, Le Sueur was appointed architect[41] and various painter-decorators submitted their estimates. Adam Frères quoted a figure of FF 70.000 including architect's fees[42] and it was this quotation which was accepted. Their bill of exactly

---

37   Commission, minutes of meeting, 31 March 1831, (F^{21} 4633).

38   D'Argout to Véron, 24 April 1831; Véron to d'Argout, 14 May 1831 (AJ^{13} 187 V).

39   The FF 30.000 was paid on 1 June 1831, (CO710 (608)). It appeared in the 1831–32 Annual Accounts under *Recettes extraordinaires*, (AJ^{13} 228 II).

40   Wilberg, op. cit., pp. 248–249 and Fulcher, op. cit., p. 68. Both authors considered that *Robert Le Diable* was subsidised in full.

41   Commission, minutes of meetings, 27 March 1831 and 31 March 1831, (F^{21} 4633).

42   Adam Frères, *peintres décorateurs*. Detailed estimate submitted to Véron, 27 April 1831, (AJ^{13} 222 VII).

FF 70.000 was paid by the Opera in instalments.[43] Meanwhile, the second instalment of FF 30.000 for *Robert le Diable* was due on 31 January 1832, but there was a problem. Véron, to conform to his 28 February 1831 *Cahier des charges*, Article 9, had to stage a grand opera in his first year to 31 May 1832 apart from *Robert le Diable*, but this seemed unlikely to happen. According to draft letters from the Commission to the Minister,[44] Véron claimed that he could not stage this second grand opera because of the prodigious effort expended on *Robert le Diable* and the holidays that were due to the singers. In any event, *Robert le Diable* was a huge success and Article 10 gave him a let-out. If a new production was very successful then a further one could be delayed or cancelled. He therefore requested that the second grand opera should be staged in his second year to 31 May 1833. The Commission agreed to accept this argument and to release the second instalment of FF 30.000. After all, the Commission had a fall-back position as the third instalment of FF 40.000, due on 31 January 1833, could be withheld if this second grand opera was not staged in time. The second instalment was duly paid on 31 January 1832.[45] The total thus far was FF 60.000 but as the redecoration had cost FF 70.000 and *Robert le Diable* had cost some FF 63.300, the lack of funding, both as to amount and timing, was very clear. Indeed Véron wrote to the Commission in July 1832, with a request for the third instalment of FF 40.000 so that he could cover the bills already paid.[46] No money was forthcoming,[47] either then or on the due date, 31 January 1833. By April 1833 relations had deteriorated to such an extent that the Minister, Adolphe Thiers, was minded to allocate the FF 40.000 to the *Théâtre Français*.[48] In the end, however, the Commission imposed a second supplement to the *Cahier des charges*, 14 May 1833, and the text of the new Article 34 spoke for itself.[49] The FF 60.000 already paid should be wholly set against the cost of refurbishment although even this was FF 10.000 short of the total. The outstanding FF 40.000 was cut to FF 20.000, and regarded as a subsidy towards one of two grand operas to be staged in Véron's third year to 31 May 1834. If this second grand opera was not staged, then the FF 20.000 would revert to the Treasury. As two grand operas were not staged in 1833–34, the FF 20.000 was never paid. Véron claimed in his memoirs that Thiers proposed a

---

43   The FF 70.000 was paid by three instalments, (CO710 (608)):

1 July 1831	FF 36.667
1 February 1832	16.667
July 1832	16.666
	70.000

     This total was charged in the 1831–32 Annual Accounts under *Dépenses extraordinaires*, (AJ[13] 228 II).

44   Draft letter, Commission to the Minister, 13 January 1832; draft letter, Commission to the Minister, 21 January 1832, (F[21] 1053).

45   The FF 30.000 was paid on 31 January 1832, (CO710 (608)).

46   Véron to the Commission, 11 July 1832, (AJ[13] 180 II).

47   D'Argout to Choiseul, 26 July 1832, (AJ[13] 180 II). He could see no justification for paying the FF 40.000.

48   Commission, minutes of special meeting, April 1833, (F[21] 4633).

49   *Cahier des charges*, 14 May 1833, second supplement, Article 34, (AJ[13] 187 I).

compromise of FF 15.000 in August 1835 to end the matter,[50] but there was no sign of this sum in the final settlement. Practically, he received nothing towards the cost of *Robert le Diable* despite the original contract, and this must have considerably soured his relationship with the Minister and the Commission.

The Annual Subsidy

The annual subsidies payable to Véron were set out in the 28 February 1831 *Cahier des charges* and covered the anticipated six years of his concession.[51] From an initial FF 810.000 in the first year, they were to fall to FF 760.000 for the next two years and FF 710.000 for the last three. However, the second supplement, 14 May 1833, enforced a major downward revision in that the last four years' subsidies were changed to an annual subsidy of FF 670.000, plus a special FF 50.000 subsidy spread over four years, rather than paid in one year by twelve monthly instalments.[52] The total shortfall would thus have been FF 160.000 with FF 77.500 of that in 1833–34. Véron had quite a lot to say in his memoirs about this reduction. Somewhat wryly he wrote that he had been too successful.[53] In other words, the Opera had been a success, he had made a lot of money and people were envious of his success, not least the Chamber of Deputies which brought influence to bear on the Minister, Thiers. As the Commission was also disenchanted with Véron, there was no sign of support for him in the minutes of their meetings or in correspondence with Thiers. The result was that the 1833–34 subsidy was reduced and Véron was left to make two further comments about Parliament and ministers in his memoirs which have stood the test of time:

> Que j'ai vu souvent sous le gouvernement parlementaire, des ministres, menacés par des conspirations de scrutin, prendre *in extremis*, sciemment, des mesures administratives qu'ils savaient désastreuses, laissant à leurs successeurs les difficultés, les désordres qu'ils créaient en se disant, presque en se frottant les mains: «Ils se tireront de là comme ils pourront.»

> Pour plaire à la Chambre, quand il était ministre, ou pour conquérir le pouvoir quand il luttait dans l'opposition, M. Thiers a compromis bien autre chose que les intérêts des beaux-arts en France, que la fortune et l'avenir de l'Opéra.[54]

The reduction in subsidy was a further symptom of the authorities' loss of confidence in Véron, whether by the Minister, the Commission or the Chamber of Deputies.

---

50 Véron, op. cit., III, p. 203.

51 *Cahier des charges*, 28 February 1831, Article 17, (AJ[13] 187 I).

52 *Cahier des charges*, 14 May 1833, second supplement, Article 17, (AJ[13] 187 I).

53 «À cette époque, l'Opéra jetait un grand éclat; j'avais eu le malheur d'être heureux.» ("At that time, the Opera was dazzling and I had had the misfortune to be happy.") Véron, op. cit., III, p. 188.

54 ("How often have I seen, under the parliamentary government, ministers who, when threatened by conspiracies at the polls, take, *in extremis* and deliberately, administrative measures that they knew would be disastrous. They then leave to their successors the difficulties and disorders that they have created, while saying to themselves and rubbing their hands together: 'They will just have to get out of it as best they can.' ") Véron, op. cit., III, p. 189.

("In order to please the Chamber when he was a minister, or in order to gain power when he was struggling in opposition, M. Thiers compromised something other than the interests of the fine arts in France and the fortune and future of the Opera.") Véron, op. cit., III, p. 190.

The Fines

The 28 February 1831 *Cahier des charges* was insistent, Article 11, that new productions must be staged with new scenery and costumes.[55] This was a decisive break from the Restoration period when the authorities had tried to compensate for their inability to impose financial discipline and to eliminate malpractices by the use of old scenery and costumes for new productions. It is not hard to imagine the pressures on Véron as a result of this new policy. Not only would the scenery and costumes inevitably cost more but this was at a time when he was seeking to please his audiences with lavish new productions. Small wonder that, in his pursuit of profit, he tried to get round this problem by cutting the costs of scenery and costumes. Unfortunately he also tried to cut corners, having underestimated the Commission's determination to enforce the terms of his 28 February 1831 *Cahier des charges* and the two supplements, not least in the number of new productions to be staged each year. He fell out with both the Minister and the Commission as a result and the fines which he incurred were symptomatic of this.

The 28 February 1831 *Cahier des charges* made it possible for fines to be imposed on Véron. They ranged between FF 1.000 and FF 5.000 and were to be taken from the caution money within three days of imposition and paid to the *caisse des pensions*. After three fines, the contract with Véron could be terminated by the Commission and the Opera's receipts seized.[56] The second supplement to the *Cahier des charges,* 14 May 1833, raised the fines to between FF 3.000 and FF 10.000 but also stated that whatever the number of fines, the contract should not be terminated.[57] When the 28 February 1831 *Cahier des charges* was drawn up, no-one could have foreseen that Véron would incur a great number of fines and that strictly speaking his contract should have been terminated after the first three. The fact was, however, that in his drive to make a fortune from the Opera, he indulged in sharp practice and was fined accordingly.

The first fine arose out of Véron's use of old scenery for *Le Serment.* The Commission met on 9 November 1832, in a special session which resulted from decisions taken at previous meetings.[58] It met as a *tribunal arbitral* in conformity with civil procedures and Véron, having joined the meeting, agreed that this tribunal had the legal powers to adjudicate on his case. He was asked whether he needed a lawyer to defend himself but declined this offer. The basis for the case against Véron, which was presented by Cavé, was that old scenery had been used for a new production without authorisation. Véron was thus in breach of Article 11 of the 28 February 1831 *Cahier des charges* and the Article was quoted in full. The case implied that Véron had used only old scenery and that he had committed two offences. He had not used any new scenery and he had not gained approval for old scenery. It was noted by Cavé that the fine could fall within the range of FF 1.000 to FF 5.000 and he asked for the maximum fine of FF 5.000. Véron then spoke in his own defence. He said that in all the new

---

55   *Cahier des charges*, 28 February 1831, Article 11, (AJ[13] 187 I).

56   *Cahier des charges*, 28 February 1831, Article 27, (AJ[13] 187 I).

57   *Cahier des charges*, second supplement, 14 May 1833, Article 27, (AJ[13] 187 I).

58   Commission, report as *tribunal arbitral,* 9 November 1832, (F[21] 1054).

productions to date he had used some old scenery mixed in with new scenery. He then put forward the somewhat disingenuous argument that old scenery could be divided into two classes. First, that which had to be changed in which case he had always sought authorisation from the Commission and second, that which needed no modification at all, either in lay-out or in painting, in which case Véron did not think he needed to seek authorisation. As for *Le Serment*, Véron advised that the old scenery had not been modified at all, only *rafraîchi,* touched up. In any event, Véron claimed that he had never had any guidance from the Commission on the interpretation of Article 11. He therefore felt there had been no breach of the 28 February 1831 *Cahier des charges*, only uncertainty over the construction of Article 11. Kératry asked whether this old scenery was still being used for the relevant old productions and Véron said that it was. Cavé and Véron then left the tribunal which, having rehearsed all the arguments again, decided that Véron had breached Article 11 and fined him FF 1.000, being the minimum possible. The Minister agreed with this fine but his suspicions were aroused. He wrote to the Commission and asked whether Véron had used old scenery prior to *Le Serment* in such a way as to breach Article 11.[59] The Commission discussed this but no conclusion was reached.[60] Finally, it wrote to the Minister with the view that Véron had not knowingly breached Article 11[61] and said that it had already sent a letter to Véron which enjoined him, in no uncertain terms, always to seek authorisation to use old scenery.[62] The Minister was still unimpressed and could not see how a fine of FF 1.000 could have taken other breaches into account. He wanted to know the truth about this matter.[63] Distrust had been created whatever the conclusion to this affair and the Minister's hard line was one reason put forward by Véron when, shortly afterwards, he offered his resignation.

In the end this fine, together with many others, contributed to the total breakdown in trust between Véron and the Commission and the Minister, and led to his premature departure in August 1835. At that time the Commission advised the Minister on the financial settlement agreed with Véron and listed the outstanding fines and other claims against him. The basis for levying such fines was FF 3.000 for the first infraction, FF 4.000 for the second, FF 5.000 for the third, and so on. The outstanding total was FF 60.000 which, together with fines of FF 22.000 already paid by Véron, totalled FF 82.000. The range and number were testimony to Véron's failure to come to terms with his 28 February 1831 *Cahier des charges* and the two supplements, and thus with the Commission itself. Included among the fines were three, totalling FF 12.000, for failure to mount the agreed number of new productions in 1833–34 and 1834–35 but the Commission went further than this. It charged Véron with two-thirds of the imputed cost of such productions for a further total of FF 43.000. Véron had thus paid, or was

59   Minister to the Commission, 30 November 1832, (F^{21} 1053).

60   Commission, minutes of meeting, 22 December 1832, (F^{21} 4633).

61   Commission to the Minister, 4 March 1833, (F^{21} 1053).

62   Commission to Véron, 15 October 1832, (F^{21} 1053).

63   Minister to Choiseul, n.d., (F^{21} 1053).

due to pay, a total of FF 125.000 which certainly made no commercial sense from his point of view. The details were:[64]

		FF
a)	Illegal redundancy, made despite the refusal of the Minister. First fine.	3.000
b)	Incomplete cleaning of theatre. Four fines in place of indemnities.*	18.000
c)	Salary reductions, without authorisation, of Légallois, Montessu and Julia. Three fines.	12.000
d)	Dismissal of Perseval, without authorisation. Second fine.	4.000
e)	Suppression of free tickets, not authorised. Third fine.	5.000
f)	Refusal to find accommodation for the *contrôleur*. Fourth fine.	6.000
g)	Delay of a second ballet in the third year; a second opera and one act of a ballet in the fourth year. Three fines.	12.000
		60.000
	Fines already imposed under d), e) and f).	22.000
		82.000
	Restitution for the second ballet, second opera and one act of ballet, evaluated at two-thirds of the imputed cost	43.000
	Total	125.000

* Under Article 19 of the 28 February 1831 *Cahier des charges*, the auditorium and foyer had to be cleaned twice a year.

The conclusion must be that Véron's drive for profit had clouded his judgement on how to handle the politics of his relationships with the Minister and the Commission.

Véron and the Fixed Personnel

On 1 March 1831 all the artists and staff assembled in the foyer of the Opera and Choiseul presented Véron to the staff. They had already been told about the *arrêté* from the Minister of the Interior which had appointed Véron and about the Minister's letter which had charged Choiseul with the task of presenting Véron to them. It must have been a dramatic moment and Choiseul picked his words carefully.[65]

He opened by saying that the Opera could no longer be directed with the mistaken ideas of the Court of Charles X. He gave credit to Lubbert for the services which he had given, or had tried to give, despite the attention of his superiors which often paralysed his efforts. He then presented Véron to the staff. He said that Véron had gained the Minister's confidence by virtue of his administrative skills, and that his uprightness and good spirit promised justice and goodwill towards the staff and a new era of prosperity for the Opera. Choiseul then explained that for the three months to 1 June 1831, Véron would manage the Opera under the authority of the Commission, and that thereafter

---

64 Commission to the Minister, 15 August 1835, (AJ[13] 180 III).

65 Commission, minutes of meeting, 1 March 1831, (F[21] 4633).

the Opera would grant a concession to him. The new director would be under the surveillance of the Commission which would act in the interests of art and of the government. Finally, he moved into a peroration which looked to the future. He expected an eradication of the many malpractices which had perpetuated and multiplied over a long period of time. He hoped that the shackles which had prevented the full development of the Opera's vast resources would be broken. He expected that existing contracts with staff would be maintained, that the rights of the staff would be assured, and that the talents of soloists and future soloists would be protected. In this way, the pomp and magnificence of the Opera would be increased. Véron then made a brief reply by thanking the Minister for the confidence placed in him. He urged the staff to be worthy of the public's favour and of the protection accorded to them. Véron was then officially installed and Choiseul asked everyone to recognise his authority.

Véron was presented as a man of uprightness, justice and goodwill. This was what the staff would have wanted to hear but it was not long before Véron's true motivation revealed itself, to the consternation of staff and Commission alike. He immediately set about the task of reducing the cost-base of the Opera on the one hand, and of strengthening the artistic side to raise receipts on the other. Lower expenses combined with rising receipts should be a recipe for financial gain and Véron, entrepreneur that he was, pursued this goal with considerable energy and ruthlessness. In modern terms, it was as though a new board of directors had been appointed to revive the fortunes of an ailing company, and a new managing-director had been parachuted in to sort out the problems.

It would be all too easy to accept Véron's version of events as described in his memoirs. They were, however, published well after the event and it would only have been human if self-justification and selective memory had not played their parts. In any event, they did not go into any detail. Fortunately, surviving archival documents yield a great deal of detailed information about the treatment meted out to the staff by Véron and it was clear that the impact was immediate and wide-ranging. Sweeping changes were made in all departments where fixed salary personnel were employed, especially in the support and administrative departments.

According to Véron, he immediately summoned the various heads of department and requested from each a programme of reforms and improvements, of cost-savings, and of confidential notes on the personnel under their care. Within a few days he was, so he claimed, then able to assess the possible cost-savings, the necessary dismissals and the urgent improvements. He also went assiduously to rehearsals in order to form his own impressions of the personnel involved. In those early days he felt that the receipts could just as well fall as increase and that it was vital to reduce the cost-base.[66] He made special reference to the savings achieved in the purchase of materials and

---

66   Véron, op. cit., III, pp. 212–213.

pointed to the fact that more was spent, in absolute terms, on the scenery and costumes for new productions.[67]

The fixed personnel were all those who were paid fixed annual salaries[68] and Véron looked very closely at the numbers employed and salaries paid. In analysing the artistic side of the Opera's activities, Véron claimed that only the chorus, corps de ballet and orchestra could have their salaries reduced without breaches of contract. He also pointed out that salary reductions would have to affect a great number of personnel for expenses to be materially reduced as the artists were already paid very modest salaries. He therefore went ahead very vigorously and in so doing claimed that he met each person individually, thus gaining a further insight into his or her feelings, character and situation.[69] These meetings needed all his courage as bad news had to be conveyed and many orchestral players and singers had just lost their jobs at the *Chapelle Royale*.[70] He found discontent most rife among the orchestral players. They had had to study for a longer period than the singers. Only the footlights separated them from the solo singers and while the latter could earn a fortune in a few years, the former could only earn modest salaries. This poor relative situation meant that the orchestral players were angry and recalcitrant. In this situation, Véron paid tribute to the firmness of Habeneck and the devotion of Halévy, both of whom managed to calm the storm especially when some orchestral players, who also served as musicians in the National Guard, petitioned the King. He, according to Véron, then wrote to the Minister of the Interior with the view that enough had already been destroyed by the July 1830 Revolution for further destruction to take place at the Opera. As only a few players had signed the petition, however, this view had no lasting impact and life at the Opera went on with renewed vigour.[71]

The way Véron set about the fixed personnel was to take a number of basic decisions.

He cut salaries wherever possible. Schedules gave details of these cuts which started as from 1 June 1831 and affected ninety-nine people from various departments:[72]

---

67   «Je pus obtenir de grandes économies sur le matériel, tout en dépensant pour les décors et pour les costumes beaucoup plus qu'on ne dépensait avant moi.» ("I managed to obtain huge savings on the materials, while spending much more than ever before on the scenery and costumes.") Véron, op. cit., III, p. 213.

68   «... soit par des traités particuliers, soit par les règlements du théâtre, qui leur garantissaient la durée de leur engagement et le chiffre de leurs appointements.» ("... either by special contracts, or by the regulations of the theatre which guaranteed them the length of their contracts and the amount of their pay.") Véron, op. cit., III, p. 213.

69   Véron, op. cit., III, p. 214.

70   "The disappearance of the royal chapel and of music specifically performed for the king led to a clear decline in court performance ...." Barbier, op. cit., pp. 26–27.

71   Véron, op. cit., III, pp. 215–216.

72   a) *Mutations survenues dans le personnel fixe pendant l'année 1830*, b) *Mutations par suite de la mise en entreprise*, c) *Détail du personnel fixe de l'année 1830*, d) *Entreprise Véron, personnel des artistes, employés et préposés 1831–32*, (PE3 (699)).

Department	Salary reductions 1831–32
Direction	6
Chant	4
Choeurs	17
Ballets	7
Orchestre	47
Salle et Théâtre	14
Costumes	3
Décorations	1
	99

It was noticeable that the greatest burden fell on the chorus, orchestra and administration. Only two soloists, the singers Dupond and Prévost, and no solo ballet dancers, had their salaries cut. The total annual savings achieved by these reductions was FF 27.070. Although the reductions in most cases were modest, the total was significant as so many people were affected: ninety-nine people was about one-fifth of the fixed personnel whom Véron inherited from Lubbert. The salary reductions gave rise to a lot of complaint, again as Véron indicated. The main one was the claim to have pension rights calculated on the higher salaries paid up to 1 June 1831. This dispute was finally brought to a head when fifty-five people submitted their case to the Commission on 10 November 1832. In order to give practical effect to this claim, a schedule detailed, in each case, the five per cent staff pension contributions based on pre-1 June 1831 salaries.[73] It is not clear from the archived material how this dispute was finally settled.

Many staff retired or were made redundant. It was only natural that changes should take place among the fixed personnel and Lubbert's tenure as director showed this clearly. For example, in 1830, the year which spanned the July Revolution, a schedule showed that forty people left the service of the Opera. Fifteen retired, ten died, fourteen left for other reasons and one left the administrative side to train as a singer.[74] A further four retired who were not on this list.[75] What was new under Véron, however, was the sheer scale of the changes. During his first year, 1 June 1831–31 May 1832, no fewer than forty-one people retired, far more than the nineteen in 1830 and the seventeen in 1829.[76] Maybe it was just coincidence that so many people had reached retirement age but the more likely reason was that many people preferred, or were forced to take, retirement rather than be made redundant. Even more significant was the number of personnel made redundant. No less than eighty-seven had left in this way by the end of Véron's first year. It is very interesting to analyse where the retirals and redundancies fell and to relate them to the total numbers employed prior to Véron's arrival. Taken

---

73 *État des artistes et préposés qui, ayant été réduits au 1ᵉʳ juin 1831, se sont soumis à l'Article 4 de l'étois de la Commission de Surveillance, en date du 10 novembre 1832, pour obtenir leur pension sur le traitement dont ils jouissaient au 31 mai 1831*, (PE3 (699)).

74 *Mutations survenues dans le personnel fixe pendant l'année 1830*, (PE3 (699)).

75 *Détail du personnel fixe de l'année 1830*, (PE3 (699)).

76 *Personnel fixe 1829*, (O³ 1696).

together, retirements and redundancies totalled 128 which constituted about a quarter of the fixed personnel:[77]

	Numbers	1831–1832	
Department	As at 1 January 1831	Retired	Redundant
Direction	17	-	7
Chant	23	-	2
Choeurs	63	2	7
Danse	31	4	3
Ballets	77	8	12
Orchestre	81	13	3
Salle et Théâtre	82	5	33
Costumes	52	7	11
Décorations	<u>75</u>	<u>2</u>	<u>9</u>
	<u>501</u>	<u>41</u>	<u>87</u>

The total of retired and redundant personnel was thus 128.

A cull of senior management took place. Concealed within these bland statistics was the demise of most senior people, including, of course, Lubbert himself.[78] Names which had featured strongly in the Restoration period such as Duplantys, Dieu, Solomé, Hérold, Ciceri, Lecomte and Gromaire all left the payroll, although Hérold was subsequently re-employed and Ciceri made a separate contract with the Opera.

There was a reduction in fixed personnel. Although many personnel retired or were made redundant, the determination of Véron to raise artistic standards was reflected in the fact that the total number of solo singers and ballet dancers, chorus and corps de ballet, actually went up in the first two years of his administration. Total numbers on the payroll went down, however, either due to genuine reductions or to the

---

77   Table of changes under Véron, (PE3 (699)).

78   Table of Véron's changes in Senior Management, (PE3 (699)).

Lubbert	*Directeur*	Redundant
D'Aubignosc	*Secrétaire Général*	-ditto-
Duplantys	*Trésorier*	-ditto-
Dieu	*Contrôleur du Matériel*	-ditto-
Solomé	*Régisseur*	-ditto-
Hérold	*Chef du Chant*	-ditto-
Aumer	*Maître de ballet*	Retired
Albert	-ditto-	-ditto-
Albert	*Premier sujet, danse*	-ditto-
Paul	-ditto-	-ditto-
Vestris	*Professeur de danse*	Redundant
Maze	-ditto-	Retired
Mérante	-ditto-	Redundant
Valentino	*Premier chef d'orchestre*	Retired
Baillot	*Premier violin, solo*	Redundant
Robert	*Contrôleur*	-ditto-
Lecomte	*Dessinateur du costume*	-ditto-
Ciceri	*Premier Peintre*	-ditto-
Gromaire	*Machiniste en chef*	Retired

contracting-out of various services to supplier-contractors. The total fell from 501 prior to Véron's arrival to 464 at the end of his first year and 465 at the end of his second year:[79]

Department	As at 1 January 1831	As at 31 May 1832	As at 31 May 1833
Direction	17	13	12
Chant	23	27	27
Choeurs	63	65	66
Danse	31	33	28
Ballets	77	82	91
Orchestre	81	78	79
Salle et Théâtre	82	39	39
Costumes	52	51	49
Décorations	75	76	74
	501	464	465

Pulling all of the above together, it is possible to make a more detailed analysis of the effect of Véron's strategy on the various departments at the Opera. Finally, the overall effect can be traced by a comparison of figures within the annual accounts.

Service de la Comptabilité et Direction.

Véron was especially severe on the central administrative and financial personnel. Although he himself received a salary of FF 12.000 per annum, which was FF 2.000 more than Lubbert, the overall effect on costs was significant as these personnel were well-paid. Numbers fell from seventeen to twelve and all the senior people were made redundant, except Bigarne the accountant who was first made redundant but then accepted a lower salary. There were seven salary reductions and although a new administrator called Mira was appointed at FF 4.000 per annum, there was an overall annual saving of some FF 21.000. Included under this heading was the loss of Solomé, the *régisseur*, although Duponchel's salary was increased from FF 2.000 to FF 6.000.

Service de la Salle et du Théâtre.

There was a very large drop in personnel from eighty-two to thirty-nine. Only around half of the total were left on the payroll, and of these fourteen had their salaries reduced. All the eighteen *ouvreuses,* the ladies who opened the doors of the boxes and allocated the unreserved seats and who, in return for a suitable tip, made sure that those who tipped well got the best seats, lost, 1 April 1832, their salaried positions. This saved FF 9.000 and the *ouvreuses* had to live on tips alone. As six *ouvreuses* had already

---

79   Table of changes in overall numbers of fixed personnel, (PE3 (699)). Note that the records in PE3 (699) were kept on the basis that everyone employed during a year was included at full salary, even although personnel both left and joined during the year. Care was therefore taken to calculate the year-end personnel numbers correctly, especially as 1830 was a special case as new personnel were not included.

retired under Véron including Roullet, the *ouvreuse de la loge du Roi*, and two had already been made redundant, savings of FF 2.050 had already been achieved. All the seven *balayeurs*, sweepers, lost their salaried positions. This saved FF 3.820 and the task was subcontracted to a supplier-contractor. All the remaining five *surveillants et surveillantes*, overseers of various parts of the theatre, lost their salaried positions, one having already been made redundant. All the six *gardiens et gardiennes des garde-robes* lost their salaried positions as did many others throughout this department. On the other hand, Véron appointed a new inspector-general called Caille and a new chief controller called Courtois.

Service des Costumes.

The changes here reflected the malpractices of the Restoration period. In summary, the *tailleurs* and *couturières* had seemed incapable of making the costumes without outside help and this was both inefficient and expensive. Out of a total staff of fifty-two, Véron retired seven, made eleven redundant and reduced the salaries of three, including Géré, the head of department, whose salary was reduced sharply from FF 3.000 per annum to FF 2.000. On the other hand, he raised the salaries of those remaining and new recruits, albeit engaged at lower salaries, kept the numbers up.

Service des Décorations.

This department included the skilled scene-changers who operated the flies, the stage and the below-stage, as well as the staff who made the sets. They were, on the face of it, highly paid but as they had very specialised skills, Véron was unable to make many changes. Only one salary was reduced, nine were made redundant and two retired. New recruits, again at lower salaries, kept the numbers up. Gromaire retired and Contant took over his position.

Service de la Scène.

Chant.

Here the thrust of Véron's policies became evident. The number of solo singers, ranked by *premiers sujets*, *remplacements* and *doubles*, rose from nineteen to twenty-three.[80] Only two soloists had their salaries cut, one of whom, Prévost, had been at the Opera since 1814 and was the oldest soloist there. Hérold, the head of singing, had been made redundant on 1 June 1831 but was reinstated on 1 March 1832. He took a salary cut from FF 5.000 per annum to FF 3.000 but it was backdated to 1 June 1831. There was thus an overall strengthening of numbers here and an improvement in the conditions of service for the soloists whose bonuses were consolidated into their salaries for pension purposes.

---

80 One singer, Valère, was made redundant and five new singers arrived: Dorus, Dérivis, Péterman, Sambet and Wartel, (PE3 (699)).

The reason why Hérold was first sacked, and then re-employed, was that he brought a case against Véron for wrongful dismissal and won. The Opera had to pay the costs of this case of FF 211 and the settlement stipulated that Hérold should be retained as *chef du chant* for a further ten and a half years. Hérold also received FF 3.750 in back-pay for the period when he was off the payroll.[81]

Choeurs.

Here again numbers increased as the total of nine who retired or were made redundant was more than offset by thirteen new chorus members. Seventeen had their salaries reduced and Véron managed to save money overall. The new singers were paid around FF 500 to FF 600 per annum, whereas those who retired or were made redundant had been paid around FF 1.000 per annum.

Danse.

Two out of the three *maîtres de ballets*, Albert and Aumer, retired, but the third, Taglioni, saw his salary doubled from FF 5.000 to FF 10.000 per annum. Although seven solo ballet dancers retired or were made redundant, seven new soloists were appointed by Véron and overall there were no salary reductions. The emergence of Taglioni as a major star led to an increase in her basic income from FF 14.000 to FF 20.000 per annum. Although her salary remained the same at FF 10.000, she was guaranteed a bonus of FF 10.000 instead of FF 4.000.

Ballets.

The numbers increased from seventy-seven under Lubbert to ninety-one as at 31 May 1833. Within these totals, twenty retired or were made redundant by Véron and a further seven had their salaries reduced. As most of the newcomers were engaged at salaries of around FF 500 to FF 600 per annum, and those who left had been earning around FF 1.000 per annum or more, Véron achieved savings here. The three teachers of dance were made redundant, saving FF 6.400, although two were subsequently re-employed on non-pensionable contracts. As for the three répétiteurs, Launer was made redundant on 1 January 1832 but immediately brought back on a contract basis as another répétiteur, Pilate, retired on the same date.

Orchestre.

Many changes were enforced by Véron here. Out of a starting total of eighty-one, no less than forty-seven had their salaries reduced, thirteen retired and three were made redundant. New players were engaged in order to keep the numbers up as the Commission had insisted on a total of at least eighty, including the conductor, in Véron's 28 February 1831 *Cahier des charges*.[82] The salary cuts were felt most of all in the strings. Out of an original total of fifty-two, seven retired, two were made redundant and thirty-four took salary cuts, although Launer was subsequently brought

---

81 *Frais dûs par Monsieur Véron pour l'affaire Hérold et l'Académie Royale de Musique,* (AJ[13] 188 VI).

82 *Cahier des charges,* 28 February 1831, Article 6, (AJ[13] 187 I).

back as first solo violin after Baillot had been sacked. Meanwhile, Véron engaged fourteen new orchestral players, of whom eleven were string players. The latter's salaries at FF 800 per annum, except for one at FF 900 per annum, were well below the FF 1.000 to FF 2.500 per annum of those who had left.

It should not be forgotten that Véron's initial room for manœuvre was not as great as his 28 February 1831 *Cahier des charges* might have indicated. From 1 March 1831 to 31 May 1831 he was only managing the Opera on behalf of the government and had to seek approval for his actions from the Commission. At a meeting of the Commission on 17 March 1831,[83] Véron advised that redundancy notices needed to be sent out by 1 April, and at a further meeting on 20 March 1831,[84] it was agreed that pensions would be honoured and that those without pension rights would get two months' salary, April and May, as indemnities. A list of retirements and redundancies was submitted by Véron on 27 March 1831.[85] At the meeting on 31 March 1831,[86] Cavé advised that he had sent out redundancy notices to twenty-four people and it had become clear that there would be appeals to the *Comité du contentieux*. At this same meeting it was decided that the Commission should authorise Véron's proposals up to 1 June and that thereafter, although the Commission no longer had a veto, it should at least be consulted. By 14 April many others, apart from the twenty-four on Véron's original list, had received redundancy notices from Cavé and a number of orchestral players sought clarification either on their pension rights or their reduced salaries.[87] By October, the Commission had become so concerned about overall numbers that it asked Véron for a list of personnel to ensure that it conformed to his 28 February 1831 *Cahier des charges*. It also asked for a list of those who had retired or been made redundant as well as a list of those newly-employed with each person's salary. At the same meeting Véron asked to be relieved of the burden, at least in part, of having to give six months' notice to personnel and of having to give indemnities to those retired or made redundant. The Commission agreed it would write a favourable report to the Minister.[88] By the end of November Véron still had not provided the list of personnel. It was still not possible to ascertain whether he had kept to his *Cahier des charges* and the Commission decided to withhold FF 2.500 from his monthly subsidy.[89] Indeed it was not until May 1832 that Véron finally sent this list of personnel[90] but by then his credibility was already damaged. At a meeting prior to this the Commission had discussed a letter from the Minister on the redundancies made by Véron and had reflected on the important question raised in this letter.[91] The net had closed as the Minister subsequently issued an *arrêté* which denied Véron the scope to make pensionable staff redundant without

83   Commission, minutes of meeting, 17 March 1831, (F²¹ 4633).

84   Commission, minutes of meeting, 20 March 1831, (F²¹ 4633).

85   Commission, minutes of meeting, 27 March 1831, (F²¹ 4633).

86   Commission, minutes of meeting, 31 March 1831, (F²¹ 4633).

87   Commission, minutes of meeting, 14 April 1831, (F²¹ 4633).

88   Commission, minutes of meeting, 6 October 1831, (F²¹ 4633).

89   Commission, minutes of meeting, 27 November 1831, (F²¹ 4633).

90   Commission, minutes of meeting, 29 May 1832, (F²¹ 4633).

91   Commission, minutes of meeting, 22 May 1832, (F²¹ 4633).

the authorisation of both the Minister and the Commission. It also forbade him to change their conditions of employment, that is to make salary reductions, without similar authorisation.[92] The Commission decided that Véron had to post three copies of this *arrêté* in the foyers of the singers, ballet-dancers and orchestral players[93] but the Minister finally decided that no publicity was needed and the *arrêté* was not posted.

Prior to this curtailment of his powers of independent action Véron had nevertheless achieved a great deal. In the short-run, it had cost money in indemnities. Véron advised the Commission in October 1831 that he had already paid out FF 38.284 in indemnities.[94] The final total for 1831–32 was FF 65.405 as shown in the 1831–32 Annual Accounts.[95] As might be expected the personnel costs for *Direction, Choeurs, Ballets, Orchestre, Salle et Théâtre, Costumes* and *Décorations* all fell in 1831–32. The increases were concentrated on *Chant*, where the arrival of Dorus cost FF 18.000 per annum, and *Danse*, where Taglioni's bonus was increased by FF 6.000 and seven new soloists arrived. In 1832–33, the arrival of Falcon was significant for *Chant* although four soloists were made redundant in *Danse*. Véron changed his policy on the *Orchestre* in this year by making ten salary increases and engaging seven new musicians. Overall, however, there was a fall in fixed personnel costs from the 1829 total of FF 900.944 to the 1831–32 total of FF 802.189:[96]

Fixed Personnel	1829*	1830	1831–32
Direction	FF 53.800	FF 56.394	FF 36.325
Chant	186.711	181.547	204.279
Choeurs	74.400	73.398	63.527
Danse	205.029	185.472	208.503
Ballets	79.179	75.406	64.526
Orchestre	131.117	129.798	83.336
Salle et Théâtre	40.755	39.441	28.613
Costumes	43.153	43.264	38.850
Décorations	86.800	86.625	74.230
Engagements nouveaux	–	20.550	–
	900.944	891.895	802.189

* In 1829, the *gratifications*, bonuses, were included in *personnel variable*. Thereafter, they were included in *personnel fixe*. To make the figures comparable, the 1829 *gratifications* have been re-allocated to *personnel fixe*.

This was a tribute to Véron's policy and management skills which should certainly not be underestimated. Although his initial purge was brutal in order to reduce the cost-base, he managed to direct the Opera by means of persuasion and he infused it with his energy and sense of purpose. Although there was a lot of opposition to the

---

92   Commission, minutes of meeting, 11 July 1832, (F^{21} 4633).

93   Commission, minutes of meeting, August 1832, (F^{21} 4633).

94   Véron to the Commission, 12 October 1831, (F^{21} 1053).

95   Annual Accounts 1831–32, (AJ^{13} 228 II).

96   Annual Accounts 1829, (AJ^{13} 146 IV), Annual Accounts 1830, (AJ^{13} 228 I), Annual Accounts 1831–32, (AJ^{13} 228 II).

redundancies and salary cuts, it said a lot for Véron's qualities as a manager that he rode out these internal squalls and took the Opera forward both artistically and financially. Despite his single-minded desire to make a fortune, Véron retained the capacity to inspire. His fellow-doctor Binet could quote Halévy who commented on Véron and on the ballerinas' mothers, who together had such an inspirational effect,[97] although another account implied that Véron took advantage of these young girls.[98] Binet also made a shrewd observation when he referred to Véron's training as a doctor and the way he could sympathise with many of his personnel who led rather miserable lives.[99] He was also astute enough to write:

> Somme toute, M. le Directeur n'a pas volé l'affection que lui porte son personnel; et cela du haut en bas.[100]

Véron and the Suppliers

In his drive to reduce expenses and be more certain of his cost-base, Véron took a number of policy decisions which affected the suppliers of goods and services to the Opera. He reviewed existing contracts whereby suppliers were paid a fixed annual sum and sought to increase the number of suppliers paid in this way. He changed suppliers at will, paid great attention to the bills submitted for payment and made frequent arbitrary reductions. Those most affected were the scene-painters and suppliers of materials for costumes and chapter 3 will cover this subject in depth. Meanwhile, Véron reviewed all the other suppliers with the same attention to detail and motivation to reduce expenses.

Within one week of his appointment on 1 March 1831, Véron wrote to certain *fournisseurs-entrepreneurs* (supplier-contractors) who were paid fixed annual sums, and advised them that he intended to cancel their contracts.[101] The letters served to give the required three months' notice and opened the way for contract renegotiations. For example, Franconi, Laloue and Bouchet had signed a further contract in May 1829 to supply two horses and two drovers as and when required, for which they were paid FF 3.600 per annum with an extra FF 50 per performance if the number of horses

---

97 Halévy commented: «Ils leur inspirent des idées et des espérances d'ambition, d'orgueil et de fortune, pour leur donner de la persévérance et du courage.» ("They inspire them with ideas and expectations of ambition, pride and fortune in order to give them perseverance and courage.") Binet, op. cit., p. 146.

98 Claudine Wayser, *L'Extraordinaire Monsieur Véron* (Paris, 1990). This story of Véron's life, written in the first person, described some of the romantic affairs which Véron had with the ballerinas.

99 «... il est permis de penser que son passage dans les hôpitaux le fait compatir avec la vraie misère, celle qui est la trame de tant de vies obscures.» ("... one may well think that his time spent in hospitals makes him sympathise with the true misery which is the fate of so many obscure lives.") Binet, op. cit., p. 149.

100 ("Taking all-in-all, the director did not lose the affection in which the staff held him; and that from top to bottom.") Binet, op. cit., p. 153.

101 Véron to various supplier-contractors, 7 March 1831, (AJ[13] 187 V).

exceeded two.[102] This had, for example, been the case with *Guillaume Tell*. This supplier-contractor might have thought that any renegotiation would lead to a re-confirmation of the long-standing relationship between the Opera and the *Cirque Olympique*, but this time Véron obtained a more favourable contract.[103] It was agreed that he would pay FF 4.000 per annum for four horses and two drovers and FF 20 for each extra horse per performance. The contract was to run for three years from 1 June 1831 to 31 May 1834. Véron must have been anticipating the need for more horses in his quest to excite and entertain his new bourgeois audiences. Another letter was sent to Mme. Floquet who had the contract to transport sets to and from the Opera, ateliers and storehouses. For this she received an annual sum of FF 1.500. Véron cancelled the contract and a new supplier called Durey was appointed at FF 1000 per annum[104] after Mme. Floquet had been sacked in November 1831. Another supplier-contractor, Merville, who was the *fourbissier,* polisher of metal, received a similar letter but in this case he was re-appointed at the same fixed annual sum of FF 1.200.[105] Finally, Jugien, *transport d'eau potable,* carrier of drinking water, at FF 600 per annum received a similar letter from Véron. In this case he was not re-appointed and the job went to Vessier at FF 300 per annum.[106]

Véron also looked to increase the number of supplier-contractors who worked for fixed annual sums. His negotiating position was strong, especially with the legacy of late payments to creditors under the Restoration. The example of Duhamel was evidence for this. He was the supplier of wood for heating and had written to La Rochefoucauld in November 1828, detailing the amounts owed to him.[107] These totalled FF 17.872 and Duhamel recalled that his *Cahier des charges* allowed the Opera only four months' credit. As he had not received any payment for eighteen months of supplies he asked for an indemnity. He then asked to be treated as a supplier-contractor and stated that he would drop his claim for an indemnity provided he could go onto a fixed annual sum, even although that would be to his financial disadvantage. Nothing came of this but it was indicative of the way suppliers viewed their relationships with the Opera and it helped Véron when he negotiated many new supplier-contractor contracts. A particular example of this was the laundering of costumes. After the 1829 and 1830 round of submissions, the cleaning of costumes, together with the dyeing and removal of grease, was awarded to four suppliers and their total bills for 1829 and 1830 were FF 12.911

---

102 Contract with Franconi, Laloue and Bouchet, 18 May 1829, (AJ^{13} 221 II).

103 New contract with Franconi, Laloue and Bouchet, 1 June 1831, (AJ^{13} 221 II).

104 List of fixed annual sums, addition to list, February 1832, (AJ^{13} 291 I).

105 List of fixed annual sums, addition to list, October 1831, (AJ^{13} 291 I).

106 List of fixed annual sums, addition to list, October 1831, (AJ^{13} 291 I).

107 Duhamel to La Rochefoucauld, 10 November 1828, (O^3 1680 I).

1827	-	Full year	FF 15.555
1828	-	1st Quarter	1.674
	-	2nd Quarter	643
		Total owing	17.872

and FF 13.062 respectively.[108] Véron negotiated fixed sum contracts for these activities, as a result of which Faure took over Fossier's work. These suppliers were paid monthly and were on one-year contracts which started in October 1831.[109] Compared with the 1829 and 1830 totals, Véron struck a hard bargain with each supplier and reduced the total expense by some twenty per cent. Worse was to come, however, for these new supplier-contractors. Véron's policy was to increase the number of singers and dancers in order to impress his audiences, and to spend more on costumes in order to dazzle them. It was not long before the supplier-contractors complained. Tournès, for example, advised Véron in October 1832 that his total costs for the eleven months to September 1832 were FF 6.132 or FF 557 per month, yet he was being paid only FF 333 per month. He sought a new contract at FF 5.000 per annum or FF 416 per month.[110] Véron was unimpressed and having accepted Tournès' resignation appointed a new supplier, Lebert, at FF 3.800 per annum.[111] This only lasted a year, however, and by December 1833 Tournès was back again, but only at FF 4.200 per annum.[112] As for Bachelier, he also complained that he was not making any money on his contract. Nevertheless, he accepted a new one-year contract, October 1832, at FF 3.544 per annum.[113]

Contracts with other new supplier-contractors emphasised the thrust of Véron's policy. As has been described, all the *balayeurs,* sweepers, were made redundant and thus came off the Opera's list of fixed personnel under the expense category of *Salle et Théâtre.* In 1829 this activity had employed seven people for a cost of FF 3.820,[114] the same being the case in 1830.[115] Véron appointed a new supplier-contractor, Lyonnet, to do this job at the higher fixed annual sum of FF 4.500. The reason for this increase was not clear, even less so as another sweeper called Destors was contracted in January 1832

---

108 *Blanchissages,* laundry, monthly expenses for 1829, (AJ[13] 404 II).

	-ditto-	monthly expenses for 1830, (AJ[13] 215 I).
		1829*	11 months 1830**
Fossier		FF 2.082	FF 2.368
Faure		1.847	2.071
Bachelier		3.957	3.354
Messeaux/Tournès***		5.025	4.437
		12.911	12.230

* Per AJ[13] 404 II and ** AJ[13] 405 II. The 1830 total of FF 13.062 was archived under AJ[13] 215 I.
*** Tournès took over from Messeaux in November 1830.

109 Contracts between Véron and Tournès, Faure and Bachelier, (AJ[13] 221 III).

Faure	FF 3.000 per annum
Bachelier	3.400 -ditto-
Tournès	4.000 -ditto-
	10.400

110 Tournès to Véron, 19 October 1832, (AJ[13] 221 III).

111 Fixed annual sums, paid monthly, December 1832, (AJ[13] 289 IV).

112 Fixed annual sums, paid monthly, December 1833, (AJ[13] 289 IV).

113 Bachelier to Véron, n.d., (AJ[13] 221 III). He referred to his monthly payment of FF 283, or FF 3.400 per annum and to the fact that his contract finished in October 1832. There was a footnote to Bachelier's original contract accepting FF 3.544 per annum.

114 Fixed Personnel 1829, (O[3] 1696).

115 *Détail du personnel fixe de l'année 1830,* (PE3 (699)).

at a further FF 240 per annum. The supply of *charbon de terre,* coal for heating, was contracted to Albouy on 10 November 1831 at FF 2.949 per annum.[116] He had previously been paid by the submission of bills, having been the successful tenderer for the two years 1829 and 1830. This sum of FF 2.949 was confirmed by the list of contracts with supplier-contractors.[117] The supply of *bois à brûler,* wood for heating, was contracted to Cléry at FF 10.000 per annum. He had not been the successful tenderer for 1829 and 1830, but had taken over from Duhamel by September 1829. He had also been previously paid by the submission of bills.[118] There were further examples which could be described but the point has been sufficiently made. It was also made through a comparison of total annual expenses as shown in the annual accounts. For instance, the overall cost of *chauffage,* heating, was FF 17.308 in 1829 and FF 20.738 in 1830. In Véron's first year 1831–32, he reduced this to FF 13.052.[119]

A special contract was negotiated with Contant, the new head machinist.[120] He was a member of the Opera's fixed personnel and was paid a salary of FF 6.000 per annum, as acknowledged in a contract for three years from 1 January 1832 to 31 December 1834. There was also an incentive clause built into this contract. Contant was entitled to five per cent of any savings achieved over a base total of FF 100.000, being the imputed cost of all the fixed and variable personnel under Contant's direction and of the cost of materials for building the sets. There was thus a real incentive for Contant to reduce the cost of materials as the strong position of the machinists meant that the numbers remained at around seventy-five and their cost at around FF 75.000. This incentive, in turn, implied the use of old sets rather than the building of new ones which could, of course, be a contravention of Véron's 28 February 1831 *Cahier des charges* unless he had gained permission from the Commission. Whether or not Contant earned more money through this incentive was not clear although it seemed unlikely as the base total was raised to FF 130.000 when the contract was renewed for a further two years from 1 January 1834 to 31 December 1836. If Albéric Second was to be believed, he was not up to the job and made his extra money through stinginess.[121] It was not clear,

---

116 Contract between Véron and Albouy, 15 November 1831, (AJ[13] 222 VII).

117 Fixed annual sums, addition to list December 1831, (AJ[13] 291 I).

118 Monthly expenses of suppliers, *chauffage,* heating, September 1829, (AJ[13] 405 II).

119 Annual Accounts 1829, (AJ[13] 146 IV), Annual Accounts 1830, (AJ[13] 228 I), Annual Accounts 1831–32, (AJ[13] 228 II).

120 Contract between Véron and Contant, 14 January 1832, (AJ[13] 22I III).

121 «On l'appelle M. Contant, et il est plus vulgairement connu sous le nom de M. Content (de lui-même). Comme homme privé, on assure qu'il est plein de qualités les plus recommandables, et je n'ai aucune raison d'en douter. Comme machiniste – ce qui est une tout autre affaire, – je n'hésite pas à déclarer qu'il n'est pas du tout à la hauteur de son emploi. Il est complètement dépourvu d'habileté et d'ingéniosité …. M. Contant, qui entend l'économie autant qu' homme du monde, lésine sur les fournitures, et met la différence dans sa poche.» ("He is called M. Contant, and he is more commonly known under the name M. Content (with himself). As a private person, one is assured that he is full of the most commendable qualities, and I have no reason to doubt this. As a *machiniste* – which is an altogether different thing – I should not hesitate to declare that he is not up to the job at all. He is totally lacking in skilfulness and ingeniousness …. M. Contant, who understands business as much as any man of the world, skimps on the supplies and puts the difference in his pocket.") Albéric Second, *Les petits mystères de l'Opéra* (Paris, 1844), p. 229.

however, whether this referred to Contant's exploitation of the incentive clause in his contract or to backhanders from suppliers.

Véron also sought to decrease the cost of goods and services by changing suppliers at will and by paying scrupulous attention to the bills submitted for payment. For example, a major expense for the Opera was lighting which was achieved through the use of wax-candles, oil and gas. Véron changed the suppliers of the first two items. Out went Deslandes and Maux St. Marc and in came Chopin as the supplier of both wax-candles and oil. Marnby and Wilson, who had taken over the supply of gas in 1830 from the *Compagnie Royale d'éclairage*,[122] were retained but Véron renegotiated the contract, having first given them notice of dismissal through a letter on 7 March 1831 which also cancelled the annual fixed sum of FF 1.800.[123] It is not clear from the archived material exactly how the savings were achieved but the total expense for lighting fell from FF 66.053 in 1829 and FF 70.567 in 1830 to FF 63.643 in 1831–32.[124] In another case the 1829 and 1830 supplier of *quincaillerie,* ironmongery, had been Juéry but he was sacked by Véron and Desforges took over. The latter's bills, together with those of many other suppliers, were subject to intense scrutiny and cut sharply.[125] Lauriou, the long-term supplier of rope, was retained by Véron but his bills were reduced sharply even although Lauriou set out, in great detail, the quantities and prices of the ropes supplied. Véron was not only concerned with large bills. He scrutinised every one, even down to the smallest amounts and did not scruple to reduce them. Thibout was retained for *lutherie,* supply and service of stringed instruments, but had his small bills reduced. Mme. Dechaux, *serrurerie,* metalwork, had put in six bills from July to December 1831 which totalled FF 2.822. Véron agreed to pay only FF 1.900 and Dechaux had to accept. She then also lost her position as supplier to the Opera being supplanted by Delfosse and Magrimaux. Albouy, *plomberie,* plumbing, had one of his maintenance bills reduced. The new supplier Magrimaux saw some of his bills sharply cut back.

It could thus be seen that Véron, free from the cumbersome procedures whereby suppliers were appointed in the Restoration period, took vigorous action to reduce expenses and eliminate malpractices. Whether through a review of existing contracts, the appointment of more supplier-contractors, the sacking of many existing suppliers or the minute scrutiny of bills, he introduced many changes which had a beneficial impact

---

122 *Mémoires versés à la comptabilité pour le mois de septembre 1830,* (AJ[13] 405 II).

123 Véron to Marnby and Wilson, 7 March 1831, (AJ[13] 187 V).

124 Annual Accounts 1829, (AJ[13] 146 IV). Annual Accounts 1830, (AJ[13] 228 I). Annual Accounts 1831–32, (AJ[13] 228 II).

125 a) Bills submitted by Desforges. One bill for FF 151 reduced to FF 145. Another bill for FF 120.70 reduced to FF 115, (AJ[13] 410); b) Bills submitted by Lauriou. One bill for FF 418.50 reduced to FF 400, (AJ[13] 410); c) Bills submitted by Thibout. One bill for FF 39.50 reduced to FF 35, (AJ[13] 410); d) Bills submitted by Mme. Dechaux covering the period July– December 1831, totalling FF 2.822. Signed *bon à payer* by Véron for FF 1.900, 25 January 1832 which Mme. Dechaux also signed *pour acquit,* (AJ[13] 289 IV); e) Bills submitted by Albouy. One bill for FF 514.50 reduced to FF 400 in early 1832, (AJ[13] 411 I); f) Bills submitted by Magrimaux. One bill, January 1833, for FF 354.05 reduced to FF 250. Another bill, June 1833, for FF 131.55 reduced to FF 100. Another bill, June 1833, for FF 763.45 reduced to FF 520, (AJ[13] 289 IV).

on the bloated situation which he had inherited. To be fair, not all bills were reduced and it is difficult to discern a consistent approach here. Some very large bills were paid in full. Nevertheless, the general policy was clear enough and becomes even clearer when the suppliers of scene-painting and of materials for costumes are discussed.

Free Seats and New Seat Prices

The July 1830 Revolution ushered in a change of politics in France in that a middle way was found between the legitimists and the republicans. Changes in society also took place which were reflected at the Opera itself. Véron believed that he could make a financial success of the Opera as he represented the new ascendant bourgeoisie and understood what it required. His policies on free seats and new seat prices were thus designed to appeal to his new audiences on the one hand and to maximise his receipts on the other. It was not clear at the start, however, whether these new policies would succeed. The onslaught on free seats could result in many unsold seats as not enough people were prepared to pay, and reduced seat prices could mean that total receipts were less as not enough people were encouraged to come. Nevertheless, Véron was a shrewd man and made a correct calculation on the willingness of his audiences to attend, and pay for, lavish new productions which appealed to the eye as well as to the ear.

In the Restoration period it was the aristocracy which made the most use of free seats and was therefore the class most likely to desert the Opera when it was forced to pay. Indeed it has been suggested by Anselm Gerhard that the *Théâtre Italien* became the preferred opera-house for the aristocracy after the July 1830 Revolution and that those with artistic and intellectual pretensions turned to concerts and chamber music.[126] This void in demand was, however, filled by a new, self-confident *haute bourgeoisie* which was prepared to come to the Opera provided it was satisfied that value for money was obtainable. The prevailing culture of this new *haute bourgeoisie* was captured by Gerhard:

> In terms of international economics, the importance of Paris was founded above all on its banking and credit services. The building of the Paris Stock Exchange – the *Bourse* – was completed in 1827 and rapidly became one of the most important institutions in European finance .... From a mere thirty-eight securities officially listed in 1830, by 1841 260 share-prices were being fixed every day. Even contemporaries like Heinrich Heine regarded the banker and the speculator as the representative figures of the July Monarchy .... Clearly, citizens who were ready to take the risks involved in stock-market speculation were the real winners of the July Revolution: one of their gains being the self-confidence that made them the leading social class alongside the aristocracy .... But it was not only at the *Bourse* that everything revolved around money: the mentality of a financially bullish *bourgeoisie* transformed the whole of society.[127]

---

126 Anselm Gerhard, *Die Verstädterung der Oper: Paris und das Musiktheater des 19. Jahrhunderts*, (Stuttgart, 1992). Translated by Mary Whittall, *The Urbanization of Opera. Music Theater in Paris in the Nineteenth Century* (Chicago, 1998), p. 31.

127 Gerhard, op. cit., p. 19.

With this new climate of opinion, Véron's gamble that the Opera could be filled by a predominantly paying public becomes understandable especially as his policy on certain seat prices encouraged the idea that value for money had been created.

Free seats

During the Restoration, the system of free seats at the Opera had led to extensive abuses which culminated under Lubbert. Two points should be repeated here in order to set the scene for the decisions taken by the Commission in the first three months to 31 May 1831, when Véron was manager on behalf of the government. First, Lubbert had an official list of *entrées de droit* and *entrées de faveur* which totalled, according to Cavé, 502 free seats. Second, due to the many abuses through *entrées de tolérance,* Cavé reckoned that the Opera, which held about 1.900 seats, could have been totally filled under the Restoration by an audience which had not paid for its seats.[128] Looking at the abuses already described, it is not hard to imagine that this could be so.

At its very first meeting after Véron had been appointed, the Commission grasped the nettle of free seats. As a first step all official free seats had to be justified:

Il sera publié par la voie des Journaux et par l'affiche du Théâtre, que ceux qui jouissent d'entrées gratuites sont invités à justifier de leurs droits au secrétaire de la Commission dans le delai de dix jours, et que faute de le faire, l'entrée sera refusée.[129]

Meanwhile, Cavé was also asked to gather information on the free boxes and seats and on the unrecorded *entrées de tolérance,* and to make a report as soon as possible:

Le secrétaire de la Commission est chargé de prendre des informations et de faire un rapport le plus tôt possible, sur les loges gratuites données journellement par le directeur précédent ..., sur les billets de service et autres, sur les entrées non-inscrites, dites de tolérance ....[130]

At a further meeting, the question of *entrées d'échange* was raised and the feeling of the Commission was that these should, in principle, cease. It was, however, realised that an advantage for the Opera could be gained by continuing this system on a limited basis, especially with the *Théâtre Italien.*[131] Discretion was given to Véron on this matter at a later meeting.[132] Although Cavé's report did not go to the Minister until 20 May 1831, the Commission was already taking decisions in March, based on his

---

128 Report of Cavé to the Minister, 20 May 1831, (AJ[13] 180 IX).

129 ("It will be published through the press and on the Theatre's posters that those benefiting from free seats are invited to justify their rights to the secretary of the Commission within ten days; and that failure to do so will result in cancellation.") Commission, minutes of meeting, 1 March 1831. (F[21] 4633).

130 ("The secretary of the Commission is charged with gathering information, and with reporting as soon as possible, on the free boxes given daily by the previous director ..., on the *billets de service* and on other non-registered free seats, the so-called *entrées de tolérance....*") Commission, minutes of meeting, 1 March 1831, (F[21] 4633).

131 Commission, minutes of meeting, 15 March 1831, (F[21] 4633).

132 The Commission encouraged Véron «... de les réduire le plus possible et d'empêcher les abus.» ("... to reduce them as much as possible and to stop the abuses.") Commission, minutes of meeting, 17 March 1831, (F[21] 4633).

research. A summary of these, contained either in the minutes of Commission meetings or in Cavé's report, makes fascinating reading.

In principle, all official *entrées de faveur* were cancelled, and the number of official *entrées de droit* drastically curtailed. As a result, Cavé could report to the Minister that the official list had been reduced from 502 to 109, the latter list being all *entrées de droit*. By the time the list was finalised, however, the number had crept up to 111. The composition of this list reflected a very strong showing from the *Conservatoire* with forty-four names. There were fifteen composers or librettists and only twenty-three people who could be described as public officials:[133]

Public Officials – Police	6	
Other officials	<u>17</u>	23
Professionals: architects, lawyers		4
Composers	8	
Librettists	<u>7</u>	15
Conservatoire – Professors	40	
Other officials	<u>4</u>	44
Commission	6	
Comité du contentieux	<u>6</u>	12
Shareholders		<u>13</u>
		<u>111</u>

All the *entrées de tolérance*, being the free seats not on the official list, were as a general rule suppressed. The unofficial *billets de faveur* and *billets de service* were thus done away with. It was, however, recognised that certain exceptions should be made to this general rule, and the number of these *entrées de tolérance* was not totally erased, as the following examples show. It was felt that latitude should be given to Véron on *billets de faveur* and *billets de service* for the first three performances of a new work. Although, in principle, free seats given to former artists and staff as well as to the families of current artists and staff were abolished, an exception was made for soloists who had retired on a full pension. Another exception was that a fourth level box was retained for the *élèves du Conservatoire*. As for the journalists, it was felt that Lubbert had abused his *entrées de faveur* through favouring his friends regardless of their use to the Opera. With Véron, the Commission gave him the latitude to do as he thought fit always provided there were no malpractices:

> La Commission propose de laisser à M. Véron le droit de concéder ou de refuser des entrées aux Journaux, amis ou ennemis. Il y va de son intérêt; on peut se reposer sur lui du soin de limiter ou de multiplier ces entrées comme il conviendra. C'est donc une affaire entre lui et les journalistes, et le gouvernement n'aurait à s'en occuper que dans le cas où il y aurait abus. La surveillance de la Commission y devra prendre garde.[134]

---

133 *Liste des entrées de droit à partir du 1er juin 1831*, (AJ[13] 180 IX).

134 ("The Commission proposes to leave to M. Véron the right to accept or refuse free entries for the press, whether friends or enemies. It is in his interest, and one can rely on him to limit or multiply these entries as is appropriate. This is therefore a matter between him and the journalists, and the government would only have to deal with it in the case of abuses. The Commission will have to watch out for this.") Extract from Cavé's report to the Minister, 20 May 1831, (AJ[13] 180 IX).

In fact there were. It was ironic that the Commission, when revising the list of *entrées de faveur* in October 1835, found that there were so many journalists that there must have been abuses under Véron. It felt that the list should be carefully examined and that the position of each journalist should be checked. In principle, it felt that two free tickets per paper was right, one for the editor and one for the music critic. Any others should be regarded as exceptional and as *entrées de faveur personelles*.[135]

Cavé's report also recommended that the Minister should have available some *entrées personelles* which could be granted to eminent men of letters and the arts. Provided not too many were granted, the presence of such people in the foyer of the Opera would be a good move in that it would indicate that merit, and not just fortune and position, was publicly acknowledged.[136] Cavé had in mind to compose a list of such people for the Minister but, as he wryly remarked in his report, Véron had got in first and planned to present his own list of such *entrées*. At that time Véron was seen as a man of good taste and experience, so Cavé raised no objection. Finally, his report made a few exceptions for certain individuals.

The initial view of the Commission was to abolish the abused system of *entrées d'échange* which, under Lubbert, had given 146 free opera seats to personnel from State-subsidised and other theatres and 126 free seats to Opera personnel for reciprocal visits. It was recognised in Cavé's report, however, that the *Théâtre Italien* should be an exception as singers from the Opera could learn from the good example set by the singers there. It was also finally felt that gain could be had from artists' exchange visits to the other State theatres and Véron was left to sort out the details. Concerning the *Théâtre Français*, the number of free Opera seats for the two years 1830 and 1831 had been set at seventy-five. After negotiations, during which Véron initially proposed a reciprocal total of thirty names and the *Théâtre Français* thirty-nine, a final compromise was reached at thirty-six names from each theatre.[137] At the *Opéra Comique*, the 1827 and 1828 total had been agreed at seventy-three. After negotiations, a reciprocal total of eighteen was the final compromise achieved in October 1831.[138] As for the *Théâtre Italien*, a reciprocal total of twelve names was agreed in April and May 1831.[139]

---

135   Commission, minutes of meeting, 3 October 1835, (F^{21} 4633).

136   «... enfin qu'il est bon que le foyer de l'Opéra soit le rendez-vous de tous les hommes éminents de la Capitale, non seulement par leur fortune ou leur position, mais aussi par leur mérit.» ("... finally, that it is good that the foyer of the Opera should be the meeting point for all the eminent men of the Capital, not only by their fortune or their position, but also by their merit.") Extract from Cavé's report to the Minister, 20 May 1831, (AJ^{13} 180 IX).

137   a) *Comédie Française, Comité d'Administration. Liste des entrées de la Comédie Française à l'Académie Royale de Musique pour l'année théâtrale 1830 et 1831*, (AJ^{13} 218); b) *Liste des Personnes qui ont droit à des entrées d'échange avec l'Opéra*, and a reciprocal list from the Opera. Total of thirty-six names, (AJ^{13} 218).

138   a) *Liste des entrées par échange du Théâtre Royal de l'Opéra Comique, à l'Académie royale de Musique pour l'année 1827 et 1828*, (AJ^{13} 218); b) Véron to Paul at the *Opéra Comique*, October 1831, in reply to a letter received in August 1831, (AJ^{13} 218).

139   *Théâtre Italien* to Véron, 14 April 1831 and 16 May 1831, (AJ^{13} 218).

Needless to say, this root-and-branch reform of the extensive use of free boxes and seats, which had come to be grossly abused under Lubbert, caused a great deal of anguish. The minutes of the Commission's meetings recorded many complaints and pleas for reinstatement. The Commission stood firm, however, and with very few exceptions the pleas were all rejected through polite but firm letters from Cavé, some of which have been archived.[140]

New Seat Prices

Véron wished to attract the wealthy bourgeoisie to the Opera but in order to achieve this he had to think carefully about the prices of boxes and seats at the box-office, the prices of *abonnements*, season tickets, and the prices for renting boxes. He had inherited a patchwork of prices which had hardly changed over thirty years.[141] Under the Restoration, it had also become less relevant due to the proliferation of free seats. His proposals were approved by the Commission[142] which had submitted a report to the Minister.[143] He, in turn, approved the new seat prices.[144] Véron's proposal to alter the configuration of certain boxes had already been approved although the alterations were to be done at his expense.[145]

The overall policy which Véron adopted was to have seat prices which represented value for money to his new audiences on the one hand, yet maintained the Opera's aura of grandeur and exclusivity on the other. He was well aware that his receipts were just as likely to fall as to rise,[146] especially if those who had lost their free boxes and seats failed to support the Opera when asked to pay. His policy was thus one of maintaining prices wherever possible; of not hesitating to reduce prices if he felt this would be beneficial; and of only raising prices if the demand was likely to be so great that higher receipts would result.

The new box-office prices for both boxes and seats reflected this policy. Véron increased the price of the *baignoires d'avant-scène,* and the *premières loges en face et d'avant-scène,* to FF 9 per seat from FF 6 and FF 7.50 respectively. The small boxes

---

140 Cavé to various former holders of an *entrée gratuite, (*AJ[13] 180 IX).

141 Report of the Commission to the Minister, 1 May 1831, (F[21] 1067). There had been only two changes: a) *Parterre* seat prices had been increased under the Empire to FF 3.60 from FF 3 to take account of the *droit des indigents*; b) Two years previously, in 1829, *quatrièmes loges* prices had been reduced to FF 2.50 from FF 3.60 as «… cette partie de la Salle était trop souvent déserte.» ("… this part of the theatre was too often empty.")

142 Commission, minutes of meeting, 8 May 1831, (F[21] 4633).

143 Report, Commission to the Minister, 1 May 1831, (F[21] 1067).

144 a) *Note*, n.d., and initialled, (F[21] 1067). The Minister was said to have approved the changes although he had a concern about a *loge de première en face*. He pointed out that if it were filled for a year with those who had paid at the box-office it would yield FF 8.200 compared with an annual rental of FF 6.100. In the end, however, he felt that Véron had a greater interest in the new seat prices than the government, and agreed the proposals; b) Commission, minutes of meeting, 30 May 1831, (F[21] 4633).

145 Commission, minutes of meeting, 10 March 1831, (F[21] 4633).

146 Véron, op. cit., III, p. 188.

were called *baignoires* because only the heads of the occupants could be seen, rather as in a bath. They were dark, secluded and private, and the activities pursued within them left little to the imagination. The comedies that could be seen from the *baignoires* were as nothing compared to the comedies enacted within them.[147] Overall, Véron must have felt he was on safe ground here as all these boxes were so sought-after, but these were the only prices to be increased:

> Il y a là augmentation. Ces places sont les meilleures, peu nombreuses et seront recherchées. La vanité et la passion payeront et dédommageront un peu de l'abaissement du prix des autres places.[148]

Those of the *balcon* were reduced to FF 7.50 from FF 10.00; of the *premières loges de côté, amphithéâtre des premières et galerie des premières* to FF 6.00 from FF 7.50, and those of the *secondes loges de côté et troisièmes loges en face* to FF 5.00 from FF 6.00. The *parterre* seat prices were left unchanged at FF 3.60. According to the report, this price might have seemed high, but this did not frighten the public. The *parterre* was the strongest and most consistent contributor to box-office receipts. Lastly, Véron changed the price of seats in his new boxes which held four people instead of six. Instead of FF 60 for six people or FF 10 each, he charged FF 32 for four people or FF 8 each.

The *abonnements* posed a special challenge to Véron. They had previously been priced at FF 600 for one year and FF 360 for six months, but this was seen to be too expensive. Not only had very few *abonnements* been sold in the Restoration period but Véron had the challenge of attracting back to the Opera all those who had lost their free seats. With this in mind he cut the prices substantially to FF 400 and FF 250 respectively. As the report observed, an annual price of FF 400 should attract many people of fortune, many of whom had previously enjoyed free entry.

As for the renting of boxes, the convention had been that the rent of a box for a single performance was one-third higher than the price paid for a seat in a box at the box-office on the day. Véron's new seat prices did not sustain this correlation and the report was careful to make this point to the Minister. Furthermore, although boxes had, by convention, been available for rent for three, six and twelve months, Véron introduced a period of two months. This, he felt, would be bound to meet the approval of the public and would enhance his receipts. As for the conventional time-periods, the prices of most were maintained, but some were reduced. Only the rents of certain *baignoires* were increased to bring them into line with the new box-office prices.

The conclusion of the report was that although total theoretical receipts had been reduced, the Opera should benefit from a pricing policy which reconciled the interests of the public with those of the Opera. It was perhaps too much to say that Véron had

---

147 Hemmings, op. cit., p. 32. This was the translation of a quotation by Joachim Duflot, *Les Secrets des coulisses des théâtres de Paris* (Paris, 1865), pp. 34–35.

148 ("There is an increase here. These seats are the best, are few in number and will be sought after. Vanity and passion will pay and will compensate a little for the fall in the prices of the other seats.") Report of Commission to the Minister, 1 May 1831, (F^{21} 1067).

introduced a sophisticated pricing policy to the Opera, based on a detailed analysis of what the public wanted and how much it was prepared to pay. It was true, however, that nothing quite like this had been tried before and Véron made a great success of his new policy. He not only had a flair for what the public wanted to hear and see but, as a bourgeois himself, he had a good feel for what the public would regard as value for money.

Véron's Decline and Fall

It has already been shown that the Commission, in appointing Véron, wanted to distance itself from the culture of the Restoration period. At the same time it had to strike a delicate balance between its role as the protector of the interests of the King and the State and its desire to put the Opera onto a sounder financial footing. On the one hand, an image of dignity and grandeur was necessary to sustain the new regime's desired image of continuity and legitimacy. On the other hand, a reduction in expenses and losses should mean that, in due course, the subsidy from the State could be reduced. Véron had presented himself as someone who was in tune with the Commission's thinking and was duly appointed. From his point of view, the opportunity to make a fortune had presented itself. His 28 February 1831 *Cahier des charges* seemed to give sufficient scope to his entrepreneurial drive and the prestige and power that went with the job had its undoubted attractions. A concession was the agreed way to satisfy the interests of both parties and Véron assumed direct control on 1 June 1831. From the start, however, the two partners began to lose confidence in each other and Véron finally resigned prematurely on 31 August 1835. There were both general and specific reasons for this.

The Commission willed the ends but not the means whereby the Opera could put its finances in order. Véron realised right from the start that drastic economies were needed and set to work accordingly. The Commission, however, was taken aback by what seemed to them his brutal, unfeeling and excessive redundancies, salary reductions and early retirements. It is not hard to imagine how the Commission must have felt when, at nearly every meeting, it spent much of its time hearing and dealing with complaints from disaffected staff or ex-staff, and this in the knowledge that many would appeal to the *Comité du contentieux*.[149] When Véron uncharacteristically wrote to the Commission to advise it that instead of immediate redundancy, he had found a further sixteen months' work for someone called Germain so that he could qualify for a pension, the Commission went out of its way to thank him and instructed Cavé to send the letter to the Minister.[150] A sense of *noblesse oblige* in the case of Choiseul and d'Henneville and of *haute bourgeoisie oblige* in the case of Bertin, Blanc and Kératry

---

149 Commission, minutes of meeting, 31 March 1831, (F^{21} 4633).

150 «… afin qu'il sache que s'il lui faut souvent se montrer sévère contre les abus, la nouvelle administration de l'Opéra ne manque ni de loyauté ni d'humanité.» ("… so that he knows that even if it must be strict against the abuses, the new administration of the Opera is not lacking in loyalty or humanity.") Commission, minutes of meeting, 7 September 1831, (F^{21} 4633).

made them all uneasy with Véron's onslaught on the staff. After all, the idea of actually reducing salaries was unheard of at the Opera. Restoration period reports for the *projet de budget* by the heads of department, which made recommendations for salaries and bonuses, had only three columns: current salary, future increase, and bonus.[151] Even if someone received a withering report, the worst that could happen was that his or her salary would be frozen.[152] When d'Henneville was asked in November 1834 to produce a report which clarified the rights of staff to pensions and redundancy payments, he questioned whether Véron could, at whim, attack the existence of what was after all a family.[153] Furthermore, as a public body the Commission was bound to pay attention to public opinion, especially as expressed in the Chamber of Deputies which voted on the subsidy to the Royal theatres in general and to the Opera in particular. As already shown, Thiers had reflected the Chamber of Deputies' envy, if not outrage, that Véron had made a fortune at their expense, and had gone along with the vote to cut the subsidy from FF 760.000 to FF 670.000.[154] Prévost, the bass singer, whom Véron tried to retire in early 1833, threatened to take a petition to the Chamber of Deputies. He could imagine their surprise were he to disclose that Véron had made a profit of FF 220.000 in his first year 1831–32: a profit which sustained Véron in luxury but the artists in misery.[155] This letter inadvertently summed up the general sense that Véron had made a fortune at the expense of the artists and other staff who sustained the Opera and of the State which subsidised it.

Véron's failure to stage two grand operas in 1832–33, one held over from 1831–32 and a new one to comply with his 28 February 1831 *Cahier des charges* and first supplement, contributed to the general loss of confidence in his ability to comply with the ground rules laid down when he accepted the post of director. Through the Commission's eyes, Véron had inherited *Robert le Diable* and had been specially subsidised to stage it. It was therefore a matter of work for Véron but not of expense

---

151 Report of the head of costumes for the 1828 budget, (AJ[13] 146 III). There were three columns: *Traitement actuel, Augmentation proposée* and *Gratification proposée*. There was no sign, in any report, of reductions proposed or contemplated.

152 Report of the heads of singing for the 1828 *projet de budget*, (AJ[13] 146 III). For example:

Singer	Comment
Cajani	«Sans talent, sans moyens; mais zélé et docile. Nous ne demandons rien pour lui.» ("Without talent, without skills; but zealous and docile. We do not ask for any increase for him.")
Georges	«Chante souvent faux. Son exactitude n'est pas grande. Cette dame se plaint toujours, nous ferons comme elle.» ("Often sings out of tune. Her punctuality is not great. This lady always complains and we shall do the same.")
Le Coq	«Cette dame a une mauvaise voix et chante faux. Elle n'a que de la bonne volonté.» ("This lady has a bad voice and sings out of tune. She only has goodwill.")

Overall, there were no proposals for any reductions in salary.

153 «...que le caprice d'un directeur ne pouvait pas porter atteinte à l'existence d'une famille.» ("...that a director's whim could not undermine the existence of a family.") Report of d'Henneville to the Commission, November 1834, (F[21] 1053).

154 *Cahier des charges*, second supplement, 14 May 1833, Article 17, (AJ[13] 187 I).

155 Prévost to the Commission, n.d., (F[21] 1053).

and thus did not count as a grand opera staged at his own expense in 1831–32.[156] In 1832–33, Véron staged *Gustave III* as a grand opera but again failed to stage a second one. What was more, he staged only a single one- or two-act opera, *Le Serment,* instead of two, and a single one- or two-act ballet, *Nathalie,* also instead of two. In his own defence, he claimed that the success of *La Tentation* the new grand ballet, of *Gustave III* the new grand opera, and of other older productions, enabled him to invoke Article 10 of his *Cahier des charges,*[157] but the Minister and Commission were unimpressed. The FF 40.000 which remained out of the FF 100.000 extra subsidy was reduced to FF 20.000 and this latter amount was never in fact paid. The annual subsidy was also reduced, from FF 760.000 to FF 670.000 from 1833–34 onwards, although FF 50.000 extra was found, to be paid in four annual instalments of FF 12.500 each.[158]

The treatment of staff and the breaches of his 28 February 1831 *Cahier des charges* and the two supplements were two major causes for the development of a mutual lack of trust between Véron and the Minister and the Commission. There were also many other specific causes for distrust, such as the use of old scenery in *Le Serment* which gave rise to Véron's first fine, and the failure of Véron to deliver the report on personnel when the Commission was concerned that a breach of his *Cahier des charges* might have taken place. Towards the end of Véron's tenure as director, this breakdown in trust was reflected in the number and value of fines imposed on Véron by the Commission, always bearing in mind that the 28 February 1831 *Cahier des charges* considered that three fines were enough for the contract to be terminated.

This sense of mistrust and recrimination was encapsulated in an undated report, probably written in early 1833, which sought to show how Véron had breached his 28 February 1831 *Cahier des charges* and first supplement, 30 May 1831.[159] This was a catalogue of his misdeeds and showed how strongly the State authorities, apart from the Commission, felt about them. First, he used old materials for his new productions before an inventory had been completed. The report felt that he should prepare an account of the materials appropriated.[160] Second, he sacked many people without authorisation, and pension costs, which were a burden on the State, had increased. He had also reduced salaries without authorisation to the detriment of pension rights. The report implied that the State could ask for indemnities from Véron as a result of these actions. Third, new productions should have new scenery and costumes but this

---

156 «Vous vous rappelez, monsieur le Ministre, qu'un traité supplémentaire passé entre vous et M. Véron le 4 mai 1831 au sujet de *Robert le Diable* dont l'état a payé une partie des frais, ne le décharge de l'obligation de faire jouer un autre grand opéra cette année sauf la condition qu'il en montera deux l'année prochaine. Ainsi *Robert le Diable* doit lui compter comme travaux mais non comme dépenses.» ("You may remember, Minister, that a supplementary agreement was made between you and M. Véron on 4 May 1831 for *Robert le Diable,* and that part of the expenses were paid for by the State. This does not release him from the obligation to stage another grand opera in this year unless he were to stage two of them in the following year. Therefore, *Robert le Diable* must count as work for him but not as an expense.") Commission to the Minister, 16 May 1832, (F^{21} 1054).

157 Véron to the Commission, 21 March 1833, (F^{21} 1053).

158 *Cahier des charges,* second supplement, 14 May 1833, Article 17, (AJ^{13} 187 I).

159 Report, n.d., (F^{21} 1069).

160 See chapter 3: Sets and Scenery under Véron's Administration.

regulation was not observed for scenery. No new work was performed without all or some old repainted scenery. Although the Commission had authorised the use of old materials to make the sets and to repaint some scenery, the State, which provided a subsidy on the basis that old materials for scenery should not be used, had a right to any benefit which Véron had gained. Fourth, Véron admitted that he had used old scenery for *Le Serment* which breached Article 11 of his 28 February 1831 *Cahier des charges.* Fifth, Véron did not always stage new productions every two months as per Article 10 of the 28 February 1831 *Cahier des charges.* Sixth, he had failed to stage, as required, six new productions in 1831–32. As the State subsidised him on this basis, it was entitled to an indemnity from Véron. Seventh, in his second year, 1832–33, Véron staged only three new productions, *Le Serment, Nathalie* and *Gustave III,* but as the Minister refused to accept *Nathalie* as a new production which qualified under the regulations, Véron effectively staged only two new productions instead of six. He had breached Articles 9 and 10 of his *Cahier des charges.* Not only should he have been fined for this, but he should have lost a part of his annual subsidy. Eighth, Véron was obliged to stage a second grand opera in his second year 1832–33 as a replacement for *Robert le Diable.* If this second opera was not staged, then the FF 40.000 not yet paid out of the extra subsidy of FF 100.000 would be confiscated. The report then took this argument further. Although the FF 100.000 had originally been granted on the basis that *Robert le Diable* would cost FF 70.000, the report maintained that the FF 100.000 was allocated as to FF 60.000 for *Robert le Diable* and FF 40.000 for the refurbishment of the theatre. As the second grand opera had not been performed, it therefore followed that the State should have withheld FF 60.000 and not FF 40.000, and the implication of this was that Véron should repay the difference of FF 20.000.[161] The report also noted that Véron was originally allocated the extra subsidy of FF 60.000 for *Robert le Diable* by d'Argout on the basis that all the scenery and costumes would be new. Véron had, however, gained the Commission's authorisation to use old scenery to make the new sets. Ninth, depreciation of sets, machines, furniture etc. should be taken into account in any settlement. Tenth, Véron had breached Article 19 of his 28 February 1831 *Cahier des charges* in that the auditorium had never been cleaned twice a year. Eleventh, Véron failed to establish *pantomime,* mime, at the Opera despite the Commission's many requests.[162] Twelfth, Véron did not fulfil the terms of a settlement with Rossini whereby he should have paid Rossini FF 10.000 per annum. Thirteenth, when the *ouvreuses* had their fixed salaries cancelled, they each received six months' salary as an indemnity. Véron should himself be accountable for this expense. Fourteenth, the state of repairs at the Opera should be verified as Véron was responsible for these expenses.

By March 1833 Véron was so disenchanted by his situation with the Minister and the Commission that, in an exchange of letters with Thiers, the Minister of Commerce and Public Works, he offered his resignation.[163] Thiers was minded to accept but was

---

161 In the event, the *Cahier des charges,* second supplement, 14 May 1833, Article 34, allocated this
      FF 60.000 entirely against the cost of refurbishing the auditorium (AJ^{13} 187 I). Véron was not
      therefore asked to repay the FF 20.000.
162 For a discussion on the importance of mime, see Gerhard, op. cit., pp. 145–150
163 Véron to Thiers, 17 March 1833 and Thiers to Véron, 19 March 1833, (AJ 187 V).

concerned that the public finances should not bear the costs of any such move. In a further letter, Véron pointed out that it would cost him a lot to resign in that the Opera had become prosperous.[164] He went out of his way to complain that Thiers had overturned Commission decisions which were not hostile to Véron's interests. He was especially critical of Thiers' decision to allow the *Théâtre Italien* to perform operas every day of the week as this would hurt the finances of the Opera. Previously, the *Théâtre Italien* could only clash with the Opera on five Mondays of the year and only with benefit performances. This new competition would, in Véron's view, hurt French composers and artists as well as himself. Whether Véron's letter expressed the real reason for his offer to resign was hard to judge. He expressed the view that one argument in favour of continuing was that the government could not break his contract, but as it was about to do just that by substantially reducing his subsidy, this argument did not really make much sense. Maybe Véron was implying that this reduction was the real reason for his disenchantment. In the end, however, a compromise was patched up. Thiers wrote that he could not allow the State to be exposed to the hazards of a resignation which had unknown consequences. Véron's resignation terms were unacceptable and he should put forward solid proposals to resolve the matter as soon as possible.[165] The result was that Véron decided to stay on. He had a reduced subsidy which was voted through by the Chamber of Deputies, he had the prospect of receiving only FF 20.000 out of the outstanding FF 40.000 to subsidise the extra grand opera, and he had a special FF 50.000 subsidy spread over four years. In financial terms he had lost heavily. It has to be said that Thiers himself was under pressure when the 1833–34 budget was debated in the Chamber of Deputies. When called on to defend the 1834–35 *Budget des théâtres Royaux* of FF 1.300.000 on 6 May 1834, he made a point of alluding to his decisions on the 1833–34 budget.[166] At that time the *Théâtre Français* and *Opéra Comique* were both in financial difficulties especially as the former had FF 500.000 of debts to pay. He had therefore raised the subsidy of the *Théâtre Français* to FF 200.000 and that of the *Opéra Comique* from FF 150.000 to FF 180.000. Given that the total *Budget des théâtres Royaux* remained the same, he had to reduce the subsidy of the Opera to offset these increases. Thiers also mentioned that as a result of his negotiations with Véron in 1833, the scenery now belonged entirely to the State. With this retrospective, Thiers gained the support of the deputies for the 1834–35 budget but still could not convince a deputy called Charlemagne who thought that the reduced subsidy of FF 670.000 was still too much. This deputy also voiced the general sense that Véron had made a fortune too readily:

> Où est la nécessité qu'un directeur d'Opéra s'enrichisse en moins de trois ans? Pourquoi ne mettrait-t-il pas dix ans à faire fortune?[167]

---

164 Véron to Thiers, 1 April 1833, (AJ[13] 187 V).

165 Thiers to Véron, 7 April 1833, (AJ[13] 187 V). This letter must have crossed with one from Véron on the same day as Thiers referred to it and to an unarchived letter from Véron, 30 March 1833.

166 *Archives Parlementaires, 2. Série (1800–1860), Tome 90*, 6 May–6 August 1834. *Séance*, 6 May 1834.

167 ("Why should it be necessary for a director of the Opera to enrich himself in less than three years? Why does it not take him ten years to make his fortune?")

It was not just the Minister, the Chamber of Deputies and Véron who were dissatisfied. The Commission also felt that its position was unclear and lacked effectiveness. Choiseul made this point to the Minister in April 1834. In his view, the Commission dealt only with obscure and petty details and that matters of substance were dealt with by the secretary, Cavé. Overall, he considered that the Commission lacked power and authority and was not able to carry out its duties properly.[168]

Véron had a strong personality and was also a fighter. Provided he continued to make his fortune year-by-year it would have been in keeping with his character to have ridden out all these problems until the end of his six-year concession. The Opera's finances, however, took a considerable turn for the worse in the financial year which ended 31 May 1835, and although no accounts were published, it was very probable that he made a loss for that year. This adverse trend would have been keenly felt by Véron, for whom money was so important a motivation, and no doubt hastened his decision to depart. In the end, he resigned on 31 August 1835, and an agreement was reached with the Commission on the terms of a settlement. The fines outstanding plus two-thirds of the imputed cost of productions which Véron did not stage totalled FF 103.000, and the depreciation of costumes inherited by Véron was estimated at FF 35.656. This gave a total due by Véron of FF 138.656.[169] On the other hand, he was entitled to receive the depreciated cost of the costumes for which he had paid and this had been calculated as FF 113.334 by Géré:[170]

Work	Total Cost of Costumes FF	Fraction Deducted	Current Value FF
Le Philtre	3.868	½	1.934
l'Orgie	9.433	¾	2.358
Robert le Diable	26.228	$7/12$	10.929
La Sylphide	7.145	½	3.572
La Tentation	38.446	$8/10$	7.689
Le Serment	3.015	½	1.508
Nathalie	3.836	¾	959
Gustave III	38.063	¾	9.516
Ali-Baba	20.256	$2/3$	6.752
La Révolte	32.686	$2/3$	10.895
Don Juan	24.759	½	12.379
La Tempête	14.301	¾	3.575
La Juive	69.340	$7/16$	39.004
Brézilia	4.527	½	2.264
	295.903		113.334

---

168 Choiseul to the Minister, 10 and 29 April 1834, (F^{21} 960).

169 Report by the Commission to the Minister, 15 August 1835, (AJ^{13} 180 III).

170 This total was presented by Géré in a report which he signed on 10 July 1835, (AJ^{13} 215 V). A formula was adopted whereby a fraction of the cost of costumes for new works presented by Véron was deducted as depreciation.

Véron claimed FF 113.000 at a meeting of the Commission in July 1835 and the total of this plus other items was finally agreed at FF 123.656. This difference of FF 15.000 between FF 138.656 and FF 123.656 was then embodied in Article 1 of a *Cahier des conditions.* It was signed by all parties and spelt out, in ten Articles, the terms of Véron's departure.[171] Véron was also due FF 25.000 for the two years still outstanding on the FF 50.000 special subsidy agreed in May 1833, and so the net figure due to him was finally FF 10.000. A notable omission was the depreciated cost of the scenery for new productions for which Véron had paid. When Véron arrived on 1 March 1831, the 28 February 1831 *Cahier des charges* gave this benefit to him. By 1835, however, the scenery belonged wholly to the State.

Throughout this chapter 2, substantial use has been made of primary sources to describe Véron's tenure at the Opera, and it is interesting to compare these sources with the comments of writers who have taken an interest in this period of the Opera's history. Crosten, for example, placed the emphasis in his book on Véron the entrepreneur, and on the effect this new style of management had on the Opera:

Under his leadership the bustle of commerce replaced the placid inertia that had characterized the Opera for so long.[172]

Crosten also agreed with Véron and Gerhard that this new style represented a triumph for the newly-confident *haute bourgeoisie*:

His attitude was at once practical for himself and representative of the bourgeois spirit which engulfed the Opera.[173]

Crosten also made the point that Véron was simply a business man and that he took the job in order to make a fortune. The evidence of the primary sources leads one to agree with Crosten, but only up to a point. By focusing entirely on Véron, he did not take all the primary sources into account and was misguided in his general conclusion that the Opera was run entirely as a business in order to satisfy the new bourgeois audiences. It is very significant that Crosten never even mentioned the Commission, the various Ministers and the Chamber of Deputies. He thus failed to recognise that the State still played a significant role and that Véron's room for manoeuvre progressively diminished as the State lost confidence in him.

Fulcher, on the other hand, realised that a conflict of interest was inherent in the 1831 *Cahier des charges* and in the setting up of a Commission:

The Cahier set up a tension between a director with the status of "entrepreneur" and an official commission, representative of the state, designed to protect its interests.[174]

Fulcher also correctly pointed out that Véron failed to realise how restrictive the *Cahier des charges* would prove to be:

---

171 *Cahier des conditions* ..., 15 August 1835, (AJ[13] 180 II).

172 Crosten, op. cit., p. 27.

173 Crosten, op. cit., p. 33.

174 Fulcher, op. cit., p. 55.

Véron, however, apparently assumed that there was a great deal more flexibility in the statutes of his *Cahier des charges* than did the official commission.[175]

The evidence of the primary sources leads one to agree with Fulcher, but again only up to a point. By focusing almost entirely on the need for the Opera to present a correct political message through its new productions, she was wrong in her general conclusion that the Opera was run by the State to achieve these political objectives. It is, again, significant that Fulcher made no reference to Véron's successful efforts to cut costs, raise receipts and make a profit.

This partial view of events by each author was highlighted in their respective comments on Véron's resignation. For Crosten, who took the commercial view, the resignation was the act of Véron the business man:

> ... he relinquished it before the expiration of his contract because he was convinced that his earnings in the theatre had reached their peak. "I did not remain there too long", he said, "...I prudently left the establishment when the subsidy was diminished." [176]

Fulcher, on the other hand, emphasised the growing conflict between Véron and the State:

> From the start, Emil (sic) Véron was on a collision course with the commission, and slowly the tensions would increase to the point of forcing Véron, in effect, to resign.[177]

Based on the primary sources extensively used in this chapter, the conclusion must surely be that it was a combination of these two views which was nearest to the truth. Véron would have been well aware that 1834–35 was a poor one from his financial point of view. Equally, the State had, by this time, had enough of him and was glad to see him go.

Now that the appointment of Véron, the practical effect of his policies, and the circumstances which contributed to his downfall, have been described in detail, the next section focuses on the Annual Accounts and what his policies and downfall meant in financial terms.

The Annual Accounts 1831–32 to 1834–35

Véron took office on 1 March 1831 but Article 2 of his 28 February 1831 *Cahier des charges* stipulated that for the three months to 31 May he should manage the Opera on behalf of the State.[178] It was only on 1 June 1831 that he should take over the Opera as director and concessionaire at his own risk, peril and fortune. During this interim period, the expenses, initially thought to total FF 466.349 were finally agreed at FF 456.428.[179] As for the receipts, these totalled FF 240.403,[180] although no subsidy

---

175 Fulcher, op. cit., p. 62.

176 Crosten, op. cit., p. 33. Véron, op. cit., III, p. 308.

177 Fulcher, op. cit., p. 62.

178 *Cahier des charges*, 28 February 1831, Article 2, (AJ[13] 187 I).

179 Expenses, 1 March–31 May 1831, (CO 343 (605)). These were described as *pour le compte du Ministère du Commerce*.

180 Receipts, 1 March–31 May 1831, (AJ[13] 233).

was included as the Ministry would, in effect, be subsidising itself. Of especial interest were the receipts and expenses for the eleven concerts given by Paganini at the Opera on his first visit to Paris. The receipts totalled FF 165.741[181] and the fee paid to Paganini was FF 124.448.[182] The basis for this fee was that he took two-thirds of the gross receipts for week-day concerts and all the gross receipts less FF 3.000 for each Sunday concert.[183] He also took all the receipts from a benefit concert for the poor of Paris and then paid these over himself.[184] An insight into the strained relations between the new Minister, d'Argout, and the Commission was revealed when d'Argout reluctantly agreed to the payment of FF 124.448. He pointed out that the contract with Paganini, although approved by the Commission, had not been approved by Montalivet, the Minister then in charge of the Opera.[185] Strictly speaking, Article 29 of Véron's 28 February 1831 *Cahier des charges* had been breached and the Commission gained an early foretaste of the fact that the Restoration principle of three levels of management was still intact.

Véron took direct control of financial affairs at the Opera as from 1 June 1831 and only had to provide certain figures on a monthly basis to the Commission to justify the caution money of FF 250.000. He opened a bank account, had his own director's account within the financial set of books and had no need to submit budgets and annual accounts for approval. He also retained control over the allocation of free seats to the press and for the first three nights of new productions. Nevertheless, he faced some daunting challenges when he took over and the fact that he succeeded was a tribute both to his management skills and to his flair as a perceptive impresario.

1831–32

As soon as Véron took over as manager on behalf of the State on 1 March 1831, he faced the probability that he would lose the receipts from the secondary theatres. As already shown, these were substantial. At around FF 180.000 per annum they were some ten to eleven per cent of total receipts in any one year.[186] Furthermore, although he stood to gain from the new policy over free seats, this would only help him if he could attract a sufficient number of extra people who were prepared to pay. Véron was cautious about this especially as he hoped to attract a new wealthy bourgeoisie who would expect value for money just as much as social acceptability.

The 1831–32 Annual Accounts showed that Véron's initial caution was fully justified. For the first five months of his concession, 1 June–31 October 1831, receipts at the box-office were distinctly lacklustre. It was only after the huge success of *Robert le Diable* that box-office receipts picked up dramatically. The first five months yielded

---

181 *Journal usuel de l'Opéra 1791–1850,* op. cit..

182 This total was included under *Matériel* in the expenses, 1 March–31 May 1831, (CO 343 (605)).

183 Jacques-Gabriel Prod'homme, *Les Musiciens célèbres, Paganini* (Paris, n.d.).

184 The accounts indicated that Paganini received the gross receipts of FF 6.105 from the concert for the poor of Paris and that he paid this over himself, (CO 343 (605)).

185 D'Argout to Choiseul, 27 April 1831, (F²¹ 1053).

186 Receipts from the secondary theatres: 1827 FF 180.995, (AJ¹³ 145 V); 1828 FF 194.673, (AJ¹³ 146 III); 1829 FF 188.895, (AJ¹³ 146 IV); 1830 FF 182.958, (AJ¹³ 228 I).

only FF 237.314, for an average of FF 47.463 per month, while the last seven months yielded FF 542.918, for an average of FF 77.560 per month:[187]

Recettes à la porte.

	FF		FF
June	44.921	November	71.063
July	40.450	December	98.554
August	48.728	January	89.121
September	50.574	February	85.384
October	52.641	March	98.776
		April	52.291
		May	47.729
	237.314		542.918
Average per month	47.463		77.560

This latter average would have been higher but for the April 1832 outbreak of cholera which reduced the April and May receipts to FF 52.291 and FF 47.729 respectively and even these totals were deceptive. April and May would have been catastrophic for Véron but for receipts of FF 52.079 from another series of concerts given by Paganini. Despite these mixed fortunes, however, Véron's gamble came off in 1831–32 and full credit should be given to him for taking the risk in the first place. When compared with the Restoration period the improvement was dramatic.[188] The combination of a dramatically reduced number of free seats and of great success at the box-office from November onwards made such a difference that the loss of receipts from the secondary theatres was more than made up. A change for the better also took place in the renting of boxes. Receipts were FF 140.044 in 1831–32 compared with FF 57.431 in 1830 and FF 129.650 in 1829. The full effect was not felt, however, until 1832–33 when the total was FF 175.179.[189] In 1831–32 Véron also received FF 60.000 out of the extra subsidy of FF 100.000 and FF 802.982[190] out of his annual subsidy of FF 810.000. With sundry other items total receipts reached FF 1.822.098.

---

187 Annual Accounts 1831–32, (AJ[13] 228 II). See Appendix IV.

188 *Recettes par représentation.* 1827 FF 499.707, (AJ[13] 145 V); 1828 FF 522.105, (AJ[13] 146 III); 1829 FF 574.155, (AJ[13] 146 IV); 1830 FF 553.956, (AJ[13] 228 I); 1831–32 FF 780.232*, (AJ[13] 228 II).
      * Receipts from the six Paganini concerns were FF 52.079 and the Opera paid away two-thirds of this, or FF 34.718 as *Frais divers, non-classés.*

189 Annual Accounts 1832–33, (AJ[13] 228 II). See Appendix IV. *Location de loges à termes, abonnements personnels,* FF 175.179.

190 Annual Accounts 1831–32, (AJ[13] 228 II).The fact that Véron received only FF 802.982, being a shortfall of FF 7.018 was due to a number of reasons, only two of which can be verified: a) He had FF 2.500 deducted from his November monthly subsidy, which was FF 65.000 instead of FF 67.500, due to his failure, as already noted, to supply the *état personnel*; b) A deduction of FF 285 was made from Véron's July 1831 subsidy which was FF 67.215 instead of FF 67.500, (AJ[13] 226 II). This was due to *oppositions* whereby certain members of the Opera's staff, who could not or would not pay personal bills, had been taken to court by their creditors and the FF 285 had been paid by *Le Payeur central du Trésor.* This was then deducted from Véron's July subsidy; c) Unable to account for the balance of FF 4.333.

On the expenses side, Véron's initial onslaught reduced the fixed personnel costs to FF 802.189. As for the variable personnel costs, the overall total remained much the same as a reduction in the total paid to soloists for *feux,* the fees paid per performance to soloists, was largely offset by higher payments to authors and composers[191] and by the extra costs of new soloists. Of the non-personnel expenses, by far the largest were those for costumes and scenery and these, as confirmed by Véron, rose sharply. They totalled FF 238.811 compared with FF 163.948 in 1830 and FF 134.609 in 1829.[192] Lastly, the extra amount paid for pensions fell dramatically. Whereas in the Restoration period extra subsidies had financed extra contributions to the pension fund, Véron only paid over the amounts deducted from salaries of FF 31.818[193] and contributed FF 12.000 in lieu of benefit performances. Total expenses, including FF 70.000 for the redecoration of the theatre and FF 65.405 for indemnities to those made redundant, were FF 1.676.999.

On the basis of these figures, which, as with all the annual accounts, should be viewed with a degree of caution, Véron made a surplus of FF 145.099 in his first full year as director. Extra figures available confirmed this total in that Véron's payments to, and drawings from, his account with the Opera can be reconciled with the Annual Accounts.[194] Given the risks which he faced initially, Véron must have been well pleased with this result and with the FF 154.093 which he drew out in cash.

---

191 Payments to authors and composers. 1827 FF 48.763, (AJ[13] 145 V); 1828 FF 50.956, (AJ[13] 146 III); 1829 FF 46.077, (AJ[13] 146 IV); 1830 FF 52.045, (AJ[13] 228 I); 1831–32 FF 68.244, (AJ[13] 228 II).

192 Expenses of costumes and scenery. 1827 FF 182.597, (AJ[13] 145 V); 1828 FF 149.995, (AJ[13] 146 III); 1829 FF 134.609, (AJ[13] 146 IV); 1830 FF 163.948, (AJ[13] 228 I); 1831–32 FF 238.811, (AJ[13] 228 II).

193 Details of the monthly deductions from salaries and of the equivalent amounts paid over to the pension fund were included in the *Comptes supplémentaires* for 1831–32, (AJ[13] 228 II).

194 The reconciliation of the 1831–32 Annual Accounts should be taken in stages, (AJ[13] 228 II). a) The first draft of the Annual Accounts showed a profit of FF 185.656, which left a cash balance of FF 31.639 after Véron had drawn FF 154.093 from his account and after various small items had been taken into account such as loans repayable by staff of FF 2.377, a small credit balance at the Banque de France of FF 1.785, fines levied on staff which Véron had not yet paid to the *Caisse des pensions* of FF 1.159 and other small items. b) Subsequent to this first draft, a revision included further expenses of FF 41.455 which related to 1831–32 but which were paid in 1832–33. These, together with a new balance of debtors and creditors, resulted in a theoretical cash deficit of FF 11.802 and a reduced profit of FF 145.099. The reconciliation of these figures was:

	FF	FF	FF
Profit – Total receipts		1,822.098	
– Total expenses		1,676.999	145.099
Cash – Drawn by Véron		154.093	
Cash deficit		11.802	
		142.291	
Balance at *Banque de France*	1.785		
Advances to staff	2.377		
Pension payments	837		
	4.999		
Fines to be paid	1.159		
Oppositions judiciaires	1.032		
	2.191	2.808	145.099

1832–33

The year started poorly due to the cholera epidemic. June receipts were only FF 36.561 and July was also relatively lacklustre at FF 54.447. Véron claimed that he did not make any request for a special subsidy[195] but the evidence indicates otherwise. One letter, while not making a direct request, left the Minister in no doubt about his difficulties. Another, written to the Commission in July after special subsidies had been made to the other Royal theatres, was more forthright in that Véron asked to be included.[196] He also claimed that he paid money to the Opera out of his own pocket and his director's account certainly showed an inflow of FF 45.970 in May and FF 44.560 in July. Nevertheless, this bore no comparison with Véron's claim that he paid in FF 50.000 per month for seven months, or FF 350.000.[197] Indeed, his account with the Opera showed substantial withdrawals over the full year.[198] This was not really surprising. Cornélie Falcon's début in *Robert Le Diable* in July 1832, and the success of *La Tentation*, *La Sylphide* and *Gustave III*, caused receipts to pick up to former levels. An analysis of the takings at the box office and of other receipts showed no evidence that any of Véron's FF 350.000 had found its way into these figures:[199]

Box-office receipts for the first five months of 1832–33:

June	FF 36.561
July	54.447
August	78.800
September	66.336
October	74.557

The claim that the Opera was deserted for seven months with only FF 500 in receipts was thus totally wide of the mark.[200] The year ended very well for Véron, especially as there were no large extra expenses as had been the case in 1831–32. The surplus was FF 275.252 and Véron took out net cash of FF 171.217 during the year. This left a cash surplus of FF 89.131 at the year-end and in July 1833 Véron took out further cash of FF 96.152. Maybe this was a timely precaution as he had already offered to resign.

1833–34

This was another very good year for Véron. His subsidy had been cut by FF 90.000 to FF 670.000 as a result of Thiers' intervention and the 14 May 1833 second supplement to the *Cahier des charges*, although there was the extra subsidy of FF 12.500. Overall receipts rose to FF 1.953.087, however, and box-office receipts were especially buoyant

---

195 Véron, op. cit., III, p. 188.

196 a) Véron to the Minister, 13 April 1832, (F²¹ 1053). While claiming no special indemnity on behalf of the Opera, he dared to count on the Minister's *honorable bienveillance*. In a P.S. he noted that out of the FF 60.000 especially granted to the Paris theatres, the subsidised *Théâtre Français* had claimed, and been granted, its share; b) Véron to the Commission, 11 July 1832, (AJ¹³ 180 II).

197 Véron, op. cit., III, p. 188.

198 Accounts of the Director with the Opera 1832–33, (AJ¹³ 228 II). Withdrawals of cash: July 1832 FF 10.000; August FF 45.967; September FF 70.000; October FF 60.000; November FF 60.000.

199 *Recettes journalières provenant des représentations 1832–33*, (AJ¹³ 228 II).

200 Gourret, op. cit., p. 122. Quoted by Fulcher, op. cit., p. 80.

at FF 965.774 compared with FF 818.262 in 1832–33. Rentals of boxes and *abonnements* were also buoyant and rose to FF 234.858 compared with FF 175.179. Although fixed personnel costs showed an increase to FF 841.155 compared with FF 831.413 and the total of variable personnel costs and other expenses were also up, the surplus was a substantial FF 370.538.[201] Véron took cash of FF 336.486 from his director's account, and the year-end cash surplus at the Opera was FF 105.612.

The 1833–34 Annual Accounts need careful analysis as the concept of receipts and expenses was intermingled with the concept of cash-flow. The total of June 1832 receipts, being the first month of the new financial year, included the cash balance brought forward from the previous year of FF 89.131. Unless this figure was taken out, the profit accruing to Véron over the course of 1833–34 would have been overstated. On the other hand, it should be included for cash-flow purposes.

1834–35

No Annual Accounts for this fourth and final year of Véron's concession were prepared. It is therefore necessary to construct them from the primary data which are scattered throughout the relevant documents. These accounts should therefore be treated with some caution where convincing proof of the accuracy of the data is not available.[202]

Data were available on the receipts at the box-office and on the rentals of boxes. A summary was contained within a single document and these figures were corroborated by other evidence.[203] A similar summary with supporting evidence was also available for 1833–34 and the figures for receipts in the 1833–34 Annual Accounts were derived from this data.[204] It is therefore reasonable to assume that the 1834–35 Annual Accounts would have been prepared on a similar basis. It was interesting to see that receipts from the box-office were down compared with 1833–34, FF 825.179 as against FF 965.774, although rentals from boxes were slightly higher, FF 246.630 as against FF 234.858. Despite the second supplement to Véron's 28 February 1831 *Cahier des charges*, 14 May 1833, which called for four new productions per year,[205] the fact was that there were only three. *La Tempête*, 15 September 1833, a two-act ballet; *La Juive*, 23 February 1835, the five-act grand opera; and *Brézilia*, 8 April 1835, a one-act ballet. Furthermore, as *La Juive* was produced late in the financial year, its success was not fully reflected in the 1834–35 Annual Accounts as there were only twenty-five performances.[206] There were no figures for the receipts from masked balls and rentals of shops. Based on previous years, estimates of FF 30.000 and FF 8.000 have been

---

201 Annual Accounts 1833–34, (AJ[13] 228 II). See Appendix IV.

202 For the construction of the 1834–35 Annual Accounts, see Appendix IV.

203 See summary of receipts, (AJ[13] 237) and box-office receipts, (CO 710 (608)). See also the *Journal usuel de l'Opéra 1791–1850*, op. cit., which included the *Location de Loges à terme* in its single total of receipts per performance.

204 The Annual Accounts 1833–34, (AJ[13] 228 II), corresponded to the figures detailed in AJ[13] 237 and CO 710 (608).

205 *Cahier des charges*, second supplement, 14 May 1833, Article 9, (AJ[13] 187 I).

206 *Journal usuel de l'Opéra 1791–1850*, op. cit., and AJ[13] 237.

taken. Extraordinary receipts were only FF 273[207] and the subsidy of FF 670.000 was the same as in 1833–34. Total receipts were thus around FF 1.780.082 compared with FF 1.953.087 in 1833–34.

The expenses of fixed and variable personnel were detailed in sets of tables which can be relied upon.[208] They were FF 927.664 and FF 279.367 respectively, compared with FF 841.155 and FF 244.557 in 1833–34. Clearly these 1834–35 figures were a setback for Véron and it is interesting to compare them with those in each year of Véron's four-year concession. Despite his drastic and brutal reductions in 1831–32, he was unable to stem the increases thereafter. The comparative expenses figures were:[209]

	Fixed Personnel FF	Variable Personnel FF	Total FF
1831–32	802.189	228.563	1.030.752
1832–33	831.413	222.734	1.054.147
1833–34	841.155	244.557	1.085.712
1834–35	927.664	279.367	1.207.031

In 1834–35 not only had total receipts fallen by some FF 173.000 over 1833–34 but the expenses of fixed and variable personnel had risen by FF 121.319 for an overall adverse swing of some FF 294.000. It would not be too fanciful to conjecture that Véron, who kept a very sharp eye on financial detail, would have been fully aware of this adverse trend when he resigned in August 1835. As for the other expenses, these have either been derived from documents which can be relied upon or estimates have been taken based on previous years. The estimated total was FF 618.575 which, again, was higher than that in previous years. Total estimated expenses were around FF 1.825.606 which gave rise to a deficit of some FF 45.524. It should again be emphasised that the 1834–35 figures are derived from primary documents as no 1834–35 Annual Accounts were prepared. Nevertheless, it would seem as though Véron achieved an overall surplus of around FF 745.000 for the four years in which he had a financial interest.

The Settlement with Duponchel

Véron resigned on 31 August 1835 and Duponchel became the new director on 1 September as per Article 1 of his *Cahier des charges*.[210] Despite this legal transfer of office, however, it was clear that the financial transfer was backdated to 1 June 1835. A schedule, 18 September 1835, was compiled to take account of these differing dates.

---

207 See table of *recettes extraordinaires*, (CO 710 (608)).

208 See tables of expenses for fixed and variable personnel for 1833–34 and 1834–35, (CO 710 (608)). These also tie-up with the figures in AJ[13] 228 IV.

209 Annual Accounts 1831–32 to 1834–35, (AJ[13] 228 II, CO 710 (608)).

210 *Cahier des charges,* 1 September 1835, (AJ[13] 187 I). Véron resigned on 31 August 1835, Article 1, and Duponchel was appointed as from 1 September 1835.

It detailed the amounts owed by Duponchel to Véron and vice-versa.[211] The schedule showed that Véron owed Duponchel FF 110.329 and Duponchel owed Véron FF 51.600 for a net balance of FF 58.729 which was recorded in the books of account.[212] The schedule made clear the reasons for this settlement. For example, Véron had received, prior to 1 June 1835, rentals for boxes and *abonnements* which covered periods after that date. These receipts totalled FF 44.875 and should be for Duponchel's benefit. Véron had also received FF 2.000 as payment for the annual right to sell opera-glasses and bouquets of flowers. FF 1.000 of this covered the six months to 30 November and should also be for Duponchel's benefit. Cléry, the supplier-contractor of wood for heating, was by now paid FF 12.000 instead of the FF 10.000 in his first contract. As at 31 May 1835, FF 4.000 was still owed by Véron, being four months at FF 1.000 per month. Duponchel, who would have to pay this bill, was thus owed FF 4.000 by Véron. It was also clear that Véron had drawn out cash of FF 56.900 from his account with the Opera after June 1835 and that this was repayable. On the other hand, Duponchel owed Véron for the expenses incurred prior to 1 June 1835 on *L'Île des Pirates*. The first night of this ballet took place on 12 August 1835 and as all the receipts would accrue to Duponchel he should also be charged with those expenses which Véron had incurred. Véron had also paid, prior to 1 June 1835, FF 5.000 to Scribe and FF 20.000 to Meyerbeer for *Les Huguenots* whose first night took place on 29 February 1836. Duponchel thus owed FF 25.000 to Véron. The annual insurance premium for cover against fire was paid in advance by Véron. Of this, FF 4.312 covered the period from 1 June 1835 to 14 May 1836 and Duponchel clearly should refund Véron for this.

Apart from the settlement of receipts and expenses pre- and post- 1 June 1835, there was another strand to the overall settlement. Véron had, from a financial point of view, resigned after four years of his six year concession. Although no background letters or contract have been archived, it seems as though Duponchel had to pay for the right to direct the Opera for these two final years. In other words, he had to buy out Véron's concession. Duponchel did not have the money to do this so a line of credit was opened for him which totalled FF 269.000. Of this amount, FF 209.000 was due to Véron for the purchase of his concession[213] which Véron referred to in his memoirs.[214] Binet also referred to the amount due to Véron, although he put it at FF 244.000.[215]

How did Véron fare in overall terms from his concession at the Opera? Although caution should again be expressed on the actual figures, there were six strands to this calculation. The overall surplus from his four years was around FF 745.000. He was paid FF 209.000 by Duponchel to buy out the unexpired period of his

---

211 Financial settlement between Véron and Duponchel, which was backdated to 1 June 1835, (AJ[13] 228 II).

212 The net sum of FF 58.729 was recorded in the books of account, (CO 568 (621)).

213 *Détail des Comptes supplémentaires, 1835–36, 1836–37*, (AJ[13] 230 I). This FF 209.000 was described as: *pour remise au directeur précédent, à raison de la cession de son traité.*

214 «J'acceptai pour ma part d'intérêts l'indemnité qu'on m'offrit.» ("For my part, I accepted the indemnity for my interests which was offered to me.") Véron, op. cit., III, p. 206.

215 Binet, op. cit., p. 163.

concession. He received income from his salary which totalled FF 54.000 from 1 March 1831 to 31 August 1835. He paid FF 58.729 to Duponchel in settlement of accrued receipts and expenses as at 31 May 1835. He paid FF 23.000 in fines prior to the final settlement, and lastly he was owed FF 10.000 by the State. The net overall surplus from these figures was an estimated FF 936.000 although this was rather more than the generally expressed view that he made a fortune of around FF 900.000.[216]

---

216 Séchan, op. cit., p. 196. De Boigne, op. cit., p. 84.

CHAPTER 3

The contrast between the management of the Opera in the Restoration period and that under Véron's leadership was more marked than has hitherto been realised by those who take an interest in the history of the Opera. The first two chapters served to highlight this contrast in both style and substance with special reference to the overall finances of the Opera. This chapter examines the two main cost components of any production at the Opera, namely the scenery and costumes, and adds credence to the thesis that there was a significant contrast between the two regimes. This is followed up, in chapter 4, by case studies of the cost of scenery and costumes in selected new productions. A summary of the terms used to describe the details of sets and scenery of individual new productions is also included in chapter 4.

Sets and Scenery in the Restoration Period

The high cost of new scenery was a recurring problem and the three levels of management never resolved it. Unable or unwilling to take decisive action, they took the decision to use, wherever possible, old scenery and materials in new productions. This defeatist policy showed signs of softening towards the end of the Restoration period and was completely reversed by the new policy written into Véron's 28 February 1831 *Cahier des charges*.

There were three main reasons for these high costs. The inefficiencies and malpractices of the painters; the French style of scene-painting; and the de facto monopoly of Ciceri. Each of these will be examined in detail.

Inefficiencies and Malpractices by the Painters

Inefficiencies and malpractices were rife in the Restoration period, whether explicitly prior to 1822, or implicitly after the new tariff had been established in that year. Prior to 1822, these abuses were laid bare in a scathing report on the scene-painting for a new production. This report served to expose a whole panoply of inefficiencies and malpractices and persuaded the authorities that action was necessary. The new production was *Aladin ou la Lampe merveilleuse*. It was first planned in 1816 although not finally performed until February 1822.

In November 1816 Choron, the *Régisseur général* at the Opera, sent a report to La Ferté. This set out the budget for a new opera called *La Lampe merveilleuse* which totalled FF 83.938.[1] The budget excluded any materials for making the sets as the report

---

1   *Le Régisseur général* to La Ferté, 23 November 1816, (AJ[13] 133).
    The total budget was:
    Scenery   FF 44.270
    Costumes   39.668
                                  83.938

considered that these could all be found from the old sets no longer in use and stored in the warehouses. It was also made clear that the cost of scene-painting included the cost of painters employed by the Opera as well as that incurred by external painters working freelance. In December 1816, a revised budget from Choron was sent to La Ferté. This time the total was FF 120.718.[2] This revision was necessary as the first budget had failed to include the cost of paint, estimated at around FF 6.000. The revised budget also included FF 30.780 as the cost of materials to make the sets and as though these materials were all new. Choron continued to think, however, that these materials could all be taken from the old sets and that the final cost would fall between FF 90.000 and FF 100.000.

The special interest in this budget was that it gave rise to a scathing anonymous report, December 1816, which revealed the inefficiencies and abuses which permeated the system for scene-painting.[3] This report both gave an insight into the state of affairs in 1816 and served as a reference for what took place thereafter. The first criticism was of Dégotti's budget for scene-painting. This had not included a detailed analysis of the scenery to be painted nor of its position on the stage. The consequence was that no-one had any idea of how much scenery would be needed for each set nor where the scenery should be positioned. Dégotti had thus only presented an overall impression of the number of chassis required for the whole production.[4] Despite this lack of information, the report then estimated that it would take 300 chassis to stage *La Lampe merveilleuse* and calculated that all the work should be completed in six months. This should take twenty freelance painters working jointly with the painters who were on salaries paid directly by the Opera: at that time the Opera had a dual system with painters who were paid an annual salary and formed part of the Opera's fixed personnel, and painters who were paid by the day and were thus freelance. Given the salaries of the former and the hourly rates of the latter, it was then possible to calculate the cost of scene-painting. It was unlikely that all the painters would be working all the time over the six-month period. Actual work would be the equivalent of five months of thirty days each for the freelance painters who were paid, on average, FF 6 per day. The calculations

---

2   *Le Régisseur général* to La Ferté, 8 December 1816, (AJ[13] 133).
     The total budget was:

Scenery, including paint	FF 50.270
Materials	30.780
Costumes	39.668
	120.718

3   *Observations sur le devis donné par Mr Dégotti, Peintre en chef, pour les décorations de l'opéra de la Lampe merveilleuse*, (AJ[13] 133).

4   «... un aperçu très idéal de la quantité de châssis qui composeront l'ensemble de l'ouvrage.» ("...an overall impression of the number of chassis which will constitute the whole work.") *Observations sur le devis* ..., op. cit., (AJ[13] 133). *Châssis* in this context had two meanings: one was a wing at the side of the stage and the other, translated as chassis, was a unit of value which applied to all the scenery.

were then set out in a table[5] and the conclusions were striking. Whereas Dégotti's budget, with the cost of paint now taken as FF 5.730, had totalled FF 50.000 for scene-painting, the new total was FF 31.000 which included only FF 18.000 for the freelance painters. This was a thirty-eight per cent reduction over Dégotti's budget and while this reduction seemed very large, if not unattainable, the thinking behind it was later vindicated by Véron when he negotiated a new tariff with Ciceri in 1831. Meanwhile, in 1816, the report went on to describe various malpractices which combined to raise the budget to FF 50.000 rather than FF 31.000. The hours of work laid down for the painters were not adhered to; a large part of each working day was spent doing nothing or working at the Opera's expense on other commissions; and there was no effective supervision. Looking back to previous years, the report made some comparisons. When, under Isabey, the scene-painting had all been contracted out to freelance painters, the cost per chassis had risen dramatically to an average of FF 177. This system lasted for three years from 1809 to 1812, whereupon a combination of freelance painters and the Opera's own painters was introduced. This was an improvement but due to the malpractices already referred to, the 1816 average cost per chassis was still around FF 135 to FF 140. For example, the opera *Natalie,* first staged on 30 July 1816, had cost FF 135 per chassis but had the time of the painters been better employed it would have cost only FF 85 per chassis. In this context the report was especially severe on the salaried painters employed by the Opera. It claimed that most of these painters produced no work at all. The calculations for *La Lampe merveilleuse* were then revised. The total cost was raised to FF 35.000 and the number of chassis to 368. This was an average of FF 95 per chassis which could again be compared with Dégotti's FF 50.000 and FF 167 per chassis. This was all conjecture, however, and the conclusion was that there was a need for more detailed information especially as the estimate of 368 chassis was likely to be an exaggeration since the total should not exceed 350. Given this uncertainty, however, the opera should not be staged until a detailed budget had been presented and approved. This would enable the Opera both to calculate the average cost per chassis and to see the layout on the stage:

		FF	FF
5			
Freelance painters: 20 x 5 x 30 x 6			18.000
The Opera's painters:			
Six months, head painter		2.500	
Six months, painter of architecture		1.800	
Three months, painter of figures		900	
Three months, painter of countryside		600	
Six months, four junior painters		3.000	8.800
			26.800
Paint			4.200
			31.000
Savings			19.000
Dégotti's budget			50.000

L'opéra de *La Lampe merveilleuse* ne doit être entrepris que lorsque l'on connaîtra tous les dessins de Mʳ Dégotti, que le genre de chaque décoration sera connu et que les plans de chacune d'elles seront fixés.[6]

In conclusion, the report made various recommendations so that the scene-painting could be carried out with order and without interruption. The Opera should itself choose the freelance painters and they should be called to work only to the extent that there was work to do. The daily rate for each freelance painter should be fixed in advance, and the hours of work for all painters should be fixed so that they did not arrive or leave at different times. There should be strict control of all the painters so that no-one could spend the day doing nothing or working on other commissions. The painters should be overseen with regard to the speed of their work and delinquents should be dismissed.

This case-study was very illuminating in that it highlighted the Opera's problems over scene-painting. The authorities were well aware of these problems and sought to curb the malpractices by the issue of a series of *arrêtés*. These had little effect and even when a new tariff was introduced it only served to consolidate, rather than reduce, the high cost per chassis for new productions.

The French Style of Scene-Painting

The high cost of scenery at the Opera was also due to the style in which it was painted. This became an issue in the 1820s as did the debate on the Italian bel canto style of singing and whether it was suitable for the Opera.[7]

The second anonymous writer who had called for a revolution in the style of singing at the Opera also called for a revolution in the style of scene-painting, not least because of the comparative cost of the French and Italian styles.[8] Ciceri was, by comparison with the Italian style, a high-cost scene-painter and was criticised for that reason. There were a number of telling points. La Scala in Milan held some 3.500 people which was about double the size of the Opera. For each set of a new ballet or new opera, new scenery was used and this scenery was never used in another production. If a new work failed and was withdrawn, the same canvas could be used again as it was painted over on the following day and used for another production. Furthermore, the Italian style of scene-painting was completely different to the French style. In Paris the Opera's scenery was full of little details, carefully worked and dazzling to the eye. At La Scala, on the other hand, everything was sacrificed to the overall effect. By way of example, the anonymous writer referred to the diorama in Paris and its scenes of Canterbury and Chartres cathedrals. These were most typical of the La Scala scenery painted by Sanquirico and Tranquillo. It was then claimed that each set at La Scala cost only thirty

---

6   ("The staging of *La Lampe merveilleuse* should only be undertaken when all the designs of M. Dégotti are known, when the genre of each set is known and the positions on stage for each one are fixed.") *Observations sur le devis* ..., op. cit., (AJ[13] 133).

7   The debate over the Italian bel canto style of singing is not germane to this thesis. See, however, for contributors to this debate: *Note*, unsigned and n.d., (AJ[13] 114 I); *Quelques observations sur l'Académie royale de Musique*, unsigned and n.d., (AJ[13] 180 II); Stendhal, *Vie de Rossini* (Paris, 1824).

8   *Quelques observations*..., op. cit., (AJ[13] 180 II).

gold sequins, or FF 360, and although La Scala made some 120 to 140 sets per year, the annual cost was only some FF 50.000 which was considerably less than that at the Opera. A similar comparison was also made by Stendhal.[9] Although he claimed that a set painted by Sanquirico or Tranquillo cost FF 400 and not FF 360, he compared this with the Opera where an equivalent set would have cost FF 3.000. He also drew attention to the cost of *Aladin ou la Lampe merveilleuse*. In his opinion, sets which may have cost FF 100.000 would have cost only FF 12.000 at La Scala. It followed from this that Ciceri was singled out for especial criticism as his French style of scenery cost so much. Meanwhile, the Opera had a very cumbersome system to mount new productions. When Viotti had been director at the Opera there had been a move to bring Sanquirico to Paris to do the scene-painting for at least eight to ten new productions within four months, but this had led to nothing. Idleness at the Opera had led to fright at the thought of putting on so many new works so quickly. Another point was that the Italian style made much greater use of backdrops to gain its effects. Not only was the cost much less but this led to simplification: the stage machinery was not used so much as there was less scenery to move.[10] Lastly, there was criticism over the length of time taken to mount productions. Since January 1825, a reprise of *Armide* had been in preparation but by the end of November it still had not been staged:

> ... une montagne serait plus facile à mettre en mouvement que l'Opéra français.[11]

The conclusion of this section is clear. From a financial point of view the Opera would have done well to have adopted the Italian style of scene-painting. This did not happen, however, and even Véron made no attempt to change this when he introduced competition to Ciceri by employing other French scene-painters.

The de facto Monopoly of Ciceri

The authorities in the Restoration period faced a fundamental problem in relation to its principal painters, who contracted to the Opera but could not be prevented from doing outside work. Ciceri emerged as the sole principal painter in 1822 and managed to create a monopoly for himself even though the terms of his contract were intended to forbid such a situation. His position became so strong that no-one was in a position to challenge his bills. Even when he was paid according to a new tariff, this was set at a rate favourable to him and he could still do outside work. He was undoubtedly a

---

9   Stendhal, op. cit.. Translated by Richard N. Coe, *Life of Rossini* (London, 1856), pp. 419 and 422. As an aside, it is interesting that the text of *Quelques observations* ... was, in many places, equivalent to, or closely related to, the text in Stendhal's book. This begs the question of whether Stendhal himself wrote *Quelques observations...*, or whether the anonymous writer relied heavily on Stendhal's book.

10 The use of backdrops led to «simplification pour le jeu des machines, car ils ne font pas tant d'usage que nous, des praticables, des pièces de décoration détachées, venant du dessus et du dessous.» ("simplification of the stage machinery as the backdrops do not require so many *praticables*, nor detached pieces of scenery which descend from the flies or rise up from below the stage.") *Quelques observations* ..., op. cit., (AJ[13] 180 II).

11 ("... a mountain would be easier to move than the French Opera.") *Quelques observations* ..., op. cit., (AJ[13] 180 II).

contributory factor to the high cost of scene-painting at the Opera and received a rude shock from Véron when the tariff was renegotiated and competition was introduced.

In the early years of the Restoration period, there were two principal painters at the Opera, of whom Ciceri was one, and an attempt was made in January 1818 to formalise their position and to resolve their ambiguous relationship with the Opera.[12] Under the new terms, they did not have the right to an annual salary as members of the fixed personnel, but were paid for their work on the designs and scene-painting entrusted to them. In other words they made private contracts with the Opera which could vary according to the amount of work done. Although they were not salaried employees, five per cent was deducted from all the amounts received by them and paid into the Opera's pension fund. Their status was thus that of being dependent on, and attached to, the Opera. They enjoyed all the advantages given to the salaried fixed personnel, not least that of pension rights which were calculated by reference to a fictitious salary of FF 6.000 per annum. In return for these benefits the two principal painters had to drop all outside commissions and work exclusively for the Opera provided one month's notice had been given. If they proposed too rigorous terms, such as too high a price or too lengthy a completion date, the administration reserved the right to make a contract with other painters. If this happened three times, a principal painter could lose his status and the advantages that went with it. He could also lose his pension rights and the deductions made towards it. The two painters, Ciceri and Daguerre, were, however, in a strong position and a later *arrêté* in January 1820 accepted the new terms which they proposed.[13] This time they gained a salary of FF 6.000 each and a tariff per production. For each act of an opera or ballet which required the same set they were paid a total of FF 1.000, and for each act of an opera or ballet which required different sets they were paid FF 1.500 regardless of the number of sets to be painted. An example was given in the text of the *arrêté*. A three-act production which had the same set for two acts and many sets for the third act would cost FF 2.500. Responsibility for restoring and touching up old scenery was given to the other salaried painters. This was a concession to Ciceri and Daguerre as neither wished to do the work. The two principal painters had thus gained a fixed salary and a fixed tariff on a piece-work basis. From the Opera's point of view there was an advantage in this as the two painters' costs could be controlled although, according to Du Rais, the idea of having two painters in charge did not work in practice.[14] Crucially, however, the

---

12 *Arrêté*, Pradel, *Directeur Général du Ministère de la Maison du Roi*, 9 January 1818, (AJ[13] 109 I).

13 *Arrêté*, Pradel, 31 January 1820, (AJ[13] 109 I).

14 Du Rais submitted a report which made a series of recommendations designed to reduce expenses and improve efficiency. As part of this report, he looked at the arrangement, introduced in 1820, whereby Ciceri and Daguerre were appointed joint-heads of scene-painting. In his view the establishment of joint-heads of scene-painting had not achieved its desired end as the two painters had fallen out due to rivalry. What is more, this had affected the other painters: «Ce fâcheux esprit presqu'inévitable dans toute institution de ce genre, gagne insensiblement tous les subordonnés. On discute, on intrigue au lieu de travailler; les ateliers sont presque déserts ....» ("This unfortunate attitude, which is virtually unavoidable in every institution of this kind, imperceptibly reaches all the subordinates. They talk and they scheme instead of working; the ateliers are almost empty....") *Rapport,* Du Rais to Lauriston, December 1821, (AJ[13] 144 IV).

new terms left a glaring loophole which was exploited to the Opera's disadvantage. The freelance painters were still paid on a daily basis and their costs vastly exceeded those of the two principal painters. The Opera then tried to close this loophole through a new overall tariff but failed to set the tariff at a sufficiently low level.

Ciceri further enhanced his position in 1822 when the new tariff was put into place. Dégotti had retired in January 1822 and the contract which Ciceri and Daguerre had had with the Opera was cancelled in May 1822.[15] Ciceri then signed a new contract with the Opera which left him as the sole principal painter. He agreed to abide by the new tariff and accepted the job of repainting the old sets in return for the salary of FF 6.000 per annum.[16] The contract was to run for ten years from 1 April 1822 to 1 April 1832, always provided that both the Opera and Ciceri could terminate it, having given one year's notice in April and further notice in the following October. The crux of the contract lay, however, in Ciceri's success in creating a de facto monopoly for himself. This had never been the Opera's intention as Article 2 in the preamble to the new tariff made perfectly plain:

> Tout artiste reconnu capable de composer et d'exécuter la décoration est admissible à entreprendre des travaux pour *l'Académie royale de Musique* qui devra, pour la distribution de ces travaux, avoir égard surtout au genre auquel chaque artiste est plus particulièrement habile. Par cette raison les décorations des divers actes d'un même ouvrage pourront être confiées à divers artistes.[17]

Any leading scene-painter could thus be employed by the Opera even to the extent that several could work on the same production. This was despite the fact that Ciceri was employed as the principal painter at FF 6.000 per annum.[18] La Ferté explained the Opera's position on this in a report to Lauriston.[19] Paris now had quite a lot of scene-painters who worked in a growing number of theatres and it was impossible to employ two principal painters at the Opera who did not undertake outside work as well. It would be better to employ a single principal painter who would be in overall charge and responsible for the restoration of the old sets, and to throw open the scene-painting to competition from other painters. This made good sense as the scenery required was to become much more varied and it was unlikely that any single painter would be sufficiently capable or experienced to paint in the required variety of genres. Through competition, the Opera would be in a position to select those painters who were judged best in particular genres. La Ferté also explained the Opera's position in a letter to

---

15 Nicole Wild, *Décors et Costumes du XIX Siècle, Tome II, Théâtres et Décorateurs* (Paris, *Bibliothèque Nationale*, 1993), pp. 297–301.

16 Contract between Ciceri and the Opera, 1 April 1822, (O³ 1685 I).

17 ("Every artist recognised as able to design and paint the scenery is eligible to work for the Opera. When it allocates the work, the Opera will take into account the genre in which each artist has especial skills. As a result, the scenery for the various acts of the same production could be given to various painters.") *Arrêté*, Lauriston, 13 March 1822, (O³ 1685 I).

18 Article 3. «Il y aura néanmoins près de l'administration de l'Académie royale, un peintre en chef ayant titre de premier peintre conservateur des décorations avec un traitement de FF 6.000.» ("There will, nevertheless, be one head-painter close to the administration of the Opera. His title will be first painter-curator of scenery with a salary of FF 6.000 per annum.") *Arrêté*, Lauriston, 13 March 1822, (O³ 1685 I).

19 Report, La Ferté to Lauriston, n.d., (O³ 1659).

Habeneck and left the latter in no doubt about the Opera's intentions. Although preference should be given to Ciceri, this should not prejudice the Opera's ability to employ other painters:

> Il est juste qu'on lui donne la préférence pour les entreprises lucratives, toutes les fois que cela se pourra faire sans préjudice du service; mais qu'on ne peut en aucun cas faire de cette préférence une obligation pour l'administration, ce serait aller contre l'esprit du nouveau règlement et l'infirmer en ce qu'il a d'utile dans l'intérêt de la scène, à savoir la faculté de faire exécuter les diverses sortes de décorations par les peintres les plus habiles en chaque genre.[20]

This intent was, however, diluted by Ciceri's insistence, perhaps based on his experience as one of two principal painters with Daguerre, that it was impossible for him to work on the same production alongside other painters on an equal basis. As this reservation was included in his signed contract, the point was conceded by the authorities. The practical result was that Ciceri used his preferential position to the full and there was no record of any bills from any scene-painter other than Ciceri in the Restoration period up to July 1830. He had created a de facto monopoly for himself despite the Opera's initial preference in favour of competition. The main reason for this new system of scene-painting, which was to attract the best painters for differing genres of scenery, was thus fatally undermined.

When the second anonymous writer made his comparison between La Scala and the Opera, he criticised Ciceri severely. Although there was a new fixed tariff per chassis which, on the face of it, should have kept the cost of scene-painting under control, this had not happened. Ciceri submitted his bills based on an approximate budget, payments in advance were made, and no-one discussed the bills for the simple reason that no-one had the competence to do so:

> ... car pour cela il faudrait être peintre des décorations.[21]

Ciceri's monopoly position had given him the ability to charge what he liked. He could not change the tariff prices but he could charge for more chassis than were actually included in the scenery or change the genre of chassis to his advantage.[22] This was a significant observation since what, in theory, should have been a successful way to control costs was, in practice, not so. A further criticism was that although the Opera provided an atelier for Ciceri, he used it to supply scenery for other theatres even to the extent of holding up work on behalf of the Opera. The first anonymous writer already referred to also criticised Ciceri. It was a great abuse to have a monopolistic principal

---

20 ("Whenever possible, and without prejudice to the service, it is right to give him the preference for the profitable work; this preference, however, must never become an obligation for the administration as that would go against the spirit of the new regulation and invalidate its usefulness: which is that the interests of the stage are best served through having the facility to mount a diversity of scenes painted by the most skilful painters in each genre.") La Ferté to Habeneck, 4 May 1822, (AJ[13] 113 I).

21 ("...because for that it would be necessary to be a scene-painter.") *Quelques observations ...*, op. cit., (AJ[13] 180 II).

22 *Quelques observations ...*, op. cit., (AJ[13] 180 II).

painter at the Opera. Ciceri's prerogative excluded other French and foreign painters and he held the Opera under a perpetual yoke. He could also charge what he pleased.[23]

There were thus three main reasons for the high cost of new sets and scenery in the Restoration period: the inefficiencies and malpractices of the scene-painters, the French style of scene-painting, and the de facto monopoly of Ciceri. The authorities were, of course, aware of these problems but the management was too weak to do much about it. With the rapid turnover of directors and the persistent interference of the authorities, this was hardly surprising. Nevertheless the Opera did try to curb the excesses, especially through the introduction of a tariff, and these attempts are the subject of the next section.

The Reaction of the Authorities

The various attempts to control, if not reduce, the cost of new scenery at the Opera were well-intentioned but unsuccessful. As a result the authorities came to rely on the only remaining option open to them which was to make extensive use of old materials and scenery in new productions. The attempts at control were, in principle, four in total. The unsuccessful one to control Ciceri has already been described and the other three were the exorbitant cost of the freelance painters; the establishment of budgets; and the new tariff.

The Exorbitant Cost of the Freelance Painters

The scathing report on Dégotti's budget for *La Lampe merveilleuse* was clearly taken to heart by the authorities. One month later in January 1817, an *arrêté* was issued which sought to correct the abuses highlighted in the report.[24] It contained detailed proposals which reflected the bureaucratic way in which the authorities tried to solve the problem of the freelance painters. A new post of inspector-general of the atelier was decreed. By preference the holder of this office should be a former scene-painter. He would join the staff of the Opera and rank after the principal painters. All the salaried painters, except for the two principal painters, all the freelance painters and generally everyone else attached to the atelier would be subject to his inspection in all matters concerning hours of work and the policing of the atelier. All the painters were required to report to the atelier at eight o'clock every day except Sunday, and work there under the orders of the principal painters. They could take one hour for lunch from ten to eleven o'clock and then work until the end of the day. The junior painters had to report at seven o'clock and could not finally leave until all the painters and the inspector-general had themselves left and everything in the atelier had been tidied up. They had to stagger their lunch hours so that there was always at least one in the atelier. The storeman had to be at his post by eight o'clock and stay there until work had finished. He could not hand over any item under his care unless ordered to do so by one of the principal painters who signed an acknowledgement of receipt which was also stamped by the inspector-general. The

---

23   The *Note*, op. cit., (AJ[13] 114 I).

24   *Arrêté*, Pradel, 3 January 1817, (AJ[13] 109 I).

storeman also had to submit a monthly inventory to the director. Here again, albeit on a small scale, was the principle of three levels of management which was applied to the overall management of the Opera. No-one could leave the atelier during the hours of work without reasonable cause and without the permission of one of the principal painters. No-one could be absent for more than a day without permission from the director which was based on a report from the principal painters. The principal painters should submit all requests for freelance painters to the inspector-general who, in turn, should submit them to the director. The latter should then decide the number, choice and daily rate of the freelance painters to be called for work.

Were all the Opera's problems to have been resolved by this wave of a Ministerial wand, then all would have been well. Unfortunately, however, the appointment of an inspector-general did little to change the culture of waste and inefficiency which characterised the Opera in the Restoration period and a further series of *arrêtés* were issued by the authorities in the early 1820s. These attempted to control the activities of scene-painting through a redistribution of responsibilities. Desfontaines, the inspector-general, was made redundant in August 1822, as was Mitoire, the storeman, and a new post of *Chef de matériel* was created as well as one called *Régisseur de la Scène*. From July 1823 to December 1825 further *arrêtés* shuffled the pack of posts and responsibilities but seemingly to no avail, especially as the tariff had already been fixed.[25] Weak management, which itself changed too often, was the real problem and it took the shock of Véron's cost-conscious regime to effect any significant improvement.

These failures were conclusively proven by the final outcome for *Aladin ou la Lampe merveilleuse* which was eventually staged in February 1822. The freelance painters started work on the scenery as early as March 1820 but did not finish until December 1821, a total of twenty-two months.[26] They were, as already noted, paid by the day at varying rates[27] and the monthly time-sheets showed the hours spent and the total costs per month. In March 1821 alone, forty-four freelance painters worked on the scenery for a total of 741 man-days and a cost of FF 4.206. The total man-days worked over the twenty-two months was a startling 13.183[28] for a cost of FF 68.726. This can be compared with the original estimate of 3.000 man-days at a cost of FF 18.000, and with the relatively small FF 7.000 bill from Ciceri and Daguerre which was in line with their agreed tariff. It can also be compared with a report which Ciceri submitted on

---

25 *Arrêté*, Lauriston, 14 August 1822, (AJ[13] 109 I). *Arrêté*, La Ferté, 10 July 1823, (AJ[13] 113 I). *Arrêté*, La Rochefoucauld, 14 March 1825, (AJ[13] 109 I). *Arrêté*, La Rochefoucauld, 26 November 1824, (AJ[13] 109 I). *Arrêté*, La Rochefoucauld, 4 April 1825, (AJ[13] 109 I). *Projet*, La Rochefoucauld, 30 December 1825, (AJ[13] 109 I).

26 *Fournitures faites par peintres externes qui ont travaillé aux décorations de la Lampe merveilleuse*, (AJ[13] 172 II).

27 The daily rates charged varied according to the status and speciality of the freelance painters, e.g.:

    Peintre de figures   FF 12 per day.
    Peintre de fleurs et architecture   8 per day.
    Peintre d'ornements   5 per day.
    Peintre garçon   2.50 per day

28 *Fournitures faites ...*, op. cit., (AJ[13] 172 II).

1 September 1821, which was countersigned by Desfontaines.[29] By that date, FF 66.867 had been spent on the scene-painting for *Aladin ou la Lampe merveilleuse*, of which FF 53.487 was for the freelance painters. Ciceri also estimated the cost of scene-painting still to be completed. This totalled FF 20.900, of which FF 12.600 was for the freelance painters who thus were estimated to cost a total of FF 66.087. As a result of this report a revised budget for scene-painting and materials, including paint and other items, was sent to Lauriston for approval. It totalled FF 114.877 of which FF 87.767 was as per Ciceri's report and FF 27.110 was for materials to make the sets. This sum must have been a great shock to the authorities and when La Ferté advised Courtin that Lauriston had approved this budget he left Courtin in no doubt about Lauriston's views:

> Son Excellence remarque combien cette dépense est exorbitante, hors de toute raison; et elle ajoute qu'elle ne donnerait pas son approbation si ce n'était chose trop avancée, pour qu'il fût possible de revenir à une exécution plus sagement ordonnée. De là naissent des observations sur la nécessité d'apporter des changements dans la partie des règlements relative aux ateliers de peinture.[30]

As the cost was indeed exorbitant, the time had come to change the way in which the scene-painting was carried out and to make a fundamental re-appraisal of how these costs could be controlled. Even although the monthly time-sheets, and Ciceri's report on the cost of the work already completed, had been signed by Desfontaines, the inspector-general, and in the case of the time-sheets, countersigned by the director, the new system of inspection and control had shown little practical benefit. As for the amount of time it took the freelance painters to complete their work, twenty-two months can be compared unfavourably with the situation at La Scala.

The Establishment of Budgets

It has already been noted that there were three levels of budget. First, the annual budget for the Royal theatres which was administered by the *Maison du Roi*. Second, the annual budget for the Opera itself which was approved by the *Maison du Roi*, and third, the budgets for each new production. The basis for the third level was laid down in the 5 May 1821 *Règlement*.[31] In the first instance, the *projet de budget* for the ensuing year should include a list of all the works submitted to the Opera and the Minister should then select four of them, two operas and two ballets, for performance.[32] At this point, the Minister would only have seen the libretto and an approximate budget,[33] but once the four works had been selected, a new budget should be prepared. Instead of a budget

---

29 *État de la situation des décorations de La Lampe merveilleuse, tant de ce qui est fait que de ce qui reste à faire à l'époque du 1ᵉʳ septembre 1821, pour ce qui concerne la partie des Peintres.* Signed by Ciceri and Desfontaines, 1 September 1821, (F²¹ 1069).

30 ("His Excellency notes to what extent this expense is exorbitant and unreasonable; and adds that he would not give his approval were it not already too late to be able to mount a production which was better controlled. It follows that there is a need to introduce changes to the regulations which govern the ateliers.") La Ferté to Courtin, 4 October 1821, (F²¹ 1069).

31 *5 mai 1821 Règlement*, Articles 23 to 27, (AJ¹³ 1186).

32 *5 mai 1821 Règlement*, Article 25, (AJ¹³ 1186).

33 *5 mai 1821 Règlement*, Article 23, (AJ¹³ 1186).

which was general and approximate, the new budget should be detailed and precise and should specify, in the greatest detail, all the costumes, materials and scenery, and the cost of each item. It should also be costed from two points of view: first, as though all the items were new; and second, as though all the usable items which were already stored in the warehouses were included, as thought fit by the various heads of department at the Opera. This second new reduced budget should then be submitted to the Minister for approval, and no expense could be incurred until this approval had been given.[34] These procedures were modified in 1826 when La Rochefoucauld tried to bring further control to the budget process. He stipulated that an inspector from the *Beaux-Arts* should attend the meetings at which the details of a production budget were discussed.[35] This detailed budget should then be further discussed in a formal *Conseil d'administration* which would seek to reduce it through the use of old scenery, costumes and materials. Finally, the modified budget should then be sent to the Minister for approval.

The practice, however, failed to conform to the theoretical regulations laid down. Lubbert had a cavalier attitude to financial matters in general, as seen especially in 1829, and was no less cavalier when it came to individual productions. There was a growing complaint from both La Bouillerie and La Rochefoucauld that the budgets for scene-painting, costumes and materials were not submitted in sufficient time for proper scrutiny, as laid down by the 5 May 1821 *Règlement*. The fact was, however, that the authorities were unable or unwilling to enforce these regulations as the analysis of individual new productions will show.

The New Tariff

Although the *arrêté* which established this new tariff was dated 13 March 1822, a great deal of discussion had taken place prior to this date. In November 1821, for example, La Ferté requested a meeting, which included Ciceri, Dégotti and Daguerre, and which discussed the setting up of a new tariff for scenery.[36] The exorbitant cost of the freelance painters for *Aladin ou La Lampe merveilleuse* had already caused considerable concern to Lauriston and the desire for change was strong. In February 1822, La Ferté, by then in possession of a detailed breakdown of the final cost of scene-painting and materials for *Aladin ou la Lampe merveilleuse* was able to send to Lauriston the details of the new tariff.[37] He compared the actual cost of the sets for *Aladin ou la Lampe merveilleuse* with what it would have been under the new tariff. The former was FF 102.225 and the latter FF 73.560. The savings of FF 28.665 were mostly as a result of the proposed demise of the salaried painters employed by the Opera as fixed personnel. Ciceri and Daguerre each cost FF 6.000 per annum so there would be a saving of FF 12.000. There were seven other salaried painters who cost FF 13.700 per annum and a man who guarded the storeroom who cost FF 1.800. The total annual saving would thus be FF 27.500. Added to this was the proposed abolition of the tariff

---

34   *5 mai 1821 Règlement*, Articles 26 and 27, (AJ[13] 1186).

35   La Rochefoucauld to Duplantys, 26 March 1826, (AJ[13] 117).

36   La Ferté to Habeneck, 9 November 1821, (AJ[13] 112 I).

37   La Ferté to Lauriston, 23 February 1822, (O[3] 1659).

for the two principal painters which was estimated at FF 12.000 per annum. The overall identifiable savings would thus be FF 39.500 per annum, but there would also be savings on paint and other materials, the cost of which would be consolidated into the new tariff rather than paid for by the Opera as separate items. From the Opera's point of view, this all made good sense but there was, again, a notable omission in these calculations. There were no proposals to reduce the costs of the freelance painters, nor to deal with the many malpractices in which they indulged. As a result, the new tariff was set at too high a level and Ciceri, having created his de facto monopoly, could take advantage of this.

On a wider canvas the Romantic movement, aided by a period of peace and prosperity under the Restoration, was ushering in a period of aesthetic change in the arts. The background to this aesthetic change has already been well described by many writers.[38] It suffices here to summarise its effect on the scenery at the Opera as being one which opened it up to outside influences. As a result, the genres in which scenery was painted were broadened and diversified. The new tariff recognised this and tried to combine the practical with the aesthetic. As it represented a radical departure from all that had gone before, it is worth a detailed analysis. In his preamble, Lauriston noted that it was more important than ever to bring order, precision and economy to the activity of scene-painting and that the way to achieve this was to determine the cost of scene-painting through a new fixed tariff, one level set for the Opera and another for the *Théâtre Italien*. Furthermore, the scene-painting, apart from Ciceri, should be carried out on a freelance basis which meant that the painters who formed part of the Opera's fixed personnel would be made redundant. As already noted, this system had already been tried for the three years 1809–1812, but with disastrous results as the cost per chassis had soared. This time the authorities sought to control the cost through a new tariff which had two basic concepts. First, the word *espèce*. In this context *espèce* meant genre, and was the Opera's response to the aesthetic changes which were taking place. There were ten genres of scenery which embraced a wide range of scenes and architecture. Second, the word *châssis*. The tariff was based on a price per chassis which varied with each genre. This was the Opera's practical attempt to quantify, in advance, the costs it would incur for the total number of chassis within each genre.[39]

It was likely that the scenery for the Opera's 1820s' productions was more elaborate than that referred to by the critic of Dégotti's budget in 1816. The new aesthetic extended the range of scenes to be painted and the amount of detail required. Nevertheless, when the critic's estimate of FF 95 per chassis for *Aladin ou la Lampe merveilleuse* is compared with the new 1822 tariff, the impression gained is of a tariff set at a very high cost per chassis. It was as though the excesses and malpractices of the freelance painters had been consolidated into this new tariff. Although the Opera had closed one loophole in that it had established a ceiling for the cost per chassis within the various genres, it had failed to reduce the ceilings to a level which represented an elimination of the many malpractices already described:

---

38   See, for example, Johnson, op. cit., pp. 336–399.

39   *Arrêté*, Lauriston, 13 March 1822, (O³ 1685 I), (AJ¹³ 109 IV), (AJ¹³ 113 I).

The 1822 Tariff

	Genre	FF per Chassis
1st	Clear Sky	35
	Storms, seas, etc	50
	Clouds	50
	Clouds with figures coloriées	130
2nd	Country scenes	100/120
3rd	Military & other camps	140
4th	Rural architecture	120/135
5th	Military architecture	160
6th	Naval architecture	160
7th	Civil architecture	200
8th	Noble & rich architecture	220/240
9th	Majestic & magnificent architecture	260
10th	Fantastical architecture	400

The new tariff also handed over enormous power to Ciceri, quite apart from his de facto monopoly. It was he who submitted the budgets and bills for all the scene-painting in a new production, based on the new tariff. The scope for him was obvious. He could over-estimate the number of chassis required when submitting his approximate and definitive budgets; he could make use of fewer chassis than the budget stipulated, as no-one had the expertise to challenge him; he was assured of a high price per chassis; he had every incentive to achieve economies from his freelance painters as he, not the Opera, would pocket the savings; and no-one was in a position to query his final bills. His monopoly position and the high cost of the new tariff were both referred to by Du Rais in another of his reports.[40] He calculated that the direct cost of scene-painting for

40 *Observations extraites d'un Rapport adressé par M. Du Rais, Chef du matériel de l'Académie royale de Musique à M.M. les membres chargés de l'examen et de l'apurement des comptes de cette administration*, $(O^3\ 1707\ I)$. Du Rais felt that the new tariff for scene-painting was more expensive than that previously in place. As an example, he drew up a table of six productions and contrasted what they had actually cost with what they would have cost were the new tariff to have been in place.

Production	Painter	No. of Chassis	Cost * FF	Cost of Tariff* FF	Difference * FF
Castor et Pollux	Dégotti	235	22.770	39.960	17.190
Achille à Scyros	- do -	154	17.552	28.125	10.573
Nathalie	- do -	225	21.528	32.100	10.572
Les Danaides	- do -	179	15.054	34.420	19.366
Proserpine	Ciceri	218	17.437	27.560	10.123
Clary	Ciceri	161	25.135	33.920	8.785
		1.172	119.476	196.085	76.609

* There were a number of addition errors in these tables which have been corrected. Du Rais also commented on Ciceri's position under the new tariff. His contract was «... à proprement parler un privilège exclusif qu'il a obtenu, pour exécuter à un prix exorbitant les décorations de l'Opéra, un vrai monopole ....» ("... strictly speaking, he had obtained an exclusive privilege to paint the scenery at the Opera at an exorbitant price; it was a real monopoly ....")

six old productions would have been some sixty-four per cent higher were the new tariff to have been used.

The Articles in the preamble to the new tariff contained other less important points. The cost per chassis included the cost of paint but the Opera would supply all the materials required to make the sets, as well as the heating and lighting of the atelier. If an old chassis needed to be entirely repainted rather than just touched up, Ciceri could charge two-thirds of the tariff price. A fixed term should be set for the completion of the scene-painting and fines for late delivery could be levied via an agreed formula. The Opera would pay one-third of the total cost at the start of work, a further one-third when the work was one-third completed and the balance after the scenery had been installed on the stage.

With this new tariff, the Restoration authorities attempted to bring order, precision and economy to the scene-painting, but this was not achieved. The authorities realised this in the later 1820s but as they were saddled with a high-cost tariff, the only way to keep costs down was to depend on old materials to build the sets and to use old scenery as much as possible.

The Use of Old Materials and Scenery

In early 1826 Ciceri took over from Blanchard at the *Théâtre Italien*.[41] As a result, his salary was raised to FF 10.000 per annum of which FF 6.000 was paid by the Opera and FF 4.000 by the *Théâtre Italien*.[42] In raising Ciceri's salary, La Rochefoucauld made two stipulations. First, Ciceri should always have a team to maintain the chassis and to touch up the scenery at both theatres. This work should be done in such a way that the public was not offended:

> ... qu'elles n'offrissent plus aux regards du public de ces disparates choquantes qui le mécontentent avec juste raison.[43]

Second, old sets and scenery which needed repair should immediately be made good by Ciceri and his team. A note on La Rochefoucauld's letter, presumably by Duplantys, requested that La Rochefoucauld's order be communicated to the various heads of department so that the old sets could be examined and those needing restoration be sent to the atelier. In September 1826 Ciceri submitted a report to Duplantys which listed the number of sets repaired since January 1826.[44] Work had been carried out on the sets of eleven old productions and covered the equivalent of 432 chassis. No prices were quoted which was in accord with Ciceri's contract when his salary was raised to FF 10.000 per annum. On the other hand, he submitted a separate bill for work done on the sets of *La Caravane* and *Clary*. In the first case, there had been an entire repaint, mostly on new canvas, which cost FF 2.182 and, in the second, part of the set had been

---

41   La Rochefoucauld to Duplantys, 9 January 1826, (AJ[13] 117).

42   La Rochefoucauld to Duplantys, 24 January 1826, (AJ[13] 117).

43   ("... so that they no longer offer to the public these shockingly ill-assorted sets which with just reason infuriate it.") La Rochefoucauld to Duplantys, 24 January 1826, (AJ[13] 117).

44   *Rapport*, Ciceri to Duplantys, 6 September 1826, (AJ[13] 119 III).

entirely repainted for a cost of FF 1.200. The normal tariff here was FF 200 per chassis, but this had been reduced to FF 150 and not by a third as stipulated in the 1822 *arrêté*.

The reason for dwelling on this work to maintain the old sets in good repair is that it gives an insight into the authorities' attitude towards the cost of new productions. This was revealed in a whole series of letters from La Rochefoucauld, of which one in January 1826 was especially relevant. He opened by asking Duplantys whether it was possible to achieve economies in the considerable cost of new productions by using all the resources in the warehouses.[45] In other words, as no-one was prepared to change the tariff, the only way to reduce the inordinate cost of scene-painting was to concentrate on using old scenery instead, especially as the cost of restoration work was included in Ciceri's salary. La Rochefoucauld then referred to the authorities' inability to evaluate the budgets for scene-painting as sufficient detail was not attached to them. Were this to be so, it would be evidence that the resources in the warehouses had been utilised and that great savings had resulted. Provided a theatrical illusion was sufficiently maintained, old scenery should be preferred as it saved so much money. Throughout most of the 1820s, La Rochefoucauld continued to harp on the need to make savings through a better scrutiny of the budgets and the use of old scenery and costumes. For instance, he referred to the forthcoming production of *Le Siège de Corinthe*, and to the need to examine and approve the budget:

> ... après avoir reconnu et décidé quels sont, parmi les objets existant dans les magasins, ceux dont on peut faire usage en déduction de la dépense. ... afin que je puisse en approuver ou modifier les dispositions, et prononcer, du moins avec quelque certitude, sur les propositions qui me sont faites.[46]

The budget, thus verified and regulated, should then be submitted to him. As already mentioned, however, his efforts were to little avail especially after Lubbert had taken over as director. Indeed, it would appear as though there was a change of heart towards the end of the Restoration period when very little old scenery was used.

In response to the aesthetic changes taking place in the 1820s, and also to the competition from the boulevard theatres, La Rochefoucauld set up a *Comité consultatif de la mise en scène* with Comte Turpin de Crissé, *inspecteur général des Beaux-Arts*, as its President.[47] It included outside members and was charged with looking at the whole question of how the Opera could improve the design and presentation of its new productions. Its remit, however, did not extend to budgets although La Rochefoucauld wrote to Lubbert in June 1828 with the suggestion that the Committee should meet in order to discuss the estimated budgets of works soon to be performed.[48] He received an interesting reply from Lubbert[49] who pointed out that the Committee had been

---

45 La Rochefoucauld to Duplantys, 24 January 1826, (AJ[13] 117).

46 ("... having identified and decided which items can be used from the warehouses in order to reduce the cost. ... so that I can approve or modify the lay-out, and decide, at least with some certainty, on the proposals put to me.") La Rochefoucauld to Duplantys, 25 March 1826, (AJ[13] 117).

47 *Arrêté*, La Rochefoucauld, 3 April 1827, (AJ[13] 109 I).

48 La Rochefoucauld to Lubbert, 9 June 1828, (O[3] 1680).

49 Lubbert to La Rochefoucauld, 11 June 1828, (O[3] 1680).

established to give advice on the plans and designs of scenery, costumes and machinery. It should not concern itself with estimated budgets and should remain completely uninformed on budgetary matters. Lubbert's reason for this was illuminating. The Committee had outside members and it would be dangerous if they, and therefore the public at large, were to be in the know on budgets. Better the budgets remained secret so that the public had the impression that they were higher than they were in reality.[50] These comments neatly summarised the Opera's position. Saddled with the need to present the theatrical illusion of pomp and grandeur to the public, the private reality of waste and abuse meant that it could only do this by skimping on new scenery and by re-using that from old productions. The Opera had every incentive to encourage the idea that it spent more on the mises-en-scène than it actually had. This attitude will be further explored in chapter 4, especially when the cost of *La Muette de Portici* is analysed.

In conclusion, the authorities failed to curb the malpractices rife in the Restoration period. The exorbitant cost of the freelance painters had been consolidated into a new tariff which was itself too high, and the new system of budgets failed to provide sufficient information on a timely basis. Ciceri gained a de facto monopoly and used it to his advantage. The only way out was to use old scenery, provided the illusion of grandeur could be maintained, but even this policy became less tenable by the end of the 1820s. All this changed dramatically, however, after Véron took over.

Sets and Scenery under Véron's Administration

The arrival of Véron and the extensive changes which affected the fixed personnel and most suppliers have already been described. Given Véron's motivation to make as much money as possible out of his six-year concession as director, it was no surprise that he soon looked at ways to reduce the cost of scene-painting and of materials to build the sets, not least because his 28 February 1831 *Cahier des charges* had signalled a complete change in policy. This has also been described through the FF 1.000 fine imposed on Véron for the use of old scenery in *Le Serment*. Nevertheless, the chain of events which led to Véron's final resignation was such that a more detailed look at the 28 February 1831 *Cahier des charges* and the two supplements is warranted, as it reveals links in the chain which concerned the use of old scenery and materials.

On the face of it, Article 11 of the 28 February 1831 *Cahier des charges* was very straightforward. New productions had to be staged with new scenery and new costumes.[51] The Commission was the supreme judge in this matter and it alone could authorise the use of old scenery. There was, however, an imprecision here as no distinction was made between the actual scenery and the materials which were used to make the sets. The Restoration period had made this distinction for the good reason that the materials used to make the sets could cost an exorbitant amount of money unless old

50   «Telles sont les dépenses de la mise en scène des ouvrages que l'on a intérêt, vous le savez, à faire croire au public plus élévées qu'elles ne le sont réellement.» ("Such are the expenses of the mises-en-scène that it is in our interests, you will understand, to let the public believe that they are higher than they really are.") Lubbert to La Rochefoucauld, 11 June 1828, (O³ 1680).

51   *Cahier des charges*, 28 February 1831, Article 11, (AJ¹³ 187 I).

materials were used. Véron thus had every incentive to take advantage of this lack of clarity and he exploited it to the full. For example, when he applied for permission to use old scenery and materials to make the new sets for *Gustave III*, he could point out that although old backdrops were used, they were completely repainted. As for the old wings and *fermes*, they were used as materials to make the new sets:

> Cet ouvrage se composera de cinq décorations; les dessins de toutes ces décorations sont originaux, aucun châssis, aucune ferme, aucun rideau de l'ancien, ni du nouveau répertoire ne concourra comme peinture à l'ensemble de ces décorations; en un mot, tous les décors de ce nouvel ouvrage seront entièrement peints à neuf. Les rideaux de l'ancien répertoire dont je demande à me servir seront lavés et imprimés à neuf pour recevoir les nouvelles peintures.
>
> Les châssis et fermes dont je demande aussi l'usage, ne seront employés que pour la construction des décors nouveaux.[52]

In all of this he was initially aided by the delay in completing an inventory of the sets and other items. His 28 February 1831 *Cahier des charges* had stipulated, Article 13, that an inventory should immediately be taken of all the sets, costumes and other items as at 1 June 1831, so that the authorities and Véron could agree on exactly what was in existence at that date.[53] Unfortunately, however, there was a considerable delay over this inventory by Adam and Contant, and it was not finalised until January 1832.[54] The authorities were very concerned about this delay and also by the fact that no inventory was made of the sets for the new productions staged by Véron. Choiseul had written to d'Argout on 20 September 1831 to advise that the inventory was virtually completed but by November 1831 d'Argout still had not received the details.[55] He was especially concerned as the commission of the Chamber of Deputies, charged with examining the annual budget, had asked about the inventory and d'Argout, wrongly as it turned out, had advised them along the lines of Choiseul's letter: it was very important to assure the Chamber of Deputies that the guarantees inherent in Article 13 of the 28 February 1831 *Cahier des charges* were fulfilled. By May 1832, although the inventory of the old sets had been completed, that for the four new productions staged by Véron had not. Montalivet impressed on Choiseul the importance of these inventories and requested the final report.[56] This was presented to d'Argout on 30 June 1832 but was still not complete. The Minister pointed out that although the inventories for the costumes and movables were done, those for the old and new sets were still to be completed.[57] As the latter should include details of the old materials used for making

---

52 ("This work will consist of five sets; the designs of all the sets are original; no wing, *ferme* or backdrop comes from the old sets and there is no painting from the scenery of the new repertoire which will be used to help create this scenery; in a word, all the scenery of this new work will have entirely new paint. The requested backdrops from the old repertoire will be washed and newly traced to be ready for the new paint.

The wings and *fermes* which I am also requesting will only be used to construct the new sets.") Véron to the Commission, 20 October 1832, (F²¹ 1071).

53 *Cahier des charges*, 28 February 1831, Article 13, (AJ¹³ 187 I).

54 *Inventaire* by Adam and Contant, 12 January 1832, (AJ¹³ 223).

55 D'Argout to Choiseul, 27 November 1831, (F²¹ 1053).

56 Montalivet to Choiseul, 24 May 1832, (F²¹ 1054).

57 D'Argout to Choiseul, 9 August 1832, (F²¹ 1053).

the new sets, this was, as it turned out, a serious failure. The fact was that Véron had a lot of scope to take full advantage of this delay in completing the inventories. Despite the fact that he had to gain permission to use the old sets to make his new ones, the authorities were not in a position to know exactly how much he had taken nor the value to him of doing so. If an anonymous report on 30 May 1832 was to be believed, he plundered the old sets. The writer was highly indignant about Véron's management and tipped off the authorities that a machinist called Chatesil could confirm Véron's deceptions. As for *Robert le Diable*, he wrote:

> M. Véron a trompé le Ministère dès son début dans sa gestion. Dans son marché avec le gouvernement, il lui a été alloué une somme de FF 80.000 pour monter *Robert le Diable* avec la condition expresse que tout serait neuf. Au lieu de remplir son engagement il a pris les matériaux …, on en estime la valeur à FF 100.000; tout a passé dans les châssis de *Robert le Diable*.[58]

As for other new productions, he wrote:

> On a détruit en plus beaucoup de plafonds, rideaux et châssis pour monter les différents ouvrages depuis l'administration Véron jusqu'à l'ouvrage de *La Tentation de St. Antoine* qu'on monte en ce moment.[59]

Out of a total estimated value of FF 2.000.000 for sets and accessories, the report estimated that Véron had, overall, appropriated materials valued at FF 300.000.

This imprecision over the scenery and the materials to make the sets was, however, even more significant when the impact of Article 13 in the 28 February 1831 *Cahier des charges* was brought home to the Minister and the Commission. This article implied that the new sets and costumes created by Véron belonged to him and that he could sell them back to the State at an agreed value when he ceased to be the director.[60] Véron had thus spotted a good opportunity to make a double profit out of the State. He could incorporate old materials into his new sets at no cost to himself and then sell the same sets to the State. The authorities came to realise this and set about redressing the imbalance. Véron was allowed to continue to use old materials to make his new sets, but the ownership of the sets was progressively changed. The first supplement to the *Cahier des charges*, 30 May 1831, created a compromise. Although the new sets were deemed to belong to the State especially as the annual subsidy contributed towards their cost, it was recognised that Véron was required to stage many new productions at considerable expense to himself. A new Article 13 resolved this difficulty by stating that the sets

---

58   ("M. Véron has deceived the Ministry right from the start of his management. In his contract with the government he was allocated FF 80.000 to stage *Robert le Diable* with the express condition that everything would be new. Instead of fulfilling his contract he has taken materials …, with an estimated value of FF 100.000, all of which have gone into the chassis of *Robert le Diable*.") Report, unsigned, 30 May 1832, (F^{21} 1054).

59   ("A lot of borders, backdrops and wings have been destroyed in order to stage other works under Véron's administration, including *La Tentation de St. Antoine*, which is now in preparation.") Report, unsigned, 30 May 1832, (F^{21} 1054).

60   «L'administration pourra, à son gré, conserver le surplus des costumes et décorations créés par l'entrepreneur, en lui payant la valeur, à dire d'experts respectivement choisis.» ("The administration will, at its own choosing, be able to retain the surplus of costumes and scenery created by the concessionaire and will pay him the value as agreed by the respective chosen experts.") *Cahier des charges*, 28 February 1831, Article 13, (AJ^{13} 187 I).

created by Véron should, at the end of his concession as director, be regarded as being owned as to fifty per cent by Véron and fifty per cent by the State.[61] At this stage Véron had thus lost half any agreed value. The second supplement, 14 May 1833, was, however, disastrous for Véron. It stated that Véron's sets belonged wholly to the State whatever the 30 May 1831 supplement had said.[62] The loss of value compared with that agreed in the 28 February 1831 *Cahier des charges* was total and this considerable change for the worse must have exacerbated the breakdown in trust between Véron and the authorities. Véron had won the battle to use old materials to make the new sets but had lost the war over the latter's ownership.

Véron also gained a pyrrhic victory over the use of old scenery in new productions. As an exception, the Commission could authorise the use of old scenery provided all the repairs deemed suitable had been carried out,[63] but this position was softened somewhat in the second supplement to the *Cahier des charges*, 14 May 1833. The old productions were divided into two categories: the first was those productions which could be re-staged and the second was those productions which had been abandoned. The first could be used in Véron's new productions provided the scenery had not been altered and only the painting had been touched up. The second could be used by Véron for new productions provided the scenery had been repainted or the sets had been used as materials to make the new sets. Exceptionally, scenery from the second category could be used in new productions without having been repainted or touched up provided that they contributed to the general effect and only after the Commission's approval had been granted.[64] Véron thus had gained much greater flexibility over the use of old

---

61 «Le moyen de concilier les deux prétentions a paru devoir consister dans un partage égal, à la fin de l'entreprise.» ("The way to reconcile the two claims seemed to consist in an equal share at the end of the concession.") *Cahier des charges*, first supplement, 30 May 1831, Article 13, (AJ[13] 187 I).

62 «L'entrepreneur, à la fin de son bail, … n'aura aucun droit de propriété sur les décorations des états ci-annexés, sous quelques formes qu'elles soient, ni sur les décorations qu'il aura fait construire à neuf pendant la durée de sa gestion: le tout appartiendra à l'État, sans indemnité ni répétitions quelconques, et nonobstant la disposition contraire insérée à l'appendice du 30 mai 1831.» ("At the end of his tenure, … the concessionaire will have no right of ownership over the scenery as annexed, whatever the form; nor over the scenery that he will have made during his concession: it will all belong to the State without any compensation or renegotiation, and despite the contrary view inserted in the appendix of 30 May 1831.") *Cahier des charges*, second supplement, 14 May 1833, Article 13, (AJ[13] 187 I).

63 *Cahier des charges*, 28 February 1831, Article 11, (AJ[13] 187 I).

64 a) «L'entrepreneur ne pourra disposer des premières que pour représenter les ouvrages indiqués sur la liste, ou pour les faire concourir partiellement à l'ensemble d'une décoration nouvelle; mais sans les altérer en rien et en rafraîchissant seulement les peintures, si besoin il y a.» ("The concessionaire will only be able to make use of the first list in order to stage the works listed, or in order to have the scenery partially included in new sets, in which case this must be done without altering the scenery in any way and only by touching up the paint if needs be;")
b) «Les fermes, châssis et rideaux de la seconde liste sont à la disposition libre et entière de l'entrepreneur, soit pour être repeints, soit pour servir à la construction de fermes ou châssis nouveaux.» ("The *fermes*, wings and backdrops of the second list are entirely at the free disposal of the concessionaire, either for repainting or for use in the construction of new *fermes* or wings;")
c) «Quant aux décorations des ouvrages nouveaux, lorsque l'entrepreneur se servira, pour leur construction, du vieux matériel mis à sa disposition (liste n° 2), les peintures devront en être nouvelles, surtout pour les grands ouvrages. Si, par exception, quelques fermes, rideaux ou châssis

scenery but, as he had completely lost the ownership of the scenery for which he had paid, he had lost overall in financial terms.

Véron's Cost Reductions

Apart from the use of old scenery and materials, Véron took other steps to reduce the cost of new productions and did indeed justify his claim that he managed to obtain great economies while spending more overall on sets and costumes. Superb negotiator that he was, he did this in five ways. He renegotiated Ciceri's contract, he renegotiated the tariff for scene-painting, he closely scrutinised the cost of individual items submitted by the scene-painters in order to reduce them, he enforced a further reduction in the total of each bill, and he introduced competition.

On the first point, Ciceri ceased to be part of the Opera's fixed personnel as from 1 June 1831. An immediate saving of FF 6.000 per annum was thus achieved, and Véron negotiated a new three-year contract directly with Ciceri.[65] This contract was finally dissolved in October 1834[66] after Véron, who had already lost a case brought by him against Ciceri in order to dissolve the contract and had been fined FF 3.000, had taken his case to appeal.[67] This case revolved round the interpretation of Ciceri's 1 June 1831 contract, and whether Ciceri had a monopoly over the painting of scenery for the Opera; or whether, as Véron contended, there was a contract which just referred to a new tariff. The question of whether Ciceri had a monopoly or not will be covered later but the reference to a new tariff gave a significant clue as to how Véron had dealt with the high cost of chassis inherited from the Restoration period. A new tariff was indeed negotiated. Véron redefined the genres and renegotiated the price per chassis contained within each genre.[68] The new tariff and a comparison with the 1822 tariff was as follows:

---

de cette liste n° 2, pouvaient concourir à l'effet général des décorations nouvelles, sans être repeints ou refraîchis, l'entrepreneur pourrait les employer sous leur ancienne forme; mais il devrait y être autorisé par la Commission de surveillance.» ("As for the sets of new works, when the concessionaire uses the old materials at his disposal (list no. 2) in order to build them, the painting will have to be new for the grand works. If, exceptionally, some *fermes*, backdrops or wings from this list no. 2 could contribute to the general effect of new sets without being painted or touched up, the concessionaire could use them in their old form; but he must be authorised by the Commission to do so.") *Cahier des charges*, second supplement, 14 May 1833, Article 11, (AJ[13] 187 I).

65 Catherine Join-Diéterle, *Les Décors de scène de l'Opéra de Paris à l'époque romantique* (Paris, 1988), p. 178. «... il signe le 1er juin avec Docteur Véron un contrat de trois ans. Il y est stipulé, article 10, que Ciceri doit exécuter seul et exclusivement toutes les décorations de l'Opéra.» ("... he signs a three-year contract with Dr. Véron on the 1st of June. It stipulates, Article 10, that Ciceri, on his own and exclusively, should paint all the scenery at the Opera.") This contract was, according to Catherine Join-Diéterle, archived under AJ[13] 109, but so far it has not revealed itself.

66 Dissolution of contract between Véron and Ciceri, 30 October 1834, (F[21] 1054).

67 *Quelques réflexions pour M.M. Ciceri et Lèbe-Gigun, Peintres Décorateurs, contre M. Véron, Directeur du grand Opéra à Paris*, (F[21] 1054).

68 The new 1831 tariff, (F[21] 1054).

The Restoration period Genre	FF per Chassis	Véron's Management Genre	FF per Chassis	% change
1st Clear Sky	35	1st	20	-43
Storms, seas, etc	50		20	-60
Clouds	50		30	-40
Clouds with figures coloriées	130		80	-38
2nd Country scenes	100/120	2nd	80	-20/-33
3rd Military & other camps	140	3rd	90	-36
4th Rural architecture	120/135	4th	80	-33/-41
5th Military architecture	160	3rd	90	-44
6th Naval architecture	160	3rd	90	-44
7th Civil architecture	200	5th	140	-30
8th Noble & rich architecture	220/240	6th	180	-18/-25
9th Majestic & magnificent architecture	260	7th	250	-4
10th Fantastical architecture	400	7th	250	-37

This new tariff, which correlated with the bills submitted by Ciceri and the other scene-painters, spoke for itself. The percentage reductions in price per chassis, as shown in the last column, were very substantial and served to highlight the malpractices which were rife in the Restoration period. Véron also used this new tariff, negotiated initially with Ciceri, to negotiate with the other scene-painters. An anonymous undated report made reference to Philastre and Cambon who had submitted their own tariff to the Opera. The report noted that there was no doubt concerning Ciceri's team of painters but that the desire to make a reputation by Philastre and Cambon had led them to reduce their prices. Unfortunately for them, however, their prices, although lower than the 1822 Restoration tariff, did not match Véron's new tariff negotiated with Ciceri.[69]

The Restoration period Genre	Restoration Tariff FF	Philastre and Cambon FF	Véron's Tariff FF
2nd Country Scenes	100/120	80	80
4th Rural architecture	120/135	120	80
7th Civil architecture	200	150	140
8th Noble & rich architecture	220/240	200	180
10th Fantastical architecture	400	350	250

Véron's new tariff was enforced on them and on every other scene-painter.[70] As for the third point, it has already been noted that none of Ciceri's bills had been challenged by the authorities in the Restoration period. This might have been expected to change after Véron took over, as the minutest detail was subject to his sharp scrutiny. It was not

69   Report, unsigned and n.d., (AJ[13] 188 III).
70   For example, contract between Véron and painters Séchan, Feuchère, Desplechin and Diéterle, 13 November 1834, (F[21] 1054).

until *Ali-Baba*, however, and a bill submitted by Ciceri in June 1833, that clear evidence emerged of this detailed scrutiny of the genre of scenery and of the number of chassis. To what extent Véron had scrutinised earlier bills prior to their submission, and whether reductions had already taken place by the time the bills were submitted, is not capable of proof on the archived evidence. On the fourth point, Ciceri's new contract was not archived and it is not possible to state whether a fixed percentage should have been deducted from each total bill, in accordance with this contract and as extended to all scene-painters. It was very clear, however, that all the bills submitted by all the scene-painters were subject to arbitrary reductions by Véron and that this had nothing to do with the genre of scenery or the price per chassis. Véron simply used his strong bargaining power and refused to pay the bills in full. This saved him a lot of money, as will be shown in chapter 4.

On point five, Véron introduced competition into the scene-painting and this gave rise to the long-running battle between Véron and Ciceri. In the first instance, Ciceri brought a case against Véron after competition had been introduced for painting the scenery of *La Tentation*.[71] After a panel of experts had given their views, the case was decided in Ciceri's favour:

> ... à l'avenir Ciceri exécutera seul et exclusivement toutes les décorations de l'Opéra.[72]

As an indemnity for Véron's misbehaviour, Ciceri's contract was extended for a further two years. A further case was heard after Ciceri took no part in the painting of scenery for *Gustave III*, but this time Véron brought the case and sought a dissolution of his contract with Ciceri. Véron again lost and was required to pay an indemnity of FF 3.000. He also lost the right to print Ciceri's name on the Opera's posters. Véron then appealed against this indemnity and a third case was heard. Again he lost. The indemnity was raised to FF 5.000, Ciceri's contract was extended for a further three years beyond 1 June 1836 and Véron had to pay legal costs which could reach FF 1.500.[73] The points made by Ciceri's lawyer at this appeal gave the dispute a vitriolic flavour as he mixed fact with personal vendetta. He first pointed out that Ciceri's reputation had been enhanced by *Robert le Diable* and that even before then Véron had thought so highly of Ciceri that, in the new contract, he had reserved the right to publish Ciceri's name on public posters. According to the lawyer, there was then a dastardly plot by Ciceri's pupils, encouraged by Véron, which accused Ciceri of monopoly and *accaparement,* cornering the market. The lawyer went on to personalise this claim:

> C'est une machination infernale pour écraser M. Ciceri...; une vile intrigue enfantée par le froid égoïsme et la noire ingratitude.[74]

---

71 The facts of the case were set out in a document, 20 July 1832, signed by all parties, (F^{21} 1072).

72 ("... in the future, Ciceri will, on his own and exclusively, paint all the scenery at the Opera.") *Quelques réflexions ...,* op. cit., (F^{21} 1054).

73 *Décision de la Cour Royale de Paris, la 3ème Chambre de la Cour*, (F^{21} 1054).

74 ("This is a diabolical plot to crush M. Ciceri ...; a vile intrigue spawned by cold selfishness and black ingratitude.") *Quelques réflexions ...,* op. cit., (F^{21} 1054).

Véron had introduced competition for the scene-painting of *La Tentation*. Ciceri had submitted the designs for two sets for *La Tentation* but they were both rejected despite the fact that, according to the lawyer, the contract gave Ciceri the sole right to design and paint the Opera's scenery. Amour-propre was also offended as it was Ciceri's pupils who had won the business and, worse still, had done the painting in the Opera's atelier on the *rue du Faubourg-Poissonière*, long occupied by Ciceri. Véron lost his appeal and was fined FF 5.000. Nevertheless, he carried on regardless. Painters other than Ciceri continued to paint the Opera's scenery, and there was no evidence of any further case brought by either Ciceri or Véron.

Relations between Véron and Ciceri had, however, been soured as a result of the introduction of competition and the various legal cases. On 30 October 1834, Ciceri's contract with Véron was dissolved and Véron had to pay an indemnity of FF 20.000, spread over two years and with four instalments of FF 5.000 each.[75] FF 5.000 was payable on the signing of the dissolution contract, FF 5.000 on 15 April 1835, FF 5.000 on 15 October 1835, and FF 5.000 on 15 April 1836. Were Véron to resign as director prior to 15 April 1836, then his successor should pay any outstanding instalments. In the event, Ciceri was paid in full and he signed as having received the FF 20.000 on 28 September 1836.

At the time when the dissolution terms were being agreed with Ciceri, Véron was also in negotiations with Séchan, Desplechin, Feuchère and Diéterle and a contract was subsequently signed with them on 13 November 1834.[76] This contract had a number of unusual features. The four painters were granted the right to do half the work of all the scene-painting at the Opera. This half was calculated by reference to the total cost of the work rather than the quantity, and the 1831 tariff for scene-painting was applied. Véron could award the other half of the scene-painting to whomever he liked, whether in whole or in part. Indeed, it could be that the four painters did all the work for one production, in which case other painters could do all the work on another production, always provided that Séchan and his three partners painted at least half of the combined total value. Another clause in the contract gave to the four painters the right to choose what scene-painting they wished to do, again up to half of the overall total value. Needless to say, however, Véron extracted some money from this contract which was a very favourable one for the four painters. The contract was linked to the FF 20.000 indemnity to Ciceri in three distinct ways. First, the four painters had to pay FF 5.000 to Véron on signing the contract, thus reducing Véron's liability to FF 15.000. Second, they had to pay interest of eight per cent on any amounts billed by them for the scene-painting of a particular production, which exceeded that half of the total to which they were entitled under the contract. This somewhat complicated formula was used, for example, to calculate the interest due on *La Juive*. Third, their liability under these two conditions was limited to FF 10.000. The method of payment stipulated to fulfil these conditions was to reduce the bills rather than to make separate payments.

---

75   Dissolution of contract between Véron and Ciceri, 30 October 1834, (F²¹ 1054).

76   Contract between Véron and Séchan, Desplechin, Feuchère and Diéterle, 13 November 1834, (F²¹ 1054).

Costumes in the Restoration Period

Of particular interest here was the way in which the suppliers of materials for costumes were appointed; what problems were encountered in the 1820s; and how the authorities failed to reduce the costs.

Just as the 5 May 1821 *Règlement* set the policy for budgets, it also set the policy for the appointment of *fournisseurs,* suppliers of goods and services to the Opera,[77] of whom about half supplied materials for costumes. Samples had to be prepared by the relevant heads of department, lodged with the secretariat and attached to each supplier's *Cahier des charges*. A successful appointment could run for five years at most and one year at least. Tenders, with samples, had to be widely distributed within the Opera for examination as to price and quality. They then had to be re-examined by the committee set up to decide which tenders to accept. Prices were subject to a discount which was set out in each *Cahier des charges*. Another *Cahier des charges*, signed by La Rochefoucauld in April 1825, laid down the detailed conditions for such appointments and gave an interesting insight into the Opera's working relationships with its suppliers.[78] The relevant phrase in the opening paragraph was *l'adjudication par voie de soumission* which meant that contracts were awarded as a result of tenders by interested suppliers. These suppliers were informed about the Opera's requirements through announcements in the press and by means of public posters. The *Cahier des charges* then went on to spell out the details of the tendering process. Tendering parties needed to submit samples which conformed, so far as was possible, to the dimensions and qualities of existing sample types at the Opera. Five examples of each sample were necessary for comparison purposes. If there was a need for additional goods or services not foreseen in the tendering process, the price should be discussed with the Opera's head of material and agreed by the director. Goods and services, for which samples were not appropriate, should, in every respect, conform to the customs and image of the trade and be supplied by good quality merchants. All supplies should be delivered directly to the warehouses or ateliers. They could only be delivered by request and via forms drawn up by the storeman or the head of costumes. The forms should be stamped by the controller and approved by the director of material. The suppliers should refuse any request for delivery of goods unless these procedures had been fulfilled. Bills with supporting documents should be sent to the storeman or the head of costumes in the first week of the month following delivery. This was mandatory and if a supplier did not conform to this, the bills would be carried over into the following month. Payment of bills would be made, at the latest, in the fourth month following their arrival. The reason given for this was to guarantee the good delivery of goods and services from the suppliers. This was a somewhat inglorious reason for delayed payment and reflected the Opera's bargaining power. Furthermore, the Opera consistently failed to pay its bills according to the timetable agreed.

---

77 *5 mai 1821 Règlement*, Article 22, (AJ[13] 1186).

78 *Cahier des charges, clauses et conditions pour les fournitures nécessaires au service de l'Académie royale de Musique*. Approved by La Rochefoucauld, 1 April 1825, (AJ[13] 116 IV).

If, after repeated requests, a supplier failed to deliver goods which formed part of his successful tender, it would then be discussed at his expense. If this did not produce a result, the contract would be put out to tender again and any damages had to be borne by the original supplier. Bills for the transport of sets should be settled in the second month after their delivery. Again, the first month served as guarantee. All requests from suppliers which could lead to price increases, or claims for compensation by reason of a rise in the price of materials or of other prices included in the tender, would be rejected. All bills were payable after a half-per cent reduction, in line with the rules established for expenses incurred by the *Maison du Roi*. The successful tenders should be submitted for approval to the *Administrateur Général des Beaux-Arts,* in this case La Rochefoucauld. He reserved the right to terminate contracts without any claims for compensation by the suppliers. They did, however, have to be made aware of such a termination one month in advance. As surety for the execution of their contracts, successful tenderers had to pledge their assets, both present and future. In cases of dispute, they had to submit to the law covering public works contracts. For the two years 1829 and 1830, a further *Cahier des charges* was compiled.[79] It was exactly the same as that approved by La Rochefoucauld in April 1825 except that a further Article was added. This enabled the administration to demand caution money from successful tenderers. The reason given was to assure the good quality and regularity of the goods supplied.

With this background of regulations and detailed procedures, the *Comité d'administration* then put in train the tendering process and it was clear that a great deal of work was entailed. The report of the committee meeting, being the last of six, which recommended suppliers to La Rochefoucauld for the period 1 April 1825 to 31 December 1826, was especially revealing as it gave the reason for each appointment.[80] It was reported that many tenders gave rise to long discussions at which officials were brought in for consultation and that research and comparison took place on the samples. It was also reported that the conditions laid down in the 5 May 1821 *Règlement* had been observed. There were a number of themes which emerged from the detailed comments on each successful tenderer. In many cases there was only one tenderer and the usual reason given was that the tenderer also supplied the *Maison du Roi*. The fact that the Opera owed money to an existing supplier counted in his favour. There was a strong inclination to re-appoint the existing supplier for whatever reason, and even if a tenderer quoted a lower price than the existing supplier, concerns over quality and reliability could rule him out.

The best way to illustrate this is to give some examples. Out of the twenty-nine categories of goods and services for the 1825 and 1826 tenders, the first was for posters and printing, and Ballard was the sole tenderer. He was printer for all the Royal theatres and was thus re-appointed. A similar situation existed for Duhamel, who supplied wood for heating and also served the *Maison du Roi*. Likewise Gameron, the sole tenderer for tallow candles, who also supplied the *Maison du Roi* and was owed a lot

---

79   *Cahier des charges, pour les années 1829 et 1830,* (AJ[13] 124 III).

80   *Comité d'administration*, report of meeting, 31 March 1825, (AJ[13] 116 IV).

of money. With that background, he could not fail to be re-appointed. Maillot, who supplied hosiery, was the sole tenderer as he supplied all the Royal theatres. Deslandes, who supplied wax-candles, was re-appointed. He had lowered his prices and in any case he merited the administration's attention as he had not yet been paid for goods supplied in 1824. Likewise with Orsel, who supplied oil and wicks for the lighting and was also owed money.

The inclination to appoint the existing supplier was borne out by the numbers. The words "previous supplier" recurred throughout as a sign of approval. Twenty suppliers out of thirty-six were described in this way and were re-appointed with little comment. Some appointments gave rise to a lot of discussion, however, and yielded an interesting insight into the concerns of the administration. Several people had tendered for the supply of embroidery. Meyer's prices were by far the lowest and well below those of Chalamel, the existing supplier. His prices were so low that the committee wondered whether he could deliver the required quality. Nevertheless, when his samples were compared with those of other tenderers, they measured up well. Then there was a question of reliability and the Opera had had no experience with Meyer. Chalamel had been appointed in 1823 despite quoting higher prices as it had been felt that his materials were more robust and thus more resistant to cleaning and the removal of grease. This time in 1825 Chalamel was in the same position but the committee finally decided to appoint Meyer, with the proviso that Chalamel would be immediately re-appointed if Meyer failed to deliver the quality required. This saga continued in the 1820s and 1830s. Chalamel was re-appointed for 1827 and 1828, lost out to Raymond for 1829 and 1830, and was reintroduced by Véron as competition to Raymond in 1831. The case of Janssen, supplier of ladies' shoes, also provoked discussion. His prices were, on the whole, higher than those of other tenderers but he had long been the supplier and had responded to the need for prompt delivery. For these reasons, and the amount owed to him, he was re-appointed. A long discussion took place over Lauriau, the existing supplier of rope. In 1823 certain tenderers had quoted lower prices than Lauriau but Gromaire, the head *machiniste*, had said that he could not be answerable for his duties, nor for any accidents, if someone else were appointed. For thirty years Lauriau's ropes had not caused any accidents. This time, in 1825, Walsberg had submitted samples which seemed perfect and although his prices were higher than those of Lauriau, the committee was minded to appoint him. Again counselled by Gromaire, however, the committee then worried about Walsberg's ropes. Although of good appearance, they might not have the required strength. As the committee had no means of assuring themselves on this point, Lauriau was re-appointed. Finally, the service of dyeing and removal of grease was re-awarded to Messeaux even although her prices were higher. It was, according to the committee, very important that this service was well done as any failure could destroy a great quantity of costumes and put productions in jeopardy. In 1823, the danger of putting this service out to tender had been foreseen and the committee felt in 1825 that it could not do better than to re-appoint Messeaux about whom there was no complaint and who had responded to every request. This report was approved by La Rochefoucauld who sent it back with a covering letter.[81]

---

81   La Rochefoucauld to Duplantys, 15 April 1825, (AJ[13] 116 IV).

The committee seemed to take a lot of trouble over these appointments, but it needed a strong case to replace existing suppliers as the records showed for the 1827 and 1828 tenders.[82] The same process also took place for 1829 and 1830. The posters were printed by Ballard, signed by Lubbert and published. Thirty-one categories of goods and services were advertised; tenders had to be received between 20 and 30 November 1828; and the appointments would run for two years from 1 January 1829 to 31 December 1830. Tenderers should visit the Opera's administration, *rue Grange-Batelière*, between 5 and 15 November to acquaint themselves with the *Cahier des charges*, the samples required, and the details of the goods and services to be supplied.[83] The result of these tenders was somewhat similar to those of 1825 and 1826, and 1827 and 1828, and detailed reasons for some of the decisions were also given.[84] Out of a total of thirty-five appointments covering thirty-one categories of goods and services, twenty-five of the 1825 and 1826 suppliers were re-appointed,[85] seventeen without any competition.[86] What also comes out of these documents, however, was the very detailed nature of these tenders[87] and what sort of lobbying took place to try and secure an appointment.

Ruggieri, *aîné,* wrote to the Vicomtesse de Laval Montmorency in November 1828.[88] He acknowledged that it was due to her benevolent protection that he had been appointed two years previously. He again solicited her help for the 1829 and 1830 appointment, hoping to gain a preferential position through her support and through the fact that he had held the position for forty years. The Vicomtesse would seem to have done her best as La Rochefoucauld enquired of Lubbert whether Ruggieri should not continue and just be re-appointed.[89] To his credit, Lubbert wrote back and said that the standard procedures should be observed.[90] La Rochefoucauld then wrote to Ruggieri, *aîné,* along the lines of Lubbert's letter and invited him to put in his tender along with the five already submitted.[91] This all sounded very proper but Ruggieri's position had

---

82 *Procès-verbal, pour les soumissions de 1827 et 1828*, 15 January 1827, (O³ 1676 III). This gave detailed comments on most suppliers.

83 *Avis aux négociants et fournisseurs*, 1829 and 1830, (AJ¹³ 179).

84 The summary of the comparisons made by the committee and the proposals on the 1829 and 1830 tendering round were submitted to La Rochefoucauld, (O³ 1685 I). He sent the list to La Bouillerie, 14 May 1829, (O³ 1685 I), who approved it. La Bouillerie to La Rochefoucauld, 22 May 1828, (O³ 1685 I).

85 *État des fournisseurs qui ont fait des propositions de fournitures pour les exercices 1829 et 1830,* (AJ¹³ 179).

86 See the summary of comparisons, (O³ 1685 I).

87 For example, the tender of Cruchet for *Modelure et Sculpture,* 30 November 1828. It detailed 164 items, each one priced as *objets neufs* and *objets à réparer.* He was the successful tenderer for 1829 and 1830, (AJ¹³ 179).

88 Ruggieri, *aîné, Artificier du Roi,* to the Vicomtesse de Laval Montmorency, 18 November 1828, (O³ 1680 I).

89 La Rochefoucauld to Lubbert, 29 November 1828, (O³ 1680 I).

90 Lubbert to La Rochefoucauld, 5 December 1828, (O³ 1680 I).

91 La Rochefoucauld to Ruggieri, 8 December 1828, (O³ 1680 I).

in fact changed. He was no longer *artificier du Roi* as Lubbert had pointed out in his letter. Had he still been so, the automatic re-appointment accorded to those who supplied the *Maison du Roi* would have obtained. In the event, Ruggieri, *aîné*, lost and Ruggieri, Claude, who had put in a separate tender, was appointed. Some tenderers did not go down without a fight. Desouches-Fayard was the sole competitor to Roussel for wood used to make the sets. He pointed out that of the sixteen items to be tendered for, he was cheaper on six and more expensive on three.[92] He therefore proposed to reduce the three to the same prices as those of Roussel. He also took a swipe at Roussel saying that he was a new merchant who used the same name as the long-standing supplier who had himself retired from business. Roussel then wrote in reply.[93] The retired Roussel was his uncle and he had taken over the business. He also reduced his own prices and finally won the tender.

The suppliers discussed above were all tenderers in the 1825 and 1826, and 1829 and 1830, rounds. Most, but not all, tendered for goods and services for costumes. There was, however, the other category of supplier called supplier-contractors who were paid by fixed amounts per annum, and had contracts with the Opera. Reference to two of them was included in La Rochefoucauld's 1825 *Cahier des charges*, Articles 9 and 10, where a quarterly fixed price was paid for the hire and maintenance of hats and metal-polishing. Other such suppliers included Renaud and Mme. Guérin, respectively men's and ladies' hairdressers, who were each paid FF 2.500 per annum for hairdressing and the hire of wigs.[94] The fact that these suppliers did not submit to the tender process was not, in itself, of great significance. Of much more significance was the fact that the Opera was a very poor payer of bills and that this strengthened Véron's hand in his negotiations with suppliers. The 1825 and 1826 report alluded to outstanding bills and this became a major issue, as already discussed. Two more examples set the scene for this general failure of the Opera to honour its debts on time, and they both served as background information to Véron's actions in relation to certain suppliers. Maillot, the supplier of hosiery, had written demanding a half per cent per month indemnity for every month his bill was not paid by the due date. Lubbert wrote to La Rochefoucauld about this and sought his advice.[95] Lubbert pointed out that this would be a dangerous precedent and as La Rochefoucauld agreed, nothing was done. Truton, the supplier of printing on fabric was due FF 579 for bills submitted in May, June and July 1828. He requested payment[96] but received a letter back from La Rochefoucauld which said that his bills were lumped in with those of all other suppliers and that he, Truton, would have to wait until payment could be made.[97]

---

92 Desouches-Fayard to Lubbert, 24 December 1828, (AJ[3] 179).

93 Roussel to Lubbert, 29 December 1828, (AJ[13] 179).

94 Dieu, *contrôleur du matériel*, to Lubbert, 7 October 1829, (AJ[13] 124 III).

95 Lubbert to La Rochefoucauld, 2 February 1828, (O[3] 1680 I).

96 Truton to La Rochefoucauld, 11 October 1828, (O[3] 1680 I).

97 La Rochefoucauld to Truton, 14 October 1828, (O[3] 1680 I).

These two examples, together with the resolution of the Opera's debts covered in chapter 1 and the example of Duhamel in chapter 2, gave an insight into the climate of opinion among the suppliers at that time. From their point of view, it would perhaps be safer, although less profitable, to have a fixed annual income and this was what enabled Véron to strike some hard bargains. Under his management, the number of suppliers on fixed income contracts went up sharply.

Costumes under Véron's Administration

When Véron took over, his 28 February 1831 *Cahier des charges* spelt out the obligations and constraints on him as director. Article 11 was emphatic that new productions should be mounted with new scenery and costumes, but whereas the same article gave a let-out in respect of the former in that the Commission could approve the use of old scenery under certain circumstances, there was no mention of such a let-out in respect of costumes. At the same time, Article 13 laid down that scenery and costumes created and paid for by Véron would be bought by the State at the end of his concession for an agreed value. The first supplement, 30 May 1831, also confirmed that the State would buy the costumes created by Véron although, as already described, the value of the scenery would be split fifty-fifty. There was no mention of the use of old costumes and the status quo was thus maintained. The second supplement, 14 May 1833, softened this stance. Article 11 reaffirmed that new costumes should be used in new productions but that old costumes could be used provided the Commission had given its authorisation. As for the sale of costumes to the State, there was no reference to any change in policy although, as already shown, the State assumed total ownership of the scenery.[98] This explained why Véron was credited with the value of costumes for which he had paid, after a fraction had been deducted for depreciation, and why he received no value at all for the scenery.

Neither the 28 February 1831 *Cahier des charges*, nor the two supplements which followed it, contained any references to the Opera's suppliers. Véron thus had a free hand to impose his own personality and policies. The cumbersome tendering procedures of the Restoration period were immediately abolished and within a week of taking over Véron had given notice of cancellation to various supplier-contractors who were paid fixed annual sums. He had to give three months' notice in each case and thus advised each supplier that his contract would terminate on 1 June 1831. Véron would have been well aware of the malpractices at the Opera, and just as he started by negotiating a new contract with Ciceri, having first made him redundant, he showed his teeth immediately by cancelling these contracts. The first two, for the hire of hats and payment for metal-polishing, were mentioned in La Rochefoucauld's two *Cahiers des charges* and related to costumes.[99]

---

98 *Cahier des charges*, 28 February 1831, Articles 11 & 13; first supplement, 30 May 1831, Article 13; second supplement, 14 May 1833, Article 11, (AJ[13] 187 I).

99 Véron, letters 7th March 1831: Merville, *fourbisserie*, annual income FF 1.200; Lacour, *chapellerie*, annual income FF 1.000, (AJ[13] 187 V).

As might be expected, Véron looked deeply into the situation of each supplier of materials for costumes and clearly arrived at four broad strands of policy. First, a complete overhaul was needed of the list of suppliers who had been successful in the 1829 and 1830 tendering round. Second, it was in his interests to have more fixed income contracts, especially given the experience of suppliers under the Restoration and the preference of some for a secure, but less profitable, contract. Third, he was in a sufficiently strong position to reduce the bills arbitrarily, just as he did for scene-painting, and he paid detailed attention to this. Fourth, competition was desirable. With these policies, he again justified the claim in his memoirs that he managed to achieve great economies.

As for the first point, Véron took his time but by 1832 substantial changes had taken place. Out of the 1829 and 1830 total of thirty-six suppliers, twenty-three had been sacked and of those retained, six went on to fixed annual sums.[100] Suppliers of materials for costumes were included in these totals and out of a total of eighteen only five were retained.[101] A comparison of prices between incoming suppliers and those who had been sacked revealed, in many cases, substantial savings.[102] It is not possible, as it is with the new tariff for scene-painting, to evaluate the total savings achieved on costumes for new productions in a precise way, but given Véron's ruthless attitude to staff and suppliers, it can hardly have been insignificant. As for the second point, a detailed analysis of the costume costs of the new productions covered in chapter 4 revealed that none of these suppliers were on fixed annual sums and so this strand of

---

100 *Tableau de la Dépense fait pour fournisseurs*, January and March 1832, (AJ[13] 411 I).

101

	1829 and 1830	Véron Administration
Supply	Supplier	Supplier*
Bonneterie	Maillot	Maillot
Broderie	Raymond	Chalamel/Rameau/Pougeois
Chaussures-hommes	Dupire	Ponsin
Chaussures-dames	Janssen	Ponsin
Draperie	Prestat	Piquet
Ferblanterie	Le Carpentier	Le Carpentier
Fleurs	Chagot	Chagot
Ganterie	Saivres	Pirenet et Farcos
Impression sur étoffe	Truton	Hourdequin
Mercerie	Gautier	Perrée-Dupuis/Valentin
Modèlerie	Cruchet	Cruchet
Parfumerie	Charlier	Villain
Papeterie	Millet	Binant
Passementerie	Raymond	Guibout/Moreau/Sinon
Plumes	Chagot	Chagot
Quincaillerie	Juéry	Desforges
Soierie et Lainage	Deslisle	Chevreux fils et Legentil
Toiles et Mousselines	Deslisle	Chevreux fils et Legentil

   * None of these were on fixed annual incomes.

102 See Appendix V.

Véron's policy did not apply.[103] All the changes in this regard have therefore been covered in chapter 2. On the third point, the bills archived for the Restoration period were, in general, very poorly prepared compared with those submitted under Véron. There were rarely any attached supporting documents, duly signed and authorised, the bills rarely had the full complement of required signatures, they were not signed *pour acquit* by the supplier, and they were paid in full after the usual discount of one-half per cent.[104] Véron, on the other hand, took the keenest possible interest in all the bills, even down to the minutest amounts. He signed them all and had no compunction in reducing the totals arbitrarily. Having already changed most of the suppliers and having negotiated, in most cases, lower prices for individual items, this further reduction in many submitted bills yielded extra savings. It only suffices to give a few examples to justify this assertion,[105] even although a few bills were paid in full and with no apparent reason.[106] Finally, under point four, Véron introduced competition just as he did for scene-painting. As the names show, there were cases of more than one supplier for a particular category of material.

Although the cost of materials for costumes for new productions formed the major item of expense, there was also a question of maintaining the old costumes in a good state of repair and renewal, and this item formed a surprisingly high proportion of the total expense on costumes in the annual accounts. Figures from Géré, the head of costumes, compiled in 1835 as part of the exercise to determine the depreciated value of the costumes paid for by Véron, threw some light on this, as did the 1833–34 Annual

---

103 *Tableau de la Dépense faite pour*   *La Sylphide*, March 1832, (AJ^{13} 201^1).
            -ditto-   *La Tentation*, June 1832, (AJ^{13} 201^2).
            -ditto-   *Le Serment*, October 1832, (AJ^{13} 201^2).
            -ditto-   *Nathalie*, November 1832, (AJ^{13} 201^2).
            -ditto-   *Gustave III*, February 1833, (AJ^{13} 201^2).
        Bills of suppliers, October–December 1831, (AJ^{13} 410).
            -ditto-   January–August 1832, (AJ^{13} 411 I).
        Impressions of suppliers 1832–33, (AJ^{13} 289, II IV V).
        Contracts with salaried suppliers, (AJ^{13} 291 I).

104 See schedules of payments to suppliers, (AJ^{13} 146 IV).

105 Bills of suppliers, October–December 1831, (AJ^{13} 410). a) *Bonneterie* – hosiery. Maillot had been retained but only on the basis that all his bills were subject to a two per cent discount; b) *Passementerie* – braid. The new supplier, Guibout, submitted a bill for FF 66, but this was reduced by Véron to FF 63, being 4.5%. Another new supplier, Sinon, had his bill of FF 315.50 reduced to FF 300 by Véron, being 3.2%. Both signed *pour acquit* for these lower amounts; c) *Fleurs* – flowers. Mme. Chagot had been retained but a tiny bill for FF 7.75 did not escape Véron's attention. He reduced it to FF 7, being 9.7%; d) *Modèlerie* – accessories. Cruchet had been retained but a bill for FF 1.787 was reduced to FF 1.700 by Véron, being 4.9%; e) *Broderie* – embroidery. Again, a tiny bill from the new supplier, Mme. Rameau, was reduced, from FF 11.75 to FF 11, being 6.4%; f) *Chaussures pour hommes* – men's shoes. The new supplier Ponsin put in a bill for FF 198, being shoes for *Robert le Diable*. As was Véron's custom, he signed the bill and all the supporting documents and reduced the total to FF 190, being 4.0%; g) *Mercerie* – haberdashery. The new supplier Perrée-Dupuis, put in two bills. One for FF 21.56 was reduced to FF 21 by Véron, being 2.6%. The other for FF 280.30 was reduced to FF 270, being 3.7%.

106 a) *Huile* – lighting oil. The new supplier, Chopin, presented a bill for FF 2.978, October 1831, and was paid in full, (AJ^{13} 410); b) *Artifices* – artifices. The new supplier, Martin, presented two bills, FF 800, October 1833 and FF 208, March 1834. Both were paid in full, (AJ^{13} 289 IV).

Accounts. Géré reckoned that the annual spend on costumes, excluding the cost of fixed personnel, was around FF 140.000 split as to FF 74.000 for new costumes and FF 66.000 for the repair and renewal of old costumes, including the cost of losses and theft. The latter figure was further broken down as to FF 20.000 for hosiery and shoes and FF 46.000 for the costumes themselves.[107] As for theft, it was a recurring problem and a number of letters from Géré to Véron attested to its frequent occurrence.[108] On the other hand, it would not be too fanciful to state that theft in the Restoration period, with its weak management and ineffective controls, was likely to have run at a much higher level than that under Véron's management. Further evidence of the high cost of repair and renewal was available in the Annual Accounts 1833–34. The total for costumes was FF 132.423 and a note on the accounts attributed FF 85.055 of this to the three new productions in that year, namely *Ali-Baba*, *La Révolte au Sérail* and *Don Juan*. FF 47.368 was thus spent on the repair and renewal of old costumes.[109] What economies were achieved in the cost of these repairs and renewals was not possible to prove from the archived material available, but it was likely to be in line with the savings achieved elsewhere.

---

107 Report by Géré, the head of costumes, 1835, (AJ[13] 215 I).

108 Géré to Véron, various letters: 9 April 1833, 27 August 1834, 7 September 1834, 4 June 1835, 24 June 1835, 30 June 1835, 31 August 1835, (AJ[13] 215 I).

109 Annual Accounts 1833–34, (AJ[13] 228 II).

CHAPTER 4

A remarkable improvement in the overall finances of the Opera took place under Véron. On the receipts side successful new productions, far fewer free seats and well-judged new seat prices all combined to raise total receipts despite a falling subsidy and the loss of the *redevance des théâtres secondaires*. On the expenses side, the onslaught on the fixed personnel costs and the reduced cost of scenery and costumes combined to offset the extra expense of lavish new productions. The result was that Véron made a substantial surplus in his first three years, 1831–32 to 1833–34, although 1834–35 saw a marked reversal of these favourable trends.

The archived primary documents on the receipts and expenses of new productions at the Opera, both in the Restoration period and under Véron, undoubtedly make it possible to compare and contrast the two regimes in a very practical way. Each production selected for analysis serves to substantiate general points already made, albeit in different ways and in more detail. Each production also serves to support the main contention of this book which is that Véron indeed wrought substantial changes at the Opera by his dramatic onslaught on the cost-structure and by his ability to raise receipts through successful new productions. Whereas chapters 1 to 3 described what happened at the Opera, this chapter describes how it happened. There is also special emphasis on *Robert le Diable* which was pivotal to the astonishing transformation achieved by Véron.

Terminology

The detailed budgets and bills for scene-painting used certain terms when referring to scenery and theatrical machinery. These were standard in the Restoration period and when Véron was director of the Opera. There is already a considerable body of well-researched work on this subject, both in general and in detail, and the terms as applied to the *Salle le Peletier* have also been extensively researched.[1] Nevertheless, any analysis of the budgets and bills of individual productions involves the use of these terms which recur throughout all the documents, and a brief explanation is needed to clarify them. There were three main components to the staging of all productions: *châssis*, the wings; *plafonds*, the borders; and *rideaux*, the backdrops. In addition there were *fermes*, painted canvas-covered wooden frames mounted on the stage itself. All of these were placed at numbered *plans*, positions, on the stage through the use of theatrical machinery.

---

1   See, for example: Marie-Antoinette Allévy, *La mise en scène en France dans la première moitié du dix-neuvième siècle* (Paris, 1938). Jean-Pierre Moynet, *L'Envers du théâtre: Machines et décorations* (Paris, 1873). Clément Contant and Joseph de Filippi, *Parallèle des principaux théâtres modernes de l'Europe et des machines théâtrales françaises, allemandes et anglaises* (Paris, 1860). Cecil Thomas Ault, Jr., *Design, Operation and Organization of Stage Machinery at the Paris Opera: 1770–1873*. Ph. D. diss., University of Michigan, 1983. Johnson, op. cit., pp. 337–346.

Châssis

This term, as already noted, could have two meanings and it is very important to understand the distinction between them. The first was a wing which could also be described as a *coulisse* – hence a wing could be referred to as a *châssis de coulisse* – although the simple term *châssis* was the one which was used in all the budgets and bills to describe these wings. These were the painted canvas-covered wooden frames which were deployed laterally on both sides of the stage, one behind the other at the various positions. The second meaning of *châssis*, already called chassis, was the term used to aggregate and evaluate all the wings, borders and backdrops by reference to the 1822 and 1831 tariffs for scene-painting. A wing, for example, was evaluated as one chassis in both tariffs; a border was evaluated as two chassis in the 1822 tariff but only one and a half in the 1831 tariff; a backdrop of sixty feet was evaluated as eight chassis in both tariffs and of sixty-six feet as nine chassis, again in both tariffs. It follows from this second meaning of *châssis* that the number of chassis used in a new production can be aggregated into a single total and that the value of this total can be derived from the *espèce*, genre, or genres, which defined each set. From this it also follows that an average cost per chassis can be calculated and comparisons made between different productions.

Plafonds

The tops of the wings as well as the fly-space above the stage were concealed by borders which were flown vertically from the stage-loft. In principle, each border was painted to blend with its corresponding wing unless the borders represented the sky. These latter were called *frises, bandes d'air* or *bandes de ciel*. They spanned the stage and were defined as genre one in both tariffs.

Rideaux

This term usually referred to the backdrops, in which case a single *rideau* could also be called a *rideau de fond, toile de fond* or simply a *fond*. There was also a *rideau d'avant-scène* which, as the name implied, was a proscenium drop, and a *rideau de manœuvre*, usually placed mid-stage. This was a signal to the audience that as a change of scenery would take place during an act, they should stay in their seats and await the new scenery which the raising of the drop would reveal.[2]

Fermes

The three main components of the scenery were wings, borders and backdrops but the overall effect could be enhanced by two-dimensional wooden frames of painted canvas called *fermes* which were stored below stage. A *ferme* was then raised through a long narrow opening by machinery underneath the stage and mounted at the assigned position on the stage. The two tariffs identified two types: a *ferme pleine* which was evaluated as six chassis and a *ferme ouverte* which was evaluated as eight chassis. The budgets and bills made frequent references to these *fermes* which, as already shown, were also evaluated in chassis. *Fermes* which represented topographical features, such

2   Allévy, op. cit., p. 182.

as a boulder, were called *terrains*. Three-dimentional *fermes* positioned on the stage such as boats, staircases and bridges, and which could be put to practical use in that members of the cast could walk or stand on them, were called *praticables*.

Accessoires

This was a term used to describe free-standing items which were either placed by hand on the stage and formed part of the expenses of scenery, or were used by the cast and formed part of the expenses of costumes. Examples of the former could be tables and chairs, and of the latter could be garlands and swords. If part of the scenery, the accessories were sometimes evaluated in terms of chassis and sometimes as separate items.

Plans

The stage floor of the *Salle le Peletier* was laterally divided from front to back into twelve *plans*, positions, with number one at the front and number twelve at the back. This was well shown in the drawings of Contant and de Filippi.[3] There was also reference to thirteen, and even fourteen, positions at the *Salle le Peletier,* but this seems very unlikely.[4]

New Productions in the Restoration Period

There were three levels of management at the Opera and tensions existed between La Bouillerie, La Rochefoucauld and Lubbert. These arose primarily out of Lubbert's mismanagement and cavalier attitude towards financial matters as shown, for example, towards the 1829 budget and accounts. It might therefore be expected that these tensions would also be present when the budgets for new productions under Lubbert were in the process of approval and when the bills had to be paid. It should also be clear that Ciceri had a de facto monopoly over scene-painting; that no-one was in a position to challenge his budgets and bills; and that the high cost of the 1822 tariff had led to the use of old scenery to save expense. As for the costumes, La Rochefoucauld insisted that old costumes should be used wherever possible to save expense, especially as the inefficiencies and abuses which abounded at the Opera prevented any significant cost reductions on new costumes.

Regulations for the third level of budget have already been described. It might be thought that these would give the authorities timely and effective control over the budgets for individual productions, especially after the inclusion of inspectors from the *Beaux-Arts* in 1826. So much for the theory, but the practice failed to conform to the prescribed regulations. Lubbert's cavalier attitude to financial matters in general extended to those concerning individual productions. A comparison between *Le Siège*

---

3   Contant and de Filippi, op. cit.. The drawing of the stage at the *Salle le Peletier* clearly showed twelve positions.

4   Wilberg, op. cit., pp. 122–123. She referred to the inconsistencies in the number of *plans* at the *Salle le Peletier* in n. 15. See also, for example, *La Tentation* and the budget and bill from Léon Feuchère et Cie. Both made reference to a backdrop at the thirteenth position for the last set, (AJ[13] 201[2]).

de Corinthe and *Moïse*, both of which were produced under Duplantys, and *La Muette de Portici*, *Manon Lescaut* and *Le Dieu et la Bayadère*, all of which were produced under Lubbert, is very instructive. It becomes a detailed indictment of Lubbert's management and highlights, yet again, La Rochefoucauld's uncomfortable position in the middle of three levels of management.

Le Siège de Corinthe

La Rochefoucauld was a poor administrator and was lampooned by his critics. Nevertheless, it was greatly to his credit that he appointed Rossini to the *Théâtre Italien* in 1824 and to the Opera in 1826. Although he was an ardent supporter of the Bourbon dynasty, his consistent support for Rossini reflected a conviction that the Opera should no longer stay within the conventions of the traditional *tragédie lyrique* but should experiment and move forward with new ideas. Just as Gluck's reform operas were described as an artistic revolution during the *ancien régime*, La Rochefoucauld hailed *Le Siège de Corinthe* as a revolution during the Restoration. It was the Opera's first performance of a Rossini opera and it broke with the conventions of the *tragédie lyrique* in three distinct ways. It took a story which was neither classical nor mythological but from fifteenth-century history; it had an unhappy ending, unlike the *tragédie lyrique* which conventionally had a happy ending, even if a contrived one through an apotheosis; and it placed the chorus as part of the plot: not just a commentator on it, but an equal and active partner with the soloists.[5] On the other hand, this artistic move forward was not matched by significant changes in the Opera's policy on scenery and costumes. Old scenery and costumes were still used in order to save expense and the claim that wholly new Greek costumes were used, based on detailed historical research, was not substantiated by the archived evidence.

Discussions began in August 1825 over the staging of this opera based on a libretto by Balocchi and Soumet. This was an adaptation of Rossini's original opera *Maometto II*, first staged in Naples on 3 December 1820, and the Paris version was first staged in French on 9 October 1826. At that time in 1825, a budget for costumes of FF 12.000 was presented.[6] Later, in November, La Rochefoucauld ordered that the opera should be put into production[7] but as neither score nor libretto were ready, it was not until the spring of 1826 that preparations began in earnest. In April, Lecomte presented his designs for costumes[8] which were the result of extensive historical research into Greek dress although it was realised that more work needed to be done before an approximate budget could be submitted to La Rochefoucauld. He had just decreed that a preliminary meeting should take place for this and all future productions which should include inspectors from the *Département des Beaux-Arts*. The main purpose was to scrutinise the costs of both costumes and scene-painting with a special emphasis on possible

---

5   For a full discussion on the significance of *Le Siège de Corinthe*, see Gerhard, op. cit., pp. 63–121.

6   Duplantys to La Rochefoucauld, 22 May 1826, (O³ 1676 I). He referred to a meeting of *the Conseil d'administration* on 30 August 1825 at which an approximate budget for costumes of FF 12.000 was discussed.

7   *Conseil d'administration*, minutes of meeting, 23 November 1825, (AJ¹³ 116 I).

8   *Conseil d'administration*, minutes of meeting, 14 April 1826, (AJ¹³ 116 I).

reductions through the use of old costumes, scenery and materials.[9] Only after this scrutiny could the Opera send the approximate budget to La Rochefoucauld for approval. In the event, the *Conseil d'administration* met to approve the approximate budget on 23 May 1826. It totalled FF 47.863: scene-painting FF 24.200, materials FF 10.045 and costumes FF 13.618. It was noted that the total for costumes had already been reduced by FF 1.867 to take account of old costumes.[10]

A more detailed look at this budget showed that Ciceri presented a budget of 120 chassis for a total cost of FF 24.000 and an average of FF 200 per chassis.[11] This was not, however, all the scenery. The first set comprised the vestibule from *Œdipe à Colone*, first staged in 1787 and with a revival in 1821,[12] for a small cost of only FF 200. The second set, a public place, used twenty chassis in the seventh genre which cost FF 4.000 but also chassis from *Le Triomphe de Trajan*, first staged in 1807,[13] at no extra cost. As for the final bill, the number of chassis had risen by then to 136½ and the total cost to FF 27.416.[14] The first set, instead of costing only FF 200, made use of fourteen new chassis for a cost of FF 2.240 and there was no mention of the vestibule from *Œdipe à Colone*, although it has to be presumed that it was used as three borders were entirely repainted and there was no mention of any wings. A new backdrop was painted, evaluated as eight chassis in the seventh genre at FF 200 per chassis. As for the second set, there was no mention of the chassis from *Le Triomphe de Trajan;* the genre was changed from the seventh to the eighth; and the final cost was twenty-three and a half chassis at FF 220 per chassis, or FF 5.170. The fourth set, the interior of the tomb, was also re-categorised in Ciceri's bill, although the number of chassis was less. Instead of twenty-six chassis in the sixth genre at FF 160 per chassis for a cost of FF 4.160, the final bill was for nineteen and a half chassis in the eighth genre at FF 220 per chassis for a cost of FF 4.290. By February 1827, Ciceri had been paid FF 22.500 to account[15] and could look forward to a final settlement of FF 4.916.

The approximate budget for costumes, based on Lecomte's designs, was FF 13.618[16] but this would have been FF 1.867 higher were it not for the expectation that all of the Turkish costumes for the ladies chorus, which would have cost FF 1.620 if new, could be found in the warehouses, and that further costumes which would have cost FF 247 if new could also be found. This budget also noted that the cost of costumes for the ballet was excluded as the designs had not been completed by the time the approximate budget was prepared. Any estimate of the cost of overtime was also left out. Although the 5 May 1821 *Règlement* had allowed for a department of fifty-two

---

9   La Rochefoucauld to Duplantys, 25 March 1826, (AJ[13] 117).

10   *Conseil d'administration*, minutes of meeting, 23 May 1826, (O[3] 1672 IV).

11   Budget for scene-painting from Ciceri, n.d., (AJ[13] 134[2]).

12   Record of operas staged at the Opera, 1754–1832, (AJ[13] 5).

13   Record of operas staged at the Opera, 1805–1807, (AJ[13] 91).

14   *Mémoire de peinture de Décorations … pour La Prise de Corinthe*, (AJ[13] 134[2]). A mistake in the title here by Ciceri.

15   Noted on the budget for scene-painting, (AJ[13] 134[2]).

16   *Devis approximatif des costumes pour le chant de l'opéra Mahomet II*, n.d., (AJ[13] 134[2]).

staff to make the costumes, even this number was always unable to cope within normal working hours. This omission of overtime from the budget for costumes was thus significant as any savings from the use of old costumes were always partially offset by the cost of this overtime. The summary of expenses for costumes reflected these points.[17] There were indeed substantial savings on the costumes for chorus and extras despite the claims for historical accuracy. The budget total was FF 10.139 but only FF 2.535 was actually spent, for a saving of FF 7.604.[18]

Costumes			Budget	Actual Expense	Savings
			FF	FF	FF
Chorus -		Men	5.002	1.638	3.364
	-	Ladies	1.292	360	932
Extras			3.845	537	3.308
			10.139	2.535	7.604

Nevertheless, the inclusion of costumes for the ballet, FF 1.471, of the cost of overtime, FF 3.000, and of many other extra expenses, meant that the final total was FF 15.449, which was FF 1.831 higher than the original budget. The inclusion of FF 690 within this total for the cleaning of costumes was another expense not previously budgeted. It was also another pointer to the number of old costumes used and raised a question mark over Lecomte's extensive research into Greek costumes and the presumption that his findings would result in new ones. As for the materials for building the sets, Gromaire had submitted a budget for FF 10.045.[19] New wings cost FF 90 each, backdrops cost either FF 302 or FF 477 according to size and borders cost FF 162 each. There was no record of the actual cost of the materials but it was likely to have been substantially less through the use of old materials.

This detailed analysis revealed some interesting points. Ciceri had a monopoly over scene-painting and it showed. There was an increase over budget in the number of chassis and changes in the genres. The total cost was over budget but nobody challenged Ciceri's bill which represented an average of FF 202 per chassis. Overall, the impression gained was of a monopolist using his position to the full. As for the costumes, there was extensive use of old costumes in line with La Rochefoucauld's policy but inefficiencies meant that overtime, which was not included in the budget, accounted for nineteen per cent of the total final cost.

La Rochefoucauld wrote to congratulate everyone on the day after the first performance but he had some criticisms.[20] The ballet was decidedly too long and its duration could be cut in half. The colour of the first set was too red especially as there was a fire in the last set which was itself too paltry. Overall, however, *Le Siège de Corinthe* was judged a great artistic success and it paved the way for *Moïse*. In

---

17 *Récapitulation* of the expenses for costumes, n.d., (AJ[13] 134[2]).
18 Details from the *Récapitulation*, (AJ[13] 134[2]).
19 *Devis approximatif de Mahomet II*, n.d., (AJ[13] 134[2]).
20 La Rochefoucauld to Duplantys, 10 October 1826, (AJ[13] 117).

financial terms, however, the success bore no comparison with those achieved by Véron. In seventy-five performances up to November 1829, it grossed FF 209.643 at the box-office, for an average per performance of only FF 2.795.[21] For Véron, such a low figure would have been a disaster.

Moïse

Although *Moïse* was the second Rossini opera to be staged at the Opera, the administration under Duplantys kept to its policy of using old scenery and costumes wherever possible. Ciceri's de facto monopoly also ensured that his budgets and bill went unchallenged and that he was paid in full. The savings through the use of old costumes were substantial, although partially offset by inefficiencies in making new costumes which led to a lot of overtime.

Moïse was in four acts, with music by Rossini, libretto by Balocchi and de Jouy and scene-painting by Ciceri. It was first performed on 26 March 1827. The translation of the Italian from the original opera *Mosè in Egitto,* first staged in Paris at the *Théâtre Italien* on 20 October 1822 and again in 1823,[22] had been entrusted to Castil-Blaze in August 1821,[23] and he completed this by March 1822 for a fee of FF 3.000.[24] There was reference to a possible staging of this work at the Opera in 1822, now called *Moïse en Égypte*, but this was postponed to 1823[25] and then discarded by the Minister.[26] The particular interest for the Opera in performing *Moïse* was that it was the second Rossini opera to be staged there after the successful *Le Siège de Corinthe* and thus aroused great expectations.

La Rochefoucauld was insistent that *Moïse* should be staged in Lent and requested that Bursay, whom he had backed against Leconte's advice,[27] should be put in charge of the scenery rather than Gromaire.[28] Duplantys was able to write back on the same day to confirm that Gromaire had given his approval to this request.[29] The first meeting of the *Conseil d'administration* devoted to *Moïse* met two days later on 13 January 1827, with other staff also attending: Gardel for the ballet, Hérold for the chorus, Ciceri for the scene-painting, Gromaire for the materials and Lecomte for the costumes. Three inspectors from the *Beaux-Arts* were also there: Turpin de Crissé, Bachelier and

---

21 Record of receipts, (CO288 (942)).

22 Record of operas staged at the *Théâtre Italien*, 1822 – 1827, (AJ[13] 137).

23 La Ferté to Courtin and Viotti, 2 August 1821, (AJ[13] 112 I).

24 La Ferté to Habeneck, 21 March 1822, (AJ[13] 112 I). The payment of FF 3.000 to Castil-Blaze was authorised on 14 April 1822, and signed by Castil-Blaze as received by him.

25 Ozanam, op. cit., p. 380. He referred to the minutes of a meeting on 2 February 1822, which contained a list of works, including *Moïse*, which could be performed in 1822. The meeting decided, however, to postpone *Moïse* until Lent 1823, (O[3] 1659).

26 Ozanam, op. cit., p. 381. The Minister to La Ferté, 27 February 1822, (O[3] 1660).

27 Report, Leconte to La Rochefoucauld, 14 September 1826. La Rochefoucauld to Leconte, 20 September 1826, (O[3] 1676 II).

28 La Rochefoucauld to Duplantys, 11 January 1827, (AJ[3] 119 I).

29 Duplantys to La Rochefoucauld, 11 January 1827, (O[3] 1678 V).

Lenormant. Rossini was also there as well as the librettists Balocchi and de Jouy.[30] After de Jouy had read the libretto, Ciceri gave a summary of his proposals for the scenery. He noted that scenery from old productions, notably *La Princesse de Babylone, L'Enfant prodigue* and *Le Laboureur Chinois* could be used. He spent some time on the machinery for the Red Sea crossing, which would be novel and would require new techniques. Finally, he estimated a cost of FF 20.000–FF 25.000 for the scene-painting. Lecomte then gave his estimate for the costumes, which was also FF 20.000–FF 25.000, although he hoped to be able to reduce this. Rossini advised that the first act score would be with the copyist in a week's time but it was noted that the copying itself was always late, either because the copyist was too slow or because changes were made in the score. Rossini sought to reassure those present that *Moïse* could be staged in Easter week provided everyone worked speedily, a view which was echoed by Duplantys. The latter then wrote to La Rochefoucauld on the same day.[31] He realised that the 5 May 1821 *Règlement* had been breached in that La Rochefoucauld had not agreed an approximate budget. Duplantys advised him that Ciceri's budget would be about FF 24.000 and that that for materials and costumes would be about FF 26.000, to give some FF 50.000 in total. He also pointed out that it would be a tour de force to stage *Moïse* within fifty days and regretted that La Rochefoucauld had not agreed to stage it in Lent 1828. Two days later, Duplantys wrote again to La Rochefoucauld.[32] Ciceri was now saying that the scene-painting would cost only FF 19.000 and Bursay felt he could make the Red Sea crossing machinery in three weeks. In the event, the *Conseil d'administration* met again on 22 February, and accepted an approximate budget of FF 54.401, being higher than Duplanty's original FF 50.000, although the cost of Bursay's machinery had not yet been finalised.[33] This budget comprised FF 20.530 for scenery, FF 20.000 for costumes and FF 13.871 for materials.

The detailed budgets and bills threw more light on these overall figures. Ciceri had indeed submitted two budgets, one for FF 27.810 and another for FF 20.530[34] but it was clear from his final bill that even more changes were made.[35] For example, his first budget for the first set placed the backdrop from *L'Enfant prodigue,* first staged in 1812 with a revival in 1822,[36] at the tenth position at no cost; there were also twelve wings, and accessories and *terrains* worth six chassis. This total of eighteen chassis was in the fifth genre at FF 160 per chassis, for a cost of FF 2.880. The second budget for the first set had a new backdrop in the second genre, with eight chassis at FF 120 each. There were twelve wings in the fifth genre and the accessories and *terrains* worth six chassis were in the second genre. The total was FF 3.600. There was also mention for the first

30   *Conseil d'administration*, minutes of meeting, 13 January 1827, (O^3 1676 III).

31   Duplantys to La Rochefoucauld, 13 January 1827, (O^3 1678 V).

32   Duplantys to La Rochefoucauld, 15 January 1827, (O^3 1678 V).

33   *Conseil d'administration*, minutes of meeting, 22 February 1827, (O^3 1676 III).

34   Budget, n.d., for *Moÿse en Égypte* from Ciceri, for four sets costing FF 27.810, (AJ^{13} 134^2). Budget, n.d., for *Moÿse en Égypte* from Ciceri, for four sets costing FF 20.530, (AJ^{13} 134^2).

35   *Mémoire de Peinture de décoration ... pour Moïse*, 6 July 1827, (AJ^{13} 134^2).

36   Record of operas staged at the Opera, 1810–1818, (AJ^{13} 93).

time of a backdrop for the fourth set which was taken from *La Mort d'Adam,* first staged in 1809,[37] and again at no cost. The final bill, however, showed a backdrop for the first set of the City of Memphis, this time in the seventh genre at FF 200 per chassis for eight chassis and a further twenty-eight chassis in various genres: the total cost was FF 5.684. The progression of this first set had thus been eighteen, then twenty-six, then thirty-six chassis, for totals of FF 2.880, FF 3.600 and FF 5.684 respectively. As for the set for the Temple of Isis, the first budget put this in the eighth genre with forty-six chassis at FF 240 each for a total of FF 11.040. The second budget did not contain any details of this set, while the final bill included it with a total of only FF 2.970. Although still defined as the eighth genre, substantial use was made of scenery from *Aladin ou la Lampe merveilleuse, L'Enfant prodigue* and *La Princesse de Babylone* which was first staged in 1815.[38] A repaint of four borders was evaluated at two-thirds of the normal cost in accordance with the 1822 tariff, or FF 160 per chassis; eight wings were only touched up for no cost at all; one backdrop was totally repainted for FF 120 and another was partially repainted at one-third of the normal cost or FF 80 per chassis. There were many other changes in the bill for the other sets and the progression was thus 165 new chassis for FF 27.810 in the first budget; 141 new chassis for FF 20.530 in the second budget; and 161½ new chassis for FF 17.625 in the final bill which totalled FF 22.149 after the inclusion of work on old scenery and of accessories.

The approximate budget for costumes was FF 20.000 but the total cost was FF 23.510.[39] FF 3.510 was then deducted to take account of the old costumes which could be taken from the warehouses. A provision of FF 2.500 was also included for the estimated overtime needed to make the costumes. In the event, the summary of expenses totalled only FF 15.317[40] as the estimate of FF 3.510 saved by the use of old costumes proved to be much too low. The chorus, corps de ballet and extras cost only FF 5.810 compared with the budget total of FF 13.496, for a saving of FF 7.686.[41]

Costumes			Budget	Actual Expense	Savings
			FF	FF	FF
Chorus	-	Men	4.296	2.447	1.849
	-	Ladies	2.554	1.610	944
Corps de ballet	-	Men	1.300	269	1.031
	-	Ladies	1.954	349	1.605
	-	Infants	508	37	471
Extras			2.884	1.098	1.786
			13.496	5.810	7.686

37 Record of operas staged at the Opera, 1808 and 1809, (AJ[13] 92).

38 Record of operas staged at the Opera, 1812–1815, (AJ[13] 94).

39 *Devis approximatif des Costumes pour l'opéra de Moïse,* 23 February 1826, signed by Géré, (AJ[13] 134²).

40 *Bordereau des Dépenses pour les Costumes de l'opéra de Moïse,* 19 April 1827, signed by Géré, (AJ[13] 134²).

41 *Bordereau des Dépenses …,* (AJ[13] 134²).

On the other hand, the overtime cost more at FF 2.987. As for the materials for the sets, Gromaire's budget, based on the second budget for scene-painting of FF 20.530, was FF 13.871.[42] This was calculated as though all the materials were new – one new wing, for example, was again estimated to cost FF 90 – but the final detailed bill from Gromaire, which clearly had made substantial use of old materials, was only FF 5.830.[43] Bursay also submitted his bill for the Red Sea machinery which totalled FF 5.050.[44] The total cost of *Moïse* was thus FF 48.346 and less than the approximate budget of FF 54.401. La Rochefoucauld was delighted with the production and wrote in effusive terms to congratulate everyone.[45]

These details highlight various points. Duplantys, unlike Lubbert, did indeed keep La Rochefoucauld informed. Ciceri continued to wield considerable power through his monopoly over scene-painting. There was no evidence that his many changes to the scenery were subject to scrutiny and his final bill was not challenged. Use of old scenery was in evidence although also subject to change. There was considerable use of old costumes to keep the costs down and the amount of overtime reflected a general inefficiency. It has also to be said, however, that the Opera did well to mount *Moïse* in only seventy-two days, an achievement which somewhat belied the general criticism of its ability in this regard.

La Muette de Portici

This was a very significant production in that it reflected many of the stresses and strains which developed at the Opera in the late 1820s. On the one hand, it was a great success and the production, first staged on 19 February 1828, remained a core production for many years to come. On the other hand, there were already clear signs of the discord which was to develop between La Rochefoucauld and Lubbert as a result of the latter's irresponsibility in financial matters and of his failure to keep La Rochefoucauld informed. Again, on the one hand, *La Muette de Portici* set new standards of historical authenticity in the scenery and costumes. On the other hand, the culture at the Opera was still such that old scenery and costumes were used in order to save money. Inefficiencies were also much in evidence: the overtime incurred to make the costumes was exorbitant and no-one challenged Ciceri's budgets and bill. The Opera had moved forward artistically but malpractices remained which the authorities failed to rectify.

La Muette de Portici, with music by Auber, libretto by Scribe and scene-painting by Ciceri, was certainly a great success. With its five acts and seven sets, it was the first of the genre of grand operas to be staged by the Opera. It was also the first opera to reflect the influence of the new *Comité de mise en scène* in that the scenery and

---

42 *Devis approximatif de Moÿse en Égypte pour Bois, Toile et Perche*, signed by Gromaire, n.d., (AJ[13] 134²).

43 *Moïse, Dépense en Bois, Toile, Ferrure*, signed by Gromaire, n.d., (AJ[13] 134²).

44 *Les Relevés des dépenses faites pour la Mer dans l'opéra de Moïse....* Signed by Bursay, 9 June 1827, (AJ[13] 134²).

45 La Rochefoucauld to Duplantys, 27 March 1827, (AJ[13] 119 I).

costumes, apart from the use of old scenery and costumes, had a reality and attention to detail not previously attempted; and of Solomé, the *régisseur*, in that the chorus was seen as actively involved in the plot. Overall, this was a response by the Opera to the Romantic movement and to the growing competition from the boulevard theatres. As a result, Lecomte and Duponchel designed the costumes to reflect historical authenticity; Ciceri visited La Scala, Milan, in 1827 to study the volcano effects created in *L'Ultimo Giorno di Pompeia*; and Solomé created crowd scenes which no longer reflected the traditional view that the chorus should line up symmetrically on the stage. After *La Muette de Portici* there was no turning back for the Opera as the audiences had seen what could be achieved and would judge future productions accordingly. Popular, spectacular drama had arrived at the Opera and this whetted the appetite for further examples of innovative stagecraft and design.[46] The artistic success of *La Muette de Portici* was undoubted and La Rochefoucauld wrote on 1 March 1828 with his congratulations on a first night triumph.[47] He went out of his way to praise all those responsible for the mise-en-scène and mentioned Solomé, Ciceri, Aumer, Duponchel and Gromaire by name. What was more, the receipts were also very encouraging. In the 122 performances up to 31 December 1830, *La Muette de Portici* took FF 540.262 at the box-office, for an average per performance of FF 4.428. Together with *Guillaume Tell* which took FF 237.918 from fifty-two performances up to 31 December 1830 for an average of FF 4.575 per performance, and *Le Comte Ory* which averaged FF 3.688 per performance from eighty-six performances up to the same date, these three operas were the main reason why the Opera's receipts improved towards the end of the Restoration.[48]

As far back as August 1827 Ciceri had prepared an approximate budget for the scene-painting which totalled FF 19.020[49] but the *Comité de mise en scène* did not meet until 19 October to review his designs.[50] Lubbert pointed out that this was an important new production for the Opera which should, strictly speaking, be staged with entirely new scenery. He recognised, however, that this would not be possible given the expense involved and although the fourth and sixth sets would be entirely new, the others would make use of old scenery wherever possible. Ciceri then presented his designs for the two new sets. For the fourth set, the market in Naples, Ciceri used an isolated *ferme* to portray shops, wagons, provisions and people, but Baron Gérard, renowned painter and member of the *Académie des Beaux-Arts*, felt that the Italian method of scene-painting would have been better in that it would have made use of a backdrop. Ciceri defended his *ferme* by saying that the French method differed from the Italian but then ran into further criticism from the *Comité*. The static people painted on the *ferme* would look rather ridiculous when compared with the cast which would be moving about. It would be better to place these painted figures further upstage on the

46 For further reading on the importance of *La Muette de Portici* see, for example, Fulcher, op. cit., pp. 11–46, and Gerhard, op. cit., pp. 122–157.

47 La Rochefoucauld to Lubbert, 1 March 1828, (O³ 1680 I).

48 Record of receipts, (CO288 (942)).

49 Approximate budget for scene-painting, August 1827, which totalled FF 19.020, (AJ¹³ 135¹).

50 *Comité de mise en scène*, minutes of meeting, 19 October 1827, (O³ 1676 III).

raised terraces. As for the sixth set, which included a *ferme* for Vesuvius, there was criticism from Gérard over the stage effects for the volcano. The end result of all these discussions was that Ciceri finally agreed to adopt the points made by the *Comité*. As for the costumes, Lecomte's designs were presented as well as some sketches by Duponchel. These sketches had been drawn while Duponchel had been in Italy and were the result of historical research. One outcome of this was to dress the fishermen in very few clothes but Lubbert felt that this might be dangerous for the Opera and advised circumspection. In the event, the *Comité* decided that Turpin de Crissé, Duponchel and Lecomte should agree among themselves what was appropriate and make the necessary changes. Two points should be made about this meeting. First, there was no discussion on any approximate budget for *La Muette de Portici*. This was in line with Lubbert's view that the *Comité de mise en scène*, which included outsiders, should not be privy to any budget details. Second, it had asked for changes to be made in the scene-painting and costumes and any changes in the scenery should have entailed a change in the provisional budget of FF 19.020.

The budget for costumes was not ready until 30 November[51] and only after then, 4 December, did Lubbert send the overall approximate budget to La Rochefoucauld.[52] It totalled FF 47.930 and comprised the same FF 19.020 for scene-painting, FF 15.610 for costumes, and FF 13.300 for materials. Lubbert indicated that various economies could reduce this total but La Rochefoucauld was unimpressed.[53] He would have liked to approve this budget but various factors prevented this. The overall total seemed too high; he did not know whether the budget had been discussed and agreed at a meeting of the *Comité d'administration* in accordance with the regulations; as some of the expenses had already been incurred, any approval would be a mere formality without purpose; he needed more detailed information as the budget was only a summary and it was impossible to assess whether Lubbert's claims that economies could be made were realistic; and finally, in a footnote, he made the general point that any decision to stage a new production should be taken well in advance so that accurate and detailed budgets could be prepared. The seeds of discord were thus sown by Lubbert's failure to provide a detailed budget for *La Muette de Portici* on time and the same complaint would be repeated with mounting frustration in the future. Lubbert never took the trouble to satisfy La Rochefoucauld and La Bouillerie on the timeliness and details of production budgets, and fell out with them as a result.

The detailed budget and bill for scene-painting confirmed Lubbert's acceptance of the need to use old scenery in order to save money. Ciceri's August 1827 approximate budget was for six sets, 112½ chassis and a cost of FF 18.620. The average cost per chassis was FF 166 and there were no accessories included in this budget. As for old scenery, the second set contained only ten chassis and a note made clear that old scenery would also be used. The third set was taken entirely from *Le Triomphe de Trajan* at a cost of only FF 400 and the fifth set used scenery from the witches' cave in *Macbeth*,

---

51   *Devis approximatif des costumes et accessoires pour l'opéra de Masanielo*, 30 November 1827, (AJ[13] 135[1]).

52   Lubbert to La Rochefoucauld, 4 December 1827, (O[3] 1676 III).

53   La Rochefoucauld to Lubbert, 10 December 1827, (O[3] 1676 III).

first staged in 1827.[54] The budget for the sixth and last set, which included the eruption of Vesuvius, contained only eighteen chassis in the seventh genre at FF 200 per chassis for a cost of FF 3.600. Given the criticism of this set by the *Comité de mise en scène* and the considerable increase in the number of chassis in Ciceri's final bill, it was all the more surprising that a revised approximate budget for scene-painting was not submitted to La Rochefoucauld on 4 December. This final bill, 20 April 1828, totalled FF 25.430 which was FF 6.410 more than the approximate budget for an overspend of thirty-four per cent.[55] The reason for this overspend was entirely due to the sixth set. The first set cost only FF 3.000 compared with the budget of FF 3.940 and mention was made of old scenery from *Clary*, first staged in 1820 with a revival in 1826.[56] The second set implied that old scenery was used although the actual old production was not specified; there was a backdrop, *terrain* and *praticable* for a total of eleven chassis but only two new wings. As the backdrop was at the eighth position, the positions in front of it must have been filled by wings from old scenery. The costs of the third, fourth and fifth sets were in line with budget but the sixth set showed a significant increase. Instead of eighteen chassis, budgeted to cost FF 3.600, there were seventy-one chassis for a cost of FF 10.790, accessories of FF 540 and a total cost of FF 11.330. It is, again, interesting to speculate whether Lubbert knew about this likely outcome when he presented the approximate budget on 4 December. As the first night was less than three months away and he had already accepted the ideas of the *Comité de mise en scène,* the strong inference must be that he would have been well aware of it especially as Ciceri's final bill showed that he painted 165½ chassis instead of 112½ for a cost of FF 24.890 instead of FF 18.620.

Géré's detailed approximate budget for costumes, 30 November 1827, was for 289 costumes at a cost of FF 15.610. He also estimated that overtime would cost FF 2.400 but that the use of old costumes would save, coincidentally, an equivalent FF 2.400. Although this budget was prepared after the changes initiated by the *Comité de mise en scène*, the summary of expenses, 7 March 1828, totalled FF 20.724: an overspend of FF 5.114 or thirty-three per cent.[57] This again invites the suspicion that Lubbert failed to take these changes into account in the 4 December budget and La Rochefoucauld implied this when he took the matter up with Lubbert later in March.[58] To avoid similar problems in the future, he requested that Duponchel should submit a detailed description of his costumes so that the approximate budget would be as accurate as possible. Lubbert's reply[59] and Géré's previous comments[60] were intended to give the reasons for the overspend. Lubbert claimed that the budget had been prepared

54   Record of operas staged at the Opera, 1827–1830, (AJ[13] 135).

55   *Mémoire de Peinture de Décoration ... pour La Muette de Portici*, 20 April 1828, signed by Ciceri, (AJ[13] 135[1]).

56   Record of operas staged at the Opera, 1816–1820, (AJ[13] 132).

57   *Bordereau de Dépense des Costumes confectionnés pour la mise en scène de La Muette de Portici, représentée le 29 fevrier 1828*, signed by Géré, 7 March 1828, (AJ[13] 135[1]).

58   La Rochefoucauld to Lubbert, 18 March 1828, (O[3] 1680 I).

59   Lubbert to La Rochefoucauld, 19 March 1828, (O[3] 1680 I).

60   Report by Géré to Lubbert, 7 March 1828, (O[3] 1680 I).

according to Lecomte's designs but as Duponchel had himself then done a lot of detailed historical research this had caused the final bill to exceed the approximate budget. In any event, wrote Lubbert, the final bill of FF 20.724 was well below that estimated by the public. He also claimed that he had produced grand effects at manageable cost. In other words, as the public had not been made aware of the true cost through figures presented to the *Comité de mise en scène*, it was advantageous for the public to think that the cost was much higher than was actually the case. As for Géré, he claimed that the overspend of FF 5.114 on *La Muette de Portici* did no more than offset the underspend of FF 4.682 on *Moïse*. He also criticised Duponchel for not disclosing the details of his designs. It is instructive, however, to compare these explanations with what actually happened. The fact was that overtime, far from costing FF 2.400, finally cost FF 4.560 or twenty-two per cent of the total cost of costumes, and accessories, budgeted to cost FF 300, finally cost FF 1.340. Out the total overspend of FF 5.114 these two items accounted for FF 3.200. Not only did Lubbert fail to submit an approximate budget for costumes which was realistic but the overspend had more to do with inefficiencies in the making of the costumes and with a failure to anticipate the accessories required. As for the materials used in building the sets, Gromaire's budget totalled FF 13.300[61] but there was no record of the actual cost. This would have been much lower as old materials would have been used.

The final bills for scene-painting and costumes totalled FF 46.154 compared with the approximate budget of FF 34.630. The approximate budget presented to La Rochefoucauld on 4 December 1827 seriously underestimated the final total cost due to Lubbert's failure to incorporate agreed changes. This failure to provide timely, detailed and realistic information created a breakdown in communication between Lubbert and La Rochefoucauld which would intensify over time. Although Ciceri accepted changes in the design of two sets, there was no control over the escalating cost of the scene-painting and Ciceri's bill, although FF 6.410 higher than budget, was not challenged. Inefficiencies in the making of costumes by the Opera's own staff were evident in the cost of overtime. Finally, the decision to use a lot of old scenery, despite the importance of *La Muette de Portici* and the creation of the *Comité de mise en scène*, was evidence of a culture which still persisted, although this was to change with *Manon Lescaut*.

Manon Lescaut

This production is a very interesting case-study of how the administration of the Opera deteriorated under Lubbert, and of how the three levels of management failed to communicate and manage in a timely and effective way. *Manon Lescaut* is also very interesting from another point of view. There was only one piece of evidence that old scenery was used and the cost of scene-painting for this three-act ballet with five sets was only slightly less than that for the five-act *La Muette de Portici*. This lack of old scenery, which was also evident in *Guillaume Tell*, was thus already anticipating the changes which were introduced in Véron's 28 February 1831 *Cahier des charges*.

---

61   *Devis approximatif*, signed by Gromaire, n.d., (AJ[13] 135[1]).

La Rochefoucauld authorised the staging of this new ballet on 9 January 1830. The music was by Halévy and La Rochefoucauld instructed Lubbert to begin rehearsals right away so that it could be staged as soon as possible.[62] Lubbert advised his staff accordingly,[63] although it was clear that a lot of preliminary work had already been done. Ciceri had, for example, submitted an approximate budget for scene-painting in 1829 which had five sets, 206 chassis and an estimated cost of FF 31.840. This had been scaled down, again in 1829, to 185 chassis and FF 26.230 and a further revision had reduced this second budget to 175 chassis and FF 23.590.[64] Another example occurred on 19 January 1830 when Lubbert wrote a note to Lecomte, the costume designer, and expressed surprise that, despite two months' notice, many designs had not yet arrived at the Opera.[65] On the same date, Lubbert submitted Ciceri's revised third approximate budget to La Rochefoucauld for approval. He pointed out that savings of FF 8.250 had been achieved as the total was FF 23.590 and not FF 31.840. This was partly due to the use of eight old *plafonds* for the fourth set which saved FF 2.360. He also stated that he was unable to send a budget for the costumes as there had been a delay in the designs but this should not hold up the production as the scene-painting would take longer to complete.[66] At this point an element of farce took over which illustrated both the failure of Lubbert to follow procedures and a breakdown in communications between the two men. La Rochefoucauld sent back the approximate budget for scene-painting with the comment that it had not yet been discussed and agreed at the *Comité d'administration* in accordance with Article 11 of the *arrêté* of 13 March 1822.[67] Lubbert replied by saying that the *Comité d'administration* no longer existed. There was only a *Comité de mise en scène* and he again requested approval.[68] This request for direct approval from La Rochefoucauld again reflected Lubbert's view of the *Comité de mise en scène*: it should not see the budgets of the Opera as it contained outsiders. Meanwhile, Lubbert was justifiably concerned about the lack of a budget for costumes which he could submit to La Rochefoucauld for approval. He twice urged Lecomte to deliver the rest of the designs[69] and sought approval from La Rochefoucauld to buy in, from the outside, some court costumes which would cost FF 2.300 rather than the FF 10.000 it would cost to make them internally.[70] Lecomte then claimed that it was not his fault that the designs were late: it was due primarily to Duponchel who had failed to give him instructions,[71]

---

62 La Rochefoucauld to Lubbert, 9 January 1830, (AJ^{13} 135^2).

63 Lubbert to Aumer, Ciceri and Gromaire, 12 January 1830. Lubbert to Duponchel, 16 January 1830, (AJ^{13} 135^2).

64 *Devis des peintures de décorations à faire pour le théâtre de l'Académie Royale de Musique, par les ordres de M. Lubbert, directeur dudit théâtre. Par Ciceri, Peintre Décorateur, 1829, pour Manon Lescaut, ballet en trois actes.* First budget for FF 31.840, (AJ^{13} 405 II), second budget for FF 26.230, (AJ^{13} 135^2), third budget for FF 23.590, (AJ^{13} 405 II).

65 Lubbert to Lecomte, 19 January 1830, (AJ^{13} 135^2).

66 Lubbert to La Rochefoucauld, 19 January 1830, (AJ^{13} 135^2).

67 La Rochefoucauld to Lubbert, 23 January 1830, (AJ^{13} 135^2).

68 Lubbert to La Rochefoucauld, 25 January 1830, (AJ^{13} 135^2).

69 Lubbert to Lecomte, 29 January 1830. Lubbert to Lecomte, 24 February 1830, (AJ^{13} 135^2).

70 Lubbert to La Rochefoucauld, 11 February 1830, (AJ^{13} 135^2).

71 Lecomte to Lubbert, 24 February 1830, (AJ^{13} 135^2).

and Lubbert reflected Lecomte's view in a note to Duponchel.[72] The row with La Rochefoucauld then escalated and revolved around the presentation of the budget for *Manon Lescaut* to the *Comité de mise en scène*. La Rochefoucauld reminded Lubbert that a meeting of this committee would shortly take place and that a budget should be presented.[73] Lubbert succcessfully sought to evade this: the meeting did take place but there was no discussion of any budget. He attached the minutes of this meeting in a letter, 1 April 1830, to La Rochefoucauld and advised him directly that the budget for scene-painting was FF 23.590 and for costumes FF 31.869, for a total of FF 55.459.[74] In reply, La Rochefoucauld was scathing. Lubbert had presented the budget for scene-painting after the sets had been completed and this was totally contrary to agreed practices. Were it not for the fact that there was a rush to produce *Manon Lescaut*, La Rochefoucauld would have refused to accept such a breach of regulations. In addition Lubbert had not sent the budget for scene-painting and costumes to the *Comité de mise en scène* as the minutes clearly showed. Finally, the budget for costumes, which Lubbert had sent directly to La Rochefoucauld, did not go into any detail: it was just a summary figure and could not possibly be presented to La Bouillerie for approval unless further details were provided.[75] In reply, Lubbert admitted that it was a mistake not to have sent the budget earlier and that work should not have been undertaken unless it had been approved. He pointed out, however, that the *Comité de mise en scène* included outsiders and should only give advice on artistic matters. It would be a real inconvenience if it saw the budget which should always be a secret within the Opera. Finally, he stated that it was impossible to give a detailed budget on the costumes until they had been completed.[76]

Lubbert had hoped that Ciceri's sets would all be completed by 24 April 1830 but he was let down. At a rehearsal on 25 April, the set for the third act had not been placed on the stage and Ciceri could only promise to deliver it on Tuesday 27 April, being one day prior to the proposed first night. Lubbert explained all this to La Rochefoucauld and asked for permission to cancel the opening night on Wednesday 28 April, and to put it off for two days. He proposed to use the Wednesday for another dress rehearsal.[77] This must have been approved but another problem arose. The *Préfet de Police* wrote to Lubbert on Wednesday 28 April, to remind him of the regulations which governed final dress rehearsals. The inspector of the *théâtres Royaux* would have to be present to confirm, as laid down by the Ministry of the Interior, that all the sets and costumes were exactly the same as those which would be used on the first night. The inspector had to submit a report to this effect to the *Préfet de Police* who would then send it to the Minister of the Interior.[78] Lubbert wrote to the *Préfet de Police* on Thursday 29 April, the day after the dress rehearsal. He had alerted the inspector to come to the rehearsal

---

72   Lubbert to Duponchel, 25 February 1830, (AJ[13] 135[2]).

73   La Rochefoucauld to Lubbert, 23 March 1830, (AJ[13] 135[2]).

74   Lubbert to La Rochefoucauld, 1 April 1830, (AJ[13] 135[2]).

75   La Rochefoucauld to Lubbert, 17 April 1830, (AJ[13] 135[2]).

76   Lubbert, draft letter to La Rochefoucauld, 22 April 1830, (AJ[13] 135[2]).

77   Lubbert, draft letter to La Rochefoucauld, 26 April 1830, (AJ[13] 135[2]).

78   *Préfet de Police* to Lubbert, 28 April 1830, (AJ[13] 135[2]).

but had had to say that there would be one rehearsal in the morning with costumes and no sets and one rehearsal in the evening with sets and no costumes. The inspector had come to the evening rehearsal and Lubbert was led to believe that he would not object to a first night on Friday 30 April. As for a further dress rehearsal with both costumes and sets, he could not bring the cast together in time. He trusted that as he was putting his personal authority on the line for whatever might befall on the first night, the authorities would be satisfied.[79] At this point there was a delay over this authorisation as the Ministry of the Interior only wrote to the *Préfet de Police* on 1 May, after Lubbert had explained the whole affair that morning at the Ministry. It was felt useless to insist on another full dress rehearsal with sets and costumes, and permission was given for the first night which finally took place on Tuesday 3 May.[80]

Despite all these problems *Manon Lescaut* must have gone well although La Rochefoucauld was maladroit in conveying his satisfaction. He wrote to Lubbert two weeks after the first night and asked that Contant, the joint-head of machinery, be congratulated on the mechanical ship which had been a great success. As only Ciceri had received flattering press comment over this ship, La Rochefoucauld felt that Contant should receive his share of the praise.[81] Lubbert's reply reflected his frustration. While pleased that Contant's work had been praised, he pointed out that La Rochefoucauld's letter was the only official mark of satisfaction that he had received since the first night. It only mentioned a *machiniste,* and made no reference to the composer, cast, designer, or Lubbert himself. He would like to convey La Rochefoucauld's congratulations to everyone involved in the production and would also appreciate a mark of satisfaction which was directed to him personally.[82] To his credit, La Rochefoucauld wrote back the next day. He expressed himself content and asked that this should be conveyed to every member of the cast. As for Lubbert, La Rochefoucauld acknowledged Lubbert's zeal in overseeing a production which was wholly worthy of the Opera.[83] Having received this letter, Lubbert then sent a note to all those principally involved in which he referred to La Rochefoucauld's special satisfaction.[84]

Manon Lescaut was also well-received by the public, although Castil-Blaze described its success as mediocre.[85] On the management side, however, it encapsulated many of Lubbert' faults and exposed the strains between the three levels of management. Although Lubbert had sent the approximate budget for scene-painting directly to La Rochefoucauld as early as January, the latter did not finally sign it until

79 Lubbert, draft letter to the *Préfet de Police*, 29 April 1830, (AJ[13] 183).

80 Ministry of the Interior to the *Préfet de Police*, 1 May 1830, (AJ[13] 183). This letter was signed by the *Maître des requêtes.*

81   La Rochefoucauld to Lubbert, 17 May 1830, (AJ[13] 135[2]).

82 Lubbert to La Rochefoucauld, 21 May 1830, (AJ[13] 135[2]).

83 La Rochefoucauld to Lubbert, 22 May 1830, (AJ[13] 135[2]).

84 Lubbert, draft notes to Aumer, Halévy, Duponchel, Lecomte and Contant, 25 May 1830, (AJ[13] 135[2]).

85 *Manon Lescaut* was performed twenty-seven times up to December 1830 and grossed FF 119.370 for an average per performance of FF 4.421, (CO289 (943)). For his comment, see Castil-Blaze, op. cit., p. 215.

17 April for the reasons already described,[86] and only sent it to La Bouillerie on 27 April, just one day before the proposed first night. He received an exasperated and sarcastic reply on 7 May.[87] La Bouillerie began with a statement of the obvious. A budget should, in principle, be approved before a work was performed. Otherwise, any exercise of authority was entirely illusory as the right to examine and control the budget had been taken away. Furthermore, he simply could not understand why the Opera, which had been working on *Manon Lescaut* for six months, could not deliver a budget for scene-painting on time. It was derisory that the budget should have been sent to him the day before the proposed first night. He then turned his attention to Lubbert and instructed La Rochefoucauld to issue yet another warning. If Lubbert failed to obtain approval to spend even the smallest amounts of money, it would be at his own expense. La Bouillerie did actually approve the budget for scene-painting but La Rochefoucauld, stuck as he was between La Bouillerie's exasperation and Lubbert's incompetence, had to pass on the former's strictures although, noticeably, he failed to pass on the threat that any failure to have expenses approved would render Lubbert personally liable.[88] This budget of FF 23.590 was thus finally approved and the final bill, after some offsetting changes, totalled FF 23.544.[89] The total number of chassis was finally 165½ and not 175. For the first set, the number of chassis was twenty-four and a half and not twenty-one and the genre was changed to the third at FF 140 per chassis and not the sixth at FF 160 per chassis. The second set included a scaled-down interior of the Opera itself and this was evaluated at fourteen chassis in the seventh genre at FF 200 per chassis and twenty-eight chassis in the third genre at FF 140 per chassis, compared with the budget total of thirty-two chassis in the seventh genre which were treated as half the normal FF 200 per chassis, or FF 100 per chassis. The third set remained in the eighth genre at FF 220 per chassis but the number of chassis was reduced from twenty to sixteen. For the fourth set, the number of chassis was twenty-one not twenty and the fifth genre at FF 160 per chassis was used. Accessories worth six chassis which were in the budget were excluded from the final bill. Finally, the fifth set remained in the second genre at FF 120 per chassis although the number of chassis was reduced from thirty-six to thirty-four. Ciceri's original bill had totalled FF 24.914 but the two changes had reduced this to FF 23.544 which was conveniently just below the budget of FF 23.590. Having deducted accessories of only FF 264, the average cost per chassis was FF 141.

Given the previous policy whereby a lot of old scenery was always used in new productions, it was very interesting that the only mention of old scenery for *Manon Lescaut* in any of the budgets or the final bill was the eight *plafonds* for the fourth set. Quite what precipitated this change of policy it is hard to say but it had already started with the six sets for *Guillaume Tell*, first performed on 3 August 1829. These had, according to Ciceri's bill, 209¾ chassis for a cost of FF 28.880 and there was no

---

86 Ciceri's budget for scene-painting, signed by La Rochefoucauld, 17 April 1830, (AJ[13] 135[2]).

87 La Bouillerie to La Rochefoucauld, 7 May 1830, (AJ[13] 135[2]). This letter acknowledged receipt of La Rochefoucauld's letter, 27 April 1830, together with the budget for scene-painting.

88 La Rochefoucauld to Lubbert, 19 May 1830, (AJ[13] 135[2]).

89 *Mémoire des Peintures de Décorations … . Par Ciceri, Peintre Décorateur*, (AJ[13] 135[2]). Ciceri's bill was submitted, May 1830, although the final total of FF 23.544 was dated 16 July 1830.

mention of any old scenery.[90] The total number of chassis for *Guillaume Tell* can be compared with *La Muette de Portici* for which a lot of old scenery was used. This opera also had six sets but the number of new chassis painted by Ciceri was only 165½. By 1829, maybe the influence of the *Comité de mise en scène*, which itself reflected the new spirit of Romanticism and the quest for historical accuracy, might have been greater. Furthermore, scenery designed for the classical mythology of the *tragédie lyrique* was not likely to be suitable for these new productions. La Rochefoucauld, who had been insistent that old scenery should be used to save expense, might also have had a change of heart. He had, after all, championed Rossini and the move away from the *tragédie lyrique*. It would have been inconsistent to have moved the Opera forward artistically without a similar move towards scenery which reflected historical accuracy. Whatever the reasons, *Manon Lescaut* was a production which anticipated the insistence on new scenery embodied in Véron's 28 February 1831 *Cahier des charges*.

Lubbert sent the budget for costumes to La Rochefoucauld on 1 April 1830. It totalled FF 31.869 and had been signed by Géré on 10 March. It so lacked detail that La Rochefoucauld felt unable to sign it and to send it to La Bouillerie for approval. Needless to say, the latter spotted this and his letter of 7 May extended his derision to this failure. La Rochefoucauld had to take this up with Lubbert on 19 May. The budget for costumes was just a single figure which gave the authorities no opportunity to evaluate and control it. He pointed out that previously directors had provided the detail required and again asked Lubbert to do likewise.[91] Astonishingly, it was not until 17 July, or over eleven weeks after the first night, that Lubbert finally provided these details.[92] By then he was in further trouble as the contract with Durand to supply court costumes for FF 2.300 had, in the event, cost FF 4.815. As this higher figure had not been approved, La Rochefoucauld again felt it was not possible to send it to La Bouillerie without a full explanation.[93] This Lubbert did by explaining that many more costumes had been required.[94] At this point the July 1830 Revolution broke out and with it came the removal of both La Bouillerie and La Rochefoucauld. The budget for costumes for *Manon Lescaut* remained, not perhaps surprisingly, unapproved.

This saga continued, however, with *Les Commissaires de la Liste Civile* as Lubbert still needed an approval in order to pay the bills. He was able to state that the budget for scene-painting had been approved – indeed Lèbe-Gigun had already written to him with the news that Ciceri had himself visited *Les Commissaires de la Liste Civile* to prove that his budget had been approved on 7 May [95] – but he was unable to throw any light on the budget for costumes beyond the fact that he had submitted it. He therefore asked *Les Commissaires de la Liste Civile* to examine their own files on *Manon Lescaut*: this was important as Lubbert could not pay any of the bills until evidence of approval had

90   *Mémoire* from Ciceri for *Guillaume Tell*, 5 September 1829, (AJ[13] 135[2]).

91   La Rochefoucauld to Lubbert, 19 May 1830, (AJ[13] 135[2]).

92   Lubbert, draft letter to La Rochefoucauld, 17 July 1830, (AJ[13] 135[2]).

93   *Maison du Roi* to Lubbert, 15 July 1830, (AJ[13] 135[2]).

94   Lubbert to La Rochefoucauld, 21 July 1830, (AJ[13] 135[2]).

95   Lèbe-Gigun to Lubbert, 4 September 1830, (AJ[13] 135[2]).

been found.[96] Over a month later, Lubbert wrote again. He still needed approval for the budget for costumes of FF 31.869 in order to pay the bills.[97] A further month later, he finally received a reply on 17 November 1830.[98] It was noted by *Les Commissaires de la Liste Civile* that Lubbert had indeed sent a detailed budget to La Rochefoucauld on 17 July, but that this had not been submitted to La Bouillerie due to the events a few days later. Approval for the budget was given although *Les Commissaires de la Liste Civile* were careful to exempt themselves from responsibility for any irregularities perpetrated by the previous regime. As for the cost of the costumes, a summary had been drawn up as early as 24 May 1830 which totalled FF 26.965 although it was noted that wigs were not included.[99] Within the total was overtime of FF 5.041 which was even higher than the FF 4.560 for *La Muette de Portici*. Another summary of these figures added the cost of wigs of FF 3.663 to give a total of FF 30.627.[100] As evidence of the fact that old costumes had been used, there was a note that there were 343 costumes, compared with 318 in the budget, but that these had actually cost FF 4.805 less than the budgeted figure.[101] Another summary in November, which spread the cost of the wigs over each costume, totalled FF 31.569 which was, again conveniently, FF 300 less than the original budget. This final bill was also approved by *Les Commissaires de la Liste Civile*.[102]

The budget for materials compiled by Gromaire, 20 November 1829, totalled FF 17.142 although a further budget, 26 February 1830, reduced this to FF 16.556.[103] Unfortunately, when Lubbert sent the budget for scene-painting and costumes to La Rochefoucauld on 1 April 1830 which totalled FF 55.459, that for materials had gone astray and was not included. On 8 May, five days after the first night of *Manon Lescaut*, Lubbert explained that this budget for materials could not be found in the papers of the former secretary-general, d'Aubignosc, and had therefore not been sent. He then enclosed it for approval and stated that the actual expense should not be more than FF 4.000.[104] La Rochefoucauld wrote to La Bouillerie for approval on the same day. Yet again he had to seek approval for a budget which was late, and yet again he blamed Lubbert.[105] This budget was actually approved on 28 May[106] and the signed document was returned to Lubbert on 3 June.[107] The actual expense was indeed very

96 Lubbert to *Les Commissaires de la Liste Civile*, 7 September 1830, (AJ[13] 135[2]).

97 Lubbert to *Les Commissaires de la Liste Civile*, 19 October 1830, (AJ[13] 135[2]).

98 *Les Commissaires de la Liste Civile* to Lubbert, 17 November 1830, (AJ[13] 135[2]).

99 Schedule of expenses for making the costumes and accessories for *Manon Lescaut*, 24 May 1830, (AJ[13] 135[2]).

100 *Récapitulation*, n.d., (AJ[13] 135[2]).

101 *Manon Lescaut, habillement*, n.d., (AJ[13] 135[2]).

102 *Récapitulation*, November 1830, for a total of FF 31.569, (AJ[13] 135[2]).

103 *Devis approximatifs*, signed by Gromaire. For FF 17.142, 20 November 1829, (AJ[13] 135[2]). For FF 16.556, 26 February 1829, (AJ[13] 405 II).

104 Lubbert, draft letter to La Rochefoucauld, 8 May 1830, (AJ[13] 135[2]).

105 La Rochefoucauld to La Bouillerie, 8 May 1830, (AJ[13] 135[2]).

106 *Devis approximatif* for FF 16.556, signed by Gromaire and La Bouillerie, 28 May 1830, (AJ[13] 135[2]).

107 La Rochefoucauld to Lubbert, 3 June 1830, (AJ[13] 135[2]).

much less than the budget of FF 16.556 as the detailed analysis totalled only FF 4.362.[108] The cost of *Manon Lescaut* was thus finally FF 23.544 for scene-painting, FF 31.569 for costumes and FF 4.362 for materials for a total of FF 59.475.

This detailed analysis of *Manon Lescaut* corroborates many of the general points already made. The strains between the three levels of management were revealed, especially those between La Rochefoucauld in the middle and La Bouillerie and Lubbert above and below him. The poor state of management into which the Opera had fallen under Lubbert, especially in financial matters, was very clear. The high cost of overtime in making the costumes was demonstrated. Lastly, there was only one mention of the use of old scenery in the budgets, bill or correspondence, and this anticipated the changes introduced in Véron's 28 February 1831 *Cahier des charges*.

Le Dieu et la Bayadère

This two-act opera with three sets was finally staged on 13 October 1830, which was after the July 1830 Revolution. Both La Bouillerie and La Rochefoucauld had gone and the Opera was under the temporary management of *Les Commissaires de la Liste Civile*. Lubbert, who again failed to provide budgets on time to La Rochefoucauld, would, nevertheless, have had the opportunity to make his mark with the new regime. After all, the change to a management based on a concession was only four and a half months away. The fact that he failed to impress the new regime and lost his position to Véron was indicative of the poor regard with which both the Restoration authorities and Lubbert himself were held. The time for change had arrived.

Le Dieu et la Bayadère had previously been scheduled for July but the Revolution intervened and forced a delay. The music was by Auber, the libretto by Scribe, and Ciceri, needless to say, did the scene-painting. La Rochefoucauld, surely mindful of the delay over the budget for *Manon Lescaut*, took the precaution to write to Lubbert on 1 April 1830. As it had been decided to stage *Le Dieu et la Bayadère*, it was a matter of urgency that the budget should be submitted without delay and he looked forward to receiving it immediately.[109] The cycle then began again. Lubbert could not provide the budget as nothing was ready.[110] La Rochefoucauld wrote again on 10 April 1830. Having reminded Lubbert of his previous failures to provide budgets on time, he again requested the budget.[111] Lubbert again wrote back.[112] His excuse this time was that it was impossible to provide the budget due to the work on *Manon Lescaut* whose first night was due at the end of April. Some eleven weeks later, La Rochefoucauld sent yet another letter on 28 June.[113] Despite Lubbert's assurances that the Opera was working on *Le Dieu et la Bayadère*, the first night of which would precede that for *Robert le Diable*, the budget still had not been received. As a result, the authorities would not

---

108 *Bois et ferrures et toiles entrées dans Manon Lescaut*, 14 July 1830, signed by Châtizel, (AJ^{13} 135^2).

109 La Rochefoucauld to Lubbert, 1 April 1830, (AJ^{13} 201^1).

110 Lubbert to La Rochefoucauld, 2 April 1830, (AJ^{13} 201^1).

111 La Rochefoucauld to Lubbert, 10 April 1830, (AJ^{13} 201^1).

112 Lubbert to La Rochefoucauld, 15 April 1830, (AJ^{13} 201^1).

113 La Rochefoucauld to Lubbert, 28 June 1830, (AJ^{13} 201^1).

have enough time to scrutinise it; there would not be enough time spent in searching
the warehouses for suitable old scenery and costumes; and too much money would have
to be spent on overtime and extra staff. Lubbert must, wrote La Rochefoucauld, send
the budget at once and he linked La Bouillerie with this demand. Some three weeks
later, on 16 July, he wrote again to request the budget.[114] The first night was due
in three weeks time and rehearsals could be jeopardized without La Bouillerie's
approval of the budget. Three days later on 19 July, Lubbert again wrote to say that
the budget was not ready[115] and at this point the July 1830 Revolution intervened. It
was not until 20 August that Lubbert could finally send the approximate budget for
approval, this time to *Les Commissaires de la Liste Civile*.[116] It totalled FF 36.025,
with FF 12.700 for scene-painting, FF 17.575 for costumes and FF 5.750 for materials.
Lubbert noted that this budget was, according to convention, compiled as though
everything was new and hoped the final outcome would be a total of around FF 34.000.
He also had the gall to suggest that the slightest delay in gaining approval would be very
prejudicial to the Opera. One week later, he was advised that the approximate budget
had been approved.[117] This further saga of procrastination and mismanagement had
finally come to an end.

Ciceri's budget for scene-painting, 11 August 1830, totalled FF 12.700 for seventy-
two chassis and an average cost per chassis of FF 176.[118] The first set, a public place,
would normally have been in the seventh genre at FF 200 per chassis but this set must
have been a lavish one as Ciceri put it in the eighth genre at FF 240 per chassis. It was
also made clear that old scenery from *Les Bayadères*, first staged in 1810 with revivals
in 1824 and 1827,[119] would be used. As for the other two sets, the second was in the
sixth genre and the third, which included an apotheosis, in the second and first genres.
The bill, 19 October 1830, totalled FF 11.530.[120] The total number of chassis was less
than budget at sixty-nine and a quarter, of which sixty-one and a half were new and cost
FF 10.300 for an average cost of FF 167 per chassis. Repaints of eight chassis from *Les
Bayadères* were included in the total. As for the costumes, the budget, 8 August 1830,
totalled FF 17.575[121] and the summary of actual expenses FF 13.822.[122] As with other
Restoration productions, it was noticeable that savings on costumes for the chorus and
corps de ballet were achieved through the use of old costumes. The budget total was
FF 10.000 but the actual expense was only FF 7.639 even though 187 costumes were

---

114 La Rochefoucauld to Lubbert, 16 July 1830, (AJ[13] 201[1]).
115 Lubbert to La Rochefoucauld, 19 July 1830, (AJ[13] 201[1]).
116 Lubbert to *Les Commissaires de la Liste Civile*, 20 August 1830, (AJ[13] 201[1]).
117 *Les Commissaires de la Liste Civile* to Lubbert, 27 August 1830, (AJ[13] 201[1]). The various budgets
     were actually approved on 24 August 1830.
118 *Devis des Peintures de Décorations à faire pour le Théâtre de l'Opéra sur les ordres de M. Lubbert,
     Directeur de ce théâtre. Par Ciceri, Peintre Décorateur. Pour La Bayadère*, (AJ[13] 405 II).
119 Record of operas staged at the Opera, 1810–1818, (AJ[13] 93).
120 *Mémoire des Peintures de Décorations …. Pour La Bayadère*, (AJ[13] 201[1]).
121 *Récapitulation du Devis des Costumes et accessoires de l'opéra de La Bayadère amoureuse, fait
     approximativement le 8 août 1830*, (AJ[13] 405 II).
122 *Récapitulation de la dépense, 187 costumes*, n.d., (AJ[13] 201[1]).

actually used against a budget figure of 177. The overtime worked was FF 1.281. As for Gromaire's budget, 18 August 1830, for materials, it totalled FF 5.750.[123]   There was no bill but it has to be assumed that the total was less.

The first point to be made on *Le Dieu et la Bayadère* was that it reflected a continuance of Lubbert's slack financial management which would not have endeared him to the authorities.   In the event, the first night took place after the July 1830 Revolution and after La Rochefoucauld had left.   The second point was that *Les Commissaires de la Liste Civile*, having had a good look at the Opera under Lubbert, would have been encouraged to think that a change in management was long overdue and that old scenery and costumes were no longer acceptable.

New Productions under Véron's Administration

One of Véron's first acts was to renegotiate a new tariff for scene-painting with Ciceri, 1 June 1831.   Corroboration of this new tariff should thus be visible in the budgets and bills for new productions from Ciceri, and also from all the other painters whom Véron employed.   It might also be expected that these budgets and bills would be subject to considerable scrutiny as part of Véron's overall drive to reduce costs and that Ciceri's, in particular, would no longer remain unchallenged.   The use of old materials to build the sets was, in general, a loophole in the 28 February 1831 *Cahier des charges* which Véron might be expected to exploit; and the use of old scenery for *Le Serment*, which gave rise to Véron's first fine, should be capable of corroboration.   As for the costumes, it was clearly stated in the 28 February 1831 *Cahier des charges* that these should all be new although there was a softening of this stance in the 1833 second supplement.   It would thus be interesting to find out whether Véron took advantage of this change and also whether the extra cost of new costumes was offset by savings in the suppliers' bills and in the overtime spent on making the costumes.   Lastly, the general claim that Véron had a phenomenal eye for detail and that no cost was incurred unless authorised by him should be visible in the documents.

Robert le Diable

The decision to stage *Robert le Diable* was taken prior to the appointment of Véron as director of the Opera.   A contract was signed by Meyerbeer, Scribe and Delavigne on 29 December 1829 for a grand opera in five acts and eight sets and Meyerbeer completed the score by May 1830.[124]   Rehearsals were due to begin in the summer of 1830 but the July Revolution intervened and the production was delayed until Véron had taken over.   *Robert le Diable* thus represented, in microcosm, many of the broader changes which took place at the Opera in its transformation from a Restoration bureaucracy to a management by concession.   It was also crucial for Véron himself. He was very astute in his public protest that *Robert le Diable* had been imposed on him by virtue of a previous contract but in reality he pinned all his hopes on a successful

---

123   *Devis approximatif pour La Bayadère, opéra*, 18 August 1830, (AJ[13] 405 II).

124   Wilberg, op. cit., pp. 245–246.

production. These hopes were, in the event, fully realised and the opera became the corner-stone of his fortune. During his concession as director from 1831 to 1835, it was performed 127 times for total receipts at the box office of FF 919.827 and an average per performance of FF 7.243. Given that total receipts were FF 3.094.956 over the same period from 566 performances for an average of FF 5.468 per performance, the significance of *Robert le Diable*, which contributed thirty per cent of this total, was all the more obvious:[125]

	Total Box-office FF	No. of Performances	*Robert le Diable* Box-office FF	No. of Performances
1831–32	507.152	82	327.979	40
1832–33	812.752	161	213.323	32
1833–34	949.873	159	216.592	31
1834–35	825.179	164	161.933	24
	3.094.956	566	919.827	127
Average per performance		FF 5.468		FF 7.243

The opera was also a triumph with press and public alike. It satisfied the contemporary craving for spectacle through the beauty and richness of its scenery and costumes. It identified closely with the spirit of Romanticism through its emphasis on the supernatural and sense of mystery, and it contained music which was new, eclectic in style, and of appeal to the emotions.[126]

The fact that Meyerbeer had signed a contract with the previous regime posed an immediate problem for the Commission when it met on the day of Véron's appointment.[127] It was accepted that the contract should be honoured but conceded that it would take at least four months to prepare the production. In the interim, the Commission agreed that Weber's *Euryanthe* should be staged in a translation by Castil-Blaze, but this then raised an immediate problem. Meyerbeer's contract had stipulated that no new opera should be performed prior to *Robert le Diable* and this would have made sense when the original plan was to stage it in 1830. By March 1831, however, this was difficult and Meyerbeer, Scribe and Delavigne were invited to meet the Commission on 3 March. Needless to say, they all initially opposed the decision to stage *Euryanthe*[128] and only agreed if three conditions were met. It must be staged prior to 1 April; a penalty of FF 30.000 should be paid to Meyerbeer if the 1 April deadline was missed; and work on the mise-en-scène for *Robert le Diable* should begin forthwith. The Commission agreed to these conditions at its meeting on 6 March and a

---

125 The takings at the box-office as from the first night, both for every subsequent performance, and for *Robert le Diable*, itself, (AJ[13] 234, AJ[13] 235, AJ[13] 237).

126 Wilberg, op. cit., pp. 235–241.

127 Commission, minutes of meeting, 1 March 1831, (F[21] 4633).

128 Commission, minutes of meeting, 3 March 1831, (F[21] 4633).

new contract was signed with Meyerbeer on the same date.[129] Meanwhile, Castil-Blaze, who was providing the translation, agreed to pay a penalty of FF 4.000 to the Opera if *Euryanthe* was not performed prior to 1 April, unless force majeure intervened. This FF 4.000 was designed to indemnify the Opera for time lost in rehearsing a production which could not then be performed until after *Robert le Diable*. He also claimed that he signed an understanding with Meyerbeer whereby he would be liable to pay Meyerbeer FF 25.000 if *Euryanthe* were not performed in time.[130]

The decision on who should pay for the expenses of *Robert le Diable*, which was another example of the problems raised by the transition to a new regime, has already been discussed, but the decision to stage *Euryanthe,* given the timescale of less than a month, remains problematic. On the one hand, Weber was a known success in Paris. As long ago as December 1824, *Der Freischütz* had been successfully staged at the *Odéon* in a French translation by Sauvage and Castil-Blaze called *Robin des Bois*.[131] *Euryanthe* was in keeping with the new spirit of Romanticism and might also be expected to succeed, although it had not been well-received when first produced in Vienna in October 1823.[132] On the other hand, there simply would not be enough time to mount a production worthy of the name. With the benefit of hindsight, it would have been better to have staged *Euryanthe* after *Robert le Diable,* but the Commission decided to go ahead on Meyerbeer's terms. The cost of the scenery was only FF 467 and of the costumes FF 1.406.[133] Admittedly, the performances were sandwiched between the Paganini concerts but receipts were poor.[134] Véron reported to the Commission that receipts from the third performance were only FF 1.400 and it was decided to withdraw the work after one more performance.[135]

When the new contract with Meyerbeer was signed on 6 March 1831, the way seemed clear for the production of *Robert le Diable* to go ahead. Although it was realised on 13 March that the Minister would need to approve the new budget of FF 70.000,[136] this did not seem to present a problem, especially after Royer-Collard's

---

129 Commission, minutes of meeting, 6 March 1831, (F^{21} 4633).

130 Commission, minutes of meeting, 3 March 1831, (F^{21} 4633). This figure of FF 4.000 is over and above Castil-Blaze's own claim that he would have to pay FF 25.000 to Meyerbeer if *Euryanthe* were not performed by 1 April 1831. See Castil-Blaze, op. cit., pp. 223–226 and Jacques-Gabriel Prod'homme, *La Première de Robert le Diable il y a cent ans. Le Ménestrel, 27 Novembre 1931, 93ᵉ Année, No. 48,* p. 497. In fact, the first performance did not take place until 6 April.

131 Spire Pitou, *The Paris Opéra, an Encyclopedia of Operas, Ballets, Composers and Performers. Growth and Grandeur, 1815–1914* (Westport, 1990), 2 vols, I, A–L, p. 541.

132 *The New Grove Dictionary of Opera* (London, 1992), ed. Stanley Sadie. 4 vols, II, pp. 88–89. *Euryanthe* was first staged at the *Kärntnertortheater* on 25 October 1823. It was not a success and was withdrawn after twenty performances.

133 Ciceri's bill, April 1831 and summary of costumes expenses, (AJ^{13} 201¹).

134 *Journal usuel de l'Opéra 1791–1850,* op. cit.. There were four performances, each coupled with a ballet. The receipts were: 6 April, FF 2.669; 13 April, FF 2.879; 18 April FF 1.484; 25 April, FF 1.032.

135 Commission, minutes of meeting, 17 April 1831, (F^{21} 4633).

136 Commission, minutes of meeting, 13 March 1831, (F^{21} 4633).

informal meeting with the Minister, reported to the Commission on 31 March.[137] Rehearsals were scheduled to start by 7 April but by then the Minister had changed. Instead of Montalivet, the new Minister was d'Argout and the Commission was unable to get formal approval for the budget. Rehearsals did not begin by 7 April and Meyerbeer asked why this was so. The Commission agreed to put the blame for this on the Minister.[138] At a further meeting, Meyerbeer complained that Véron intended to stage a two-act opera and a three-act ballet before *Robert le Diable*, despite the 6 March 1831 contract. The Commission was divided on this, with support for both Meyerbeer and Véron.[139] Its own position was then undermined by d'Argout's letter which arrived during the meeting. This has already been discussed in relation to the FF 100.000 subsidy which was agreed by the Minister on 24 April, but there were other points. D'Argout felt that the Commission had exceeded its powers in that it had not obtained ministerial approval for certain decisions:[140] it had agreed the FF 30.000 penalty were *Euryanthe* not to be performed by 1 April; it had accepted the validity of Meyerbeer's contract with the previous regime; and it had concluded a new contract on 6 March with Meyerbeer to stage *Robert le Diable* as soon as possible. It had thus breached Article 29 of the 28 February 1831 *Cahier des charges*[141] on three occasions and the decisions had no validity. In any event, wrote d'Argout, the original contract signed with Meyerbeer on 29 December 1829 was itself invalid. It had only been signed by La Rochefoucauld but the regulations had required the signature of La Bouillerie as well. This was an awkward turn of events for the Commission and Cavé was instructed to write to Meyerbeer with the unwelcome news. All of this meant further delay and a third contract was finally signed with Meyerbeer on 14 May 1831.[142] This included a provision to stage Auber's *Le Philtre* and Carafa's *L'Orgie*, the first by 20 June and the second by 5 July. The first night of *Robert le Diable* did not finally take place until 21 November 1831.

Robert le Diable should have been staged in 1830 and three budgets for scene-painting were submitted. The first by Ciceri, undated, totalled FF 51.880 for 272 chassis, eight sets and an average cost per chassis of FF 183.[143] This high figure was mainly due to the palace in the sixth set and the church in the eighth set. Together these had 110 chassis in the eighth genre at FF 240 per chassis. There was no evidence of any old scenery in this budget and no accessories. The second budget, also undated, contained figures which overlaid those in the first budget and totalled FF 50.200 for 261 chassis and an average cost per chassis of FF 185. The genres and sets remained

---

137 Commission, minutes of meeting, 31 March 1831, (F²¹ 4633).

138 Commission, minutes of meeting, 17 April 1831, (F²¹ 4633).

139 Commission, minutes of meeting, 28 April 1831, (F²¹ 4633).

140 D'Argout to Choiseul, 27 April 1831, (AJ¹³ 201¹).

141 *Cahier des charges*, 28 February 1831, (AJ¹³ 187 I). See Appendix III.

142 Wilberg, op. cit., p. 253.

143 *Devis des Peintures de Décorations …. Par Ciceri, Peintre Décorateur. Pour Robert le Diable (Opéra)*, n.d., (AJ¹³ 289 IV).

the same.   The third budget by Ciceri, February 1831, totalled FF 45.395 for seven
sets, 248 chassis and an average cost per chassis of FF 175.[144] The confusion over
the number of positions on the Opera's stage was reflected here.   The backdrop for the
last set was described as at the twelfth position although this backdrop was said to be
at the thirteenth position in the first two budgets. As for the costumes, no budget has
been found and a claim that the budget totalled FF 49.395 would appear to be
erroneous.[145]   A budget for materials, submitted by Gromaire and based on the first
budget for scene-painting, totalled FF 19.080 for wings and borders, although Gromaire
noted that the use of old materials would reduce this to FF 9.000.   An overlay reduced
this to FF 6.000.   Materials for backdrops totalled FF 3.190 and the reduced total was
FF 9.190.[146]

      The question of a total budget for *Robert le Diable* assumed great significance after
Véron was appointed on 28 February 1831. The sequence of events whereby Véron
was granted an extra subsidy of FF 100.000 to stage *Robert le Diable* and to refurbish
the Opera has already been described.   It suffices to say that the Commission, at its
meeting on 10 March 1831, took note of a total budget of FF 84.550 but felt this was too
high.[147] As a result, Ciceri, Lèbe-Gigun, Duponchel and Contant were invited to re-
examine their budgets and to present new figures on 13 March. This they did and the
Commission set a ceiling of FF 70.000 for the budget[148] which was then incorporated
in the document which set out the terms for the FF 100.000 extra subsidy.   The point
about this new ceiling, was, however, that the meeting on 13 March took place only
thirteen days after Véron had been appointed. The figures for scene-painting could
not have taken the new 1 June 1831 tariff into account; nor could the effect of Véron's
drive to reduce the cost of costumes through the appointment of new suppliers and
negotiations over the cost of individual items of material have been calculated; nor
the extensive plundering of old sets for materials to build the new sets. Véron, through
his subsequent vigorous action to reduce costs, created a situation whereby the reduced
budget of FF 70.000 was not so restrictive as it would initially have appeared. For
example, were the February 1831 budget of FF 45.395 for scene-painting, which would
have been included in the total budget of FF 84.550, to have been based on the 1 June
1831 tariff, the total would have been only FF 31.720:[149]

---

144 *Devis des Peintures de Décorations .... Par Ciceri, Peintre Décorateur, Pour Robert le Diable,*
      Opéra, February 1831, (AJ[13] 289 IV).

145 Wilberg, op. cit., p. 251, n. 65. Wilberg stated that the costumes budget was FF 49.395. This would
      appear to be confused with the third budget for scene-painting of FF 45.395, especially as the first 5
      looks like a 9.

146 *Devis approximatif pour bois et toile de l'Opéra de Robert le Diable,* n.d., signed by Gromaire,
      (AJ[13] 289 IV).

147 Commission, minutes of meeting, 10 March 1831, (F[21] 4633).

148 Commission, minutes of meeting, 13 March 1831, (F[21] 4633).

149 Based on the February 1831 budget, (AJ[13] 289 IV), and on the 1 June 1831 tariff, (F[21] 1054).

	No. of Chassis	1831 tariff Genre	Price per Chassis	Amount
			FF	FF
1st Set	17	3rd	90	1.530
	5	2nd	80	400
	5	1st	20	100
	8	2nd	80	640
	35			2.670
2nd Set	38	3rd	90	3.420
3rd Set	22	2nd	80	1.760
4th Set	-	-	-	2.000
5th Set	44	3rd	90	3.960
6th Set	36	6th	180	6.480
7th Set	19	3rd	90	1.710
	54	6th	180	9.720
	73			11.430
Total	248			31.720

Average per chassis   FF 120

In fact, Véron signed a contract with Ciceri on 1 July 1831 for a budget of FF 32.910 and an initial down-payment of FF 9.000.[150] The scene-painting for *Robert le Diable* should be completed by 5 September with a FF 2.000 fine for each performance delayed by any failure to deliver the sets on time. Whether or not this budget included accessories was not made clear. In the end, Ciceri's bill for *Robert le Diable*, November 1831, showed that the third budget's fourth and third sets were amalgamated. There were thus six sets and the bill totalled FF 37.474[151] with accessories included of FF 5.312. The total number of chassis was 252 ¼ for a cost of FF 32.162 and an average of FF 128 per chassis. Véron then showed his bargaining power by refusing to pay the bill in full. Ciceri settled for FF 37.000, thus reducing the average cost per chassis to FF 126. Given the details in Ciceri's bill, it is possible to calculate the cost of *Robert le Diable* were the 1822 tariff to have been in force, assuming the accessories would have cost the same. This total would have been FF 46.445 for an average cost of FF 184 per chassis. Together with the accessories, the total would have been some FF 51.757, for an increase of some FF 14.757 or forty per cent:[152]

---

150 Contract signed by Ciceri, 1 July 1831, (AJ[13] 289 IV).

151 *Mémoire des Peintures de Décorations .... Par Ciceri et Lèbe-Gigun, Peintres-Décorateurs. Pour Robert le Diable, Opéra*, (AJ[13] 201[1]).

152 Based on Ciceri's bill, (AJ[13] 201[1]), and the 1822 tariff, (O[3] 1685 I).

	No. of Chassis	1822 Tariff Genre	Price per Chassis	Amount
			FF	FF
1st Set	21	4th	135	2.835
	12¼	5th	160	1.960
	33¼			4.795
2nd Set	27	8th	240	6.480
	10	7th	200	2.000
	10	4th	135	1.350
	47			9.830
3rd Set	24	2nd	100	2.400
	8	1st	50	400
	32			2.800
4th Set	51	5th	160	8.160
5th Set	25	8th	240	6.000
	5	3rd	140	700
	30			6.700
6th Set	59	8th	240	14.160
	252¼			46.445
			Accessories*	5.312
				51.757
			Average per chassis	FF 184

* Assuming accessories would have cost the same.

The cost of the costumes for *Robert le Diable* can be calculated from two sets of figures and one hypothesis. First, the summary totalled FF 26.228.[153] This was taken from detailed analyses of the various users of these costumes: soloists, chorus, ballet, extras and so on. Accessories of FF 1.435 were included within the total, although the cost of any overtime was not shown separately in this schedule. Fortunately, another document did show this figure which was only FF 328.[154] The impact of Véron's drive to reduce costs was immediately apparent. When this figure of FF 328 is compared, for example, with the FF 4.560 for *La Muette de Portici* and the FF 5.041 for *Manon Lescaut,* the impact is stark and clear. Second, a table of expenses for costumes, which was a new source of information, listed the suppliers' invoices in date order, and totalled FF 25.339.[155] This table was always likely to be somewhat less than the summary which was inclusive of various other items such as overtime. The hypothesis for the final actual cost relates to the suppliers' bills, which were not listed in the table of expenses and which were subject to arbitrary reduction by Véron. As with all the productions under Véron, the bills were either paid in full, or had a discount of between

153 *Récapitulation*, n.d., (AJ[13] 201[1]).

154 *Relevé de la dépense des costumes et accessoires pour les ouvrages montés pendant l'administration de M. Véron ...*, 10 July 1835, (AJ[13] 215 V).

155 *Table de la dépense pour Robert le Diable*, n.d., (AJ[13] 201[1]).

two to five per cent within the bill so that the net amount was submitted for payment, or were reduced arbitrarily by Véron. An average reduction of some three per cent would seem about right, based on a significant sample of all the bills submitted for payment during Véron's concession.[156] The total cost of costumes for *Robert le Diable* would thus have been around FF 25.500. One last point: it was fascinating to discover that Véron, despite Article 11 of his 28 February 1831 *Cahier des charges,* which decreed that new productions should have new costumes,[157] made use of three costumes from *L'Orgie* and *Le Comte Ory* for the men's ballet, and twenty-eight veils taken from the store of costumes made available for general use.[158]

The Restoration estimate for materials to build the sets was FF 9.190. This was based on the assumption that old materials would be used wherever possible, but the problem for Véron was that his 28 February 1831 *Cahier des charges* stipulated that the scenery for new productions should all be new.[159] As already described, however, the wording was rather ambiguous as it did not clearly stipulate that the materials for building the wings, borders, backdrops, *fermes* and other items should also be new. Having obtained approval on 11 April and 26 July 1831, Véron seized the opportunity to take full advantage of this.[160] The list of old sets used for *Robert le Diable* was lengthy,[161] and said by one critic to have had a value of FF 100.000.[162] The final cost for materials was only FF 831, being the figure derived from the table of expenses.[163]

The total cost of *Robert le Diable* has to remain an estimate due to uncertainty over the suppliers' bills for costumes. Nevertheless, it can be said that scene-painting cost FF 37.000 and materials for building the sets FF 831. Taking the estimate of FF 25.500 for the costumes, the total is around FF 63.300. There was much speculation over the

---

156 Bills of suppliers, 1831–1835, (AJ[13] 409–AJ[13] 416).

157 *Cahier des charges*, 28 February 1831, Article 11, (AJ[13] 187 I).

158 *État des costumes qui servent d'une pièce dans une autre, pour les ouvrages du nouveau répertoire,* (AJ[13] 215 III).

159 *Cahier des charges*, 28 February 1831, Article 11, (AJ[13] 187 I).

160 *Inventaire*, 12 January 1832, signed by Adam and Contant, (AJ[13] 223). The two dates, 11 April and 26 July, were written in the margin.

161 *Inventaire*, 12 January 1832, signed by Adam & Contant, (AJ[13] 223). The old sets, from which materials were taken, together with the inventory number, were as follows:

Alceste 6.	*Castor et Pollux*, 163, 166.
Démophon 9.	*La Caverne* 195.
Le Déserteur 72.	*Jérusalem délivrée* 201.
Adrien 79.	*Sapho* 242, 243, 244, 245.
Sémiramis 122.	*Ipsiboé* 254, 255, 256.
Achille à Scyros 153.	*La Belle au bois dormant* 264.
Zéloide 219.	*Pharamond* 265, 266, 268, 269.
Roger de Sicile 220.	*Le Retour de Zéphire* 6D.
La Muette de Portici 225.	*Médée* 13.L.

162 Report, unsigned, 30 May 1832, (F[21] 1054).

163 *Table de la dépense pour Robert le Diable*, n.d., (AJ[13] 201 [1]).

cost of *Robert le Diable*, with totals quoted of between FF 50.000 and FF 200.000.[164] What can be said for certain is that Véron made an onslaught on costs which showed the Restoration management in a poor light. The new 1831 tariff for scene-painting and refusal to pay Ciceri's bills in full; the appointment of new suppliers, reduction in the price of materials for costumes, refusal to pay the bills in full and reduction in overtime; and the plunder of old sets to build the new ones all contributed to Véron's success. *Robert le Diable* really was the corner-stone of his fortune.

La Tentation

Véron realised that lavish new productions were the best way to attract a paying audience but that costs had to be reduced to make such productions financially worthwhile. *La Tentation*, an *opéra-ballet* in five acts, first performed on 20 June 1832, fulfilled these requirements. It was a sumptuous production designed to attract and please the Opera's new bourgeois audiences and succeeded in so doing.[165] The music was by Halévy and Gide, and Cavé, the secretary to the Commission, and Duponchel were involved in the libretto and staging. It had 338½ chassis which vastly exceeded any recent production at the Opera except for *Aladin ou la Lampe merveilleuse*. Even *Robert le Diable* had only 252¼ chassis and it was imperative for Véron that the average cost per chassis for *La Tentation* should be as low as possible. The special point to be emphasised here is that Véron was astonishingly successful. He plundered the old sets to reduce the cost of making the new sets; the genres of scene-painting under the 1831 tariff, especially for the 103½ chassis in the fifth set, were comparatively low; and he arbitrarily reduced the final bill from Léon Feuchère et Cie. The result was that the average cost per chassis was only FF 99 which was unheard of at the Opera from the Restoration onwards.

The fact that Léon Feuchère et Cie did all the scene-painting gave rise to the action brought by Ciceri against Véron. It was also clear that these painters were subject to the same new tariff for scene-painting which Ciceri had agreed with Véron on 1 June 1831. This was Léon Feuchère et Cie's first contract with the Opera for scene-painting and its budget, except for the second set, and bill were meticulous in the lay-out of all the details.[166] This was very helpful as a direct comparison can be made between the budget and bill under the new tariff and those which would have pertained were the

---

164 See Wilberg, op. cit., p. 252, n. 68. She referred to Castil-Blaze in the *Journal des Débats*, 23 November 1831, who quoted the range of FF 50.000–FF 200.000. See also Marie-Hélène Coudroy, *La Critique parisienne des «grands opéras» de Meyerbeer: Robert le Diable, Les Huguenots, Le Prophète, L'Africaine*, (Saarbrücken, 1988), p. 83. She referred to *Le National*, 4 December 1831, which quoted a figure of 50.000 écus, or FF 150.000. See also Prod'homme, *La Première de Robert le Diable il y a cent ans*, p. 499. Prod'homme quoted *Le Corsaire*, 22 November 1831, which put the cost of *Robert le Diable* at more than FF 80.000.

165 For the first year of performances, *La Tentation* was staged forty-two times and grossed FF 216.109 for an average of FF 5.145 per performance, (AJ[13] 235).

166 *Devis approximatif des décorations à exécuter pour le ballet de la Tentation .... Par Léon Feuchère et Cie*, 8 February 1832, (AJ[13] 201[2]).

1822 tariff still to have been in force. For example, the budget, 8 February 1832, totalled FF 37.040 but would have been an estimated FF 53.310 under the 1822 tariff:[167]

	No. of Chassis	1822 Tariff FF	1831 Tariff FF
1st Set	43	4.460	2.940
2nd Set	65 est.*	11.400 est. **	8.000
3rd Set	38	5.120	3.460
4th Set	21	4.620	3.780
5th Set	51	13.220	10.700
6th Set	36	4.320	2.880
7th Set	66	7.920	5.280
	320	51.060	37.040***

Borders in various categories each
evaluated as two chassis and not
one and a half   1.250
                                                                53.310

* Based on actual bill of FF 123 per chassis.   ** Based on estimated thirty per cent savings under Véron.   *** There was a FF 200 addition error in Léon Feuchère et Cie's budget which totalled FF 36.840.

The final bill totalled FF 38.072 but would have been an estimated FF 53.322, for an increase of FF 15.250 or forty per cent:[168]

	No. of Chassis	1822 Tariff FF	1831 Tariff FF
1st Set	46	4.375	3.005
2nd Set	60½	10.600 est. *	7.440 **
3rd Set	48	6.960	4.840
4th Set	80½	17.240	13.550
5th Set	103½	8.710	5.630
	338½	47.885	34.465
Accessories, heating		3.607	3.607***
Total		51.492	38.072

Borders in various categories each
evaluated as two chassis and not
one and a half   1.830
                                                                53.322

* Estimated thirty per cent savings under Véron. ** The genre was not given. There were forty-four and a half chassis at FF 140 per chassis, being *rehaussés* and *paillonnés*, enriched and tinselled, and sixteen ordinary chassis at FF 80 per chassis. *** No savings estimated.

167 Details of the budget and tariffs for *La Tentation*, (AJ[13] 201[2], O[3] 1685 I, F[21] 1054).

168 *Mémoire de Peintures de Décorations faites par Léon Feuchère et Cie*, (AJ[13] 201[2]). The two tariffs, (O[3] 1685 I, F[21] 1054).

In fact, the savings were even greater as Véron refused to pay the bill in full: he reduced it arbitrarily from FF 38.072 to FF 37.000 and the increase was FF 16.322 or forty-four per cent. Payments to account of FF 27.000 had already been made so FF 10.000 remained outstanding.[169] Apart from the budget for the second set, Léon Feuchère et Cie was indeed meticulous in the details of the number of chassis evaluated for *La Tentation*. As the budget estimated 320 chassis and the bill detailed 338½, the average cost per chassis can be calculated and compared. The budget of FF 37.040, which had no accessories within it, yielded an average cost per chassis of FF 116, while the actual bill, less the FF 1.072 which Véron refused to pay, the FF 3.107 for accessories and the FF 500 for heating the atelier, yielded an average cost per chassis of only FF 99. The equivalent figures under the 1822 tariff would have been FF 167 and FF 147 respectively. Véron's achievement in both driving down the cost per chassis to below FF 100 and in breaking Ciceri's monopoly was thus fully demonstrated in *La Tentation*.

There was no budget for the costumes, although Véron paid great attention to the day-book which gave details of the materials ordered to make them: he signed every day's total without fail.[170] He thus ensured that the price reductions which he had negotiated with the many new suppliers were put into effect. As with *Robert le Diable*, the costume expenses were also listed in a table by supplier and by date.[171] This was in addition to the usual summary of expenses which was laid out in the same way as under the Restoration, that is by each soloist, the chorus, corps de ballet, extras, accessories and other items.[172] The table for costumes totalled FF 47.049, but it was made clear that the cost of materials for building the sets, FF 7.402, was included within this amount, thus leaving FF 39.647. The summary showed a total of FF 38.925 and the total for overtime was only FF 781.[173] Given the considerable amount of money spent on costumes, this was a very small amount when compared with the overtime paid, for example, for *Manon Lescaut*, and was ample proof of Véron's drive to eliminate inefficiencies and reduce costs thereby. The total cost of *La Tentation*, estimated by some at FF 150.000,[174] was thus around FF 82.700 if the total in the table for costumes were taken and three per cent were deducted as a result of Véron's refusal to pay many of the bills in full. This huge sum reflected the number of chassis required and the lavishness of the production, but was still not the full story. Véron had already taken advantage of the loophole in his 28 February 1831 *Cahier des charges*. Having gained approval, he had destroyed some old sets in order to provide the materials for

---

169 *Mémoire, Léon Feuchère et Cie*, (AJ[13] 201[2]). Véron noted on the bill that FF 27.000 had already been paid out of the total of FF 37.000.

170 Authorisations to order materials for the costumes were noted by date and called *Autorisation des dépenses pour la confection des costumes, accessoires et ustensiles*, (AJ[13] 201[2]). Each daily total was signed by Véron, however small.

171 *Tableau de la Dépense faite pour le Ballet de La Tentation*, n.d., (AJ[13] 201[2]).

172 *Récapitulation*, n.d., (AJ[13] 201[2]).

173 See table from the *Bureau de l'habillement*, 10 July 1835, (AJ[13] 215 V).

174 See, for example, Binet, op. cit., p. 130.

the sets of *Robert Le Diable*.[175]   This process was, however, taken to extreme in *La Tentation*.[176] Given that Gromaire had estimated FF 90 for a new wing, FF 162 for a new border and either FF 302 or FF 477 for a new backdrop, *La Tentation*, with 338½ chassis, would have been very expensive were all the materials to have been new and Véron saved a fortune through his plunder of the old sets. This provoked the report which estimated that he had destroyed scenery worth FF 300.000 since taking over as director.[177] It should be emphasised that approvals were sought and obtained for this on 6 February and 16 May 1832,[178] but the extent of the plunder must have taken the authorities by surprise and it eventually provoked a hostile reaction.

La Tentation was thus evidence of some of the general points already made. The new tariff was put into effect; Véron kept an eye on his suppliers; the amount of overtime for making the costumes was insignificant and Véron made great savings by the use of old materials for making the sets. It also proved a great success with the Opera's new audiences and gave evidence of Véron's flair in providing what they wanted.

Le Serment

Véron had been very successful with his first three big new productions: *Robert le Diable*, *La Sylphide* and *La Tentation*. His confidence must have been high, especially as the cost-base was much reduced through the onslaught on the fixed personnel, the new 1831 tariff for scene-painting, and the lower prices for materials to make the costumes. As an entrepreneur who was used to taking risks, he must also have felt that his 28 February 1831 *Cahier des charges* enabled him to do just that and was not a constraint on his ambitions. With *Le Serment*, however, an opera in three acts with

---

175 *Cahier des charges*, 28 February 1831, Article 11, (AJ[13] 187 I).

176 *Inventaire*, 12 January 1832, signed by Adam and Contant, (AJ[13] 223). Changes after this date were noted in the margin, and the full extent of Véron's plunder of old sets was revealed. The productions from which materials were taken, together with the inventory number, were as follows:

Tarare 1.	*Orphée* 12.	*Sémiramis* 124.
Les Danaïdes 3.	*Proserpine* 27, 125, 135, 143.	*Tamerlan* 128.
Alceste 6.	*La Fille mal gardée* 31.	*Daphnis et Pandrose* 133.
Démophon 9.	*Pâris* 86.	*Achille à Scyros* 152.
Castor et Pollux 161, 165, 166	*Les Bayadères* 191, 192.	*Aladin ou la Lampe merveilleuse* 231.
La Mort d'Adam 178, 180.	*Jérusalem délivrée* 202.	*Alfred le Grand* 240.
Olympie 182, 271.	*L'Heureux retour* 209.	*Cendrillon* 246.
Persée et Andromède 188.	*Nathalie* 211, 212.	*Vendôme en Espagne* 252.
Ipsiboé 254, 255, 256.	*Les deux Salem* 257.	*La Belle au bois dormant* 263, 264.
Pharamond 267.	*Manon Lescaut* 299.	*Guillaume Tell* 295.
Manon Lescaut 299.	*Iphigénie en*	*Le Retour de Zéphire* 6.D.
Paul et Virginie 6.L.	*Tauride* 1.E.	*La Mort d'Abel* 38.L.
Praxitèle 34.L.	*Lasthénie* 40.B.	

177 Report, 30 May 1832, n.d., (F[21] 1054).

178 *Inventaire*, 12 January 1832, (AJ[13] 223).

music by Auber and libretto by Scribe, he seriously overestimated his freedom to do as he pleased.

Le Serment was first performed on 1 October 1832, some sixteen months after Véron had taken over at the Opera. It was performed fifteen times in 1832–1833 with total receipts of FF 69.105 for an average of FF 4.607 per performance. This average was deceptive, however, as it was always paired with a ballet. Of these La Sylphide, the new ballet in which Marie Taglioni had a great triumph, accounted for seven and La Tentation for two. On these occasions, receipts were well above the average and the conclusion must be that it was these two ballets, and not Le Serment, which attracted the audiences.[179] Indeed, Le Serment was not performed again until February 1834, when it was paired with the ballet La Révolte au Sérail, itself another great success.

Le Serment gave rise to the fine of FF 1.000 against Véron on the grounds that he had breached Article 11 of his 28 February 1831 Cahier des charges through the use of old scenery without approval. The Commission, which sat as a tribunal arbitral, heard the case and Véron, in his own defence, made a distinction between old scenery which was modified and that which had not been modified except that the painting had been rafraîchi, refreshed, through a repeint, repaint, or retouche, touching up. If modified, Véron felt that approval was required but if not, then he was entitled to go ahead without approval. Given Véron's distinction, the presumption must be, unless proved otherwise, that the scenery for Le Serment, even if old, was not modified. Apart from the question of scenery and although the tribunal arbitral did not investigate this there was also evidence of the use of old costumes in Le Serment which, again, would have been a breach of Véron's 28 February 1831 Cahier des charges. Given these two possible breaches, it is hard, at this distance in time, to understand Véron's motivation to take these risks. The cholera epidemic was over, his new productions had been successes and he was making a lot of money. Was he so keen to make money that he was prepared to take a risk for the sake of a three-act opera which would only cost FF 6.013? Or did he calculate that breaches of his 28 February 1831 Cahier des charges were not a serious matter? Or was he just naïve in thinking that the Commission would do nothing about it? There are no clear answers to these questions, although Véron's character was such that a combination of all three reasons was the most likely motivation.

As for the scenery, it was clear from Ciceri's bill that old scenery was indeed used in abundance.[180] The first set came straight out of the ballet La Sylphide which had only opened six months previously on 12 March 1832. The rustic room was, according to Ciceri, transformed into an inn through the use of appliques, additional features. This use of the set from La Sylphide was hard to understand as Le Serment was, as already noted, paired with La Sylphide for seven performances in 1832–1833. The audiences would have seen the same set twice on the same night, albeit in a different production and with some modifications. Ciceri had, according to his bill, taken the

---

179 Receipts for the year 1832–1833, (AJ[13] 235).
180 *Mémoire des Peintures de Décorations faites pour le Compte et par les Ordres de M. Véron …. Par Ciceri et Lèbe-Gigun, Peintres-Décorateurs. Pour Le Serment ou les faux monoyeurs*, (AJ[13] 201[2]).

chambre rustique from *La Sylphide* and transformed it into the interior of an *auberge* by means of *retouches* and *appliques*. This blatant use of scenery from another production which had itself only recently been staged in March 1832, was not likely to have endeared Véron to the Commission, given the terms of his 28 February *Cahier des charges,* and made the imposition of a fine more understandable. Use was also made of old scenery from *Cendrillon,* first staged on 3 March 1823,[181] and there was some repainting done on this. Ciceri also painted extra wings, a backdrop, a *ferme* and various accessories and added to some of *Cendrillon's* scenery by means of *appliques*. Together with the second set, the cost was FF 2.543. As for the third set, scenery from *La Dansomanie, La Somnanbule* and *Nina* was used and the words *repeint* and *retouche* were much in evidence. These works were first staged in 1800, 1827 and 1813 respectively,[182] and there was no evidence that sets from these four productions were destroyed, as was the case with *Robert le Diable* and *La Tentation*. This set cost only FF 418. The total was thus FF 2.961 of which Véron was only prepared to pay FF 2.600.

The costumes cost only FF 3.015 according to the summary.[183] This was a very low figure given the fact that all the costumes were supposed to be new. Overtime only cost FF 39.[184] The table of expenses figure was even lower at FF 2.413[185] and only FF 398 was spent on materials for the sets. According to the summary, there were forty-one costumes for the male chorus dressed as villagers and forty-two costumes for them dressed as sailors. Yet the total costs were only FF 176 and FF 457 respectively. The total cost of twenty-seven costumes for the female chorus dressed as villagers was only FF 352. The costumes for eight male members of the corps de ballet dressed as merchants was only FF 89. These were all very low figures and invite the suspicion that old costumes were used.

Le Serment thus presents a number of problems. Véron's motivation is one, the use of a set from *La Sylphide* so soon after its opening is another and the cost of some of the costumes yet another. Its production served as one element in the souring of relations between Véron on the one hand and the Minister and the Commission on the other. With the benefit of hindsight it was a production which, in the short-term, saved a lot of money but which, in the longer term, contributed to Véron's downfall.

Ali-Baba

This was a production which served to make the point that Véron made every effort to reduce the cost of scene-painting. The new 1831 tariff had already achieved this when compared with the 1822 tariff, but this was not enough for Véron. With *Ali-Baba,* an opera in four acts and with five sets, Véron paid detailed attention to the bills from Ciceri and Philastre and Cambon and reduced them substantially. *Ali-Baba,* with music

---

181   Record of operas staged at the Opera, 1820–1823 (AJ[13] 133).

182   Record of operas staged at the Opera, (AJ[13] 55, 94 and 135).

183   *Récapitulation,* (AJ[13] 201²).

184   See table from the *Bureau de l'habillement,* 10 July 1835, (AJ[13] 215 V).

185   *Tableau de la Dépense faite pour l'opéra Le Serment,* (AJ[13] 201²).

by Cherubini and libretto by Scribe was not, however, a success. First staged on 22 July 1833, it could not be compared with previous productions such as *Robert le Diable*, *La Tentation* and *Gustave III*. It was performed only eleven times with total receipts of FF 61.526. These tapered off badly and for the eleventh performance the receipts were only FF 1.713.[186] *Ali-Baba* was certainly not an opera which enhanced Véron's fortune.

Ciceri submitted his budget on 29 March 1833.[187] This was for three sets and totalled FF 13.520. He had, however, still not come to terms with the 1831 tariff and evaluated the borders incorrectly. He looked back to the 1822 tariff when a border was worth two chassis, rather than to the 1831 tariff which reduced a border to one and a half chassis. The consequence was that Ciceri's budget, which contained 126 chassis for an average of FF 107 per chassis, should have been for 117½ chassis, a reduced total of FF 12.380, and an average of FF 105 per chassis. Needless to say, Véron was quick to correct this error when the bill came in. Over and above this, Véron had already saved a great deal of money through the new 1831 tariff. Ciceri's budget of 126 chassis would have cost FF 19.960 under the 1822 tariff for an average cost of FF 158 per chassis. The increase would have been FF 7.580 or sixty-one per cent:[188]

	No. of Chassis	Genre	Cost per Chassis	Total cost
			FF	FF
1st Set	37	2nd	120	4.440
3rd Set	38	3rd	140	5.320
4th Set	51	7th	200	10.200
	126			19.960

Ciceri had established a monopoly position under the Restoration and the 1822 tariff favoured him. His bills went unchallenged and the Opera just paid up in full. All of this changed under Véron and the bill for *Ali-Baba*, 27 June 1833, was severely scrutinised.[189] First, the number of chassis was reduced from 141¾ to 125 as Véron simply did not accept Ciceri's numbers. He re-evaluated the borders as already shown, struck out some chassis which, so it seems, did not exist, and changed the genre of others. The consequence was that Ciceri's bill was reduced from FF 16.155 to FF 14.295. This was not all, as Véron was only prepared to pay a total of FF 13.000 which Ciceri had to accept. He had already received FF 11.500 to account and settled for only FF 1.500 more.[190] As a result, Véron paid only FF 104 per chassis rather than

---

186 Receipts for the year 1833–34, (AJ[13] 237).

187 *Devis des Peintures de Décorations à faire pour l'Académie Royale de Musique et par les ordres de M. Véron, Directeur. Par Ciceri et Lèbe-Gigun, Peintres-Décorateurs. Pour Ali-Baba: Opéra,* (AJ[13] 201[2]). This budget was signed by Ciceri and dated 29 March 1833.

188 The calculation under the 1822 tariff, (O[3] 1685 I).

189 *Duplicata du Mémoire des Peintures de Décorations faites ..., pour le Compte de M. Véron, Directeur,* (AJ[13] 201[2]).

190 The bill for Ciceri's scene-painting had a footnote to the effect that the bill was agreed at FF 13.000; that Ciceri had received FF 11.500 to account, and that FF 1.500 remained to be paid. This was signed by Véron and Ciceri, (AJ[13] 201[2]).

FF 114 and saved a total of FF 3.155 on Ciceri's original bill. This FF 13.000 can also be compared with the 1822 tariff on the reasonable assumption that Ciceri would have not have had the number of chassis reduced and would have been paid in full.

This total would have been FF 23.120 for an average of FF 163 per chassis. The increase would have been FF 10.120 or seventy-eight per cent:[191]

	No. of Chassis	Genre	Cost per Chassis	Total cost
			FF	FF
1st Set	37¼	2nd	120	4.470
2nd Set	3½	8th	240	840
	14	8th	2/3 x 240*	2.240
4th Set	30½	3rd	140	4.270
5th Set	56½	7th	200	11.300
	141¾			23.120

* The bill showed *l'ancienne ferme repeinte*, that is to say a repaint of an old *ferme*. This was in the eighth genre in the 1822 tariff which, Article 9, indicated that a repaint would be charged at two-thirds of the normal rate.

As for Philastre and Cambon, who painted the third set, they were also severely dealt with. Their bill of FF 4.760 was for thirty-five chassis and included accessories of FF 210. This was reduced by Véron to thirty-four chassis for a total of FF 4.620 including accessories of FF 180.[192] The average cost per chassis on the revised bill was FF 131. Véron then treated Philastre and Cambon in the same way as he treated Ciceri. He would pay only FF 4.000 and as these painters had already received FF 1.500, they settled for a further FF 2.500.[193] The average cost per chassis thus fell further to FF 112. Were the 1822 tariff to have been used and the bill paid in full, the total cost of the thirty-five chassis would have been FF 6.580 for an average of FF 188 per chassis and the total bill FF 6.790 for an increase of FF 2.790 or seventy per cent:[194]

	No. of Chassis	Genre	Cost per Chassis	Total cost
			FF	FF
3rd Set	28	7th	200	5.600
	7	3rd	140	980
	35			6.580
			Accessories	210
				6.790

Taking the FF 13.000 and FF 4.000 together, the overall conclusion is clear. Véron paid FF 17.000 for the scene-painting of *Ali-Baba* instead of a Restoration estimate of

---

191 The calculation under the 1822 tariff, (O³ 1685 I).

192 *Mémoire de peintures de la Décoration du Bazar dans l'opéra d'Ali-Baba, faite pour le compte de Monsieur Véron, Directeur, par Philastre et Cambon, peintres décorateurs*, n.d., (AJ¹³ 201²).

193 A note on the bill showed that Philastre and Cambon had already received FF 1.500 and that FF 2.500 was due. This was signed by Véron and Philastre and Cambon, (AJ¹³ 201²).

194 The calculation under the 1822 tariff, (O³ 1685 I).

FF 29.910. He did this by use of the 1831 tariff, by detailed scrutiny of the bills and by a refusal to pay the revised totals in full.

There was no budget for costumes and the summary totalled FF 20.318.[195] The overtime cost only FF 208.[196] Véron's drive for efficiency and lower costs had certainly borne fruit here, although this was offset by the cost of the new costumes for the chorus, men and ladies, and the corps de ballet, men and ladies, which absorbed FF 13.920 or sixty-nine per cent of the total. Véron had re-negotiated terms with the suppliers of materials for costumes and had appointed many new suppliers. Nevertheless the cost, when compared with Restoration totals, remained high. As for the table of expense for costumes, this totalled FF 19.804 after deduction of FF 2.700 for materials used to make the sets.[197] This latter figure would have been much higher but for the use of materials from old sets which had been destroyed and for which Véron sought and gained approval.[198] A schedule provided by Contant gave details of operas plundered as well as the inventory number of the sets[199] but this did not fully tie up with the inventory itself.[200]

The 1833–34 Annual Accounts tended to corroborate the figures above. A note to the accounts put the cost of the sets including materials at FF 19.634, and that of costumes, after Véron's arbitrary reductions, at FF 20.066.[201] The former can be compared with the cost of scene-painting FF 17.000 and of materials FF 2.700 for a total of FF 19.700. The latter can be compared with the summary of FF 20.318 and the table of expenses of FF 19.804. In all of these cases, the totals are sufficiently close to give credence to the view that the total cost of *Ali-Baba* was around FF 40.000.

---

195 *Récapitulation*, n.d., (AJ[13] 201[2]).

196 See table from the *Bureau de l'habillement*, 10 July 1835, (AJ[13] 215 V).

197 *Tableau de la Dépense faite pour Ali-Baba*, (AJ[13] 201[2]).

198 *Inventaire*, 12 January 1832, signed by Adam and Contant, (AJ[13] 223). Approvals were granted on 16 March, 30 April and 18 June 1833. Véron to the Commission, 16 March 1833, (F[21] 1053).

199 *Service des Décorations. Demande de l'autorisation d'employer à la confection des décorations de l'opéra d' Ali-Baba, les nombres des décorations de l'ancien matériel ...*, signed by Contant, (F[21] 1053).

200 *Inventaire*, 12 January 1832, signed by Adam and Contant, (AJ[13] 223). The old sets used *for Ali-Baba*, together with the inventory number:

Psyche 11.	*Adrien* 79.
Amphitryon 19.	*Zirphile et Fleur de myrrhe* 134.
Calypso 47.	*La Vestale* 171.
Le Seigneur bienfaisant 58.	*Les Bayadères* 190.
Électre 59.	*Roger de Sicile* 220.
Les Abencérages 206.	*Les Fiancés de Caserte* 223.
Nathalie 213.	*La Muette de Portici* 225.
Alfred le Grand 240.	*Le Laboureur Chinois* 4.D., 5.D.

201 Note to the Annual Accounts 1833–34, (AJ[13] 228 II).

La Révolte au Sérail

This ballet in three acts, initially called *Azélie et Nadir,* had music by Labarre and was first performed on 4 December 1833. The staging was lavish and it was a great success at the box-office.[202] The scenery was painted by Ciceri and although no budget was archived, his bill revealed some of the ways in which Véron imposed his stringent regime.[203] Ciceri's bill totalled FF 24.892 but again he had difficulty in coming to terms with the new tariff. He described his first set as being in the seventh genre at FF 200 per chassis, being a palace in very rich Moresque architecture, but this confused the 1822 and 1831 tariffs. Under the Restoration tariff, this would have been in the eighth genre at FF 240 per chassis, but under Véron's tariff it should have been in the sixth genre at FF 180 per chassis. Véron again picked this up and Ciceri's bill was reduced accordingly. The total number of chassis was also reduced. Ciceri billed for 150 $^{11}/_{12}$ chassis which cost FF 24.892. With no accessories included, this meant an average of FF 165 per chassis which reflected the very lavish sets which Ciceri painted. These would have cost FF 36.930 under the 1822 tariff or FF 245 per chassis:[204]

	No. of Chassis	Genre	Cost per Chassis	Total cost
			FF	FF
1st Set	35 $^{1}/_{6}$	8th	240	8.440
2nd Set	38	10th	400	15.200
	19¾	7th	200	3.950
3rd Set	32½	2nd	120	3.900
	10	1st	35	350
4th Set	15½	8th	240	3.620
	150 $^{11}/_{12}$			35.460

Borders in various categories, each evaluated as two
chassis and not one and a half   1.470

                                                                          36.930

Véron then set to work on Ciceri's bill. He reduced the total number of chassis to 143 $^{5}/_{12}$ and revised the first set tariff to FF 180 per chassis. The new total was FF 22.690[205] but Véron had still not finished. He arbitrarily cut this total to FF 21.500 with a final payment of FF 6.500 as FF 15.000 had already been paid to account.[206] The overall result was that the average cost per chassis fell further to FF 150 and Véron had saved the difference between FF 21.500 and FF 36.930, being FF 15.430 or an increase of seventy-two per cent.

---

202 Over its first year, this ballet was performed thirty-two times and total box-office receipts were FF 220.370 for an average of FF 6.886 per performance, (AJ[13] 237).

203 *Mémoire des peintures de décorations pour l'Académie Royale de Musique pour le compte de Monsier Véron, Directeur. Pour Nadir et Azélie, ballet en 3 actes,* (AJ[13] 202¹).

204 The calculation under the 1822 tariff, (O³ 1685 I).

205 *Ballet de la Révolte des femmes,* (AJ[13] 202¹). A schedule detailed the way in which the number of chassis was reduced to 143 $^{5}/_{12}$, and the change from FF 200 per chassis to FF 180 per chassis for the first set.

206 Statement signed by both Véron and Ciceri, 28 December 1833, (AJ[13] 202¹).

As for the costumes, the summary totalled FF 32.853 out of which the corps de ballet, men and ladies, cost FF 18.432.[207] The overtime cost FF 419.[208] It would be hard to imagine such a large total for costumes under Lubbert and such a small total for overtime, when old costumes would have been used to keep the costs down. This total was therefore an interesting reflection on Véron's policy and on his 28 February 1831 *Cahier des charges*. His policy was to encourage the artistic side and to produce the lavish productions which his audiences demanded. His 28 February 1831 *Cahier des charges* insisted, however, that new costumes should be used for new productions and this entailed a lot of money. The second supplement, 14 May 1833, softened this policy in that old costumes could be used after approval from the Commission, but there was no evidence that Véron sought and obtained such an approval. There was also a big bill for accessories, which cost FF 5.195.

Two other features of Véron's regime were in evidence here. First, he had a great eye for detail and nothing escaped his attention. Even the smallest request which entailed expense was only authorised with his signed approval.[209] Second, he again made use of materials from old scenery which had been destroyed, although not on anything like the same scale as that for *La Tentation*.[210] According to the inventory, approval for this was given on 14 August and 21 August 1833, although no correspondence was archived as with *Gustave III* and *Ali-Baba*.

As for the table of expenses, this totalled FF 31.310 for costumes and FF 3.086 for the materials to make the sets.[211] Further details on the cost of *La Révolte au Serail* were also contained in a note to the 1833–34 Annual Accounts. Of the figures available, these were the highest, being FF 32.305 for costumes and FF 25.932 for scene-painting and materials, for a total of FF 58.237.[212] This can be compared with FF 57.440 using the summary figure for costumes and FF 55.896 using the table of expenses figure for costumes. Whether Véron actually saved money on the costumes when compared with the Restoration is hard to judge. On the one hand he had renegotiated terms with his suppliers, there was hardly any overtime and he would not have paid many bills in full. On the other the costumes were all new and would have cost a great deal more.

La Révolte au Sérail was a success and gave credence to a number of the general points made about Véron's concession. Ciceri, whether he liked it or not, had to use the

---

207 *Récapitulation*, n.d., (AJ[13] 202[1]).

208 See table from the *Bureau de l'habillement*, 10 July 1835, (AJ[13] 215 V).

209 *Autorisations pour la Confection des costumes et accessoires de la scène du Ballet d'Azélie et Nadir*, (AJ[13] 202[1]). Véron signed each day's requests, however small.

210 The old sets used, together with inventory number, (AJ[13] 223):

   Psyché 105, 184, 185.   *Les Bayadères* 191, 192.

   Sémiramis 123.   *Les Abancérages* 204.

   La Dansomanie 140, 141.   *La Mort d'Adam* 178.

211 *Tableau de la Dépense faite pour le Ballet d'Azélie et Nadir*, (AJ[13] 202[1]).

212 Note to the Annual Accounts 1833–34, (AJ[13] 228 II).

new 1831 tariff and saw his bill whittled away further by Véron after scrutiny and a refusal to pay even the revised lower total in full. Véron's eye for detail was very apparent and he cracked down on the overtime spent in making the costumes. He also continued to make use of materials from old sets to help construct the new sets and saved a lot of money thereby. Véron's overall policy was also in evidence. He was prepared to spend money on a lavish production in the belief that audiences would be attracted by it. He was right, as was shown by the average receipts per performance of FF 6.886, and also by the number of performances.

La Juive

Véron set great store by this grand opera in five acts, with music by Halévy and the libretto by Scribe. The first night was on 23 February 1835 and the press was kept well-informed beforehand:

> Right from the start of rehearsals in October 1834, a good five months before its opening, the *Opéra* director Dr. Véron kept feeding the press with stories of scenic splendour, authentic costumes, cost of production. There was hardly a Paris paper which did not regale its readers with details of armoury and live horses on stage. One worked out the cost to the *Opéra* of having the fountain flow with wine every night, while others published 'reliable figures' revealing an overall production cost of FF 100.000, FF 150.000, FF 170.000 ....[213]

Véron's talents as an impresario and publicist were thus fully in evidence,[214] and although the initial receipts showed caution from the public, *La Juive* soon became a mainstay of the Opera's repertoire.[215] The opera took FF 158.447 from twenty-five performances in the period up to 31 May 1835, for an average of FF 6.338 per performance,[216] but Véron did not personally benefit from its continuing popularity thereafter.

Philastre and Cambon painted the third set and the other five sets were painted by Séchan, Feuchère et Cie. The latter submitted a bill in February 1835 for FF 37.107 but this was again subject to great scrutiny by Véron. As a result the number of chassis in each set was changed, first under the heading of *Règlements* and second under the heading of *Vérification*.[217] Further schedules supported the detailed calculations[218] and it was the *Vérification* figures which were used by Véron to settle the bill even although the *Règlements* figures were lower. The bill was based on 181 chassis for a cost of FF 30.005, an average cost of FF 166 per chassis and a total, including accessories and other items, of FF 37.107; the *Règlements* were based on 161 chassis for a cost of

---

213 Ruth Jordan, *Fromental Halévy, His Life and Music 1799–1862*, (London, 1994), p. 62.

214 For a full discussion on the background to *La Juive* and the role of Véron, I am indebted to Diana R. Hallman and her Ph.D. diss., *The French Grand Opera 'La Juive' (1835). A Socio-Historical Study* (The City University New York, 1995).

215 For example, the sixth performance on 6 March 1835 grossed only FF 5.950 from the box-office and hire of boxes for the evening, whereas the twenty-fifth performance on 29 May 1835 grossed FF 7.319, (AJ[13] 237).

216 Summary of Receipts, 1834–35, (AJ[13] 237).

217 *Mémoire*, February 1835, submitted by Séchan, Feuchère et Cie, (AJ[13] 202[1]).

218 *Résumé des totaux généraux pour décoration y compris les accessoires*, (AJ[13] 202[1]). *Résumé du présent mémoire pour la décoration seulement*, (AJ[13] 202[1]).

FF 25.750, an average cost of FF 160 per chassis and a total, including accessories, of FF 29.316; the *Vérification* was based on 179¼ chassis for a cost of FF 28.210, an average cost of FF 157 per chassis and a total, including accessories and other items, of FF 36.467.[219] Were the 1822 tariff to have been in force, these totals would have been substantially higher especially as the differential between the tenth genre under the 1822 tariff of FF 400 per chassis was very great when compared with the equivalent seventh genre under the 1831 tariff of FF 250 per chassis. The elaborate sixth set was mostly in this genre: it contained 34½ such chassis in the bill and 30½ in the *Vérification*. Under the 1822 tariff, the bill for 181 chassis would have totalled FF 43.863 for an average of FF 242 per chassis, compared with FF 30.005.[220] The increase would have been FF 13.858 or forty-six per cent. The 179¼ chassis in the *Vérification* would have cost FF 41.176 for an average of FF 230 per chassis compared with FF 28.210. The increase would have been FF 12.966 or again forty-six per cent. Although the final overall total was agreed at FF 36.467, Véron actually paid FF 35.517, with a final payment of FF 5.517 after payments to account of FF 30.000.[221] The difference of FF 950 was the same as the sixth months' rent charged by Séchan, Feuchère et Cie in its bill. Véron's refusal to pay this made sense as the contract signed with these painters on 13 November 1834 made free space available to them in the Opera's own ateliers. There was thus no need to pay rent for the painters' own atelier in the *rue de Provence*. As for the third set painted by Philastre and Cambon, the archived bill was incomplete with only one page which did not reach a final total. This was a bill for 54½ chassis which cost FF 5.050 and a *Vérification* for 50½ chassis which cost FF 4.640.[222] It is possible, however, to derive the total paid to Philastre and Cambon from a schedule which detailed payments to account and the final settlements to both teams of painters.[223] This schedule was drawn up to work out the eight per cent due by Séchan, Feuchère et Cie to Véron under Article 11 of the 13 November 1834 contract which itself was linked to the FF 20.000 which Véron should pay to Ciceri when his contract was dissolved on 30 October 1834. It was clear from this schedule that the total paid to Séchan, Feuchère et Cie was FF 35.517 and that to Philastre and Cambon was FF 8.776. Half of this combined total of FF 44.293 was FF 22.146 and Séchan, Feuchère et Cie was due to pay eight per cent on FF 13.371, or FF 1.070, being the difference between FF 35.517 and FF 22.146. This schedule thus provided the clue to the total cost of scene-painting for *La Juive* which was FF 44.293.

As for the costumes, the summary total was a massive FF 69.769.[224] The most significant amount within this total was the huge cost of costumes for the extras of FF 30.057. Possibly connected with this total was the suggestion that the armour worn in *La Juive* also cost FF 30.000:

---

219 Details of these calculations are as per Appendix VI.
220 Details of these calculations are as per Appendix VI.
221 Schedule, n.d., headed *La Juive*, (AJ[13] 188 III).
222 *Mémoire de peinture faite pour l'opéra La Juive*, (AJ[13] 202[1]). Incomplete and unsigned.
223 Schedule, n.d., headed *La Juive*, (AJ[13] 188 III).
224 *Récapitulation*, n.d., (AJ[13] 202[1]).

La mise en scène de *La Juive* coûte FF 150.000, dont FF 30.000 sont employés pour l'acquisition d'un bel assortiment d'armures en cuivre, en fer, accessoires de théâtre jusqu'alors fabriqués en carton. C'était de l'argent bien placé, puisque tout cet appareil devait contribuer puissamment au succès de l'ouvrage.[225]

There was, however, no evidence for this in the documents. The table of expenses clearly showed that Granger, the supplier of armour, submitted invoices which totalled only FF 12.103,[226] and maybe the cost of the costumes for the extras, who wore a great deal of armour, was mistakenly taken as the cost of the armour itself. Be that as it may, the lavishness of the costumes, combined with the overall scale of the spectacle, contributed to some derogatory press comment, not least by Castil-Blaze who referred to it all as an excess of *duponchellerie*.[227] The table of expenses identified FF 3.774 as materials to make the sets and FF 65.397 for costumes and so the ostensible total cost for *La Juive* was some FF 115.800: FF 44.293 for scene-painting, some FF 67.750 for costumes after a notional three per cent reduction due to Véron's enforcement of discounts and refusal to pay some bills in full, and FF 3.774 for materials. Whatever the exact final figure, it was less than generally believed at the time. Séchan thought the mise-en-scène for *La Juive* cost FF 150.000[228] and the *La Quotidienne* for 27 February 1835, four days after the first night, put it at FF 180.000 or more.[229]

Given Véron's propensity to cut costs by cutting corners, it was always reasonable to suspect that he may have made use of some old costumes in his new productions, but no fines were ever levied on Véron as a result of breaching Article 11 of his 28 February 1831 *Cahier des charges*. After the second supplement, 14 May 1833, however, it became clear that old costumes were used for *La Tempête*, a two-act *ballet-féerie*, and later, in 1835, for *La Juive*. A document listed the number and cost of the old costumes contained within the summary totals of FF 14.302 and FF 69.769 respectively.[230] For *La Juive*, there were 524 new costumes which cost FF 66.317 and 76 partly new, partly taken from stock, costumes which cost FF 2.432. Overtime of FF 1.020 accounted for the balance. It was also likely that Véron would have made use of old materials to build the sets for *La Juive*, just as he had done with all his previous new productions, and this

---

225 ("The mise-en-scène for La Juive cost FF 150.000, out of which FF 30.000 was spent on the purchase of a good assortment of armour made of copper and iron. These were accessories which were previously made of cardboard. It was money well spent as all this display contributed powerfully to the work's success.") Castil-Blaze, op. cit., p. 246.

226 *Tableau de la Dépense faite pour La Juive*, (AJ[13] 202[1]).

227 «... en 1835 on n'était pas encore habitué, même à l'Opéra, à ces débauches de décors et de costumes.» ("... in 1835 and even at the Opera, no-one was accustomed to scenery and costumes which were so excessive.") Séchan, op. cit., p. 301. According to Séchan, Castil-Blaze referred to these extravagancies as *duponchellerie*.

228 Séchan, op. cit., p. 301.

229 «Cette piece n'a coûté, dit-on, que FF 180.000 à monter. Le double de la dépense ne nous aurait pas surpris ....» ("This production, so they say, cost only FF 180.000. We should not be surprised if it had cost double that amount ....") Karl Leich-Galland, *La Juive, Dossier de presse parisienne (1835)* (Saarbrücken, 1987), p. 147. Quote from *La Quotidienne*, 27 February 1835.

230 Note on breakdown of costume expenses, (AJ[13] 215 V).

was the case.[231] Without so doing, the materials cost of FF 3.774 would have been considerably higher.

Véron thus had another artistic success in *La Juive* but, paradoxically, it did not help him financially. The huge cost of *La Juive* was not recovered sufficiently in the last months of his concession up to 31 May 1835. With only twenty-five performances from which to benefit, Véron would have been well aware of this when he resigned and of the fact that the 1834–35 Annual Accounts would not have enhanced his fortune.

Summary

The above analyses of various new productions, both from the Restoration period and under Véron, serve to substantiate, in a very detailed way, the general points made in chapters 1 to 3. In particular, the analyses show how Véron achieved substantial cost savings for his new productions and also how he raised receipts. The overall contention of this book, which is that Véron's sweeping changes at the Opéra had a far greater impact than has hitherto been recognised, is thus reinforced.

Concerning the scenery in the Restoration period, the regime was saddled with a high-cost structure through the 1822 tariff and with Ciceri's monopoly. The only way to reduce costs was to use a lot of old scenery, as the analyses of *Le Siège de Corinthe*, *Moïse*, and *La Muette de Portici* all demonstrate. There was, however, a gradual change in this policy in that less old scenery was used, for example, in *Manon Lescaut*. The effect of Ciceri's monopoly was also very evident. None of his bills were challenged, he was paid in full, and no other painter was mentioned. Véron, on the other hand, achieved huge savings through the 1831 tariff, his scrutiny of bills and his refusal to pay bills in full. The comparison between the 1831 tariff and the 1822 tariff, applied through detailed analyses of the various budgets and bills, has never been attempted before and yielded startling results. The fact that the average cost per chassis for *La Tentation,* for example, was only FF 99 was testimony to Véron's success. Véron also introduced competition for the scene-painting, as already discussed in chapter 3. The new painters had to abide by the 1831 tariff, as is clearly shown by the detailed budgets and bills.

As for the costumes, the policy adopted by La Rochefoucauld in the Restoration period was to use old costumes whenever possible, and the tables of savings for *Le Siège de Corinthe* and *Moïse* clearly show this. On the other hand, inefficiencies were rife at the Opéra. Overtime of FF 4.560 for *La Muette de Portici* and FF 5.041 for

---

231 The old scenery used, together with the inventory number, (AJ[13] 223):

Alceste 43.	*Tamerlan* 129.
La Caravane 50.	*Olympie* 136, 182, 184.
Les Mystères d'Isis 36, 114.	*Achille à Scyros* 152.
Psyché 64.	*Clary* 224, 225.
Œdipe à Colone 234.	*Alfred le Grand* 238, 241.
La Mort du Tasse 237.	

Approvals to use old materials were granted on 4 July, 21 July and 23 December 1834.

Manon Lescaut were good examples of this inability to deliver costumes without a lot of extra work. Véron's arrival, however, changed this situation dramatically. Appendix V shows the sort of price reductions which were achieved, either with new or existing suppliers, and although it is not possible to quantify these cost savings exactly through the analyses of Véron's new productions, it is reasonable to assume that the savings were substantial. What is more, there was hardly any overtime worked to make the costumes, which was a further saving. The overtime for *Robert le Diable* was, for example, only FF 328. Lastly, as with the scene-painting, Véron refused to pay many bills in full. He made arbitrary reductions which further reduced the cost.

Some further points should be made in this summary. The detailed analysis of *Manon Lescaut* gives practical support to the contention that Lubbert was a poor administrator and the pivotal position to Véron's fortune of *Robert le Diable* is clearly demonstrated by the table of box-office receipts. An average of FF 7.243 per performance, with total box-office receipts of FF 919.827 from 127 performances, leaves nothing more to be said, especially when compared, for example, with the Restoration period average box-office receipts of FF 4.428 from 122 performances for *La Muette de Portici*. Lastly, Véron's qualities as entrepreneur, administrator and impresario can, through these analyses, be balanced by his failings to satisfy the authorities. The substantial use of old sets to build the new ones, evidence for which is documented for all the new productions analysed, is testimony to Véron's all-consuming ambition to make a fortune and helps to explain why he created such distrust in so doing.

CONCLUSION

For most of the Restoration period, the Opera could be said to have had weak management, too rapid a turnover of directors, and an inability to overcome the culture of waste and abuse through tighter controls and more decisive action. On the expenses side, the budgets for new productions were ineffective as sufficient information was not made available on a timely basis. The new 1822 tariff for scene-painting, which failed to deal adequately with the inefficiencies and malpractices of the scene-painters, was set at too high a level and enabled Ciceri to create a monopoly for himself. As for the expenses of the new costumes, the suppliers of materials overcharged and the Opera's own staff incurred excessive overtime in making them. The consequence was that La Rochefoucauld and the Opera's management were obliged to use old scenery and costumes in order to save money, as clearly demonstrated in the analyses of various new productions in chapter 4. On the receipts side, there were also many problems. Despite the subsidies and extra funds made available by the *Maison du Roi*, whether through extra subsidies, outright gifts, loans, or the assumption of the Opera's debts, there were never enough receipts to put the Opera onto a sound financial footing. This situation was made worse by the liberal distribution of free boxes and seats, especially under Lubbert, and by the practice of selling free tickets on the black-market. With these deficits and debts, the Opera was thus a continual drain on the resources of the *Maison du Roi*, although the appointment of La Bouillerie in 1827 led to an improvement from the Opera's point of view. Loans were written off, debts paid, and receipts were enhanced by successful new productions, most notably *La Muette de Portici, Guillaume Tell* and *Le Comte Ory*. This improvement took place despite Lubbert's cavalier attitude towards management and finances, and can be verified from the analyses of the annual accounts from 1828 onwards.

The new administration under Louis-Philippe was determined to change the way in which the Opera was managed and to improve its finances. The appointment of Véron and his 1831 *Cahier des charges* reflected this new approach in that it was an attempt to balance the interests of the State with those of an entrepreneur. The initial result was that Véron, having seized the initiative with great determination and flair, wrought substantial changes. On the expenses side, the new 1831 tariff for scene-painting resulted in a very substantial reduction in costs and served to confirm the misjudgements inherent in the 1822 tariff. New suppliers of materials for the costumes were appointed and their prices were, in the main, much lower than those of previous suppliers. Meanwhile, brutal redundancies and salary reductions reduced the overall costs of the fixed personnel. On the receipts side, the abuse of free seats was tackled and successful new productions raised box-office receipts, aided by a new policy on seat prices. The annual accounts and analyses of the cost of new productions were a tribute to Véron's success, which was achieved despite the loss of the *redevance des théâtres secondaires* and the fact that, by 1834–35, the financial situation had deteriorated. Nevertheless, there was a price to pay for Véron's success. The balance of interests so carefully constructed when Véron was appointed had, for the reasons described in chapter 2, moved too much in Véron's favour. It was increasingly felt by the Commission, the government and the Chamber of Deputies that Véron had taken undue advantage of his position and had been less than honest in his dealings with them. Confidence in Véron was progressively lost and it was never restored.

Véron was a very remarkable man. Having become director of the Opera at thirty-two, he applied all his prodigious energies and leadership skills to create a vibrant opera-house which would especially attract his new self-confident bourgeois audiences. His motivation to do this was to make a fortune and it was by no means clear at the outset whether this was achievable. He had inherited a *Salle le Peletier* which was over-manned, inefficient and riddled with abuses. It had also been poorly managed and subject to too much bureaucracy. Nevertheless, Véron succeeded in his motivation to make money and joined the ranks of *grands notables* in Paris by virtue of his new wealth. His policies had a greater impact than has, perhaps, hitherto been recognised. He also had a substantial piece of luck. Through no initiative of his own, he had inherited *Robert le Diable*. This opera proved to be a stunning success both artistically and financially. It really was the corner-stone of his fortune.

It is, nevertheless, very difficult, if not impossible, to manage any opera-house successfully over any length of time. Four separate interests have to be sustained and satisfied: artistic integrity, management necessity, sponsors' demands, and audience enthusiasm. These four interests rarely run in tandem and the constant juggling of priorities can eventually defeat even the most able of directors. Sponsors' demands can result in a loss of artistic integrity; too forward an artistic policy can cause a headache for management as audiences dwindle and losses mount; the management never has enough money and must constantly struggle with rising costs and insufficient receipts; it must also keep the artistic side vibrant, the sponsors happy and the audiences enthused.

How did Véron cope with these separate and potentially conflicting interests? As a director who had a concession to manage the Opera at his own risk, peril and fortune, his prime concern was to attract a large paying audience to every evening when a production was staged and at a cost which would enable him to prosper. Out of the four separate interests, management and audiences were in tandem and Véron exploited this convergence with great skill, flair and success. On the artistic side, he also had some success given the time and place in which he lived. Not all of his new productions succeeded and it could be said that he pandered to the tastes of his new audiences by providing them with lavish spectacles which were not too demanding. Nevertheless, *Robert le Diable* was a real innovation for the Opera which succeeded triumphantly and the ballerina Marie Taglioni raised the artistic side through the quality of her dancing. On the other hand, his resignation was prompted by his failure to satisfy two of the four interests. Even his management could not stem the inexorable tide of rising costs and he made a loss in 1834–35; and he fatally fell out with his sponsors, the State.

Véron was too single-minded and failed to appreciate fully what the State's interests required of him. He had signed the 28 February 1831 *Cahier des charges* but consistently failed to fulfil his obligations towards it. He took neither the time nor trouble to humour and appease the government, the Commission, and the Chamber of Deputies. As an entrepreneur, he lacked the political sense to realise that these interests were very important and had to be balanced against his own. For all his success at the Opera, he ran out of friends in high places. Whether he resigned simply because the finances had turned against him, as Crosten believed, or whether he was sacked because the State wished to see the back of him, as Fulcher believed, is a moot point. The practical result was the same and he left well before the end of his six-year concession.

APPENDIX I

Translation of Dubois' Report to the Comte de Lastoret, (AJ^{13} 114 I).

The management of a theatre, like any business whose organisation is complex and whose ways of working are infinitely varied, needs stability and security so that a systematic routine and a noticeable improvement can be established. People have rightly complained for a long time that the Opera has not been moving towards its desired goal of high art combined with good house-keeping. The constant changes in management and in the appointment of directors is the principal and indeed the only reason for the stagnation in the development of this enormous establishment. In only ten years since 1814, there have been five different directors. Messrs. Picard, Choron, Persuis, Viotti and Habeneck have directed the theatre during this time. The average term of office of a director is therefore two years.

When a well-meaning Minister appoints as directors men who are favoured with his confidence and who are worthy of it by virtue of their knowledge, ability and enthusiasm, is this all for the good? No. The potential is created and increases, but is its growth assured? No. Everything conspires to halt and destroy it right from its birth. Let me explain. As soon as a new director is given legitimate power, the staff, who are in general very fickle, welcome, celebrate and rejoice over the new appointment. At first, there is hard work, obedience, and even respect, but one must not be deceived. This first spark of enthusiasm is due less to the trust inspired by the new director than to the hate which usually inspired the fall of his predecessor. This fall of the previous director is such a triumph for the staff that they are initially ready to submit to the new yoke, however tiring and however despotic.

I can provide evidence of this from my own experience. During the first year the staff are on the look-out. Hoping for much from the goodwill or rather the weakness of their new director, they obey, they appear satisfied and they seem to consider the new director as their liberator. So far, so good. In order to be made welcome by the staff during his first year, the director observes without complaint and directs without too much severity. In effect, he governs the Opera in a paternalistic way which means that the abuses are tolerated. The second year leads to some minor changes and a few reforms as a result of observations made during the first year. The staff, who notice that the director has not turned a blind eye as they had thought, begin to mutter under their breath, give voice to their fears and attempt some slander. Their obedience comes with a bad grace and is somewhat strained. Sick-leave reappears and complaints of over-tiredness are heard. Finally the quiet sense of duty begins to break down and the director is seen as demanding and unfair. Two years have passed and the third opens. It is now that the revolution becomes general.

There is no doubt that any director who is attentive, perceptive and well-informed must have noticed the detailed vices and abuses of the staff. He therefore feels it his duty to act decisively as dictated by common sense and good-housekeeping. He should no longer tolerate either the long period of time spent in a state of disorder or the fact that services are paid for by illegal favours. Dangerous ring-leaders are removed, suspect staff are dismissed and new duties are allotted to those who remain or to those who replace them. The new system, it is not hard to imagine, is then criticised, ridiculed and slandered. New problems arise from the recent allocation of duties to the new staff. This unrest is called <u>anarchy</u>. The director is loudly declared to be useless and lacking in skill and the only thought is to replace him. How do they set about achieving this desired aim? By slander, by anonymous letters, by articles in the newspapers.... They shout a lot, and very loudly. The protests reach the ears of the highest authorities who initially reject them but the director, who is attacked at length on a daily basis with slander, poisoned words and false evidence, begins, despite his better self, to have less confidence, less peace of mind and less goodwill. Using the widespread hatred as a pretext, a new director then seems necessary and the old director is replaced.

This is a true and honest picture, and is in no way exaggerated. Might not the director, who has to leave at a time of major changes, be at least consoled by the preservation of his new way of doing things and the new duties he has allocated? Indeed not. The obvious confusion which arises when one is setting up and outlining new responsibilities becomes chaos as the director who has had these innovative ideas has not lasted long enough to explain his intentions, nor to define his aims, nor to set his plans in place. The changes made with a view to the general good are then blamed because they have not achieved their full effect and the old erroneous ways are re-established in full force despite their dangers. What might have been fruitful seems bad and everyone is astonished that the previous director could have had such harmful thoughts and such disorganised plans. It is therefore inevitable that this instability of management at the Opera should produce such unfortunate results. How can one hope for steadfast obedience, sustained enthusiasm and sincere loyalty from a staff who know from experience that the authorities will change the director every two or three years? Those who have no patience wait for the downfall of the director. The quieter staff await the expected dismissal with a lack of concern and with no enthusiasm for work. As for the director who is in the middle of these squalls, he works towards his goal but secretly feels the greatest possible anxiety since he expects, any day, the fate predicted for him, the fate which had struck his predecessors.

What is the remedy for this chaos, this lack of discipline and these fears which are born of this lack of stability? There is only one way. It is to make the management of the Royal theatres similar to that of other theatres by a contract of *privilège* for a fixed number of years. It will be seen in the history of the Opera that this suggested solution is not new, that formerly the King did grant a *privilège* to this theatre, and that Paris itself, when in charge of the Opera, also used this means of fostering it. Were the management of the Opera to enjoy an assured ten-year *privilège* these incessant abuses would cease in the face of a sustained management effort which was not impeded. One would also see the artists obliged, in their own self-interest, to submit to an authority which was more enduring. The higher authority, which will have established an appropriate regime for the good of the company, will be able to ask the management of the Opera, whose jobs are now guaranteed except in cases of embezzlement, for an accurate account of their stewardship of the Opera and the management would have the time to make the Opera profitable for both art and good-housekeeping. Finally, the Minister, encouraged by the hope of an improvement, will have appointed a director whose work he can guide and whose new plans he can approve. The director, on the other hand, promoted by the King to further high office, would retain the certainty that his plans would have been carried through. Instead, he currently experiences the chagrin of seeing his work suddenly ruined and his hopes dashed. As for his staff, who have enjoyed his trust and might have hoped for a better reward, they are ignominiously dismissed.

Les administrations Théâtrales, comme toute entreprise dont les rouages sont nombreux, dont les détails d'exécution sont variés à l'infini, ont besoin de stabilité, d'une certitude d'existence qui permette d'établir un ordre de choses durable, une amélioration sensible.

Depuis longtemps on se plaint et avec raison que l'Académie Royale de Musique ne marche pas au bien désiré sous le rapport de l'art comme sous celui de l'économie.

La première la seule cause même de cette stagnation dans la marche de ce vaste établissement, c'est la mutation successive des administrations appellées à le gouverner.

En dix années seulement, depuis 1814, on compte cinq administrations

MM. Picard, Choron, Persuis, Viotti, et Habeneck ont, dans cet espace de temps, dirigé le Théâtre.

Le terme moyen de l'existence de ces administrations est donc de deux années.

Lorsque la bienveillance d'un Ministre appelle à des fonctions d'administrateurs de Théâtre, des hommes honorés de sa confiance et qui sont dignes d'elle par leurs connaissances, leur aptitude et leur zèle, le bien est-il fait? non, il naît, il commence. Son accroissement

en il certain? non; tout peut s'arrêter et le détruire
dès sa naissance. Je m'explique.

Aussitôt qu'une administration nouvelle est investie
de pouvoir honorable, les administrés, en général
très inconstants, accueillent fêtent, célèbrent les nouveaux
membres qui la composent. Il y a d'abord ardeur de
travail, soumission, respect même; mais il ne faut pas
s'y tromper. ce premier feu de zèle est moins dû à
la confiance qu'inspirent les nouveaux Directeurs, qu'à
la haine qui, habituellement, poursuit le pouvoir déchu.
La chute des anciens administrateurs est un tel triomphe
pour les administrés, qu'ils sont d'abord prêts à plier
sous un nouveau joug, fut il même plus fatigant,
plus despotique.

Je puis, par expérience donner une preuve de ce que
j'avance ici.

Pendant la première année les artistes ou employés
sont aux aguets. Espérant tout de la bonté ou plutôt
de la foiblesse de leur nouveau chef, ils obéissent,
paroissent satisfaits, et semblent regarder la nouvelle
administration comme leur libératrice.

Jusques là tout va bien. Pour se faire accueillir

ses administrés, il est juste de convenir que pendant cette
première année l'administration observe sans se plaindre,
commande sans trop de rigueur, enfin gouverne
paternellement, ce qui veut dire au théâtre conserve
respecter les abus.

La seconde année, le résultat des observations
faites pendant la première année déjà quelques légers
changements, quelques réformes. Les administrés qui
commencent à s'appercevoir que la direction n'a pas
fermé les yeux comme ils le croyaient, murmurent
tous bas, témoignent des craintes, essayent quelques
calomnies, en un mot plus qu'une soumission de mauvaise
grâce ou forcée. Les indispositions renaissent, les
plaintes de trop de fatigue se font entendre; Enfin la
position calme du devoir commence à cesser, et
l'administration paroit exigeante et injuste?

Ces deux époques passées, la troisième année
arrive, et c'est alors que la révolution devient générale.

Il n'est pas douteux qu'une administration
attentive, prévoyante, éclairée, a dû remarquer dans
tous leurs détails, les vices, les abus de chaque partie,
il est de son devoir de porter enfin un coup décisif, et
de ne plus respecter, puisque la raison, l'économie le

commandent, ni une ancienneté qui s'est passée dans le
désordre, ni des services qui ont été payés par des
avantages illicites. Des chefs dangereux sont donc éloignés,
des employés peu sûrs sont renvoyés, et de nouveaux
devoirs sont tracés à ceux qui restent ou à ceux
qui remplacent. Le nouveau système, comme il est
facile de le concevoir est critiqué, ridiculisé, calomnié,
les troubles du moment, trouble qui résulte d'une
nouvelle répartition des droits à de nouveaux employés
est appellé anarchie. l'administration est déclarée
tout haut inhabile, incapable, et l'on ne pense plus
qu'à son remplacement.

Comment arriver à ce but si désiré ? par des
calomnies, par des lettres anonimes, par des articles
de journaux .... On crie beaucoup, et très fort.
les clameurs finissent par arriver jusqu'à l'oreille
qui les repoussoit, et le chef suprême assailli longtems,
chaque jour, de dénonciations, de discours envenimés,
de fausses preuves, a, malgré lui, moins de confiance
de sécurité, de bienveillance: sous le prétexte d'une
haine générale, une nouvelle administration paroit
nécessaire, l'autre est changée.

Ce tableau est vrai, fidele, et n'a rien de le

couleurs de l'exagération.

L'administration qui succombe au moment de mutations très considérables, de changements très importants, sera-t-elle, au moins, consolée dans sa retraite par la conservation du chemin qu'elle a tracé, des nouveaux droits qu'elle a prescrits? non: des embarras indispensables quand on crée, quand on trace des fonctions, deviennent un désordre quand ceux qui ont eu ces idées régénératrices, n'ont pas eu le temps d'expliquer leurs intentions, de régler leurs desseins, d'asseoir leurs projets.

Les changements qu'ils ont faits par l'idée du bien sont-donc blâmés parcequ'ils n'ont pu avoir leur entier effet, en les anciennes erreurs sont rétablies dans toutes leurs forces, malgré tout leur danger? Ce qui aurait pu être fructueux, paroît mauvais, et l'on s'étonne que l'administration précédente ait eu des pensées si nuisibles, des projets si désordonnés.

Il est donc bien constant que la mobilité des administrations de l'académie Royale de Musique produit ces résultats fâcheux. Comment, en effet, espérer une obéissance constante, un zèle soutenu, un attachement sincère de sujets qui, par expérience, savent que l'autorité déplace tous les deux ou trois ans le

chefs qu'on leur a donnés. Ceux qui n'ont pour de
patience, travaillent à la déchéance de leur administration,
les Sujets tranquilles attendent les renvoi certain avec
insouciance en sans aucune ardeur de travail

Des leur côté les administrateurs qui, au milieu
de ces orages, marchent à leur but, éprouvent
secrètement les plus vives inquiétudes, puisqu'ils
doivent s'attendre, chaque jour, au sort qui leur est
prédit en qui a frappé leurs prédécesseurs.

Comment remédier à ce désordre, à cette
indiscipline, à ces craintes qui naissent de l'instabilité
des chefs de l'établissement?

Il n'est qu'un moyen. c'est d'assimiler la
direction des théatres royaux à celle des autres
Spectacles sous le rapport des privilèges pour un
certain nombre d'années.

On verra dans les annales de l'opéra que ce
moyen présenté aujourd'hui n'est point une innovation,
que le Roi accordoit jadis des privilèges pour ce
Théâtre, en que la ville de Paris elle même, quand
elle étoit chargée de l'académie Royale de musique
employoit aussi ce moyen protecteur de l'établissement.

Que l'administration de l'opéra jouisse pend.ᵗ

dis au d'un privilège assuré, et l'on verra les abus,
poursuivis avec constance, cesser sous des efforts soutenus
et sans entraves. On verra les artistes forcés dans leurs
intérêts de se soumettre à une puissance durable.
l'autorité Supérieure qui aura établi un ordre de choses
convenable au bien du service pourra demander à des
fonctionnaires, qu'il aura garantis dans leur place
Sauf le cas de malversation, un compte exact de
leur gestion qu'ils auront eu le temps de rendre profitable
à l'art comme aux autres parties économiques. Enfin
le Ministre qui, animé par l'espoir d'une amélioration,
aura nommé une administration, l'aura guidée dans
ses travaux, l'aura approuvée dans ses vues nouvelles,
Conservera, si le Roi l'appelloit à d'autres dignités,
la certitude que ses projets seront réalisés, au lieu
d'éprouver le déplaisir de voir briser, tout à coup, son
ouvrage, détruire ses espérances, en renvoyer
ignominieusement ceux qui, honorés de sa confiance,
Devaient espérer une autre récompense.

Source: *document conservé au Centre historique des Archives nationals à Paris, (AJ[13] 114).*

APPENDIX II

Budget and Annual Accounts 1827, (AJ[13] 145 V).

	Budget	Accounts
	FF	FF
RECETTES		
Recettes à l'entrée	667.838	499.707
Location de loges à l'année	50.000	47.990
Bals Masqués	42.000	37.378
Concerts spirituels	17.000	10.963
Location de boutiques	5.050	4.925
Redevances des théâtres secondaires	170.000	180.995
Redevances de l'opéra Italien pour costumes	15.000	11.250
Subvention royale	750.000	750.000
Recettes extraordinaires	9.000	172.041
	1.725.888	1.715.249
DÉPENSES		
Administration et Service	54.200	50.033
Artistes du chant	156.511	134.910
des choeurs	72.620	72.362
de la danse	203.691	188.981
des ballets	80.500	79.162
de l'orchestre	132.500	132.496
Service de la salle et du théâtre	37.290	36.680
des costumes	42.548	41.965
des décorations	85.450	85.447
Total de personnel fixe	865.310	822.036

	Budget	Accounts
	FF	**FF**
Gratifications annuelles aux premiers sujets	63.375	56.596
Feux	80.000	91.263
Artistes externes par représentation	5.000	2.985
Élèves de la danse	9.000	8.990
Comparses de la danse	10.000	12.887
Honoraires des auteurs et compositeurs	40.000	48.763
Encouragements aux surnuméraires du chant	6.000	5.250
aux élèves de la danse	4.000	3.898
Indemnités aux anciens artistes choeurs et ballets	3.000	2.900
Travaux extraordinaires des services divers	19.500	21.751
Gratifications éventuelles	15.000	19.415
Total de personnel variable	254.875	274.698
Éclairage	65.000	68.661
Chauffage	20.000	20.569
Copie de musique, Lutherie	12.000	17.824
Frais de costumes et décorations	190.000	182.597
Frais de mobilier et bâtiment	5.000	24.012
Total de matériel	292.000	313.663
Droit des indigents	65.000	50.226
Affiches, frais de bureau	12.000	13.654
Frais de sûreté	28.000	27.669
des bals masqués	12.000	23.367
des concerts spirituels	7.000	8.502
imprévus et éventuels	40.000	33.073
Impôt foncier	703	635
Fonds commun d'insuffisance	25.000	51.960
Total dépenses diverses	189.703	209.086
Indemnités aux réformés et héritiers	4.000	2.854
Subvention à la caisse des pensions	120.000	120.000
	124.000	122.854
Totaux	1.725.888	1.742.337
Déficit		(27.088)

Budget and Annual Accounts 1828, (AJ¹³ 146 III).

	Budget	Accounts
	FF	FF
RECETTES		
Recettes à l'entrée	540.000	522.105
Location de loges à l'année	50.000	82.880
Bals Masqués	40.000	33.584
Concerts spirituels	15.000	9.370
Location de boutiques	4.925	2.675
Redevances des théâtres secondaires	188.000	194.673
Subvention royale	850.000	850.000
Recettes extraordinaires	10.000	10.461
	1.697.925	1.705.748
DÉPENSES		
Direction et service	47.900	46.787
Artistes du chant	133.705	115.851
des choeurs	73.300	72.495
de la danse	186.333	158.140
des ballets	81.417	78.820
de l'orchestre	132.800	130.348
Service de la salle et du théâtre	38.090	37.948
des costumes	42.418	41.184
des décorations	86.912	84.576
Total de personnel fixe	822.875	766.149

	Budget	Accounts
	FF	FF
Gratifications annuelles aux premiers sujets	64.206	45.829
Feux	80.000	102.770
Artistes externes, par représentation	3.000	2.247
Élève des choeurs, par mois	4.000	2.449
Élève des ballets, par représentation	9.000	8.985
Comparses - do -	12.000	9.939
Honoraires des auteurs et compositeurs	55.000	50.956
Encouragements aux surnuméraires		
des choeurs	4.000	3.958
des ballets	3.000	2.973
Indemnités aux anciens artistes,		
* choeurs et ballets*	2.900	2.650
Travaux extraordinaires des services divers	15.000	9.391
Gratifications éventuelles	20.000	25.890
Total de personnel variable	272.106	268.037
Éclairage	65.000	62.520
Chauffage	15.000	18.073
Copie de musique, Lutherie	15.000	14.726
Frais de costumes et décorations	180.000	149.995
Frais de mobilier et bâtiment	12.000	10.891
Droit des indigents	50.500	55.747
Affiches, frais de bureau	12.000	11.882
Frais de sûreté	28.000	27.353
des bals masqués	23.000	19.940
des concerts spirituels	10.000	8.916
imprévus et éventuels	30.000	33.743
Impôt foncier	635	616
Fonds commun d'insuffisance	32.896	69.771
Indemnités aux réformés et héritiers	2.000	4.906
Subvention à la caisse des pensions	126.913	126.913
	602.944	615.992
Totaux	1.697.925	1.650.178
Surplus		55.570

Budget and Annual Accounts 1829, (AJ[13] 146 IV).

	Budget	Accounts
	FF	**FF**
RECETTES		
Recettes à l'entrée	540.000	574.155
Location de loges à l'année	75.000	129.650
Bals Masqués	34.000	31.760
Location de boutiques	4.925	5.225
Redevances des théâtres secondaires	185.000	188.895
Subvention royale	817.925	817.925
Recettes extraordinaires	13.000	57.850
Total des Recettes	1.669.850	1.805.460
DÉPENSES		
Direction	45.800	45.800
Service de la scène	8.000	8.000
Chant	131.259	142.511
Choeurs, études et service	74.400	74.358
Danse	186.300	176.688
Ballets, écoles et service	80.150	78.512
Orchestre	130.400	131.117
Service de la bibliothèque	2.000	2.000
de la salle et du théâtre	38.265	38.655
des costumes	43.882	43.141
des décorations	86.800	86.800
Total du personnel fixe	827.256	827.582

	Budget	**Accounts**
	FF	**FF**
Gratifications annuelles aux 1ers Sujets du	55.000	70.858
du Chant et de la Danse		
Feux ou droit de présence	100.000	129.766
Artistes externes par représentation	2.000	3.357
Élèves des Choeurs, par mois	3.000	2.733
des Ballets, par représentation	9.000	8.989
Comparses, par représentation	10.000	10.102
Honoraires des auteurs et compositeurs	50.000	45.972
Encouragements aux surnuméraires		
des choeurs	4.000	2.467
des ballets	3.000	2.917
Indemnité fixe aux anciens artistes		
des Choeurs et des Ballets	2.650	2.367
aux réformés et héritiers	5.500	1.349
Travaux extraordinaires des divers services	10.000	15.574
Gratifications éventuelles	20.000	20.000
Total du personnel variable	274.150	316.451
Éclairage	60.000	66.053
Chauffage	15.000	17.308
Copie de musique, lutherie	10.000	10.167
Frais de Costumes et Décorations	170.000	134.609
Frais de mobilier et de bâtiment	12.000	21.272
Droit des indigents	56.590	65.430
Affiches, frais de bureau	12.000	12.084
Frais de sûreté	27.000	26.454
des bals masqués	20.000	19.089
Dépenses divers non susceptibles de classement	30.000	38.341
Impôt foncier (magasin Louvois)	616	608
Fonds de réserve	6.538	65.955
Subvention à la caisse des pensions	148.700	148.700
	568.444	626.070
Totaux	1.669.850	1.770.103
Surplus		35.357

Budget and Annual Accounts 1830, (AJ[13] 228 I).

	Budget	Accounts
	FF	**FF**
RECETTES		
Recettes à l'entrée	560.000	553.956
Loges de la Maison du Roi	48.000	48.000
Location de Loges à l'année	100.000	57.431
Bals Masqués	30.000	27.102
Location de boutiques	4.925	4.525
Redevances des Théâtres secondaires	190.000	182.958
Recettes extraordinaires	13.000	3.252
Subvention royale	<u>778.919</u>	<u>778.919</u>
Totaux	<u>1.724.844</u>	<u>1.656.143</u>
DÉPENSES		
Direction	47.000	46.194
Service de la Scène	10.200	10.200
Chant	132.908	137.497
Choeurs	73.450	73.398
Danse	164.767	158.206
Ballets	77.100	75.406
Orchestre	131.000	129.798
Salle et Théâtre	38.865	39.441
Costumes	43.683	43.264
Décorations	86.800	86.625
Engagements nouveaux	20.000	20.550
Gratifications fixes – Premiers sujets	<u>75.500</u>	<u>71.316</u>
Total du personnel fixe	<u>901.273</u>	<u>891.895</u>

	Budget	**Accounts**
	FF	**FF**
Feux par représentation	110.000	114.393
Artistes externes	3.000	3.236
Élèves des ballets – par représentation	9.000	8.969
des choeurs – par mois	3.000	2.754
Comparses, par représentation	10.000	9.882
Honoraires des Auteurs et Compositeurs	48.000	52.045
Encouragements, par mois aux surnuméraires	3.000	3.000
des choeurs		
des ballets	3.000	2.700
Indemnités, pour répétitions du matin, aux)	2.200	1.950
anciens artistes, choeurs et ballet)		
aux réformés, héritiers	3.000	760
Travaux extraordinaires	12.000	11.607
Gratifications éventuelles	20.000	20.000
Total du personnel variable	226.200	231.296
Éclairage	66.000	70.567
Chauffage	18.300	20.738
Copie de Musique, Lutherie	12.000	12.295
Costumes et Décorations	170.000	163.948
Mobilier et Bâtiment	17.600	18.833
Droit des indigents, sur les recettes	60.909	56.103
à l'entrée et location de loges à l'année		
Affiches, frais de Bureau	12.000	11.365
Sûreté et Police	31.500	26.558
Bals Masqués	16.362	16.362
Dépenses diverses	27.000	26.530
imprévues	-	1.620
extraordinaires	17.000	17.000
Rachat de Congés	-	18.000
	448.671	459.919
Caisse des Pensions	148.700	148.700
Totaux	1.724.844	1.731.810
Déficit		(75.667)

APPENDIX III

Translation of Conditions of Contract of the Opera.

28 February 1831, (AJ^{13} 187 I).

M. Véron

Copied from the example at the
Bureau des Théâtres (1880)

Conditions of Contract for the Director of the Opera, run as a public service on a concessionary basis, as decreed by the Commission and approved by the Minister of the Interior.

Article 1

The management of the *Académie Royale de Musique*, the so-called Opera, will be entrusted to a Director who will run it for six years at his own risk, peril and fortune, while observing the following clauses and conditions.

Article 2

The six years will start from 1 June 1831. The Concessionaire will, however, begin his duties on 1 March 1831 and, during the period prior to 1 June, will act only as Manager and will be accountable each month to the authorities. During this interim period, refurbishment of the auditorium, deemed necessary by the Commission appointed under Article 3, will be undertaken.

Article 3

The Commission appointed by the Minister of the Interior, under the decree of 28 February 1831, will supervise the enforcement of the conditions listed below. The Duc de Choiseul, Edmond Blanc, Hyp. Royer-Collard, Armand Blanc, d'Henneville, all members of the Commission, and Cavé, secretary, cannot be dismissed during the lifetime of the concession.

Article 4

The Concessionaire will be required to maintain the Opera in the state of pomp and luxury appropriate to this National Theatre.

Article 5

He will respect the commitments already validly entered into. As a result, from the day he takes up office as Director, the contracts and agreements with all authors, artists, soloists and staff will be his responsibility for the time they still have to run.

Article 6

The number of musicians, singers and dancers will always be maintained at the following levels:

One conductor.

Seventy-nine musicians of whom a first violinist can replace the conductor.

Two heads of singing who can accompany for rehearsals and studies.

Sixty-six members of the chorus, male and female and not including the students from the *Conservatoire*.

One ballet-master.

Forty female ballet-dancers and thirty male ballet-dancers, not including children.

A teacher of dance and mime for the corps de ballet.

Article 7

The students from the *Conservatoire* will remain available to the Concessionnaire so long as their presence is deemed useful by the Commission.

Article 8

Only those genres hitherto deemed appropriate for this Theatre will be staged.

1. Grand or little opera with or without ballet.

2. Ballet with mime.

The Director will not be allowed to introduce any other genre, even for benefit performances, without the express written authorisation of the Commission.

Article 9

In each year of his concession, the Director will be responsible for staging at least the number of new works described below:

1. One grand opera in three or five acts.

2. One grand ballet in three or five acts.

3. Two little operas in one or two acts.

4. Two little ballets in one or two acts.

Notwithstanding, the little works could be replaced by translated works.

Article 10

The Concessionaire will have to direct in such a way that there is at least one new production every two months.

The Commission can, however, release the Concessionaire from the obligation to stage some of these works in any year when the success of one or several of them is sufficient to sustain the pomp and brilliance of the Opera.

Article 11

New productions must be staged with new scenery and new costumes.

The Commission will be the supreme judge in all the decisions which affect the Director and the authors and it alone will be able to authorise the Director to use old scenery, for which it may demand all the repairs it deems necessary.

Article 12

The Director will be able to stage as many productions per week as is suitable for him, but the number must not fall below three.

He will also be able to hold Balls and Concerts on days and times suitable for him.

Article 13

The Director will enjoy the full use of the scenery, costumes, accessories, musical instruments, libretti and music scores, and generally of all the movables which currently belong to the administration of the Opera. An inventory will be done immediately, on a shared expense basis, by two experts, one chosen by each party, so that the Concessionaire will be able to use those movables that suit him. As for the costumes, he will have total use of them, with the proviso that he must return, at the end of his concession, costumes to a value which is equal to the estimated original value, or pay the difference.

The administration will be able to retain the surplus of costumes and scenery created by the Concessionaire by paying him the value as agreed by experts chosen by each party. The movables regarded as useless by the Commission will, after consultation with the Concessionaire, be sold for the profit of the State.

Article 14

The Concessionaire will be able to add machinery to the Theatre, according to his needs and after he has obtained authorisation from the Commission. The latter will seek the advice of experts concerning the strength and security of the building.

In all cases, the fixtures and fittings will remain as part of the premises.

Article 15

The Concessionaire will be required to keep and be in charge of those *entrées de droit* which have been decreed by the Commission in the annex to these articles. The box used by the *Intendant de la Liste Civile* will be transferred to the Minister of the Interior.

Article 16

The Concessionaire will be required to stage, each year, four performances for the benefit of the *Caisse des Pensions*. Only his expenses will be paid for these productions. The Commission will fix the days and will decide what should be staged.

Article 17

So that the Concessionaire can manage the Opera, he will be granted a subsidy of FF 810.000 for his first year, FF 760.000 for the second and third years and FF 710.000 for the last three years. This subsidy will be paid each year to the Concessionaire in twelve monthly installments.

He will be required, at the end of each month, to submit to the Commission a signed duplicate of the salaries paid in the previous month. The Commission will give this to the Minister of the Interior.

Article 18

The Concessionaire will deposit caution money when he takes over as Director, in order to guarantee the payment of salaries. The amount will be agreed between now and 1 June 1831. It will not be less than FF 150.000 and not more than FF 250.000. The agreed sum will be interest-bearing and will be deposited with the *Caisse des Consignations*.

Article 19

During his tenure, the Concessionaire will be able to benefit from the value created by renting out any part of the Opera. He will be solely responsible for all the expenses of upkeep of the building and adjacent rooms, the heating, the lighting, the fire department and the police security. He will be required to maintain the building in a good state of repair and to warn the Commission of any large repairs which might be necessary. He will also be required to clean thoroughly the auditorium and foyer twice a year, under the supervision of the Commission.

Article 20

The Commission will be responsible for the payment of taxes of all kinds, both current and future.

Article 21

He will take financial responsibility for all accidents caused by fire, which may occur for whatever reason, except when he makes a claim on the insurance company. He will be required to pay an annual premium to cover this as from 1 June 1831 and will be required to renew the cover as soon as the existing one expires.

Article 22

He will also be required to pay the expenses to guard and maintain the warehouses that are currently used to store the scenery and costumes of the Opera.

Article 23

At the end of his concession, he will be required to leave the premises in a good state of repair and to pay for any repairs that might be necessary.

Article 24

The Concessionaire will not be responsible for the payment of pensions, whether in whole or in part, to artists and staff of the Opera by virtue of contracts and obligations entered into prior to his management. The administration alone will be directly responsible for such pensions as well as for the payment of existing pensions.

As a result, the Concessionaire will be required to hand over, on a monthly basis to the person chosen by the Commission, the deductions made on the salaries of artists and staff who were hired prior to his assumption of office.

Article 25

The Concessionaire will only be required to respect those statutes and regulations of the Opera which affect the personnel legitimately hired by the previous regime. He will thus be free to impose, on those personnel whom he will hire in the future, such rules and conditions as seem more suitable for him.

Article 26

In the event of a dispute over the execution of the different clauses in this contract, the Concessionaire will, as a last resort, be judged by way of arbitration. He will not have recourse to any appeal to the Court against the judgement of the members of the Commission who will be the arbitrators in accordance with civil legal proceedings.

The period of grace of three months, as decreed by Article 1007 of the *Code de Procédure*, will only begin from the day when either the authorities or the Concessionaire will have submitted their conclusions to the arbitrators.

Article 27

Each breach of this contract may lead to a fine on the Concessionaire of between FF 1.000 and FF 5.000. The fine will be decided by the Commission and will be immediately taken from the caution money within three days. The fine will be credited to the *Caisse des Pensions*.

After three breaches, the Commission could pronounce this contract terminated, without prejudice to all expenses, damages and interests.

In such a case, the receipts could be seized on the request of the Minister of the Interior who may also, on the Commission's advice, take further protective measures that are deemed appropriate, at the Concessionaire's expense, risk and peril.

The present contract will have to be terminated whenever the legislative power refuses to give to the Minister of the Interior the means to implement it.

In this case, a liquidation will be carried out and the Concessionaire will bear any losses he may have incurred prior to the date of the termination.

Article 28

All registration fees of this contract will be at the expense of the Concessionaire.

Article 29

None of the decisions authorised by the Commission can be implemented without the authorisation of the Minister of the Interior.

Approved, six words crossed out as void.	Done in triplicate in Paris on 28 February 1831
The Members of the Commission.	Peer of France, Minister, Secretary of State at the Ministry of the Interior.
Signed: The Duc de Choiseul 　　　Edmond Blanc 　　　Hipp. Royer-Collard 　　　Armand Bertin 　　　D'Henneville 　　Cavé, Secretary	*Signed*: Montalivet. Approved the words above. *Signed*: L. Véron.

*Cahier des Charges
de l'Opéra.*

—

28 février 1831.

Mr. Véron.

*Copié sur l'exemplaire
du Bureau des Théatres.
(1830)*

28 Février 1831

Cahier des Charges de la Direction
de l'Opéra, en régie intéressée, arrêté
en commission et approuvé par
Monsieur le Ministre de l'Intérieur

───────◀═══════════▶───────

Art. 1

l'Administration de l'Académie Royale
de musique, dite Opéra, sera confiée
à un Directeur-Entrepreneur qui
l'exploitera pendant six ans, à ses
risques, périls et fortune aux charges
clauses et conditions suivantes :

Art. 2.

Les six années commenceront à
courir du 1er Juin Dix huit cent trente
un. Néanmoins l'entrepreneur entrera
en jouissance le premier Mars dix huit
trente-un, et pendant l'espace de temps qui
précédera le terme ci-dessus fixé
il ne sera que gérant et devant compter
chaque mois avec l'autorité —

Pendant ces intervalles seront faites
les réparations et peintures de la Salle
jugées indispensables par la commission
instituée par l'art . 3.

Art. 3.

La commission nommée par le
Ministre de l'Intérieur par arrêté du
vingthuit février dix huit cent trente un
sera chargée de surveiller l'éxécution
des conditions ci-après déterminées .
M.Mrs. le duc de Choiseul, Edmond
Blanc, Hyp. Royer-Collard, Armand
Bertin, D'henneville, membres de
la Commission et M. Cavé secrétaire,
ne pourront être révoqués pendant
la durée de l'entreprise.

Art. 4.

L'Entrepreneur sera tenu de
maintenir l'Opéra dans l'état de
pompe et de luxe convenable à
ce théâtre National.

Art. 5.

Il devra respecter les engagements
valablement faits jusqu'à ce jour.
En conséquence, à compter du jour
de son entrée en jouissance les
traités ou conventions avec tous

présence sera jugée utile par la
Commission de surveillance.

Art. 8.

Il ne pourra être exploité sur
la scène de l'Opéra que les genres
attribués jusqu'à ce jour a ce théâtre:

1°. Le grand ou le petit Opéra avec
ou sans ballet.

2°. Le Ballet pantomime.

Le Directeur ne pourra introduire
aucun autre genre même dans les
représentations à bénéfice, sans
l'autorisation expresse et par écrit
de la Commission de surveillance.

Art. 9

Dans chaque année d'exploitation
le Directeur sera tenu de monter
au moins le nombre d'ouvrages nouveaux
ci-après spécifié.

1°= un grand Opéra en trois ou
cinq actes.

2°= un grand Ballet en trois ou
cinq actes.

3°= deux petits opéras soit en
un acte, soit en deux actes.

4°= deux petits ballets soit en
un acte soit en deux actes.

Néanmoins

présente sera jugée utile par la
Commission de surveillance.

Art. 8.

Il ne pourra être exploité sur
la scène de l'Opéra que les genres
attribués jusqu'à ce jour a ce théâtre:

1°. Le grand ou le petit Opéra avec
ou sans ballet.

2°. Le Ballet pantomime.

Le Directeur ne pourra introduire
aucun autre genre même dans les
représentations à bénéfice, sans
autorisation expresse et par écrit
de la Commission de surveillance.

Art. 9

Dans chaque année d'exploitation
le Directeur sera tenu de monter
au moins le nombre d'ouvrages nouveaux
ci-après spécifié.

1°= un grand Opéra en trois ou
cinq actes.

2°= un grand Ballet en trois ou
cinq actes.

3°= deux petits opéras soit en
un acte, soit en deux actes.

4°= deux petits ballets soit en
un acte soit en deux actes.

Néanmoins

Néanmoins les petits ouvrages
pourront être remplacés par des
ouvrages traduits.

Art. 10.

l'Entrepreneur devra diriger
ses travaux de manière qu'il y ait
au moins une représentation nouvelle
tous les deux mois.

Toutefois la commission de
Surveillance pourra dispenser
l'Entrepreneur de monter dans
l'année une partie de ces ouvrages
lorsque le succès d'une ou plusieurs
pièces suffira à la pompe et à
l'éclat du Spectacle.

Art 11.

Les ouvrages nouveaux devront
être montés avec des décorations
nouvelles et des costumes nouveaux

La Commission de surveillance
sera juge suprême en cette matière,
tant vis à vis du Directeur que
des auteurs et pourra seule
autoriser le Directeur à se servir
d'anciennes décorations auxquelles
elle pourra exiger toutes les

réparations qu'elle croira convenables.

Art. 12

Le Directeur pourra donner par semaine autant de représentations qu'il lui conviendra, mais le nombre n'en pourra être au dessous de trois.

Il aura en outre la faculté de donner des Bals et Concerts aux Jour et heure qui lui conviendront.

Art. 13.

Le Directeur aura pendant la durée de son entreprise la jouissance des décorations, costumes, accessoires, instruments, livres et partitions et généralement de tout le mobilier appartenant actuellement à l'administration de l'Opéra. Il sera fait immédiatement et à frais communs par deux experts respectivement choisis, état de tout ce mobilier, au moyen de quoi l'entrepreneur pourra faire usage du dit mobilier comme bon lui semblera. Quant aux costumes il pourra en disposer d'une manière absolue sauf à rendre à la fin de son entreprise une quantité de costumes égale

en valeur au montant de l'estimation
ou à payer la différence.

L'Administration pourra à son
gré, conserver le surplus des
costumes et décorations créés
par l'entrepreneur en lui en payant
la valeur à dire d'experts, respec=
=tivement choisis.

Le Mobilier reconnu inutile
par la Commission sur la demande
de l'Entrepreneur sera vendu au
profit de l'État.

Art. 14.

l'Entrepreneur aura la faculté
de faire machiner le théâtre
selon les besoins de son service,
après avoir obtenu l'autorisation
de la Commission qui consultera
à cet égard des gens de l'art
dans l'intérêt de la solidité et
de la sureté de la Salle.

Dans tous les cas, tout ce
qui sera scellé ou de construction
fixe restera la propriété de
l'établissement.

Art. 15

L'Entrepreneur ne sera tenu

à conserver que les entrées de droit
dont il lui sera donné État
arrêté par la commission qui
restera annexé aux présentes.

La loge dont jouissait l'intendant
de la Liste Civile sera affectée au
Ministre de l'Intérieur.

Art. 16

L'Entrepreneur sera tenu
pendant la durée de son entreprise
à donner chaque année quatre
représentations au profit de la
Caisse des Pensions. Il ne lui
sera pour ces représentations
tenu compte que de ses frais. La
commission de surveillance en
fixera les jours et elle indiquera
la composition du spectacle.

Art. 17.

Pour fournir à l'Entrepreneur
les moyens d'exploiter l'opéra il
lui est accordé une subvention de
huit cent dix mille francs pour
la première année, sept cent
soixante pour la seconde et
la troisième année, et sept
cent dix mille francs pour
les trois dernières années.

Cette subvention sera payée

chaque année par douziemes
à la fin de chaque mois à
l'Entrepreneur.

Il sera tenu de remettre à
la fin de chaque mois à
la commission de surveillance
qui le transmettra au Ministre
de l'Intérieur un double de
l'État émargé d'appointements
du mois précédent.

Art. 18.

L'Entrepreneur devra fournir
au moment de son entrée en
jouissance pour la garantie
de l'execution de ses engagements
un cautionnement ~~de~~ ~~Cent~~
~~cinquante mille francs~~ en
Inscriptions de rentes sur l'État
qui seront déposées à la Caisse
des Consignations.

Art. 19.

Pendant tout le temps de
son exploitation l'Entrepreneur
jouira des produits de toutes
les locations faisant partie
des batiments de l'Opéra. Il

dont le montant sera reglé du présent jour au premier Juin et qui
ne pourra être au dessous de Cent
cinquante mille francs, ni au dessus
de deux cent cinquante mille francs.

sera seul chargé de tous les
frais d'entretien de la salle et de
ses dépendances, du chauffage
de l'Éclairage, des frais de
Pompiers et de gardes de police.
Il sera tenu d'entretenir les
batiments en bon état de répa=
=rations locatives et de prévenir
la Commission de surveillance
des grosses réparations qui
pourraient être nécessaires. Il
sera tenu également de faire
deux fois par an et sous la
surveillance de la Commission un
nettoyage général de toutes les
parties de la salle et du foyer.

Art. 20

L'Entrepreneur sera chargé
du payement des impositions
de toute nature, présentes et à
venir.

Art. 21.

Il sera responsable des
accidents d'incendie qui pourraient
survenir pour quelque cause
que ce soit, sauf son recours
envers la Compagnie d'assurances

avec laquelle il sera tenu
d'entretenir l'abonnement +existant+ 6
et d'en former un nouveau, lors
de l'expiration de celui actuel.

tel qu'il existera au premier Juin
prochain.

Art. 22

Il sera également tenu des
frais de garde et d'entretien
des magasins servant actuelle =
= ment aux décorations et costumes
de l'Opéra.

Art. 23

À la fin de sa jouissance, il
sera tenu de laisser les lieux
en bon état de réparations
locatives ou de payer celles
qu'il y aurait lieu de faire.

Art. 24.

L'Entrepreneur ne sera en
aucune manière tenu de fournir
soit intégralement, soit en partie,
les pensions auxquelles pourront
avoir droit les artistes, et
employés de l'Opéra en vertu
des engagements antérieurs
à sa gestion. l'administration
y pourvoira seule et directement.

ainsi qu'au paiement des anciennes
pensions.

En conséquence, l'Entrepreneur
sera tenu de verser chaque mois
entre les mains de la personne
qui lui sera indiquée par la
commission de surveillance le
montant des retenues qui, d'après
leurs engagements doivent être
faites sur les traitements des
artistes ou employés engagés
avant son entrée en jouissance.

Art. 25

l'Entrepreneur sera tenu
d'observer les statuts et règlements
particuliers à l'opéra qu'envers
les personnes engagées valablement
sous ce régime. Dès lors il sera
libre d'imposer à ceux qu'il engagera
à l'avenir telles règles et condi=
=tions qui lui sembleront plus
convenables.

Art. 26.

En cas de contestation sur
l'exécution des différentes clauses
du présent traité l'Entrepreneur
sera jugé par voie d'arbitrage

en dernier ressort et sans
recours aucun par voie de
demande en cassation ou de
requête civile par les membres
de la commission de surveillance
lesquels procéderont comme arbitres
volontaires conformément
au code de Procédure civile

Le délai de trois mois
fixé par l'article 1007 du code
de Procédure n'aura cours
que du jour où, soit l'autorité
soit l'Entrepreneur aura fait
signifier ses conclusions
déposées es-mains des arbi=
= tres.

Art 27.

Chaque contravention aux
présentes pourra entraîner contre
l'Entrepreneur une amende de
mille francs à cinq mille
francs qui sera prononcée
par la commission de surveillance
et prise immédiatement sur
le cautionnement, qui, dans
ce cas devra être complété
dans les trois jours. l'amende

sera versée à la Caisse des
Pensions.

Après trois contraventions
constatées, la commission de
surveillance pourra prononcer
la résiliation du présent traité,
le tout sans préjudice de tous
dépens, dommages et intérêts. -

Au dit cas, les recettes pour-
=ront être saisies à la requête
du Ministre de l'Intérieur qui
pourra en outre sur l'avis de la
Commission, prendre telles autres
mesures conservatoires qu'elle
jugera convenables et aux frais
risques et périls de l'Entrepreneur.

Le présent traité sera
nécessairement annullé dans
le cas où le pouvoir législatif
refuserait au Ministre de l'Intérieur
les moyens de l'exécuter.

Ce cas arrivant, une liquidation
sera faite et il sera tenu compte
à l'Entrepreneur des pertes qu'il
aurait pû supporter jusqu'au
jour où la résiliation aura

ça lieu.

Art. 28.

Tous les frais d'enregistrement du présentes seront à la charge del'Entrepreneur.

Art. 29.

Aucune des décisions que la commission de surveillance est autorisée à prendre ne pourra être exécutée sans l'autorisation du Ministre de l'Intérieur

Approuvé six mots rayés comme nuls ————

Fait triple à Paris le vingt huit février mil huit cent trente un

Le Pair de France, ministre, secrétaire d'État au ministère del'Intérieur.
Signé: Montalivet

approuvé les écritures ci dessus
signé: L. Véron

Les membres de la Commission de surveillance.
Signé: Le Duc de Choiseul
Edmond Blanc.
Hipp. Royer Collard
Armand Bertin.

Dheunville

Cavé Secrétaire

Source: *document conservé au Centre historique des Archives nationals à Paris, (AJ*[13] *187).*

APPENDIX IV

Annual Accounts 1831–32, (AJ[13] 228 II).

1 June 1831–31 May 1832

	FF
RECETTES	
Recettes à la porte	780.232
Location de loges à terme	140.044
Bals Masqués	23.070
Sous-location de boutiques	8.646
Recettes extraordinaires	67.124
Subvention	802.982
	1.822.098
DÉPENSES	
Administration	36.325
Chant	204.279
Choeurs	63.527
Danse	208.503
Ballets	64.526
Orchestre	83.336
Salle et Théâtre	28.613
Costumes	38.850
Décorations	74.230
Total du personnel fixe	802.189

	FF
Feux des Artistes – chant, danse	92.880
Droits de présence – Artistes externes	8.680
– Élèves des ballets	5.897
– Comparses	7.877
Honoraires – Auteurs, Compositeurs	68.244
Travaux extraordinaires	15.564
Traitements supplémentaires – Primes	9.814
Gratifications, Indemnités, Rachat de Congés	19.607
Total du personnel variable	228.563
Éclairage	63.643
Chauffage	13.052
Copie de musique, Lutherie	15.426
Costumes et Décorations	238.811
Affiches, Impressions, Papeterie	19.218
Droit des Indigents	31.769
Sûreté et Police	25.037
Bals Masqués	11.036
Mobiliers et Bâtiments	4.898
Divers non-classés	58.097
Extraordinaires	87.855
	568.842
Indemnités aux réformés	65.405
Contribution à la caisse des pensions	12.000
	77.405
Totaux	1.676.999
Surplus	145.099

Annual Accounts 1832–33, (AJ¹³ 228 II).

1 June 1832–31 May 1833

	FF
RECETTES	
Recettes journalières provenant des représentations	818.262
Location de Loges à termes, Abonnements personnels	175.179
Recettes provenant des Bals Masqués	23.303
Location de Boutiques, Concessions et Privilèges	7.684
Subvention ministérielle	760.000
Recettes extraordinaires	20.227
	1.804.655
DÉPENSES	
Appointements de la Direction et du service de la Scène	36.783
des Artistes du Chant	214.900
des Choeurs	66.352
de la Danse	196.080
des Ballets	70.316
de l'Orchestre	100.277
du service de la Salle et du Théâtre	25.582
des Costumes	45.129
des Décorations	75.994
Total de personnel fixe	831.413

	FF
Feux des Artistes du chant et de la danse	93.075
Jetons de présence des Artistes externes	9.392
Élèves des Ballets	5.734
Comparses	8.908
Honoraires des Auteurs et Compositeurs	60.049
Travaux extraordinaires des divers services	15.986
Traitements supplémentaires Primes	6.830
Gratifications éventuelles, Indemnités	
Rachat de Congés	22.760
Total du personnel variable	222.734
Éclairage	67.176
Chauffage	11.045
Copie de musique, Lutherie	14.560
Costumes et Décorations, mise en scène	112.394
entretien	64.773
Affiches, Impressions, fourniture de bureau	18.664
Frais de sûreté et police	19.136
Droit des indigents sur les recettes	
journalières et locations de loges à terme	89.044
Frais de bals masqués	14.086
de Mobilier et Bâtiment	6.686
divers, non-classés	20.786
Dépenses extraordinaires	25.037
Indemnités aux réformés	1.369
Contribution à la Caisse des Pensions	10.500
	475.256
Totaux	1.529.403
Surplus	275.252

Annual Accounts 1833–34, (AJ[13] 228 II).

1 June 1833–31 May 1834

	FF
RECETTES	
Recettes des representations	965.774
Location de Loges à terme)	234.858
Abonnements personnels)	
Bals Masqués	43.946
Location de boutiques	8.300
Recettes extraordinaires	30.209
Subvention ministérielle	670.000
	1.953.087
DÉPENSES	
Direction	36.808
Chant	228.133
Choeurs	71.468
Danse	177.045
Ballets	79.829
Orchestre	101.879
Salle et Théâtre	23.895
Costumes	45.942
Décorations	76.156
Total du personnel fixe	841.155

	FF
Feux du chant et de la danse	116.060
Jetons de présence des Artistes externes	14.143
Élèves des ballets	4.744
Comparses	8.493
Honoraires des Auteurs et Compositeurs	56.668
Travaux extraordinaires	13.030
Traitements supplémentaires Primes	9.279
Gratifications, Indemnités, Rachat de Congés	22.140
Total du personnel variable	244.557
Éclairage	60.947
Chauffage	15.116
Copie de musique, Lutherie	10.995
Costumes	132.423
Décorations	83.512
Affiches	19.575
Droit des Indigents	105.339
Sûreté et Police	19.547
Bals Masqués	-
Mobilier et Bâtiment	3.801
Divers non-classés	19.591
Dépenses extraordinaires	11.724
Total matériel et dépenses divers	482.570
Indemnités aux réformés	267
Contributions à la Caisse des Pensions	14.000
	14.267
Totaux	1.582.549
Surplus	370.538

Annual Accounts 1834–35.

1 June 1834–31 May 1835

	FF
RECETTES	
Recettes des représentations	825.179[a]
Location de Loges à terme	246.630[a]
Bals Masqués	30.000*
Location de boutiques	8.000*
Recettes extraordinaires	273[b]
Subvention ministérielle	670.000[c]
	1.780.082
DÉPENSES	
Direction	37.150[d]
Chant	256.100[d]
Choeurs	74.389[d]
Danse	218.837[d]
Ballets	86.192[d]
Orchestre	104.274[d]
Salle et Théâtre	23.351[d]
Costumes	47.570[d]
Décorations	79.801[d]
Total du personnel fixe	927.664

	FF
Feux du chant et de la danse	123.587[d]
Artistes externes	17.650[d]
Élèves des Ballets	6.650[d]
Comparses	12.881[d]
Auteurs et Compositeurs	47.590[d]
Travaux extraordinaires	19.945[d]
Traitements supplémentaires	21.559[d]
Gratifications, Indemnités, Rachat	29.505[d]
de Congés	
Total du personnel variable	279.367
Éclairage	43.020[b]
Chauffage	12.950[b]
Copie de musique, Lutherie	10.703[b]
Costumes)	362.665[e]
Décorations)	
Affiches	9.204[e]
Droit des Indigents	97.498[f]
Sûreté et Police	19.500*
Bals Masqués	12.000*
Mobilier et Bâtiment	5.000*
Divers non-classés	20.485[e]
Dépenses extraordinaires	8.279[f]
Indemnités aux réformés	3.271[e]
Contributions à la Caisse des Pensions	14.000[e]
	618.575
Totaux	1.825.606
Déficit	(45.524)

a. AJ[13] 237, CO 710 (608), *Journal usuel de l'Opéra 1791–1850*, op. cit..

b. CO 710 (608).

c. *Cahier des charges*, second supplement, 14 May 1833, Article 17, (AJ[13] 187 I).

d. AJ[13] 228 IV, CO 710 (608).

e. AJ[13] 228 IV.

f. AJ[13] 291 II.

* Estimate based on previous years.

APPENDIX V

There were many examples, spread among the bills of suppliers of materials appointed by Véron, where the prices showed a substantial reduction over those of the Restoration suppliers who had been retained or replaced. The relevant references used for these examples were: Restoration period, 1829 bills from suppliers, (AJ[13] 404 I). Veron's administration, 1831–32 bills from suppliers, (AJ[13] 411 II).

Specific examples from among the many reductions achieved by Véron.

	Supplier/Supplies under Restoration	Supplier/Supplies under Véron
a) *Mercerie*	Gautier	Perée-Dupuis
Épingles – No. 18	FF 10 per 12 *milles*	FF 9 per 12 *milles*
Épingles – Drapières	17 per 12 *milles*	16 per 12 *milles*
Épingles – Hourzeaux	22 per 12 *milles*	21 per 12 *milles*
Lacets file ferrés	9 *la grosse*	7 *la grosse*
Lacets à coulisse	4.50 *la douzaine*	3.80 *la douzaine*
Ruban de fil blanc	3 *la douzaine*	2.65 *la douzaine*
Padoux de file – No. 25	3 *la douzaine*	2.50 *la douzaine*
Padoux de file – No. 45	6.25 *la douzaine*	3.75 *la douzaine*
b) *Chaussures pour dames*	Janssen	Ponsin
Satin blanc unis	FF 4.00 *la paire*	FF 3.25 *la paire*
Blancs unis	3.50 *la paire*	3.25 *la paire*
Puces unis	3.50 *la paire*	3.25 *la paire*
Prunelle noire unis	3.88 *la paire*	3.25 *la paire*

These were major items of expense for both opera and ballet.

c) *Bonneterie*	Maillot	Maillot

He was retained by Véron, and his prices remained the same, but all his bills were subject to a 2% reduction under Véron, which was a change.

d) *Bois à ouvrer*	Roussel	Roussel
Planches de sapin, 12 pieds et 12 lignes	FF 3.15 per *planche*	FF 2.90 per *planche*
Planches de sapin, 12 pieds et 15 lignes	4.00 per *planche*	3.50 per *planche*
Voliges de peuplier	0.65 *le toise*	0.55 *le toise*

Roussel was retained by Véron, but his prices were reduced. This wood was used in the construction of the sets and was included under scenery.

e) *Quincaillerie*	Juéry	Desforges
Clous rivets effilés	FF 1.50 per *kilo*	FF 1.20 per *kilo*
Crin noir	3.40 per *kilo*	3.20 per *kilo*

f) *Toiles et Mousselines*	Deslisle	Chevreux fils et Legentil
Mousseline blanche claire en ¾	FF 1.90 *à l'aune*	FF 1.70 *à l'aune*
Mousseline blanche double, 2ème qualité	1.90 -ditto-	1.40 -ditto-
Calico blanc en ¾, 2ème qualité	1.40 -ditto-	1.00 -ditto-
Calico blanc en ⁵/₄, 1ère qualité	2.90 -ditto-	2.00 -ditto-
Calico blanc en ⁴/₄, 2ème qualité	2.00 -ditto-	1.40 -ditto-
Calico blanc en ¾, 3ème qualité	1.05 -ditto-	0.70 -ditto-
Toile Cretonne blanche en ⁷/₈	2.80 -ditto-	2.25 -ditto-
Percaline noire en ¾	0.90 -ditto-	0.85 -ditto-

In every new production, these materials were a significant part of the total cost. From the few examples quoted above, it was clear that Véron negotiated substantial price reductions from the new supplier.

g) *Soierie et Lainage*	Deslisle	Chevreux fils et Legentil
Crèpe Lisse blanc, 1ère qualité	FF 4.00 *à l'aune*	FF 3.70 *à l'aune*
Satin blanc, 1ère qualité	8.00 -ditto-	6.40 -ditto-
Gaze de soie blanche	1.40 -ditto-	1.15 -ditto-
Gros de Naples blanc	6.50 -ditto-	6.00 -ditto-
Satin, rose/bleu ciel/noir/bois/blanc	7.00 -ditto-	6.00 -ditto-
Satin ponçeau fin	8.75 -ditto-	8.50 -ditto-

As in *toiles et mousselines* above, Véron dismissed and appointed the same suppliers.

APPENDIX VI

Details of these Calculations, (AJ[13] 202[1]).

Genres	No. of new Chassis	Bill	No. of new Chassis	Règlements	No. of new Chassis	Vérification
		FF		FF		FF
1st Set						
5th at FF 140	57½	8.050	52¼	7.315	54¾	7.665
1st at FF 20	1½	30	4½	90	4½	90
	59	8.080	56¾	7.405	59¼	7.755
Accessories		1.220		1.020		1.220
		9.300		8.425		8.975
2nd Set						
5th at FF 140	23	3.220	19	2.660	20	2.800
Accessories		241		216		256
		3.461		2.876		3.056
4th Set						
6th at FF 180	29	5.220	26¾	4.815	29¾	5.355
1st at FF 30	1	30	1	30	1	30
	30	5.250	27¾	4.845	30¾	5.385
5th Set						
6th at FF 180		540		450		540
Six chassis charged at only FF 90/FF 75, as cancelled						
5th at FF 140	30½	4.270	25½	3.570	27¾	3.885
1st at FF 20	-	-	1½	30	6½	130
	30½	4.270	27	3.600	34¼	4.015
6th Set						
7th at FF 250	34½	8.625	27	6.750	30½	7.625
5th at FF 140	4	560	3½	490	4½	630
	38½	9.185	30½	7.240	35	8.255
Accessories		2.290		1.880		2.340
		11.475		9.120		10.595
Total, sets & accessories	181	34.296	161	29.316	179¼	32.566

Sundries authorised by Véron	2.691	-	2.691
Repaint of borders, six chassis at FF 20	120	-	120
Six months' rent of atelier *rue de Provence*	-	-	950
Small items	-	-	140
Total	37.107	29.316	36.467
Of which			
New chassis	30.005	25.750	28.210
Accessories	4.291	3.566	4.356
Other items	2.811	-	3.901
	37.107	29.316	36.467
Average cost per chassis	FF 166	FF 160	FF 157

Details of these Calculations, with the 1822 tariff.

Genres	Cost per Chassis	Bill No. of Chassis	Cost	*Vérification* No. of Chassis	Cost
	FF		FF		FF
1st Set					
7th	200	57½	11.500	54¾	10.950
1st	35	1½	53	4½	158
		59	11.553	59¼	11.108
2nd Set					
7th	200	23	4.600	20	4.000
4th Set					
8th	240	29	6.960	29¾	7.140
1st	50	1	50	1	50
		30	7.010	30¾	7.190
5th Set					
7th	200	30½	6.100	27¾	5.550
1st	35	-	-	6½	228
		30½	6.100	34¼	5.778
6th Set					
10th	400	34½	13.800	30½	12.200
7th	200	4	800	4½	900
		38½	14.600	35	13.100
Total		181	43.863	179¼	41.176
Average cost per chassis			FF 242		FF 230

BIBLIOGRAPHY

Primary Sources

Paris, *Archives Nationales*

AJ^{13} 5

Record of operas staged at the Opera, 1754–1832, with special reference to *Œdipe à Colone*.

AJ^{13} 91

Record of operas staged at the Opera, 1805–1807, with special reference to *Le Triomphe de Trajan*.

AJ^{13} 92

Record of operas staged at the Opera, 1808 and 1809, with special reference to *La Mort d'Adam*.

AJ^{13} 93

Record of operas staged at the Opera, 1810–1812, with special reference to *L'Enfant prodigue* and *Les Bayadères*.

AJ^{13} 94

Record of operas staged at the Opera, 1812–1815, with special reference to *La Princesse de Babylone* and *Nina ou la folle par amour*.

AJ^{13} 109

Administration of the Opera, 1814–1829, including various *arrêtés*, *ordonnances* and *accords*, and the creation of the *Comité consultatif de la mise en scène*.

AJ^{13} 112

General administration of the Opera, including correspondence and ministerial decisions. There was special reference to the atelier and Ciceri's nomination as principal painter.

AJ^{13} 113

General administration of the Opera 1822–1825, including correspondence, minutes of meetings of the *Comité d'administration*, and the new 1822 tariff for scene-painting.

AJ^{13} 114

Ministerial decisions, correspondence and other administrative matters for the Opera 1823–1825, including various budgets, a report on the direction of the Opera and choice of principal painter, and details of *entrées d'échange* 1824.

AJ^{13} 116

Various *ordonnances* and *arrêtés* for the Opera by La Rochefoucauld, 1825–1827, minutes of meetings of the *Comité d'administration*, the submission of tenders by suppliers for 1825 and 1826, and a report by the Committee on the results with an explanation for each successful tender. Details of *entrées d'échange* 1825.

AJ¹³ 117

General correspondence on the Opera by La Rochefoucauld in 1826, including letters to Duplantys on the use of old sets and costumes.

AJ¹³ 118

Various, including the 1826 lists of *entrées de droit* and *entrées de faveur* and the *projet de budget* for 1826.

AJ¹³ 119

General correspondence of La Rochefoucauld on the Opera in 1827, especially letters concerning the budget for *La Muette de Portici* and decisions concerning administration, productions and personnel. The work of Ciceri in restoring and touching up old sets in 1826, and a 1827 report by Géré, the head of costumes. Details of *entrées d'échange* with other theatres 1825–1827.

AJ¹³ 121

General correspondence and reports on the Opera in 1828, including the decision by the *Cour Royale* on the *redevance*.

AJ¹³ 122

General correspondence including reports on the *projet de budget* for 1829.

AJ¹³ 123

Correspondence, minutes of meetings and other matters 1829 and 1830. In particular, a letter from La Rochefoucauld to Lubbert which criticised him on many aspects of his management.

AJ¹³ 124

Various, including correspondence in 1830, preparation of the 1830 budget, *entrées de droit et de faveur* to the Opera, and the 1829 and 1830 *Cahier des charges* for suppliers by La Rochefoucauld.

AJ¹³ 132

Record of operas staged at the Opera, 1816–1820, with special reference to *Clary*.

AJ¹³ 133

The budgets and report thereon for *Aladin ou la Lampe merveilleuse*. *Livrets*, designs and other documents for new productions at the Opera 1820–1823.

AJ¹³ 134

Livrets, designs and other documents for new productions at the Opera 1823–1827, including *Le Siège de Corinthe* and *Moïse*.

AJ^{13} 135

Livrets, designs and other documents for new productions at the Opera 1827–1830, including *La Muette de Portici, Le Comte Ory, Guillaume Tell, Manon Lescaut* and *Macbeth*.

AJ^{13} 137

Record of operas staged at the *Théâtre Italien*, 1822–1827, including *Mosè in Egitto*, first performed on 20 October 1822.

AJ^{13} 142

Information on the building of the *Salle le Peletier*, including work to be done to improve public safety.

AJ^{13} 144

Budgets and accounts of the Opera under the Restoration. The deficit of FF 431.708 as at 31 March 1823, and reports by Du Rais.

AJ^{13} 145

Annual accounts of the Opera and other financial information for 1826 and 1827, including monthly summaries of receipts and expenses, and reports from the various heads of departments in preparation for the 1827 budget.

AJ^{13} 146

Various books of account of the Opera for 1828, including receipts and expenses, payment mandates/journals of payment July/August 1827–February/April 1830. Documents in support of budget preparations 1828–1830, including a report from the heads of singing for 1828.

AJ^{13} 148

Various reports relating to the *redevance* and the *droit des indigents*, with schedules showing the amounts collected in 1818.

AJ^{13} 172

Schedules of payments to freelance painters 1816–1822 including man-hours and payments for *Aladin ou la Lampe merveilleuse*.

AJ^{13} 179

Submission of tenders by suppliers for 1829 and 1830 and the results thereof.

AJ^{13} 180

Reports and correspondence covering Véron's tenure as director, including letters on the outstanding FF 40.000 from the FF 100.000 supplement, details of fines and the review of *entrées gratuites*. Here also is *Quelques observations...*, anonymous and undated, which called for a revolution in singing and scene-painting at the Opera in the Restoration period. The position on the *redevance*, post July 1830, is also included.

AJ^{13} 183

Productions and other matters dealt with by the Commission, 1830–1854, including a report on *Moïse* by the Ministry of the Interior to the *Préfet de Police* in May 1830.

AJ[13] 185

Correspondence on the mise-en-scene of various productions 1833–1849. Documents relating to the *Salle le Peletier*, including the 9 August 1820 *Ordonnance du Roi* which opened a credit of FF 900.000 to construct the *Salle le Peletier*.

AJ[13] 187

Organisation at the Opera 1829–1853, including *ordonnances* and regulations, Véron's 28 February 1831 *Cahier des charges* and two supplements, the suspension of various suppliers' contracts and correspondence between the Minister, the Commission and Véron.

AJ[13] 188

Correspondence, contracts and bills for scenery by various scene-painters including Ciceri, Philastre and Cambon and Séchan, Feuchères et Cie.

AJ[13] 201

Documents, correspondence and other information on the new productions under Véron 1831–1833.

AJ[13] 202

Documents, correspondence and other information on the new productions under Véron 1833–1835.

AJ[13] 215

The Opera's department for making costumes 1822–1874. Correspondence, reports, inventories and other items including reports by Géré, the head of costumes.

AJ[13] 218

Correspondence between the Opera and those theatres with which it had reciprocal *entrées d'échange*, especially in 1831 when Véron renegotiated the basis for such *entrées*.

AJ[13] 221

Contracts with various supplier-contractors, including those between Véron and the suppliers of laundry services and that between Véron and the new head machinist, Contant.

AJ[13] 222

Further contracts between Véron and various supplier-contractors, including Albouy.

AJ[13] 223

Inventories of scenery classified by production and in chronological order. In particular, an inventory signed by Adam and Contant, January 1832, which, with subsequent additions, detailed the old scenery used by Véron for his new productions.

AJ[13] 226

Dossiers on artists and staff from 1831 to 1847. These related to deductions from salary for a variety of reasons and some were connected with a reduction of FF 285 from Véron's July 1831 subsidy.

AJ^{13} 228

Annual accounts 1830, 1831–32, 1832–33, and 1833–34. Monthly schedules of expenses June 1832–January 1837 and various other financial documents which covered Véron's tenure as director.

AJ^{13} 230

General accounts for receipts and expenses 1834–1853, including references to the sum paid by Duponchel to Véron as a result of the former's purchase of the concession to direct the Opera.

AJ^{13} 233

The receipts for the period 1 March–31 May 1831, when Véron was manager of the Opera on behalf of the State.

AJ^{13} 234

Summary of receipts for 1831–32.

AJ^{13} 235

Summary of receipts for 1832–33.

AJ^{13} 237

Summary of receipts for 1833–34 and 1834–35.

AJ^{13} 289

Expenses covering the period 1831–1835, including lighting and heating and certain expenses for scene-painting and costumes.

AJ^{13} 291

Schedules of monthly payments to supplier-contractors, 1831–1835, and various other expenses including payments to those made redundant.

AJ^{13} 404

Bills from suppliers in 1829, filed monthly.

AJ^{13} 405

Bills from certain suppliers in 1830, filed monthly. Also bills for the 1830 mise-en-scene of *Guillaume Tell, Manon Lescaut* and *Le Dieu et la Bayadère*.

AJ^{13} 409–AJ^{13} 416

Bills from suppliers, 1831–1835, filed monthly.

AJ^{13} 1027

Report in the *Gazette des Tribunaux*, July 1831, of a case before the *Conseil d'État*. This concerned the *droit des indigents* and the claim to tax the free seats.

AJ^{13} 1186

Laws and regulations, with special reference to the Opera, 1750–1888. Includes the *5 mai 1821 Règlement*.

C 731

Minutes of meetings of the *Commission du Budget* for the 1822–23 budget, and other documents.

C 733

Dossier 4. Minutes of meetings of the *Commission du Budget* which examined the 1824–25 budget for the various Ministries, and other documents.

C 758

Dossier 21. Minutes of meetings of the *Commission du Budget* which examined the projected 1833–34 budget for the various Ministries, and other documents relating to the annual budgets.

F^{13} 1273

Documents on the construction of the *Salle le Peletier*, and the payment of bills.

F^{21} 960

Commission des Théâtres 1817–1851, including information on the subsidies to the Royal theatres. Also comments on the position of the Commission vis-à-vis the Opera and Véron in 1834.

F^{21} 1053

Various reports and correspondence which covered Véron's tenure as director, including one by d'Henneville to the Commission, one by Prévost to the Commission, and correspondence between the Minister, the Commission and Véron, 1831–1834.

F^{21} 1054

Various reports and correspondence which covered Véron's tenure as director, especially documents relating to the Véron-Ciceri dispute and the new 1831 tariff for scene-painting.

F^{21} 1067

Reports, letters and other documents which related to Véron's new seat prices.

F^{21} 1069

General correspondence on works produced or proposed. Details of works produced 1819–1865. Contracts, scenery and costumes, including the estimated costs of scene-painting for *Aladin ou la Lampe merveilleuse*.

F^{21} 1071

Various reports and correspondence on the Opera 1828–1860, including Véron's request to use old scenery for *Gustave III*.

F^{21} 1073

Documents on the construction of the *Salle le Peletier*, the overrun on costs and who should bear the extra expense: whether the Ministry of the Interior or the *Maison du Roi*.

F^{21} 1075

Various budgets, annual accounts, general correspondence. Reports by the Commission on Véron's administration 1832–33 and 1833–34.

F^{21} 1112

Report to the King, February 1818, which set out the change of policy over the *Théâtre Italien* whereby it was annexed by the Opera.

F^{21} 4633

Commission, minutes of meetings as from 1 March 1831.

O^3 1599

A comprehensive set of documents on the *Budgets des Théâtres Royaux* during the Restoration period, including correspondence, budgets, supplements and other information.

O^3 1601

General affairs of the Royal theatres with correspondence and reports. The setting up of the *Commission des Théâtres Royaux* 1827, and the 1830 budget for the Royal theatres.

O^3 1605

Théâtres Royaux: reports, decisions, *arrêtés* of the *Maison du Roi*, 1819–1820. Action taken as a result of the assassination of the Duc de Berry on 18 February 1820.

O^3 1620

Théâtres Royaux: correspondence and various matters, 1814–1830. Report by Leconte to La Rochefoucauld which recommended that the number of free seats issued to authors, composers and artists should be reduced.

O^3 1644

Finances of the Opera and various other matters, 1815 and 1816. Confirmation of position of La Ferté.

O^3 1649

Reports, correspondence and accounts for 1818, including a reference to the *redevance des théâtres secondaires*.

O^3 1650

Various letters and reports. Budgets of the Royal theatres 1818–1827 (1819 missing). Monthly receipts for 1819 and various *arrêtés*.

O^3 1651

Correspondence, financial and other affairs, 1818–1821. Move of the Opera to the *Salle Favart*.

O^3 1662

Correspondence, finances, various documents, all relating to 1823, including receipts from individual performances. The calculation of the *droit des indigents*, and budgets for various 1823 productions.

O^3 1663

The *devis approximatif* for various productions in 1823. Correspondence, including a letter which indicated that extra financial help for the Opera would be forthcoming in case of urgent need.

O^3 1666

Correspondence 1824 and 1825 and the Opera's expenses 1824–1827. Report, October 1824 by La Rochefoucauld, on the debts of the Opera totalling FF 340.000.

O^3 1671

Files concerning the finances of the Opera 1816–1829 and correspondence over free seats. Annual Accounts 1826.

O^3 1672

Various documents relating to 1826, including Lubbert's request for a three-year concession, meetings of the *hospices*, and reports by Leconte to La Rochefoucauld.

O^3 1676

Various letters and reports 1826 and 1827. The separation of the *Théâtre Italien* and its debts. Summary of expenses and reference to the *redevance* on the secondary theatres and the *droit des indigents*. Submissions of suppliers for 1827 and 1828.

O^3 1678

Opera and *Théâtre Italien*. Various financial matters, 1822–1827. Duplanty's successful request to La Rochefoucauld that he be appointed treasurer of the Opera after Lubbert had supplanted him as director.

O^3 1679

Opera and *Théâtre Italien*. Various financial matters, 1827 and 1828. The December 1828 report by La Bouillerie to the King which called for a more strict regime of accounting and supervision.

O^3 1680

Various correspondence and reports on financial matters 1828–1830. Submissions by suppliers for 1829 and 1830, and an *arrêté* on the *redevance* levied on the secondary theatres.

O^3 1681

Budgets and other financial matters 1826–1830, with correspondence about the free seats at the Opera and the number of personnel taken on by the Opera in 1829.

O^3 1685

Various documents and letters on the *droit des indigents*. An *arrêté* fixing the price of scenery through the new 1822 tariff.

O^3 1690

Various documents on financial and other matters in 1830, including problems over the *droit des indigents*.

O^3 1691
Various documents on financial matters, including some expense categories for 1830. Correspondence between La Bouillerie and La Rochefoucauld on the subject of free seats.

O^3 1694
Personnel and financial matters at the Opera for 1829. Various reports about the sums granted or lent to the Opera by the *Maison du Roi*, including the FF 252.409 owed by the *Théâtre Italien* to the Opera, and the settlement of outstanding debts to suppliers.

O^3 1696
Agreed budgets for the Opera, 1815–1829, excluding 1827 and 1828.

O^3 1704
Journals of receipts of which one, 1825, showed that the *droit des indigents* was raised on ball receipts.

O^3 1707
Various reports, *règlements, arrêtés* and other documents, including reports by Du Rais on the *droit des indigents* and the *redevance*.

O^3 1708
Projet de budget for the Opera 1830. Correspondence on various matters including the *entrées de faveur*, and other financial reports.

O^3 1716
Various financial reports and other documents 1815–1824, including the *projet de budget* for 1824.

O^3 1724
Jury littéraire and various other matters, 1822–1830. A calculation of the debts of the Opera as at 31 March 1823, totalling FF 426.649.

O^3 1736
Financial and other affairs of the *Théâtre Italien*, 1814–1818. Report to the King by Pradel, February 1818, which recommended that the Opera should annex the *Théâtre Italien*.

Bulletin des lois
  2ème Semestre 1811, No. 385
  2ème Semestre 1820, No. 428
  Juillet à Septembre 1824, No. 687
  1er Semestre 1827, No. 163

Paris, *Bibliothèque de l'Opéra*

CO 288 (942)
    Receipts by performance of operas, 1803–1830.

CO 289 (943)
    Receipts by performance of ballets, 1803–1830.

CO 343 (605)
    Grand Livre 1831, which gave details of the expenses for the period 1 March–
31 May 1831.

CO 568 (621)
    Grand Livre 1835–36. This recorded the net sum owed by Véron to Duponchel of
FF 58.729.

CO 710 (608)
    Grands livres, recettes et dépenses par articles, 1 June 1831–31 December 1835.

PE2 (698)
    Personnel classified by category of employment, 1818–1829.

PE3 (699)
    Personnel classified by category of employment, 1830–1844.

Journal usuel de l'Opéra 1791–1850
    Details of receipts per performance.

Paris, *Archives Parlementaires*

2. Série (1800–1860).
    Tome 35 26 February 1822 – 29 March 1822
    Tome 41 28 May   1824 – 6 July 1824
    Tome 90 6 May   1834 – 6 August 1834

Paris, *Conseil d'État, Bibliothèque et Archives*

Recueil des Arrêts du Conseil, par M. Deloche.
    Tome Premier, 2ème Série, Année 1831.

Secondary Sources

Quoted Books, Articles and Dissertations

Allévy, Marie-Antoinette. *La mise en scène en France dans la première moitié du dix-neuvième siècle.* Paris, 1938.

Ault, Cecil Thomas, Jr. *Design, Operation and Organization of Stage Machinery at the Paris Opera: 1770–1873.* Ph.D. diss., University of Michigan, 1983.

Barbier, Patrick. *La vie quotidienne à l'Opéra au temps de Rossini et de Balzac: Paris, 1800–1850.* Paris, 1987. Translated by Robert Luoma. *Opera in Paris, 1800–1850. A Lively History.* Portland, 1995.

Binet, Maurice E. *Un médecin pas ordinaire, Le Docteur Véron.* Paris, éditions Albin Michel, 1945.

de Boigne, Charles. *Petits mémoires de l'Opéra.* Paris, 1857.

Bossuet, Pierre. *Histoire des théâtres nationaux.* Paris, 1909.

Castil-Blaze, François Henri Joseph. *L'Académie Impériale de Musique.* 2 vols. Paris, 1855.

Chantavoine, Jean and Jean Gaudefroy-Demombynes. *Le Romantisme dans la musique européenne.* Paris, 1955.

Collingham, Hugh A.C. *The July Monarchy, a Political History of France 1830–48.* New York, 1988.

Contant, Clément and Joseph de Filippi. *Parallèle des principaux théâtres modernes de l'Europe et des machines théâtrales françaises, allemandes et anglaises.* Paris, 1860.

Coudroy, Marie-Hélène. *La Critique parisienne des «grands opéras» de Meyerbeer: Robert le Diable, Les Huguenots, Le Prophète, L'Africaine.* Saarbrücken, 1988.

Crosten, William L. *French Grand Opera: An Art and a Business.* New York, 1948, reprint 1972.

Dandelot, Arthur. *La Société des Concerts du Conservatoire de 1828 à 1897. Les grands concerts symphoniques de Paris.* Paris, 1898.

Daumard, Adeline. *La Bourgeoisie Parisienne 1815–48.* Paris, 1963.

—— *Les Fortunes Françaises aux XIXe Siècle.* Paris, 1973.

Duflot, Joachim. *Les Secrets des coulisses des théâtres de Paris.* Paris, 1865.

Ehrhard Auguste. *L'Opéra sous la direction Véron (1831–35).* Extract from the *Revue Musicale de Lyon,* 1907.

Fétis, François-Joseph. *Biographie universelle des musiciens et bibliographie générale de la musique.* 8 vols. Paris, 1863.

Fulcher, Jane F. *The Nation's Image: French Grand Opera as Politics and Politicized Art.* Cambridge, 1987.

Gautier, Théophile. *Mademoiselle de Maupin.* Paris, 1834.

Gerhard, Anselm. *Die Verstädterung der Oper: Paris und das Musiktheater des 19. Jahrhunderts.* Stuttgart, 1992. Translated by Mary Whittall. *The Urbanization of Opera. Music Theater in Paris in the Nineteenth Century.* Chicago, 1998.

Gourret, Jean. *Ces Hommes qui ont fait l'Opéra 1669–1984.* Paris, 1984.

Hallman, Diana R. *The French Grand Opera 'La Juive' (1835). A Socio-Historical Study.* Ph.D. diss., The City University New York, 1995.

Hemmings, Frederic W. J. *The Theatre Industry in Nineteenth-Century France.* Cambridge, 1993.

–––––– *Theatre and State in France, 1760–1905.* Cambridge, 1994.

Johnson, Janet Lynn. *The Theatre Italien and Opera and Theatrical Life in Restoration Paris, 1818–1827.* Ph.D. diss., University of Chicago, 1988.

Join-Diéterle, Catherine. *Les Décors de scène de l'Opéra de Paris à l'époque romantique.* Paris, 1988.

Jordan, Ruth. *Fromental Halévy, His Life and Music 1799–1862.* London, 1994.

Laforêt, Claude. *La Vie musicale au Temps romantique (Salons, Théâtres et Concerts).* Paris, 1929.

Lasalle, Albert de. *Les Treize Salles de l'Opéra.* Paris, 1875.

Leich-Galland, Karl. *La Juive, Dossier de presse parisienne (1835).* Saarbrücken, 1987.

Lettre sur l'Opéra et sur le danger auquel il n'a pas encore échappé, adressée à l'auteur d'un écrit sur l'Opéra et sur le danger auquel il vient d'échapper. Paris, 1829.

Malliot, André L. *La Musique au Théâtre.* Paris, 1863.

Martin, Félix. *Historique des Salles de l'Opéra.* Paris, *Bibliothèque de l'Opéra,* Rés 1049 [4].

Merle, Jean-Toussaint. *Lettre à un compositeur français sur l'état actuel de l'Opéra.* Paris, 1827.

Mongrédien, Jean. *La Musique en France des Lumières au Romantisme.* Paris, 1986. Translated by Sylvain Frémaux. *French Music from the Enlightenment to Romanticism 1789–1830.* Portland, 1996.

Moynet, Jean-Pierre. *L'Envers du théâtre: Machines et décorations.* Paris, 1873.

d'Ortigue, Joseph. *Le Balcon de l'Opéra.* Paris, 1833.

Ozanam, Yves. *Recherches sur l'Académie royale de Musique (Opéra Français) sous la seconde Restauration.* 3 vols. Thèse, École des Chartes. Paris, 1981.

Pélissier, Paul. *Histoire administrative de l'Académie Nationale de Musique et de Danse.* Paris, 1906.

Pitou, Spire. *The Paris Opéra, an Encyclopedia of Operas, Ballets, Composers and Performers. Growth and Grandeur, 1815–1914.* 2 vols. Westport, 1990.

Prod'homme, Jacques-Gabriel. *L'Opéra (1669–1925).* Paris, 1925.

—— *Les Musiciens célèbres, Paganini.* Paris, n.d.

—— *La Première de Robert le Diable il y a cent ans. Le Ménestrel, 93ᵉ Année, No. 48.*

Revue musicale. Published by François-Joseph Fétis. Paris, 1828.

Roullet, Pierre N. *Récit historique des événements qui se sont passés dans l'administration de l'Opéra, la nuit du 13 février 1820.* Paris, 1820.

Royer, Alphonse. *Histoire de l'Opéra.* Paris, 1875.

de Sauvigny, Guillaume de Bertier. *Nouvelle Histoire de Paris. La Restauration, 1815–1830.* Paris, 1977.

Séchan, Charles P. *Souvenirs d'un homme de théâtre, 1831–1855.* Paris, 1883.

Second, Albéric. *Les petits mystères de l'Opéra.* Paris, 1844.

Stendhal. *Vie de Rossini.* Paris, 1824. Translated by Richard N. Coe. *Life of Rossini.* London, 1856.

Sur l'Opéra et sur le danger auquel il vient d'échapper. Paris, 1829.

The New Grove Dictionary of Opera. Ed. Stanley Sadie. 4 vols. London, 1992.

Véron, Louis. *Mémoires d'un bourgeois de Paris.* 6 vols. Paris, 1856.

Wayser, Claudine. *L'Extraordinaire Monsieur Véron.* Paris, 1990.

Wilberg, Rebecca S. *The 'Mise en scène' at the Paris Opéra – Salle Le Peletier (1821–73) and the Staging of the First French Grand opéra: Meyerbeer's "Robert le Diable".* Ph.D. diss., Brigham Young University, 1990.

Wild, Nicole. *Décors et Costumes du XIX Siècle, Tome II, Théâtres et Décorateurs.* Paris, *Bibliothèque Nationale,* 1993.

Nico Schüler (Ed.)

Computer-Applications in Music Research

Concepts, Methods, Results

Frankfurt/M., Berlin, Bern, Bruxelles, New York, Oxford, Wien, 2002. 180 pp., num. fig., num. tab.
Methodology of Music Research. Edited by Nico Schüler. Vol. 1
ISBN 3-631-39032-7 · pb. € 32.–* / DM 63.– / US $ 27.95 / £ 20.–
US-ISBN 0-8204-5478-8

At the conference „Musicology 1966–2000: A Practical Program," on May 26, 1966, Jan LaRue speculated „that computer analysis will become one of the most important directions in musicology for the next generation…" Having passed the year 2000, we have to realize that LaRue's prediction did not come true: neither for computer-assisted music analysis, nor for computer-applications in music research in general. This volume is intended to initiate a more critical discussion of computer-applications in music research and to present concepts, methods, and results of newest research in this area.

Contents: Musicology, Computers, and Interdisciplinarity · Information Theory and Aesthetics · Timing in Contemporary Music Performance · Melodic Analysis · Structural Analysis and Performance · Comparative Analysis with Neural Networks · DAPHNE: A Music Analysis System with Real Score · Classifying Methods of Computer-Assisted Music Analysis · Searching for Hidden Regularities in Music · Bibliography

Frankfurt/M · Berlin · Bern · Bruxelles · New York · Oxford · Wien
Auslieferung: Verlag Peter Lang AG
Moosstr. 1, CH-2542 Pieterlen
Telefax 00 41 (0) 32 / 376 17 27

*inklusive der in Deutschland gültigen Mehrwertsteuer
Preisänderungen vorbehalten

Homepage http://www.peterlang.de